JAVASCRIPT

Developer's Resource

JAVASCRIPT

⛏Developer's Resource

CLIENT-SIDE PROGRAMMING USING HTML, NETSCAPE PLUG-INS AND JAVA APPLETS

Prentice Hall PTR
Upper Saddle River, NJ   07458
http://www.prenhall.com

Kamran Husain
Jason Levitt

Husain, Kamran.
    JavaScript developer's resource : client-side programming using
HTML, Netscape plug-ins and Java applets / Kamran Husain, Jason Levitt.
        p.   cm.
    Includes index.
    ISBN 0-13-267923-X
    1. JavaScript (Computer program language)   2. Client/server
computing.   I. Levitt, Jason. II. Title
QA76.73.J39H87   1997
005.2—dc20

                                                                96-38437
                                                                CIP

Editorial/Production Supervision: Raymond Pajek
Acquisitions Editor: Mary Franz
Development Editor: Ralph E. Moore
Buyer: Alexis Heydt
Cover Design: Anthony Gemmellaro
Cover Design Direction: Jerry Votta
Art Director: Gail Cocker-Bogusz
Series Design: Meg VanArsdale

© 1997 Prentice Hall PTR
Prentice-Hall, Inc.
A Simon & Schuster Company
Upper Saddle River, NJ 07458

The publisher offers discounts on this book when ordered in bulk quantities.
For more information, contact

    Corporate Sales Department
    Prentice Hall PTR
    One Lake Street
    Upper Saddle River, NJ 07458
    Phone: 800-382-3419; Fax: 201-236-714
    E-mail (Internet): `corpsales@prenhall.com`

Printed in the United States of America

10 9 8 7 6 5 4 3 2 1

ISBN 0-13-267923-X

Prentice-Hall International (UK) Limited, *London*
Prentice-Hall of Australia Pty. Limited, *Sydney*
Prentice-Hall Canada Inc., *Toronto*
Prentice-Hall Hispanoamericana, S.A., *Mexico*
Prentice-Hall of India Private Limited, *New Delhi*
Prentice-Hall of Japan, Inc., *Tokyo*
Simon & Schuster Asia Pte. Ltd., *Singapore*
Editora Prentice-Hall do Brasil, Ltda., *Rio de Janeiro*

This book is dedicated to my father,
Dr. Bilal Riaz Husain.

May he go to Heaven.

Kamran Husain

For the places: Flight Path, Ro, Flipnotics,
and Ruta Maya;

And the people: Flint, Linda, and Natasha.

Jason Levitt

CONTENTS

JAVASCRIPT DEVELOPER'S RESOURCE

Appendix B   Some Helpful Web Sites and Newsgroups   541

Appendix C   Debugging JavaScript   543

Acknowledgments

The authors would like to thank Mary Franz at Prentice Hall for her encouragement and tenacity. They would also like to thank Norreen, Ralph, and Ray for keeping up with strict deadlines and ever morphing versions of Navigator. Additionally, they would like to thank Brendan Eich, Fanny Wu, Len Feldman, and the brave Netscape Public Relations group for their technical assistance. And last, but definitely not least, Kamran thanks his wife Uzma, and his twin daughters, Haya and Hana, for putting up with odd schedules, deadlines, and missed trips to the swimming pool.

ABOUT THE AUTHORS

Kamran Husain

Kamran is an independant software consultant specializing in UNIX systems programming. He has developed applications and turn key systems in all sorts of software environments including C, C++, Real Time Systems, Windows NT, 95, Java, X Windows and Motif. He has a BSEE from the University of Texas at Austin and an MSCS from the University of Houston. He can be reached via e-mail at khusain@ikra.com

Jason Levitt

Jason Levitt started his career as a software developer and consultant before finally yielding completely to the joys of journalism. Before joining Open Systems Today in 1990, he freelanced technology reviews for such publications as Unix/World and Byte Magazine, and was a correspondent for Byte's MicroBytes Daily, one of the early online news services. He currently writes for InformationWeek Magazine in which he pens a bi-monthly column on Internet technology, entitled "InternetView." He can be reached at jlevitt@cmp.com

INTRODUCTION

Welcome to the *JavaScript Developer's Resource*, a book designed for Web developers who desire a quick introduction to JavaScript and the technology behind it, along with in-depth discussions of its functionality and real examples intended to put that functionality to work. This book will provide you with the both the knowledge and the tools required to create powerful JavaScript scripts, enabling you to take full advantage of the capabilities inherent in JavaScript and to develop useful and interesting Web sites that push the limits of Web development.

JavaScript is a powerful scripting language that is quickly gaining mindshare among Internet users. Much of its popularity can be attributed to the ease with which developers and non-developers alike can tap into its power. A JavaScript interpreter is built into today's most popular Web browsers: Netscape's Navigator 2.0 and 3.0, and Microsoft's Internet Explorer 3.0. Unlike most other scripting and programming languages, you don't need any other tools, aside from one of these browsers, in order to get started writing and executing JavaScript scripts. JavaScript scripts, of course, are already all over the Internet, being used to enhance the impact and delivery of Web pages at countless sites and, after reading this book, you will have the skills to enable your site to compete with the best of them.

JavaScript exists in both client and server implementations. This book is based on the client-side JavaScript implementation that is contained in the Navigator 2.0 and 3.0 browsers. We do, however, introduce server-side JavaScript in the final chapter.

We wrote this book at a time when JavaScript was still evolving. This evolution required us to revise the contents several times to reflect new or changed features in the various beta releases of the Navigator 3.0 browser, and to accomodate security fixes in the Navigator 2.0 browser. In fact, the Navigator 3.0 browser was just released as this book went to press. Therefore, our exploration and discusssion of JavaScript is based primarily on the beta 6 release of Navigator 3.0, as well as the release version of Navigator 2.02. Although Microsoft's Internet Explorer 3.0 for Windows 95 supports JavaScript, it was backwards-engineered by Microsoft to be compatible with the JavaScript implementation in Navigator 2.02. Some of the examples in this book don't work properly with it.

There are several audiences who may find this book useful. Web page developers and Internet application developers should find this book suitable both as a tutorial on the language and as a guide to its more advanced applications. Developers with limited programming experience, and even casual Web addicts, will find usable code and can go directly to those JavaScript features that interest them. Finally, seasoned developers will find interesting, and certainly more advanced, material in Part III.

How this Book is Organized

Part I of this book, "The JavaScript Basics," which contains Chapters 1 through 4, covers just that: the basics of JavaScript. This part is designed to get you grounded in the JavaScript language, including an introduction to the language and its tools and syntax, as well as a solid treatment of its variables, operators, statements, and objects. An understanding of the material presented in Part I will prepare you for the more advanced chapters contained in Parts II and III.

Part II, "The JavaScript Objects," contains Chapters 5 through 9, and picks up right where Chapter 4 left off. In this part, we get into heavy detail about the objects built in to JavaScript, including the basic navigational objects, event handlers that enable interactive Web pages, and more advanced uses of objects for creating on-the-fly

HTML, windows and frames, and even a section on creating your own objects. By the end of Part II, you should have everything you need to begin creating dynamic Web pages using JavaScript.

But wait, there's more . . . Part III, "Advanced JavaScript: Using Live-Connect and LiveWire," which contains Chapters 10 through 12, provides you with a beyond-the-basics look at what's probably the most powerful feature of JavaScript: its ability to interact within Netscape's Internet Application Architecture to create Internet applications that offer far greater capabilities than JavaScript alone can provide. With the introduction of Navigator 3.0 and it's LiveConnect capabilities, Netscape gave JavaScript developers the tools to let their scripts communicate with Java applets and plug-ins. In this part, we'll explore what this means to JavaScript developers who wish to add sound, video, animation, and more to their Web sites. Finally, we'll take a brief look at server-side JavaScript implementation with the LiveWire tool.

How to Use This Book

You'll notice as you read this book that there are a number of elements and we've tried to be consistent about attaching certain conventions to certain elements to make them stand out. These conventions have been used to make especially useful material easier to read and to find later on when referring back to our book during your programming sessions.

Source Code

All source code, whether it be complete Program listings or just code snippets, has been styled in a special font, as follows:

```
<HTML>

<BODY>

<APPLET CODE= xxx>

</APPLET>

</BODY>

</HTML>
```

Please note also that all set-off source code appearing in the body of this book has been included on the accompanying CD-ROM for easy reference and use.

As well, we often use coding terms that run into the main text in our discussions. These terms have also been set in a special font, like so: "You can address the properties of the `aHouse` object using any number of `myHouse` statements." This applies to filenames and URLs as well.

Icons and Other Conventions

A number of special icons have been created and set in the margins of this book to call your attention to particularly useful and important information that might otherwise get lost in the running discussion of the text. As well, we've styled other key information distinctively so that you won't have to weed through the main text as you quickly scan for relevant Tips and Notes. These conventions are as follows:

This icon alerts readers to software bugs and possible methods of avoiding them.

This icon flags information that, while useful, may cause unexpected results or serious frustration.

Tip   This convention is used to highlight particularly useful information that will save the reader time, emphasize a valuable technique, or offer some special advice.

Note This convention highlights information that deserves special attention, such as an interesting fact about the topic at hand, or information that you may want to keep in mind while programming.

And Finally . . .

In the true spirit of online presentation, this book is accompanied by two forms of online media that we know you will find useful: the CD-ROM that accompanies this book, and a special Web supplement that has been created especially for this book.

Look for additional information related to JavaScript at this book's web site: www.prenhall.com/developers_resource_series

About the CD-ROM

The CD-ROM contains the source code for all the code samples in this book. Hopefully, these samples will provide the basis for writing useful JavaScript applications. The code is provided for the Navigator 2.02 and 3.0 browsers running under Windows, Macintosh, and Unix, and has been tested to the best of our abilities.

Even though we made the best effort to get the source code on the CD-ROM to work across Windows, Macintosh, and Unix systems, you should be aware that the code will not always run consistently across platforms. That's because there are incompatibilities between the JavaScript implementation in Netscape's Navigator (versions 2.x and 3.0) and Microsoft's Internet Explorer 3.0. Alas, in some cases, even the same version of browser on different operating systems behaved differently! If you are running a Windows 95 system with the Netscape Navigator 3.0 browser, you are most likely to get all the examples to work right. Macintosh and Unix users should definitely read the errata files on the disc.

Perhaps when all the subtle and the not-so-subtle differences are ironed out, we can confirm that our JavaScript code will work regardless of platform for a given version number. There are still folks out there on the Net who use Navigator 2.02 because of all the "reported bugs" in Navigator 3.0.

Finally, writing JavaScript code is not a black art. It's a simple, yet uniquely powerful language to work with. Despite its power, JavaScript has its limitations and you should be aware of them before deciding to write a major application in it. JavaScript is simply a tool and you should know when to use it and when to use something else like Perl, Java or even C! Hopefully, this book will provide you with enough information to get you started.

Also, to help you along, we have added a number of shareware plug-ins. You should carefully read the notices and requirements for each plug-in before installation and use.

PART ONE

The JavaScript Basics

Show myHome

Show myHut

Show myLodge

Show myEstate

Learning a new language is never easy, so we tried to make Part I a vehicle that eases the reader into the more difficult second and third parts of the book. For people with at least a bit of programming experience, Part I holds no surprises. For others, it may require more study, but is still a relatively gentle introduction to JavaScript.

Chapter 1, "JavaScript and the Internet Application Framework," looks at JavaScript from a broad perspective, as part of Netscape's Internet Application Architecture; more closely, it defines exactly what JavaScript is (a powerful scripting language), and what it isn't (it isn't Java). Chapter 1 also looks at what tools are available for JavaScript development and what capabilities they offer the developer.

Chapter 2, "Getting Started with JavaScript," is the first hands-on JavaScript chapter and it also serves as a lexicon for the various syntactical peculiarities of the language. We first introduce a simple JavaScript script and meticulously work through its execution from start to finish. We look closely at the flow of script execution, how the <SCRIPT> tag is used, and how various special characters are used to seamlessly incorporate JavaScript into Web pages. It is important to be familiar with the material in Chapter 2 so that you will be able to "read" the more complex JavaScript scripts in later parts of the book.

While Chapters 1 and 2 introduce the language and its syntax, Chapters 3 and 4 introduce variables, operators, statements, and delve deeper into the concept of objects, the building blocks of the JavaScript language. Chapter 3, "JavaScript Language Basics," introduces concepts that are common to nearly all modern computer programming languages: data types, variables, control-flow statements, built-in functions, string operations, and user-defined functions. Developers already familiar with languages such as C or Perl will find Chapter 3 familiar territory.

Chapter 4, "JavaScript and Objects," branches off into new territory with an introduction to JavaScript's instance-based object implementation. While JavaScript is not a fully object-oriented language in the same league as Java or C++ (JavaScript offers no inheritance, overrides, or virtual functions, for example; these mechanisms are typical in other object-oriented languages), it still offers a rich hierarchy of built-in objects suitable for Internet programming. This set of built-in objects, sometimes referred to as the JavaScript Object Model, along with their associated methods and properties, are the tools we use to create powerful JavaScript scripts in Parts two and three.

CHAPTER

JAVASCRIPT AND THE INTERNET APPLICATION FRAMEWORK

- JavaScript and Its Uses

- Netscape's Internet Application Framework

- JavaScript is Not Java

If you're reading this book, you're probably used to hearing the hype about Java. Well, JavaScript isn't Java (we'll discuss the differences later), but it is a useful scripting language that can be used to add bells and whistles (and even full-blown applications) to your Web pages. By the time you get to the end of this book, you'll see how JavaScript can be used with Java applets, plug-ins, and server-side JavaScript, to create powerful Internet applications. But for now, we'll start with the basics. In this first chapter, we will attempt to tell you what JavaScript is and what it's used for. We'll also describe how JavaScript fits into Netscape's Internet Application Framework, and we'll attempt to bring home the point (once again!) that: JavaScript is not Java.

What Is JavaScript?

JavaScript is a lightweight, object-oriented, scripting language developed by Netscape Communications. JavaScript is similar in spirit to other lightweight scripting languages such as Perl, Bourne Shell, Lingo, and Tcl. JavaScript lets you add interactivity to web pages, making them more compelling and more efficient.

Typical uses of JavaScript include form field validation, on-the-fly creation of HTML, forms that calculate values based on user input, and toolbars that manage Web navigation and browser attributes. These types of applications previously required time-consuming trips back to the Web server to run Common Gateway Interface (CGI) scripts, which is the usual method for a Web browser to communicate with a Web server.

Interest in JavaScript has soared because of the popularity of the Navigator browser and the ease with which JavaScript can be integrated into existing Web pages. Even Microsoft has chosen to implement JavaScript and has incorporated it into their Internet Explorer 3.0 browser.

One of the reasons for JavaScript's popularity is that it gives programmers easy access to the properties of Web pages, such as the hypertext links, background colors, and windows, in a way that can be easily integrated into existing Web sites. JavaScript scripts often reside within Web pages and consist of JavaScript source code surrounded by a special <SCRIPT> tag.[1] To facilitate the acceptance of JavaScript, Netscape has given JavaScript a syntax and object-oriented programming style similar to the popular Java language.

---

1. As we'll find out in Chapter 2, "Getting Started with JavaScript," the <SCRIPT> tag has a SRC attribute in the Navigator 3.0 implementation of JavaScript, which lets you put scripts in a separate file. Also, we'll see in Chapter 12, "An Introduction to Server Side JavaScript and Livewire," that server-side JavaScript uses the <SERVER> tag and gets interpreted by the Web server instead of Navigator.

A Bit of History

Although JavaScript shares much of the same syntax and flexibility of Sun's Java language, JavaScript and Java are not directly related. JavaScript was originally called LiveScript and was intended as a general scripting language for use in Netscape's Navigator browser. However, the rise in popularity of Sun's Java language, coupled with Netscape's decision to implement the Java Virtual Machine inside the Navigator browser, prompted Netscape to rename LiveScript to JavaScript.

Early beta versions of Navigator 2.0 contained the first implementations of the LiveScript interpreter, but by the time Navigator 2.0 was released in early 1996, the implementation was called JavaScript. Navigator 3.0, which was released in the summer of 1996, adds additional capabilities to JavaScript as well as LiveConnect, Netscape's name for Navigator 3.0's capability for communication between Java applets, Plug-Ins, and JavaScript scripts.

Netscape's Internet Application Framework

JavaScript is just one technical component of Netscape's Internet Application Framework, a hefty buzzword that encompasses Netscape's entire product line of Web servers and browsers. Although Microsoft has implemented client-side JavaScript in their Internet Explorer 3.0 browser, only Netscape offers a server-side implementation of JavaScript and an enterprise-wide strategy for incorporating JavaScript into both their clients and their servers.

The Internet Application Framework refers to all of Netscape's servers and browsers and to the many APIs, protocols, standards, and technologies available on them. It has three parts: the Network Platform, the Client APIs, and the Server APIs. The Network Platform consists of Java, JavaScript, and HTML, as well as Internet protocols, security standards, and database access APIs. The Client APIs are Netscape's Plug-In API and the proprietary Interprocess Communication APIs, such as Apple Events on the Macintosh, OLE on Windows, and X-Events on Unix/X-Windows systems. The Server APIs are CGI (Common Gateway Interface) and NSAPI (Netscape Server API). Netscape's LiveWire, an application that runs alongside the Netscape Web server, handles execution of server-side JavaScript scripts. Table 1.1 lists and describes the various components of Netscape's Internet Application Framework.

Table 1.1 Components of Netscape's Internet Application Framework. The Framework has three parts: The Network Platform, The Client Platform, and the Server Platform. (This table is taken mostly from Netscape's white paper on the subject.)

The Network Platform	Description
Java	A programming language created by Sun Micro-systems that enables the creation of powerful network-centric applications.
JavaScript	A scripting language for the creation of simple applications that may be entirely embedded in HTML documents.
HTML	(HyperText Markup Language), the nearly ubiquitous language for creating richly formatted documents on the World Wide Web. It is an international standard whose specification is maintained by the Internet Engineering Task Force (IETF).
Internet protocols	A collection of fundamental protocols and standards such as TCP/IP, SMTP, POP3, NNTP, FTP, IRC, Telnet, and MIME. The Internet Application Framework will incorporate emerging protocols as products and services become available to support them.
Database Access APIs	Server-side JavaScript defines objects that allow developers to access databases. Netscape is also working to define standard ways for accessing cross-platform databases such as ODBC and Sun's emerging Java Database Connectivity (JDBC) technology.
Electronic commerce standards	A collection of standards and protocols are necessary to make the Internet a viable platform for electronic commerce. Netscape is working with electronic payment solution providers to define standards to make electronic commerce a reality.

(Continued)

The Network Platform	Description
Security standards that enable private communication to occur over the public Internet.	SSL (Secure Sockets Layer) is an open, widely endorsed channel security protocol originally defined by Netscape, and in the process of being signed over to the Internet Engineering Task Force, that provides message encryption, client and server authentication, and message integrity services to many application protocols such as HTTP, FTP, and NNTP.
LiveMedia	A standard proposed by Netscape for creating interoperable real-time data servers and clients over the Internet.
Live3D	An open platform for writing visually exciting 3D applications that combines VRML viewing technology and powerful 3D extensions with Java, JavaScript, and Netscape's Plug-in application programming interfaces (APIs).

Client APIs

Inline Plug-in APIs	Provides a means of incorporating dynamically loadable modules into the client process itself. Together with Java and JavaScript facilities, plug-ins enable high-performance application delivery of performance-intensive rich content, such as sound, graphics and video.
Netscape Client APIs	Operating system-specific APIs that let applications communicate via Apple Events (Macintosh), OLE Automation and DDE (Dynamic Data Exchange) (Windows), and X Events (Unix/X-Window).

Server APIs

CGI (Common Gateway Interface)	The Internet standard interface for invoking server-based scripts or compiled programs at the request of clients.
Netscape Server APIs (NSAPI)	Provides developers with the ability to extend the native capabilities of the server. NSAPI is a highly granular API that allows developers to exert a great deal of control over the server's behavior by creating high-performance extensions.

As Table 1.1 shows, the Internet Application Framework encompasses a wide range of APIs, protocols, and other standards. However, this book concentrates on only a few of those standards, namely JavaScript, and to a lesser extent, HTML, Java, and plug-ins. Figure 1.1 illustrates how these standards, along with a few other related standards, such as CGI, fit into a web client/server architecture.

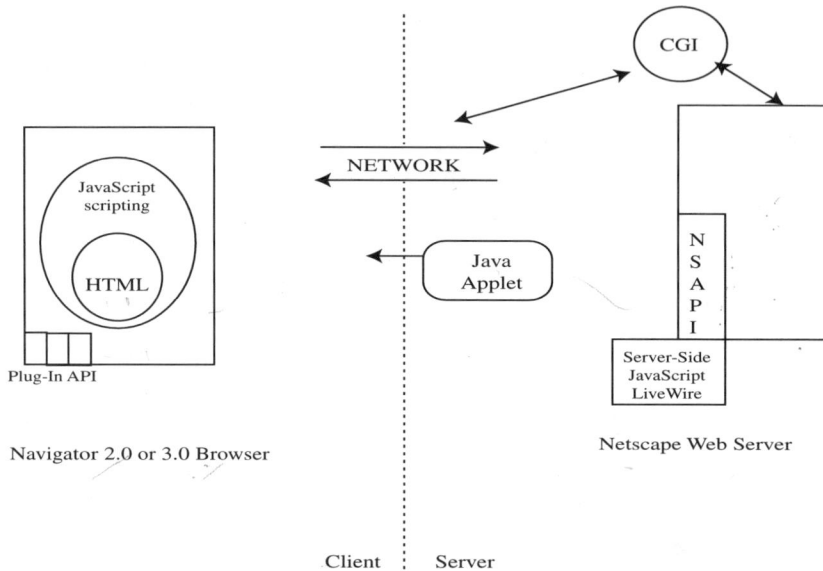

Figure 1.1 Important development APIs and languages in Netscape's Internet Application Framework

Development Components of Navigator 2.0 and 3.0

Netscape's Internet Application Framework encompasses many development technologies and JavaScript is the glue that holds the major components together. Because this book is concerned primarily with the client-side implementation of JavaScript, we're mainly interested in the client-side technologies contained in the Navigator browser. Those technologies are the Java Virtual Machine, which runs Java Applets; Plug-Ins, which are platform-specific code modules that extend the functionality of Navigator by supporting new

MIME (Multimedia Internet Mail Extensions); and the JavaScript interpreter, which executes JavaScript scripts.

Figures 1.2 and 1.3 show the major technical components of the Navigator 2.0 and 3.0 browsers and how JavaScript facilitates communication between them.

In Navigator 2.0, JavaScript can write directly to Plug-Ins. Unfortunately, in Navigator 2.0, there are no other communication channels between JavaScript scripts, Java Applets, and Plug-Ins.

In Navigator 3.0, Netscape introduced LiveConnect, which offers a way for JavaScript script, Java Applets, and Plug-Ins to send and receive data. With LiveConnect, JavaScript scripts can alter properties and methods of Java Applets, and vice versa. JavaScript can also reference public Java methods defined in Plug-Ins, as well as query the installed Plug-Ins to see if a particular one is loaded.

The basis for LiveConnect technology is straightforward. Any Java applet that is downloaded into the Navigator 3.0 browser becomes an object that can be referenced from a JavaScript script. All Java classes defined using the "public" identifier are available to JavaScript scripts.

Communication with Plug-Ins is somewhat similar. Netscape has implemented the Java Runtime Interface (JRI), which lets developers define Java classes in their C++ Plug-In code. The JRI, coupled with a modified Plug-In API, lets Plug-Ins include public Java classes that can be referenced from JavaScript scripts as well as Java Applets.

The potential applications of LiveConnect are innumerable. One that comes to mind is an online instructional system that takes advantage of an audio Plug-In. The user could select, start, and stop audio instructions through a JavaScript script that controls the audio Plug-In. Meanwhile, a Java Applet would receive quiz scores and other user entries that it would relay back to a server for immediate feedback.

Javascript in Navigator 2.0

Javascript Interpreter

<SCRIPT LANGUAGE="JavaScript">
- - - - - - - - - - - - -
- - - - - - - - - - - - -
<SCRIPT>

Javascript event handler inside of HTML tag calls function in JavaScript

JavaScript can check for existence of a Plug-In and write directly to a Plug-In

<BODY>

<FORM>
<INPUT TYPE="button"
onClick="scriptoutline()"
</FORM.

/BODY>

HTML Interpreter

Plug-In
modules

Live3D | mBED | Shockwave | Acrobat | Real Audio

Java Virtual Machine

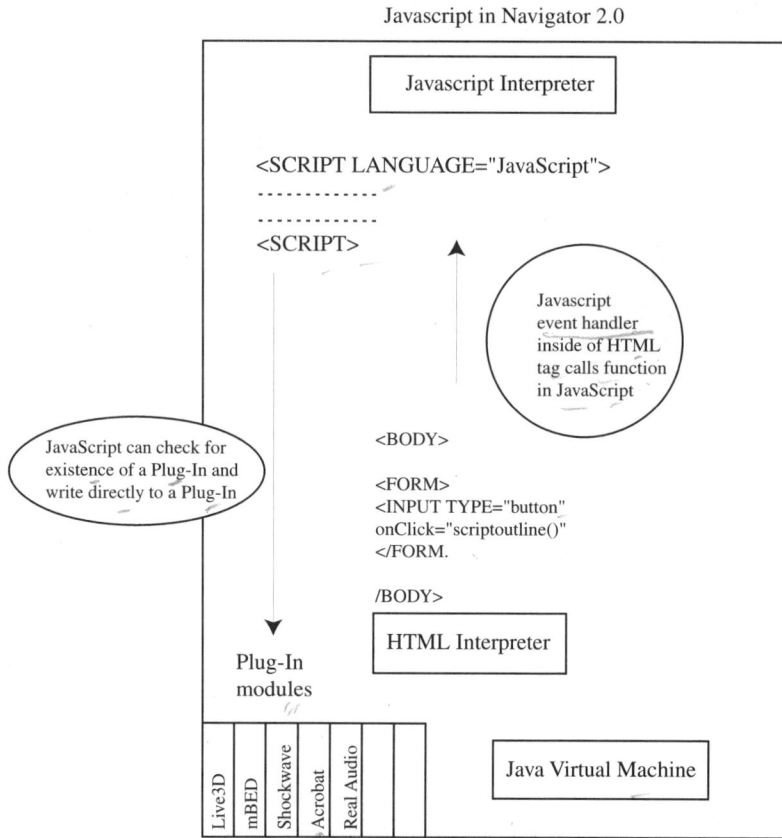

Figure 1.2 How components of the Navigator 2.0 Browser interact with JavaScript

Developing With JavaScript

JavaScript is executed by a JavaScript language interpreter, which is part of your Web browser software. Currently, the only browsers that have JavaScript language interpreters are Microsoft's Internet Explorer 3.0 and Netscape's Navigator 2.0 and 3.0. Table 1.2 shows which versions of these browsers have implementations of JavaScript, Netscape Plug-Ins, and Java Applets.

Javascript in Navigator 3.0

| Javascript Interpreter |

```
<SCRIPT LANGUAGE="JavaScript">
-------------
-------------
<SCRIPT>
```

Javascript event handler inside of HTML tag calls function in JavaScript

JavaScript can access Java public variables and methods and vice versa.

JavaScript can check for existence of a Plug-In and write directly to a Plug-In. Plug-Ins can define public Java Classes and JavaScript can access those classes.

```
<BODY>

<FORM>
<INPUT TYPE="button"
onClick="scriptoutline()"
</FORM.

/BODY>
```

| HTML Interpreter |

Plug-In modules

| Live3D | mBED | Shockwave | Acrobat | Real Audio |

| Java Virtual Machine |

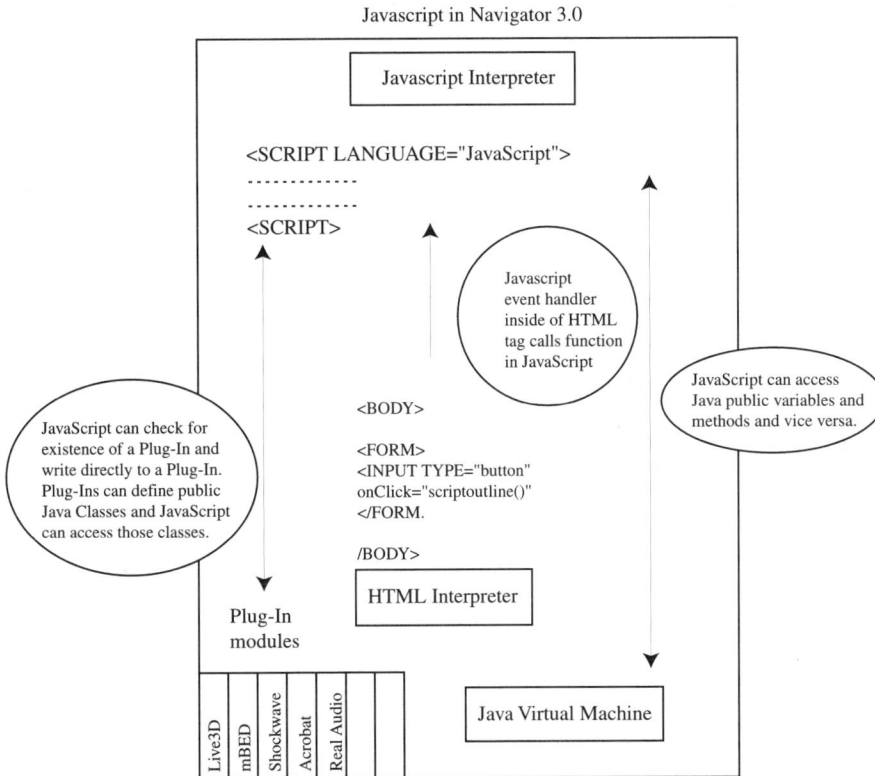

Figure 1.3 How components of the Navigator 3.0 Browser interact with JavaScript

Table 1.2 JavaScript, JavaApplets, and Plug-In Support by Navigator and Internet Explorer Browsers[a]

Browser	Version #	Platform	Java-Script	Plug-Ins	Java Applets	Live-Connect
						no
Navigator	1.x	All	no	no	no	no
	2.0	Windows95/NT	yes	yes	yes	no
		Macintosh	yes	yes	no	no
		Unix/X-Window	yes	yes	yes	no
		Windows 3.1	yes	yes	no	no
	2.01	Windows95/NT	yes	yes	yes	no

(Continued)

Browser	Version #	Platform	JavaScript	Plug-Ins	Java Applets	Live-Connect
		Macintosh	yes	yes	no	no
		Unix/X-Window	yes	yes	yes	no
		Windows 3.1	yes	yes	no	no
	2.02	Windows 3.1	yes	yes	no	no
		Windows 95/NT	yes	yes	yes	no
		Macintosh	yes	yes	no	no
	3.0	Windows 95/NT	yes	yes	yes	yes
		Macintosh	yes	yes	yes	yes
		Unix/X-Window	yes	yes	yes	yes
		Windows 3.1	yes	yes	yes	yes
Navigator Gold	2.01	Windows95/NT	yes	yes	yes	no
	2.01	Windows 3.1	yes	yes	no	no
	2.02	Windows 95/NT	yes	yes	yes	no
	3.0	Windows95/NT	yes	yes	yes	yes
	3.0	Macintosh	yes	yes	yes	yes
	3.0	Unix/X-Window	yes	yes	yes	yes
	3.0	Windows 3.1	yes	yes	yes	yes
Internet Explorer	2.x	Windows95	no	no	no	no
		Macintosh	no	yes	no	no
		Windows 3.1	no	no	no	no
	3.0	Windows 95	yes	yes	yes	no

[a]NOTES: Unix systems are: Solaris 2.3 and 2.4, SunOS, Irix, HPUX, Linux, AIX, BSDI, and OSF1. For Navigator 2.x, Java support in all Unix systems except AIX and BSDI. Only released versions are listed; however, there were many interim beta and alpha versions released for testing and development. We advise against using any beta or alpha version.

As of the publication of this book, Navigator 3.0 is the best choice for development and testing of examples in this book, though it would be useful to have Navigator 2.02 and Microsoft's Internet Explorer 3.0 to test for compatibility of your scripts.

Because the JavaScript interpreter is built right into your browser, developing with JavaScript is quick and easy. JavaScript scripts are plain text files, so they can be typed in quickly, using whatever text editor is handy, and then loaded immediately into Navigator for execution. The JavaScript development process requires switching back and forth between your editor and the Navigator browser.

> **Tip** Netscape's Navigator Gold browser contains a built-in editor, so it is particularly convenient to use for editing JavaScript scripts. Once you have a Web page containing a JavaScript script loaded into Navigator Gold, you simply select the Edit Document menu selection to expose and edit the JavaScript script.

JavaScript Is Not Java

Despite the fact that both JavaScript and Java share the word "Java" in their names, JavaScript is not Java. Unfortunately, the hype surrounding the Java language has been deafening, even though, as this book goes to press, there are still only a minuscule number of really useful applications written in Java, and few stable environments for running them. This hype, combined with a vast array of products with the word Java in their name, has caused many people to think that JavaScript and Java have some direct relationship.

Yes, Java and JavaScript are both languages used by programmers, but they are very different kinds of languages. Even their origins are different. Java was developed by Sun Microsystems. JavaScript was developed by Netscape Communications. Table 1.3 outlines the key differences between the two languages.

Table 1.3 Differences Between JavaScript and Java (taken from the Netscape documentation)

JavaScript	Java
Interpreted (not compiled) by client browser	Compiled on server before execution on client browser
Object-based. Code uses built-in, extensible objects, no classes or inheritance	Object-oriented. Applets consist of object classes with inheritance
Code integrated with, and embedded in, HTML	Applets distinct form HTML (accessed from HTML pages)
Variable data types not declared (loose typing)	Variable data types must be declared (strong typing)
Dynamic binding. Object references checked at run-time	Static binding. Object references must exist at compile-time

A Bit About JavaScript

JavaScript is a relatively simple, interpreted language similar in spirit to interpreted languages such as John Ousterhaut's Tcl (Tool Control Language), the Unix C Shell and Bourne Shell, and Larry Wall's Perl. JavaScript scripts are usually interspersed in Web pages as plain text surrounded by the <SCRIPT>...</SCRIPT> tag. JavaScript event handlers, which respond to certain user-initiated events such as clicking on a form button, can be added to standard HTML form tags. JavaScript is extensible, but does have classes or inheritance. To a developer, this means that you can't really add any new functionality to JavaScript, just new versions of whatever objects JavaScript already makes available to you.

JavaScript scripts are executed by a JavaScript interpreter, which resides within the Navigator 2.0 and 3.0 browser. Microsoft's Internet Explorer 3.0 browser also has a JavaScript interpreter.

JavaScript is used to add interactivity to Web pages by attaching JavaScript statements to user events, such as clicking on a form button. You can also use JavaScript to help users navigate, and change the attributes of, Web pages, because most objects available to JavaScript are Web pages loaded into the Navigator browser. Attributes of

Web pages include background color, hypertext links, and the date it was last modified. JavaScript is best used in conjunction with HTML constructs such as IMG tags and forms.

A typical use of JavaScript is to validate and calculate values based on numbers or text entered into an HTML form, such as an IRS tax form.

Like most scripting languages, JavaScript is not very good at tasks that require a lot of screen I/O or memory-intensive text or number manipulation. You might, for example, be able to write a spreadsheet program in JavaScript, but it would be clumsy and slow.

A Bit About Java

Java is a compiled, extensible, object-oriented programming language that can be used to write full-scale enterprise applications, such as spreadsheet programs, as well as smaller, downloadable programs known as applets. Java applets are executed by the Java Virtual Machine, which is Sun's name for the engine that isolates Java applets from their operating system environment and executes them. The Java Virtual Machine makes applets portable by isolating them from the details of their execution environment. There is an implementation of the Java Virtual Machine within the Navigator 2.0 and 3.0 browser that executes Java applets that you download into Navigator. Microsoft's Internet Explorer 3.0 browser also has an implementation of the Java Virtual Machine.

Java is an object-oriented language that uses object classes with inheritance. It uses strong typing (variable types must be declared) and static binding (object references must exist at compile-time). Most importantly, Java programs must be compiled before they can be executed by the Java Virtual Machine. (As we'll see in Chapter 12, "An Introduction to Server-Side JavaScript," server-side JavaScript is also compiled before execution. However, it is still fundamentally an interpreted scripting language.)

Hello World in JavaScript and Java

As an example of the differences between Java and JavaScript, let's look at the most basic of programs, the venerable "hello world" program. It simply prints the string "hello world" in our browser.

`Hello.jav` (Program 1.1) is the program written in the Java language. `Hello.htm` (Program 1.3) is the same program written in the JavaScript language.

For Java, we need two files, `hello.jav` and `hellojava.htm` (Program 1.2). We use the Java language compiler, which is part of Sun Microsystem's Java SDK (Software Development Kit), to compile our `hello.jav` program. By convention, the resulting file is named `hello.class`. `Hello.class` is a Java applet. An applet is a small program that is executed inside of the Navigator browser by the Java Virtual Machine. In order to make the Java Applet download into Navigator, we have to reference it from within a Web page using the <APPLET>....</APPLET> tag shown in the file `hellojava.htm`. When Navigator loads the file `hellojava.htm`, the <APPLET> reference fetches the hello.class file from the Web server and it is executed within Navigator. It's necessary to include the Java Graphics class to draw on the screen.

Program 1.1: The `hello.jav` program is compiled to create an applet that will be called by the HTML file to write "hello world" to the Navigator browser

```
import java.awt.Graphics;

import java.applet.Applet;


public class hello extends Applet {

    public void paint(Graphics g) {

    g.drawString("hello world", 25, 25);

    }

}
```

Program 1.2: `hellojava.htm` **is a web page containing a reference to the Java Applet using the <APPLET> tag**

```
<HTML>

<BODY>

<APPLET CODE="hello.class" WIDTH=100 HEIGHT=25>

</APPLET>

</BODY>

</HTML>
```

In contrast, getting the same result from JavaScript is trivial. We simply create a one-line JavaScript script that uses the write method of the current document object to write the string "hello world" to the browser window.

Program 1.3: `hello.htm` **contains one JavaScript script that writes "hello world" to your Navigator browser**

```
<HTML>

<BODY>

<SCRIPT LANGUAGE="JavaScript">

document.write("hello world")

</SCRIPT>

</BODY>

</HTML>
```

As you can see, the differences between using JavaScript to write the simple "hello world" string and using Java to accomplish the same task are very clear.

Summary

Based on the discussion in this chapter, we now know that:

- *Netscape's Internet Application Framework includes Java, JavaScript, HTML, as well as many other standards.*

- *JavaScript is one component of Netscape's Internet Application Framework.*

- *JavaScript can be used to embed useful applications in your Web pages.*

- *Navigator 3.0 is the best browser to use to run examples in this book.*

- *JavaScript is not Java. The differences between the two are very clear, and can be seen in the summary in Table 1.3.*

Coming Up

The next chapter is a primer that introduces all the basics of the JavaScript language as well as details on how to write and execute JavaScript scripts.

CHAPTER
2
GETTING STARTED WITH JAVASCRIPT

- JavaScript Scripts

- Referencing Objects

- JavaScript Syntax and Structure

- JavaScript Entities

JavaScript is a convenient and powerful language that you can use to add spice to your Web pages. The beauty of JavaScript is that, while it's possible to write fairly complex JavaScript scripts, you need only use a few JavaScript statements to add interactivity to your pages. In this chapter, we guide you through the editing and execution of a simple JavaScript example as well as use simple scripts to demonstrate the structure of JavaScript scripts. The goal here is to get you programming with JavaScript as quickly as possible while, at the same time, demonstrating the power of the language.

In our first JavaScript script, we create a simple form with some JavaScript interactivity. Our script illustrates many of the core concepts of JavaScript. It also introduces a few important objects and shows how they can be used in scripts.

Before We Begin

In order to execute a JavaScript script, you'll need a copy of Netscape Navigator version 2.0 or higher. All of the examples in this book have been tested on Navigator and Navigator Gold versions 2.0, 2.01, 2.02, and 3.0 for Macintosh and Windows 95. Most have also been tested under the Sun Solaris version. The Windows95 version of Navigator 3.0 also runs under Windows NT 4.0. To run the Navigator 2.0 examples, we recommend you use Navigator 2.02 because it has important security and bug fixes. As of the publication of this book, Navigator 2.02 is also the most stable release of Navigator. However, if you use Navigator 2.02, you will not be able to run examples that contain the new JavaScript features in Navigator 3.0. If you decide to do some serious JavaScript development, it's a good idea to have both Navigator 2.02 and 3.0 on your computer.

When using Navigator 3.0, make sure that JavaScript is enabled so that your JavaScript scripts will be interpreted when they are loaded into Navigator. You enable JavaScript by selecting "Enable Java-Script" on the Languages tab in your Network Preferences, as shown in Figure 2.1. You can find the Network Preferences by pulling down the Options menu in Navigator 3.0. In Navigator 2.0, there is no checkbox for enabling JavaScript, as it is always "on"—there is no way to disable it.

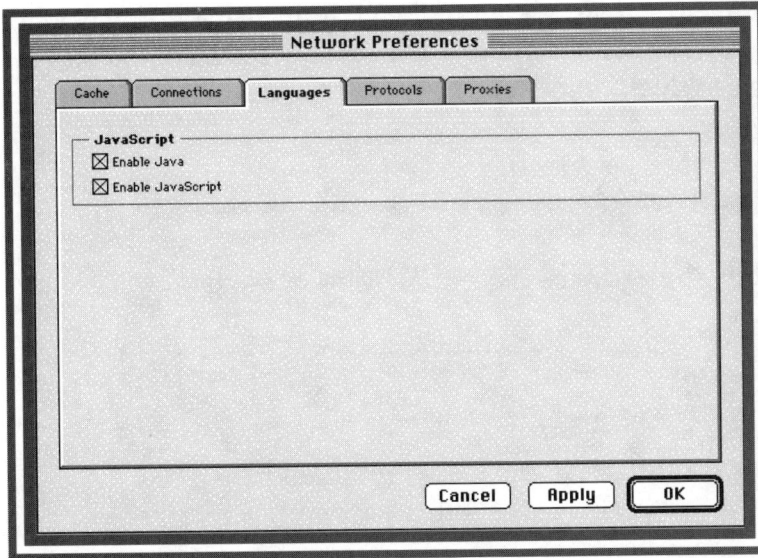

Figure 2.1 In order to use JavaScript with Navigator 3.0, you must enable it in your Network Preferences

You can download Navigator from Netscape Communications' web site at:

```
http://www.netscape.com/
```

Or their ftp site at:

```
ftp://ftp.netscape.com/
```

Navigator Gold is identical to Navigator, with the addition of a built-in HTML editor. The editing capabilities of Navigator Gold make it convenient for editing HTML pages containing JavaScript. However, you can also use a text editor, such as Notepad under Windows, or SimpleText under Macintosh, to create and edit your scripts.

One advantage of using a separate text editor instead of Navigator Gold to edit your scripts is that there is less of a chance of losing your work if Navigator decides to crash.

Navigator Gold Lets You Edit JavaScript

Once you've loaded an HTML page containing JavaScript, select "Edit Document" from the File menu to edit the JavaScript script. Select "Browse Document" and the JavaScript is instantly interpreted! To enter new JavaScript scripts, select "Edit Document" from the File menu and then select "Text" from the Format menu and select the Client JavaScript radio button.

While the Microsoft Internet Explorer 3.0 browser also contains a JavaScript implementation that is roughly equivalent to the implementation in Navigator 2.0, owing to architectural differences in Microsoft's and Netscape's Internet architectures, examples in Chapters 10, 11, and 12 will not work with Internet Explorer, so we recommend you use Navigator to run the examples in this book.

A Simple Example

For our first example, let's suppose that you want to display the current date and time on your Web page whenever a user loads it into their browser. Before JavaScript was added to Navigator, you had to write a server-side CGI (Common Gateway Interface) program to obtain the current time and date and then add it to your Web page before sending it to the user. With JavaScript, it requires just a few lines of code and all of the logic is contained in your Web page. There is no longer any need to query the Web server to obtain the date and time.

If you have a text editor or Navigator Gold handy, type in the HTML document shown in Program 2.1, which contains a JavaScript script, and save it as date.htm. We will analyze each part of the document once you have typed it in.

Program 2.1: The date.htm[1] program

```
<HTML>

<HEAD>

<TITLE>A Page With The Date And Time</TITLE>


<SCRIPT  LANGUAGE="JavaScript">

function FillDate() {

this.document.dform.dateandtime.value = new Date()

}

</SCRIPT>

</HEAD>
```

(continued)

1. You could simplify date.htm by putting the function routine directly into the onLoad statement, like: <BODY onLoad=" document.dform.dateandtime.value = new Date()">, but for purposes of learning the language, the function call is more instructive.

```
<BODY onLoad="FillDate()">

<FORM NAME="dform">

The current date and time is:

<INPUT TYPE="text" NAME="dateandtime" VALUE="You Do Not Have
JavaScript" SIZE=42>

</FORM>

<BR>

This page is brought to you by Prentice Hall. Thanks for stop-
ping by!

</BODY>

</HTML>
```

The first thing to note about date.htm is that it looks almost like your usual Web page. It has the usual <HTML>, <HEAD>, <TITLE>, and <FORM> tags, but there are several important additions.

The first new tag we encounter, and perhaps the most common one you'll see in this book, is the <SCRIPT> tag. In date.htm, the <SCRIPT> tag is used as a container tag. That means that everything between the <SCRIPT Language="JavaScript"> tag and its closing tag, </SCRIPT>, is JavaScript. The Language parameter is necessary to differentiate between JavaScript and other scripting languages.[2]

Navigator 3.0 also recognizes a "SRC=" attribute to the <SCRIPT> tag so that JavaScript scripts can reside in files separate from the Web page where they are referenced. We'll discuss the SRC attribute later in this chapter.

---

2. The only scripting language supported by Navigator 2.0 and 3.0 is JavaScript. Without the language attribute, Navigator assumes JavaScript is the scripting language. Browsers such as Microsoft's Internet Explorer browser 3.0 support both JavaScript and Visual Basic Script. If it contained Visual Basic Script statements, it would be <SCRIPT Language="VBS"> instead.

Let's take a closer look at the JavaScript script that's in our `date.htm` example. In it, we define one function, named `FillDate`, that does nothing more than set the value of the form field named `dateandtime` to the current date and time.

```
<SCRIPT  LANGUAGE="JavaScript">

function FillDate() {

this.document.dform.dateandtime.value = new Date()

}

</SCRIPT>
```

The next element that we encounter is the unusual <BODY> tag, which contains a JavaScript event handler called `onLoad`. The `onLoad` event handler is executed immediately after the Web page is loaded into the browser window. In this instance, our function `FillDate()` is executed immediately after the page is loaded.

```
<BODY onLoad="FillDate()">
```

The main part of our Web page is a simple HTML form, named `dform`, with a single text field, named `dateandtime`. It uses standard HTML syntax. We give the text field the initial value of "You Do Not Have JavaScript" so that it will display if you load the page into a browser that does not support JavaScript, such as Navigator version 1.1.

```
<FORM NAME="dform">

The current date and time is:

<INPUT TYPE="text" NAME="dateandtime" VALUE="You Do Not  Have
JavaScript" SIZE=42>

</FORM>
```

Finally, we print a carriage return and text, just for fun:

```
<BR>

This page is brought to you by Prentice Hall. Thanks for stop-
ping by!

</BODY>
```

Let's go ahead and execute our JavaScript script by loading `date.htm` into our browser. In Navigator, go the file File menu and select "Open File In Browser". If it executes properly, you should see something close to Figure 2.2.

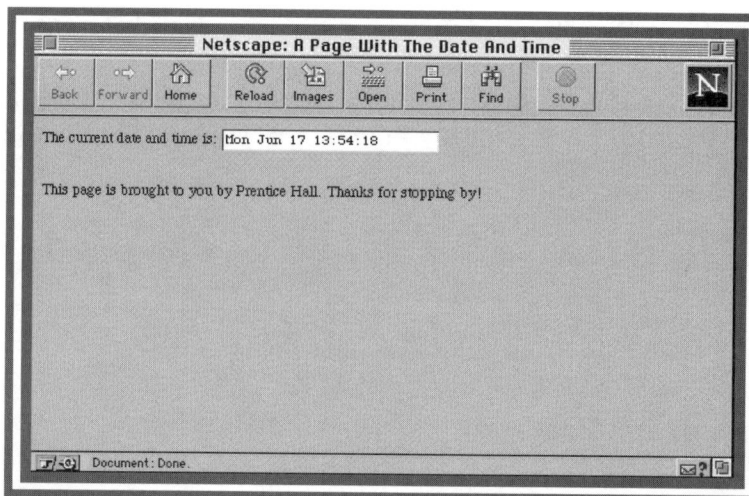

Figure 2.2 The page `date.htm` running in Navigator 3.0 for Macintosh

Our first JavaScript example is now finished and executed. We'll return to our `date.htm` example again in subsequent sections of this chapter, adding to it to illustrate additional features of JavaScript. Next, let's examine how JavaScript scripts are loaded and executed from within HTML documents.

How JavaScript Is Loaded and Executed

Navigator loads and interprets Web pages from top to bottom. That's important to understand when you are writing your scripts because you want to make sure that your scripts are interpreted in a predictable order. Functions must be defined before they are called, output must be written at appropriate times, and events must only occur when referenced functions and variables are available.

You can take advantage of the top-to-bottom interpretation of Web pages by putting multiple JavaScript scripts in your Web pages. That way, you can be sure that the scripts are interpreted at the right time.

Let's look at a different version of `date.htm`, this one containing two scripts. We'll call it `date2.htm`, as in Program 2.2. We'll replace the form in `date.htm` with a script that writes directly to the current document. `Date2.htm` produces the same output as `date.htm` by writing directly to the document instead of filling in a form field. The order of interpretation is important here because we want the `top.document.write` method to occur immediately after the string "The current date and time is:" is loaded into our browser.

> **Note** Functions are never executed until they are called; therefore, the `top.document.write` does not occur until we call it from the second script.

A Web page can be logically divided into two regions. The top region is enclosed by the <HEAD>...</HEAD> tags. The bottom region is enclosed by the <BODY>...</BODY> tags. As a general rule, you want your function definitions to come first in the <HEAD> portion of your document, so that they are available to event handlers and other JavaScript statements that reference the functions.

Define Your Functions In the <HEAD>

As a general rule, it is best to define your JavaScript functions in the <HEAD> portion of your Web page to ensure that they are defined before event handlers or scripts in other parts of your Web page call them.

Program 2.2: `Date2.htm`, a revised version of `Date.htm`

```
<HTML>

<HEAD>

<TITLE>A Page With The Date And Time</TITLE>

<SCRIPT  LANGUAGE="JavaScript">

function FillDate() {

dateandtime=new Date()
```

(continued)

```
top.document.write(dateandtime)

}

</SCRIPT>

</HEAD>

<BODY>

The current date and time is:

<SCRIPT LANGUAGE="JavaScript">

FillDate()

</SCRIPT>

<BR><BR>

This page is brought to you by Prentice Hall. Thanks for stop-
ping by!

</BODY>

</HTML>
```

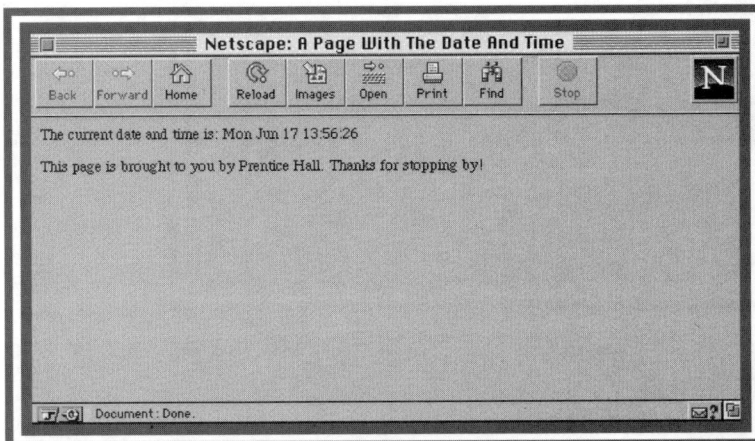

```
┌──────────────────────────────────────────────────────────────┐
│ ▢▢  Netscape: A Page With The Date And Time          ▢▢      │
│  ⇦○    ○⇨    🏠     🔄      🖼      ⇨○     🖨      🔍    ⊘   Ⓝ  │
│  Back  Forward Home  Reload  Images  Open   Print   Find  Stop  │
│                                                                │
│  The current date and time is: Mon Jun 17 13:56:26            │
│                                                                │
│  This page is brought to you by Prentice Hall. Thanks for stopping by! │
│                                                                │
│                                                                │
│                                                                │
│                                                                │
│                                                                │
│                                                                │
│  ⌐/⊸  Document: Done.                               ✉?▤       │
└──────────────────────────────────────────────────────────────┘
```

Figure 2.3 The page `date2.htm`

Navigator interprets `Date2.htm` in the following order:

1. `top.document.title` *is set to "A Page With The Date And Time".*

2. *The function* `FillDate()` *is defined.*

3. *"The current date and time is:" is displayed.*

4. *The function* `FillDate` *is executed, which displays the string stored in the variable* `dateandtime`.

5. *"This page is brought..." is displayed.*

We can also take advantage of the fact that Navigator loads and interprets our Web page from top to bottom to place scripts with `document.write` statements strategically within our Web page. Because the evaluation of the page proceeds from top to bottom, we know that the output of the scripts in our Web page will occur sequentially. In Program 2.3, `date3.htm`, we'll add another script to the end of `date2.htm` to show how you can take advantage of top-to-bottom evaluation to write the output of scripts into your page. The additional script displays the version of the Navigator browser you are using. Figure 2.4 shows the output of `date3.htm`.

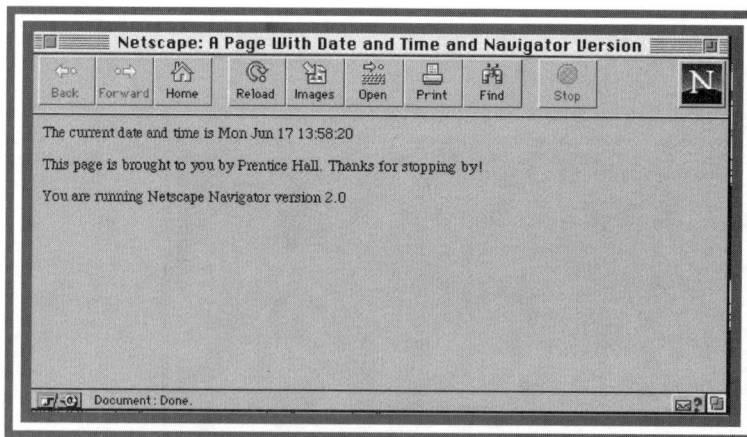

Figure 2.4 The page `date3.htm` running in Navigator 2.0 for Macintosh

Program 2.3: `Date3.htm` takes advantage of the top-to-bottom evaluation of JavaScript.

```
<HTML>

<HEAD>

<TITLE>A Page With Date and Time and Navigator Version</TITLE>

</HEAD>

<BODY>

The current date and time is

<SCRIPT LANGUAGE="JavaScript">

dateandtime=new Date()

top.document.write(dateandtime)

</SCRIPT>

<BR><BR>

This page is brought to you by Prentice Hall. Thanks for stopping by!

<BR><BR>

You are running Netscape Navigator version

<SCRIPT LANGUAGE="JavaScript">

var place=0

place=navigator.appVersion.indexOf(" ")

document.write(navigator.appVersion.substring(0,place))

</SCRIPT>

</BODY>

</HTML>
```

Introduction to Objects

The Navigator browser imposes a simple object model on any Web page that is loaded. The object model, which we'll discuss in more detail in Chapter 4, "The JavaScript Object Model" along with the various properties and methods of objects, is a convenient way for JavaScript to reference the various components of a Web page. Using JavaScript, you can reference such built-in Navigator objects as forms, documents, and dates, and, as you'll see in Chapter 4, you can also create your own objects. To get at the various attributes of the Navigator objects, you can reference their properties. There are also specific operations, called methods, that act upon objects.

For now, let's take a quick look at the objects in our sample page, date.htm. When date.htm is loaded into Navigator, several objects are instantiated and made available using JavaScript. If you are familiar with programming in a language such as C, it is useful to think of objects as a specific data type. Some objects are strings, some are structs, and others are arrays.

Our text field is a text object that is referenced by its NAME attribute. Our form is a form object and is also referenced using its NAME attribute. Further, when we load date.htm, it becomes the current document object. The browser window is yet another object and is referred to with the keyword "this," which means the window in which we are currently working. We will discuss how to reference other browser windows, as well as subwindows (frames), in later chapters.

Let's take another look at date.htm in which the function Fill-Date is defined. We can see that the left side of the statement begins to make sense:

```
this.document.dform.dateandtime.value = new Date()
```

Taking just the left side of the assignment statement, we can put it into plain English by reading it from right to left as: "the value (value) of the text field named `dateandtime` (dateandtime), in the form named `dform` (dform), in the current document (document), in the current window (this)".

So what does the right side of that statement mean? Date is a built-in object of Navigator. It is a string object containing the date and time and has a format that looks like this:

```
"month day, year hours:minutes:seconds"
```

Calling Date with no parameters, `Date()`, returns the current date and time in the format above.

The keyword "new" creates a new instance of the object Date, so the right side of the statement returns a string containing the current date and time in the above format.

The <SCRIPT> Tag

As we've seen in previous examples, JavaScript scripts are placed directly into Web pages using the container <SCRIPT>...</SCRIPT> tag. All JavaScript scripts, except those inside of HTML tags, are referenced using the <SCRIPT> tags, so it is important to understand its attributes and usage. We discuss JavaScript inside of HTML tags later in this chapter. Table 2.1 shows the attributes of the <SCRIPT> tag.

Table 2.1   <SCRIPT> Tag Attributes

<SCRIPT> tag attribute	Description	Example
LANGUAGE = language	Determines what script interpreter is used. Some possible values are "JavaScript" for JavaScript scripts, and "VBS" for Visual Basic Scripts. Microsoft's Internet Explorer 3.0 recognizes VBS. This attribute should always be used, though some browsers assume JavaScript if it is missing.	<SCRIPT LANGUAGE= "JavaScript">
SRC = URL (Navigator 3.0 only)	The URL of a JavaScript source file, which must contain only JavaScript statements. Even if this attribute is used, a closing </SCRIPT> tag is required. If the LANGUAGE attribute is missing, the filename extension, such as .js, will be used to determine the script interpreter	<SCRIPT LANGUAGE= " JavaScript" SRC="http:// mymachine.com/ mysource.js"> </SCRIPT>

All Web browsers that understand JavaScript will attempt to evaluate scripts placed between the <SCRIPT> tags. The purpose of the LANGUAGE attribute of the <SCRIPT> tag is to tell the browser what scripting language is used. For Navigator 2.0, the LANGUAGE attribute is ignored and JavaScript is always assumed. Microsoft's Internet Explorer 3.0, on the other hand, recognizes both Visual Basic Script and JavaScript. A good rule of thumb is to always use the LANGUAGE attribute with the <SCRIPT> tag because future browsers may support many scripting languages.

The SRC attribute is a new attribute that was added in the Navigator 3.0 implementation of JavaScript. The SRC attribute lets you put your JavaScript scripts into a separate file instead of in your Web page. This makes your Web pages easier to read and maintain. It also makes it easy for several files to share the same JavaScript script. As an example, we'll take our `date.htm` program and put the Java-Script script into a separate file that we'll call `date.js` (Program 2.4). By convention, the file extension `.js` is used for JavaScript source files. Note that when you use the SRC attribute, the <SCRIPT> tag is still a container; that is, a closing </SCRIPT> is necessary. We'll call our modified `date.htm` program, `sdate.htm` (Program 2.5). It now has a <SCRIPT> tag with the SRC attribute set to `date.js`.

Program 2.4: `date.js` is a JavaScript script

```
function FillDate() {

this.document.dform.dateandtime.value = new Date()

}
```

Program 2.5: `sdate.htm` uses the SRC attribute of the <SCRIPT> tag, which causes the contents of the file `date.js` to be loaded and interpreted.

```
<HTML>

<HEAD>

<TITLE>A Page With The Date And Time</TITLE>

<SCRIPT SRC="date.js">

</SCRIPT>

</HEAD>

<BODY onLoad="FillDate()">

<FORM NAME="dform">

The current date and time is:

<INPUT TYPE="text" NAME="dateandtime" VALUE="You Do Not Have
JavaScript" SIZE=26>
```

(continued)

```
</FORM>

<BR>

This page is brought to you by Prentice Hall. Thanks for stop-
ping by!

</BODY>

</HTML>
```

A single Web page can contain any number of scripts enclosed by the <SCRIPT>...</SCRIPT> tag. You can also have a Web page where there are some scripts using <SCRIPT>...</SCRIPT> and some using the SRC attribute. Because the Navigator 2.0 browser does not recognize the SRC attribute of the <SCRIPT> tag, it will ignore the SRC attribute.

Navigator 3.0 will ignore the closing </SCRIPT> tag if the SRC attribute is used. For more advanced techniques for handling Navigator 2.0 and 3.0 compatibility issues with the <SCRIPT> tag, see Appendix E, "Useful Tables and Other Info."

The <NOSCRIPT> Tag

The <NOSCRIPT> tag can be used to display HTML to a non-JavaScript capable browsers (such as Navigator 1.1). It will also display HTML to JavaScript-capable browsers that have JavaScript disabled in their options panel.

In Program 2.3, for example, we could add the <NOSCRIPT> tag to warn users who loaded a page that requires JavaScript, or who have disabled JavaScript in their browser and may not know it.

```
The current date and time is

<SCRIPT LANGUAGE="JavaScript">

dateandtime=new Date()

top.document.write(dateandtime)

</SCRIPT>

<NOSCRIPT>

<B>**Sorry, this page requires JavaScript to retrieve the cur-
rent date and time.

you need to get Netscape Navigator 2.0 or later! If you are
using Navigator 2.0

or later, and you see this message, you need to enable JavaS-
cript in your Network

options.

</NOSCRIPT>
```

Using Comments, Punctuation, and Special Characters in JavaScript

JavaScript has its own punctuation and syntactic peculiarities, and it's important to learn them so that, as our scripts get more complex in later chapters, you can concentrate on the language and not on syntax or punctuation details. In order to get a handle on reading and writing JavaScript, this section covers the basics of structuring JavaScript scripts, using comments in your scripts, using special characters, and delimiting strings. Understanding how scripts are structured and how punctuation is used will make it much easier to read scripts presented in later chapters of this book and to create your own (we hope!) error-free scripts.

Those readers who are very familiar with the syntax and structure of other languages such as Java, Perl, and C++ may not need to read the following sections. For them, the quick review in Tables 2.2 and 2.3 should suffice. Table 2.2 outlines the key points of this section. Table 2.3 shows the special punctuation characters used for comments, string delimiting, and statement separation that we will discuss.

Table 2.2   Key Points Covered in this Section

Topic	Key Point(s)
Using Comments in Java-Script	Use // to start a comment on a line. You can use C style, /* ... */, comments for comments that span more than one line.
Hiding your scripts from non-JavaScript capable browsers	Surround your JavaScript scripts with HTML comments, <!-- ... --> , to hide them.
Putting multiple JavaScript statements on a single line	Use a semicolon to separate multiple JavaScript statements.
Case sensitivity	JavaScript is a case-sensitive language. JavaScript keywords must have the appropriate case. HTML is not a case-sensitive language.
Using single and double quotes to enclose string literals	You can use single and double quotes interchangeably. You must alternate single and double quotes when strings are nested. You can "escape" quotes if you don't want them interpreted by JavaScript. Preceed the quote with a "\" to escape it.
Using special characters in JavaScript	JavaScript only has special characters for a handful of non-printable characters, such as tabs. See Table 2.8 for a list. HTML character entities may be used in JavaScript string literals.

Table 2.3 JavaScript Punctuation

JavaScript Punctuation	Characters Used	Example
Comments	//	temp = new Date() // Here is a comment
Comments	/*.......*/	/* More comments here */
String delimiter	"..."	document.write("<h1>HELP!</h1>")
String delimiter	'...'	document.write('<h1>HELP!</h1>')
Statement separator	;	temp = new Date(); return temp
Statement separator	end of line terminator	temp = new Date()
return temp		

Using Comments in JavaScript

Placing comments in your JavaScript scripts is easy. Comments in JavaScript scripts can use either "//" or the familiar C programming comment, "/* ... */". Comments starting with "//" may begin anywhere on a line and lasts until the end of the line. Comments enclosed with "/* ... */" may span multiple lines. The following is our program date.htm with comments.

```
<HTML>

<HEAD>

<TITLE>A Page With The Date And Time</TITLE>

<SCRIPT  LANGUAGE="JavaScript">

/* This script contains a single function

   called FillDate() that merely sets the

   form field dateandtime to the current

   date and time                             */
```

(continued)

```
// Function FillDate()

// FillDate retrieves the current date and time

function FillDate() {

this.document.dform.dateandtime.value = new Date() // Set the
current date and time

}

</SCRIPT>

</HEAD>

<BODY onLoad="FillDate()">

<FORM NAME="dform">

The current date and time is:

<INPUT TYPE="text" NAME="dateandtime" VALUE="You Do Not Have
JavaScript" SIZE=42>

</FORM>

<BR>

This page is brought to you by Prentice Hall. Thanks for stop-
ping by!

</BODY>

</HTML>
```

How to Hide From Other Browsers

In a perfect world, everyone would be running Navigator 2.0, or some other browser that recognizes JavaScript. However, the reality is that there are other browsers in use on the Internet, and most of them neither understand the <SCRIPT> tag nor execute JavaScript. So what happens when one of those browsers loads a page containing a JavaScript script?

When a browser encounters an unrecognized tag, the default action is to ignore it, which means that the <SCRIPT>...</SCRIPT> tags will be ignored in browsers that cannot handle JavaScript. Unfortunately, the JavaScript statements within the <SCRIPT> tags will be treated like any other text and therefore will be printed out on in the user's window. Let's take a look at the output of our example, date.htm, when it is viewed with the Navigator 1.12 browser for Macintosh (Figure 2.5). Navigator 1.12 does not have a JavaScript implementation, so it does not understand the <SCRIPT> tag.

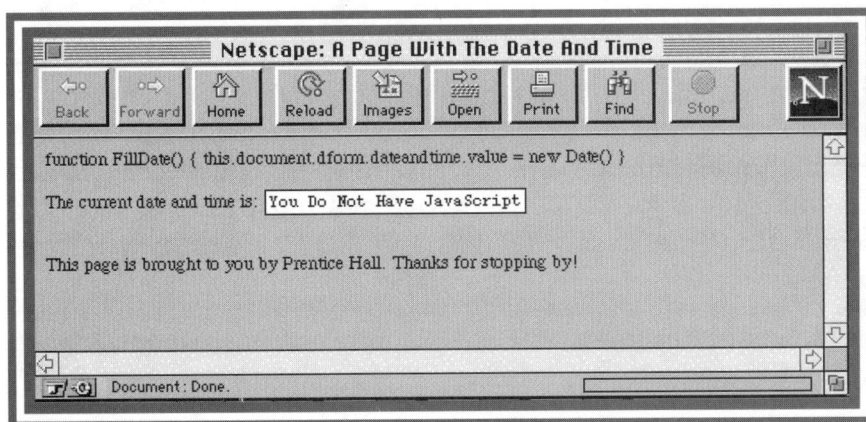

Figure 2.5 Uncommented JavaScript scripts display their source in non-JavaScript browsers, such as Navigator 1.12

The JavaScript statements get printed out as if they were regular text. Note that because we are unable to place the date value in the text field, it defaults to its value, which is the string "You Do Not Have JavaScript."

We can fix this problem by surrounding the script with comments. Standard HTML comments on Web pages are surrounded by "<!--" and "-->" strings. The <!-- string must have a space after it, and the --> string must have a space before it.

Because non-JavaScript capable browsers will ignore the <SCRIPT> tag, and also anything between these two comment strings, using the HTML comment strings will successfully hide our JavaScript script from them.

> **Tip** Some older browsers improperly implement HTML comments. They check for a single closing ">" instead of the three closing characters "-->". Users of those browsers will see JavaScript source code in their pages if you happen to use a ">" within your JavaScript script.

JavaScript-capable browsers such as Navigator 2.0 and 3.0 will ignore the first comment string, "<!--" inside the <SCRIPT> tag, but are unable to lookahead and successfully recognize the closing HTML comment tag, "-->". Therefore, we must hide the closing comment string from Navigator 2.0 and 3.0 by using a JavaScript comment string, "//".

Let's look at our example, date.htm, fully commented and hidden from other browsers.

```
<HTML>

<HEAD>

<TITLE>A Page With The Date And Time</TITLE>

<SCRIPT  LANGUAGE="JavaScript">

<!--  Here is the beginning of the comment to hide this script
from browsers without JavaScript

// Function FillDate()

// FillDate retrieves the current date and time
```

(continued)

```
function FillDate() {

this.document.dform.dateandtime.value = new Date()  // Set the
current date and time

}

/* We can also use these

C programming style comments   */

// Here is the end of the comment that hides this script from
other browsers -->

</SCRIPT>

</HEAD>

<BODY onLoad="FillDate()">

<FORM NAME="dform">

The current date and time is:

<INPUT TYPE="text" NAME="dateandtime" VALUE="You Do Not Have
JavaScript" SIZE=42>

</FORM>

<BR>

This page is brought to you by Prentice Hall. Thanks for stop-
ping by!

</BODY>

</HTML>
```

We don't have to worry about the JavaScript statement inside the
<BODY> tag or those that we might put inside other common HTML
tags (we'll discuss JavaScript inside HTML tags later in this chapter).

When browsers encounter tag attributes they don't understand, they ignore them. So, when browsers that don't understand JavaScript see the <BODY onLoad="FillDate()"> tag, they ignore the onLoad="Fill-Date()" and treat it as a normal <BODY> tag.

Always Surround Scripts with HTML Comments

Surrounding your scripts with the HTML comment strings will insure that non-JavaScript-capable browsers will not see JavaScript statements displayed in their browser window.

Multiple Statements on a Line

The syntax of JavaScript scripts is very similar to the Java and C programming languages. In general, one JavaScript statement is put on each line. The end-of-line terminator or a curly brace separates each statement. Multiple statements can be put on a single line using semicolons to separate the statements. To best illustrate this, we need to add a statement to our date.htm example because the function FillDate only contains a single statement. Let's add some more JavaScript statements to date.htm by modifying the function FillDate to append the current year to the date. In our revised FillDate function, we create a local variable named temp that is assigned the current date object.

```
var temp = new Date()
```

We then use the appName method to add the application name to the date string. The "+" sign is used to append strings together.

```
this.document.dform.dateandtime.value = temp + "from" +
navigator.appName
```

We'll call our new version of date.htm, date4.htm. It's shown in Program 2.6.

Program 2.7 is the scrunched-together version of date4.htm. It uses no line terminators, so all the statements run together and wrap around at the end of each line.

Program 2.6: date4.htm with one statement per line

```
<HTML>

<HEAD>

<TITLE>A Page With The Date And Time</TITLE>

<SCRIPT  LANGUAGE="JavaScript">

function FillDate() {

var temp = new Date()

this.document.dform.dateandtime.value = temp + "from" +
navigator.appName

}
```

(continued)

```
</SCRIPT>

</HEAD>

<BODY onLoad="FillDate()">

<FORM NAME="dform">

The current date and time is:

<INPUT TYPE="text" NAME="dateandtime" VALUE="You Do Not Have
JavaScript" SIZE=55>

</FORM>

<BR>

This page is brought to you by Prentice Hall. Thanks for stop-
ping by!

</BODY>

</HTML>
```

Program 2.7: `date4.htm` with all the HTML and JavaScript
statements scrunched onto a single line

```
    <HTML><HEAD><TITLE>A Page With The Date And Time</
TITLE><SCRIPT LANGUAGE="JavaScript">function FillDate() { var
temp = new Date() ; this.document.dform.dateandtime.value =
temp + "from" + navigatr.appName } </SCRIPT> </HEAD><BODY
onLoad="FillDate()"><FORM NAME="dform">The current date and
time is:<INPUT TYPE="text" NAME="dateandtime" VALUE="You Do
Not Have JavaScript" SIZE=55></FORM><BR>This page is brought
to you by Prentice Hall. Thanks for stopping by!</BODY></HTML>
```

Case Sensitivity

An important aspect to keep in mind while scripting with Java-Script is that it is case sensitive. Variable and function names such as bob and Bob are different. As well, all JavaScript objects, properties, and methods are case senstive. Note the following line of code:

```
place=navigator.appVersion.indexOf("123")
```

The JavaScript indexOf method must have an uppercase "O" because that is the way it is defined in the JavaScript language. Using a lowercase "O", as in indexof, would cause a syntax error. In contrast, HTML tags, and any attributes of HTML tags, whether inside of outside of JavaScript statements, are not case sensitive.

To illustrate this, note that the Web page version.htm as shown in Programs 2.8 and 2.9 is equivalent.

Program 2.8: version.htm with normal capitalization

```
<HTML>

<HEAD>

<TITLE>What version of Navigator?</TITLE>

<SCRIPT LANGUAGE="JavaScript">

function GetVersion() {

        var place=0

        place=navigator.appVersion.indexOf(" ")

return (navigator.appVersion.substring(0, place))

}
```

(continued)

```
document.write("<h2>You are running Navigator")

document.write(" version " +  GetVersion() + "</h2>")

</SCRIPT>

</HEAD>

<BODY>

</BODY>

</HTML>
```

Program 2.9: Funky capitalization is allowed in HTML statements, but not in JavaScript statements

```
<HTml>

<hEAD>

<TItLE>What version of Navigator?</TiTLE>

<SCRIPT lanGUAGE="javascriPT">

function GetVersion() {

          var place=0

          place=navigator.appVersion.indexOf(" ")

  return (navigator.appVersion.substring(0, place))

}
```

(continued)

```
document.write("<H2>You are running Navigator")

document.write(" version " +  GetVersion() + "</h2>")

</scRIPT>

</HEAD>

<BoDY>

</BODY>

</HtmL>
```

The LANGUAGE attribute of the SCRIPT tag is not case sensitive, nor is the heading tag, <h2> inside the JavaScript document.write statement.

Using Single and Double Quotes

It's a good idea to get a handle on how single and double quotes are used in JavaScript so that you will be able to decipher JavaScript statements containing multiple and nested string literals. String values are used frequently in JavaScript and, when literal string values are used in a script, they are enclosed with either single or double quotes. Single and doubles quotes can be used interchangeably to enclose string values, as well as nested in a single statement, and that can make scripts quite difficult to read.

We can see the use of quotes to surround a string literal in this line from Program 2.9 in the previous section.

```
document.write(" version " +  GetVersion() + "</h2>")
```

We can use any combination of single or double quotes to write three different, yet equivelant, versions of the same statement:

```
1) document.write(' version ' +  GetVersion() + '</h2>')

2) document.write(' version ' +  GetVersion() + "</h2>")

3) document.write(" version " +  GetVersion() + '</h2>')
```

All three versions are equivelant to the original.

Things get more complicated when you have a string within a string, or a *nested string*. Nested string literals require that you alternate your use of single and double quotes. Use one type of quotes for the nested string and another type for the enclosing string. In the following example, we use the JavaScript document.write statement to write a hypertext link to our Web page. The syntax of the document.write statement requires that we surround the string with quotes, but the string, a hyptertext link, also contains a string literal.

```
document.write("<A HREF='http://www.netscape.com/
'>Netscape Home Page</A>")
```

We could also exchange the quotes to make an equivelant statement.

```
document.write('<A HREF="http://www.netscape.com/
">Netscape Home Page</A>')
```

If you want to use single or double quotes as part of a string and not have JavaScript interpret its usage as a delimiter, you can use a backslash before the quote to "escape" the character and keep JavaScript from interpreting it. JavaScript will then treat the quote as a plain character rather than a delimiter. This is especially useful if you have a text string that contains several kinds of quotes and you don't want JavaScript to interpret any of the quotes.

Program 2.10, which we'll call `quote.htm`, is a very simple example that demonstrates escaping isolated single quotes that are used as apostrophes. Figure 2.6 shows the output of Program 2.10.

Program 2.10: `quote.htm`: escaping single quotes when they are used as apostrophes

```
<HTML>

<SCRIPT LANGUAGE="JavaScript">

document.write('"Ain\'t that too bad," he said. "You\'re miss-
ing a hubcap"')

</SCRIPT>

</HTML>
```

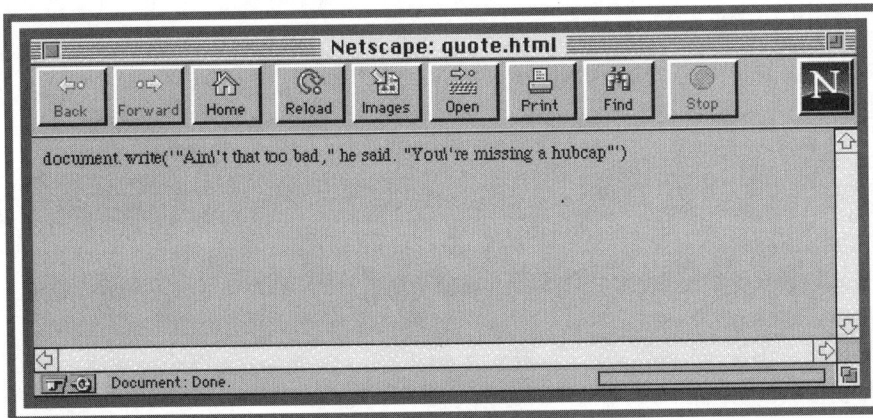

Figure 2.6 The output of `quote.htm`

Special Characters in JavaScript

JavaScript allows only a handful of non-printable characters. Table 2.4 shows those characters.

Table 2.4   Non-Printable Characters in JavaScript

Character	Value
\ b	backspace
\ f	form feed
\ n	new line
\ r	carriage return
\ t	tab

These non-printable characters can appear within JavaScript string literals. The following example, `special.htm`, shown in Program 2.11, shows how you can use the tab character to write some preformatted text to a Web page using tabs for spacing. Figure 2.7 shows the output.

Program 2.11: `special.htm` uses the JavaScript tab character to format output

```
<HTML>

<SCRIPT Language="JavaScript">

document.write("<h2>First Quarter Totals</h2>")

document.write("<PRE>Jan\tFeb\tMar</PRE>")

document.write("<PRE>$213.00\t$455.00\t$600.00</PRE>")

</SCRIPT>

</HTML>
```

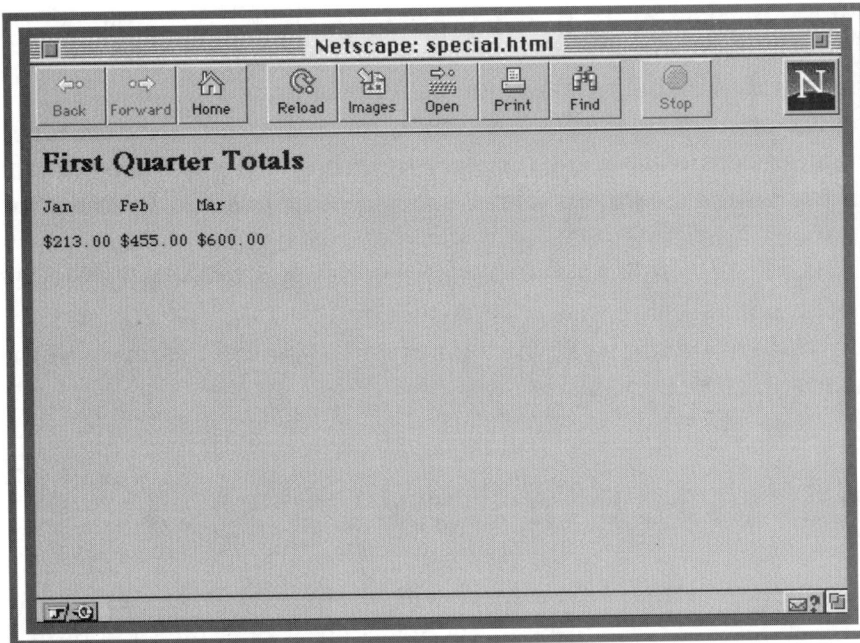

Figure 2.7 Output of `special.htm`

You can also use HTML character entities within JavaScript statements. In the following example, we want to write the string "Don't "preach" to me!" to a document. However, we get a syntax error because the apostrophe in "Don't" causes the statement to have mismatched quotes. One way around it is to encode the apostrophe using its character entity, &#039 and then alternate single and double quotes for the rest of the string.

```
<SCRIPT>

document.writeln('Don&#039;t  "preach" to  me!')

</SCRIPT>
```

Mastering the syntactical issues discussed in this section is an important step to creating error-free JavaScript scripts. As with any programming language, syntax is the key to getting the operating system to understand what you are telling it to do. There are two basic categories of JavaScript error messages, which will be explained in more detail in Appendix D, "Debugging JavaScript": Syntax error messages and Variable or Function Reference error messages. Avoiding syntax error messages is something even the most experienced programmer cannot possibly do every time. Now that you are familiar with these issues, however, you can begin to at least understand the importance of proper syntax and, while it's not always obvious where the problem lies, you'll have a better idea of what to look for should you get a syntax error message. Again, refer to Tables 2.2 and 2.3 when investigating the cause of your error for a brief overview of the key issues presented in this section.

JavaScript in HTML Tags

JavaScript statements can be used within some HTML tags to add instant feedback to user-initiated events, such as clicking on a button or hypertext link. JavaScript statements within HTML tags always take the following form:

```
<TAG  EventHandler="JavaScript statements">
```

In our first example program, date.htm, we saw the following JavaScript statement within the <BODY> tag.

```
<BODY onLoad="FillDate()">
```

The onLoad statement is a JavaScript event handler, a type of JavaScript statement that we will cover in detail in Chapter 6, "Events, Input, and Output." In this instance, it means that when this Web page is loaded into Navigator, the function FillDate() should be called. Don't worry if you don't understand yet how all the event handlers work. We introduce the concept here simply to help make scripts easier for you to read.

JavaScript event handlers can be embedded inside several common HTML tags. Tables 2.5 and 2.6 show the HTML tags that can contain JavaScript event handlers and the names of the JavaScript event handlers they can contain. JavaScript event handlers execute JavaScript functions and/or statements when their associated event occurs. They do not require the use of a <SCRIPT> tag.

Navigator 2.0 only recognizes JavaScript in the HTML tags listed in Table 2.5 and will ignore JavaScript embedded in the HTML tags listed in Table 2.6. Browsers that do not understand JavaScript will ignore any JavaScript within HTML tags.

Table 2.5   HTML Statements That Allow Embedded JavaScript for Navigator 2.0

HTML Statement	Event Handlers	Example
<INPUT TYPE= "button"...>	onClick	<INPUT TYPE="button" VALUE= "GO"NAME="go Button" onClick="history.go (eval(sform.nstring.value))">
<INPUT TYPE="checkbox"...>	onClick	<input type="checkbox" NAME="Red" onClick="if (this.checked) { showshirt()}">
<BODY...>	onLoad, onUnload	<BODY onUnload= "clearstatus()">
<FORM...>	onSubmit, onReset	<FORM NAME="dform" onSubmit= "return checkData()">
<FRAMESET...>	onLoad onUnload	<FRAMESET ROWS="30%,50%" onUnload="if (window.confirm ('Would you like me to open another browser window and load a URL?')) { loadURL() }};">
<A HREF=....>	onClick, onMouseover	<A HREF="http://www.netscape. com/" onMouseOver="window.status='Netscape Home Page'; return true">
<INPUT TYPE="radio"...>	onClick	<INPUT TYPE="radio" NAME= "sselect" VALUE="altavista(newstring)">AltaVista
<INPUT TYPE="reset"...>	onClick	<INPUT TYPE="reset" NAME="RESET" VALUE="RESET" onClick="setVarsToZero()">
<SELECT...>	onBlur, onChange, onFocus	<SELECT NAME="Month" SIZE="1" onFocus="if (!checkbox()) alert('You need to check a size first!')">
<INPUT TYPE= "submit"...>	onClick	<INPUT TYPE="submit" NAME= "sname" VALUE="Submit" onClick ="return checkdata(this.form)">
<INPUT TYPE="text"...>	onBlur, onChange, onFocus, onSelect	<INPUT TYPE="text" NAME= "year" VALUE="1996" SIZE=4 onFocus=" window.status='We use the Gregorian Calendar'; return true" onBlur="checkval(this.value)" >

(Continued)

HTML Statement	Event Handlers	Example
<TEXTAREA...>	onBlur, onChange, onFocus, onSelect	<TEXTAREA NAME="editfield" ROWS="10" COLS="20" onSelect= "alert('Do not edit. This field is for display only!)"></TEXTAREA>
<INPUT TYPE="button"...>	onClick	<INPUT TYPE="button" VALUE= "GO" NAME="goButton" onClick= "history.go(eval(sform.nstring.value))">
<INPUT TYPE="checkbox"...>	onClick	<input type="checkbox" NAME="Red" onClick="if (this.checked) { showshirt()}">
<BODY...>	onLoad, onUnload	<BODY onUnload="clearstatus()">
<FORM...>	onSubmit	<FORM NAME="dform" onSubmit="return checkData()">
<FRAMESET...>	onLoad onUnload	<FRAMESET ROWS="30%,50%" onUnload="if (window.confirm ('Would you like me to open another browser window and load a URL?')) {loadURL() }};">
<A HREF=....>	onClick, onMouseover	<A HREF="http://www.netscape.com/" onMouseOver ="window.status='Netscape Home Page'; return true">
<INPUT TYPE="radio"...>	onClick	<INPUT TYPE="radio" NAME= "sselect" VALUE="altavista(newstring)">AltaVista
<INPUT TYPE="reset"...>	onClick	<INPUT TYPE="reset" NAME= "RESET" VALUE="RESET" onClick= "setVarsToZero()">
<SELECT...>	onBlur,onChange, onFocus	<SELECT NAME="Month" SIZE="1" onFocus="if (!checkbox())
HTML Statement	Event Handlers	Example

Table 2.6   Additional HTML Statements That Allow Embedded JavaScript in Navigator 3.0

HTML Statement	Event Handlers	Example
<IMG SRC="..." ...>	onAbort, onError, onLoad	<IMG SRC="pic.gif" onError="loadaltpage()">
<MAP NAME="..."><AREA ....></MAP>	onMouseOver, onMouseOut	<MAP NAME="BigMap">< AREA COORDS="12,34,45,78" HREF="firstpage.htm" onMouseOver="jump start()"></MAP>

JavaScript entities allow you to use a JavaScript expression as the value for an HTML attribute. This gives you more flexibility when designing pages with HTML and JavaScript.

JavaScript entities are identical to HTML character entities except you replace the code with a JavaScript expression. As with HTML entities, JavaScript entities start with an ampersand and end with a semicolon, but instead of a name or number, you use a JavaScript expression enclosed in curly braces {}. You can use JavaScript entities only where an HTML attribute value would normally go. For example, suppose you wanted to change some of the numeric attributes of an HTML table. Instead of hard-coding them, you could use Java-Script as follows in Program 2.12. `Table.htm` displays a weekly calendar. You can change the table size quickly by simply editing the four JavaScript variables.

Program 2.12: `table.htm` uses JavaScript entities to display an HTML table whose size can be easily adjusted

```
<HTML>

<HEAD>

<TITLE>Weekly Schedule</TITLE>

<SCRIPT LANGUAGE="JavaScript">

var twidth="4"  //Width of table border

var color="FF712E" //Background color

var cwidth="100"  //Cell width

var cheight="108"  //Cell height

</SCRIPT>
```

(Continued)

```
</HEAD>

<BODY>

<CENTER><h2>WEEKLY SCHEDULE</h2></CENTER>

<TABLE BORDER="&{twidth};" BGCOLOR="&{color};">

<TR><TD width="&{cwidth};" align=center><B>Sunday</B></TD>

<TD width="&{cwidth};" align=center><B>Monday</B></TD>

<TD width="&{cwidth};" align=center><B>Tuesday</B></TD>

<TD width="&{cwidth};" align=center><B>Wednesday</B></TD>

<TD width="&{cwidth};" align=center><B>Thursday</B></TD>

<TD width="&{cwidth};" align=center><B>Friday</B></TD>

<TD width="&{cwidth};" align=center><B>Saturday</B></TD>

</TR><TR><TD height="&{cheight};" valign=top><BR></TD>

<TD height="&{cheight};" valign=top><BR></TD>

<TD height="&{cheight};" valign=top><BR></TD>

<TD height="&{cheight};" valign=top><BR></TD>

<TD height="&{cheight};" valign=top><BR></TD>

<TD height="&{cheight};" valign=top><BR></TD>

<TD height="&{cheight};" valign=top><BR></TD></TR>

</TABLE>

</BODY>

</HTML>
```

Summary

By now, you should be aware of the syntactic peculiarities of Java-Script and the structure of Web pages containing scripts. Much of the material in this chapter will help you read and understand scripts that you'll encounter in later chapters. It's a good idea to go back and run the examples in this chapter to ensure that you are familiar with the basics of JavaScript programming. Keep the following points in mind when scripting with JavaScript:

- *All JavaScript scripts are placed directly into Web pages using the <SCRIPT> tag, or referenced from Web pages by using the SRC attribute of the <SCRIPT> tag.*

- *Because Web pages are interpreted from top to bottom, you must write so that all of your scripts are executed in a predictable order: Functions should be defined within the <HEAD>, output must be written at appropriate times, and events must only occur when referenced functions and variables are available.*

- *Using JavaScript, you can reference such built-in Navigator objects as forms, documents, and dates, as well as create your own objects.*

- *Syntax is the key to error-free scripting. Refer to Tables 2.2 and 2.3 in this chapter for a review of the main JavaScript syntax issues.*

- *JavaScript can be used within some HTML tags to respond to user-initiated actions.*

- *JavaScript entities allow you to use a JavaScript expression as the value for an HTML attribute, giving you more flexibility when designing pages with HTML and JavaScript.*

Coming Up

In the next chapter, we present the core objects and statements of the JavaScript language and show how they can be used to create scripts that add interesting interactivity to your Web pages.

CHAPTER 3

JavaScript Language Basics

- Variables
- Statements
- Looping Constructs
- Functions
- Using Built-in Objects
- Evaluating Expressions

This chapter will cover JavaScript operators, variables, and language constructs. The contents of this chapter will serve as reference material for the rest of the book. If you are already a C or Perl programmer, this chapter will be an overview of much of what you already know about programming in general. If you are new to programming, don't worry; doing the examples and experimenting on your own will get you started with JavaScript very quickly.

Variables

A *variable* in JavaScript stores an item of data and is the basic building block of any JavaScript program you write. There are only three fundamental data types in JavaScript: *number, string,* or *Boolean.* A variable must be one of these variable types or it's nothing. Numbers can be either integers or floating-point numbers. Strings are a sequence of text characters specified between double quotes. Boolean variables can either be *true* or *false.* A value of *null* shows that a variable has no value, though it may still have a type. All other complex variable types are built on these three data types.

Variables in JavaScript are referred to by *names.* A variable name can start with a letter or an underscore (_). A variable name can also contain digits, but it cannot start with a digit because the variable will then be misinterpreted by the interpreter. Symbols such as * ,% , or / are reserved for use as operators and therefore cannot be used in variable names.

As well, JavaScript has some reserved words that you cannot use as variable names because reserved words have special meanings and functions. Because the language is still under development as of this writing, the list of reserved words in Table 3.1 may not be complete. Even so, you should be aware of at least these variable names as being sacrosanct.

Table 3.1   Reserved Words in JavaScript

abstract	boolean	break	byte
case	catch	char	class
const	continue	default	do
double	else	extends	false
final	finally	float	for
function	goto	if	implements
import	in	instanceof	int
interface	long	native	new
null	package	private	protected
public	return	short	static
super	switch	synchronized	this
throw	throws	transient	true
try	var	void	while
with			

It's important at the very start of this chapter to distinguish between variables that are *not defined*, versus those variables that are *defined but have no value assigned to them*. When examining a variable with no assigned value, you will be returned a null value. Always remember that a variable in JavaScript comes into existence when it is assigned to, not when it's used or examined in any other way. When attempting to use a variable that has not been assigned to, you will most likely run into a JavaScript error message. It's never a good idea to use uninitialized variables in JavaScript anyway, so always initialize a variable before you use it.

Statements

A *statement* in JavaScript is something that manipulates variables in a single operation. Each statement in a JavaScript program that exists on one line does not have to be terminated with a semicolon. Statements that span multiple lines, however, must be terminated with a semicolon. More than one statement can be placed on one line as long as each individual statement is terminated with a semicolon. Blocks of statements can be enclosed in curly braces ({}).

At the time of this writing, there are known problems in NT with spanning one statement over several lines. New lines in the middle of a statement are not interpreted correctly. When in doubt, turn line-wrapping ON in your editor and make the statement fit in one line, no matter how long the line gets.

Some examples of statements assigning values are shown below:

```
iq = 10;        // Assign a number 10 to iq

pi = 3.14159; // Assign a floating point number

nuthin  = null;    // No value in nuthin

name = "My name is Gomer";

  /* String assignment shown above. This is

    a long comment line terminated at this

    line */
```

JavaScript variables are *loosely typed*. That is, variables do not have to be formally declared before being used. A JavaScript variable comes into existence the moment it is referred to or assigned a value to. The value of a variable depends on how the variable is being used. We will cover using variables in a moment, but first let's see how to manipulate variables using operators.

Operators

Variables are manipulated through the use of *operators*. This section is a quick overview of the three types of operators available to you in JavaScript. Just as there are three data types, there are three types of operators: *arithmetic*, *string*, and *logical*. For each type of operator, there are two classes of operators: *binary* and *unary*.

A binary operator requires two *operands*, one to the left and one to the right of the operator. For binary operators, use the following style:

```
operand1 operator operand2
```

A quick note about comments:

Comments in JavaScript code can be specified in one of two ways.

1. Using standard C comments by enclosing them in between /* and */ characters.

2. Using // as in C++ for ignoring everything up to the end of a line.

You should use the style with which you feel most comfortable. There are really no hard and fast rules about which method to use. To maintain good coding style, you should attempt to use comments that are concise, easy to read, and written in a style that does not interfere with the code. See Table 2.2.

For example, in the statement a + b, a and b are the operands and the plus (+) sign is the operator.

A unary operator works on a single operand and can be specified either to the left or right (but not on both sides) of an operator. Therefore, some unary operators will be used in either of the two ways:

```
operator operand        // e.g. ++x

operand operator        // e.g  x++
```

Arithmetic Operators

JavaScript has these standard arithmetic binary operators available in all but the most bizarre of languages: addition (+), subtraction (-), multiplication (*), division (/), and Modulus (%). The modulus operator returns the remainder of the result of dividing an integer operand by another integer in the operation. Consider the example in the statement: 10 % 3 returns a 1. In the example a % b, a and b are operands and the % is the operator.

C/C++ programmers will also find the unary increment (++) and decrement (--) operators very familiar. Both post-increment (*var++*) and pre-increment operations (++*var*) are supported. For example, in the two statements below, a will be assigned the value of b before b is incremented by 1, and c will be assigned the value of d after d is incremented by 1.

```
a = b++; // a is set to value of b,then b is incremented.

c = ++d; // c is to value of d after d is incremented.
```

Just like the increment operator, JavaScript supports the decrement (--) operator with both pre- and post-decrement operations. For example, in the two code lines below, a will be assigned the value of b before b is decremented by 1, and c will be assigned the value of d after d is decremented.

```
a = b--; // a is set to b, then b is decremented.

c = --d; // a is set to d after d is decremented.
```

The unary negation (-) operator used to negate an operand must always be specified before the operand. For example, the following line of code will negate the value of a. (If a was 4, it will be set to –4). It's more efficient to negate than to multiply by –1.

```
a = -a
```

An assignment statement is of the plain form a = b, where a is assigned the value of b. Assignment operators can be combined with arithmetic operators to shorten code segments. These short-hand statements are listed below:

```
a *= b      really does this:   a = a * b

a /= b      really does this:   a = a / b

a += b      really does this:   a = a + b

a -= b      really does this:   a = a - b

a %= b      really does this:   a = a % b
```

Bit Operators

Bit operations, though system dependent, are very important when working with colors. JavaScripts bitwise operators let you set, clear, or shift bits in a number. A few key points to remember are that all the numbers in a bit operation are converted to 32-bit entities and bits are matched from right to left.

The three standard bitwise operators supported in JavaScript are:

1. & *for the bitwise AND operation.*

2. | *for the bitwise OR operation.*

3. ^ *for the bitwise XOR operation.*

The table of operations on a pair of bits are listed in Table 3.2

Table 3.2   Bitwise Operands

Operands				
#1	#2	AND	OR	XOR
0	0	0	0	0
0	1	0	1	1
1	0	0	1	1
1	1	1	1	0

For example, Given two numbers 10 (in bits, 1010) and 7 (in bits, 111), we will get the following results:

```
a = 10;

b = 7;

c = a & b; // c = 2,  1010 & 0111 = 0010

d = a | b; // d = 15, 1010 | 0111 = 1111

e = a ^ b; // e = 13, 1010 ^ 0111 = 1101
```

Note how the seven in Item b is used as at least a four-bit entity even though it's possible to represent it in three bits.

Bits can be shifted to the left or right to achieve a multiplication or division by 2, respectively. Three bitwise shift operators are supported in JavaScript:

1. *Left Shift a by b times, with zeroes shifted in from right. (a << b)*

2. *Zero-fill Right Shift a by b times, stuff zeroes on high-order bits. (a >>> b)*

3. *Sign-propagating Right Shift a by b times (a >> b). If the topmost bit is set, do not stuff zeroes.*

Shift operators convert all their operands into 32-bit integers, even though results are returned in the same type as that of the left-hand operand. Bits shifted off on the right or left side of an operand are discarded.

For example, 7<<2 yields 28, because 111 shifted two bits to the left yields 11100, which is 28 decimal. 7 >> 1 will give 011, the right-most bit being discarded, to give the value of 3.

JavaScript has shortcut assignment operators for bitwise operations that are very similar to those for it's arithmetic operators. The permitted shortcut operators are:

1. $a \mathrel{<<=} b$ *actually does this* $a = a << b$

2. $a \mathrel{>>=} b$ *actually does this* $a = a >> b$

3. $a \mathrel{>>>=} b$ *actually does this* $a = a >>> b$

4. $a \mathrel{\&=} b$ *actually does this* $a = a \mathrel{\&} b$

5. $a \mathrel{\text{^}=} b$ *actually does this* $a = a \text{ ^ } b$

6. $a \mathrel{|=} b$ *actually does this* $a = a \mid b$

Logical Operators

Logical operators perform Boolean actions on Boolean operands and return a logical value of either *true* or *false*. The logical "AND" operator is the use of two ampersands together (&&). The && operator returns true if both Boolean operands *op1* and *op2* are true; otherwise, it returns false. The operands *op1* or *op2* can be expressions or returned values from functions. The logical "OR" operator returns true if either logical operand *op1* or *op2* is true. Only if both *op1* and *op2* are false does the ‖ return a false value. The logical "NOT" operator is a unary operator that is used to negate its Boolean operand value. That is, if the variable is true, return false, and if the variable is false, then return true.

This is important: JavaScript is smart enough to figure out whether or not to continue in a series of logical statements. Be careful when placing actions in a boolean statement.

For example, consider the three calls to boolean functions in the statement below:

```
a = eval1() && eval2() && eval3();
```

JavaScript processes the statement above from left to right. At the very first false value, JavaScript will stop processing the line. This means that if *eval1()* returns false, then *eval2()* and *eval3()* are **not** called and the statement returns true immediately. Don't program your code to rely on *eval2()* and *eval3()* being called all the time.

Likewise, for a series of OR operations together, the very first true evaluation will stop processing on the order from left to right. For example, in the following below:

```
a = eval1() || eval2() || eval3();
```

if *eval1()* returns true, then *eval2()* and *eval3()* will not be called. This type of coding can spell disaster, especially if you are relying on eval2() and eval3() to always do something for you.

Comparison Operators

A *comparison operator* returns a logical value based on the result of the comparison of values in two operands. Numbers are compared on the basis of their numeric values, and strings on the basis of their standard lexicographical ordering. Table 3.3 lists comparison operators.

Table 3.3   Comparison Operators

Oper	Description
a == b	Returns true if a and b are equal.
a != b	Returns true if a and b are not equal.
a > b	Returns true if a is greater than b.
a < b	Returns true if a is less than b.
a >= b	Returns true if a is greater than or equal to b.
a <= b	Returns true if a is less than or equal to b.

Tertiary statements allow the assignment of a value based on a condition. For example, consider the following statement:

```
a = (condition) ? b : c;
```

If condition is true, then the value of a is assigned the value of b. If the condition is false, a will be assigned the value of c. Strings can also be used in tertiary statements, as in:

```
status = (kills >= 125) ? "ace" : "durn good"
```

This statement assigns the value "ace" to the variable status if the value in kills is greater than or equal to 125, otherwise it assigns the string "durn good" to status.

String Operations

Strings are just a series of characters. You can concatenate strings together, truncate them, and assign them to other strings. Strings are encased in double quotes and can include spaces. For example, to assign the value of "Be Prepared" to a variable x, you would use the command:

```
x = "Be Prepared";
```

Use the plus sign (+) to concatenate two strings. For example, given a variable with a string "down" in it, you can change the value to "down home" with any one of the following commands:

```
x = "down "; // Given this statement

         /* you can make y equal to "down home" with

         ** any of the following commands: */

y = "down " + "home";

y = x + "home";

y += "home";

y += x;
```

Empty strings are defined as two double quotes together. To clear a string, simply set it to "" as shown here:

```
empty = "";
```

Strings can also use special character codes to further format the data. These codes are very similar to those found in C or C++. Notably absent are the formats of the audible bell (\a) and the vertical tab (\v). The escape formats that can be applied to strings in the current version of JavaScript are listed in Table 3.4.

Table 3.4   Escape Codes for Characters in Strings

Character	Function
\b	Backspace
\n	New line
\t	Tab
\r	Carriage return
\f	Form Feed
\\	A backslash
\'	Single quote
\"	Double quote
\ooo	Octal number
\hh	Hex number

Treat strings like the objects they are. (Sounds mean, doesn't it?) Strings have methods that can be called using the syntax:

```
stringObject.method()
```

For example, the toUpperCase() and toLowerCase() functions are methods that can be called on a string to return a value that is in all caps or all lower-case characters. To use these methods, you can call the methods as shown below.

The comments following the line show the value of the variable after executing the statement:

```
var a = "Happily Married" // an oxymoron to begin with

b = a.toUpperCase() // b = "HAPPILY MARRIED"

b = a.toLowerCase() // b = "happily married"

b = "Happily Married".toLowerCase() // b = "happily married"
```

It's easy to get the length of a string with a call to the `string.length` member. Empty strings have a length of 0. Carriage returns (\n) are one character each. Don't try to get the length of null objects.

```
len = a.length  // len = 15

len = "Happily Married".length // len = 15

len = "".length // len = 0

len = "New\nLine" // len = 8   (NOT 9)

var x = null

len = x.length  // will cause an error.
```

Strings can be sliced and indexed to get substrings. First, to get an offset into a string, you can use the method:

```
string.indexOf( stringToSearch [, startIndex])
```

The `startIndex` is optional and defaults to 0 (i.e., the first character of the string if not specified). The search is conducted from left to right. A returned value of –1 indicates that the offset was greater than the length of the string.

To get an offset of a character from the end of a string, you have to search from right to left. This is where you can use the function:

```
string.lastIndexOf( stringToSearch [, startIndex] )
```

Let's try both of these functions in an example:

```
offset = "bubba".indexOf("b") // offset = 0

offset = "bubba".indexOf("u") // offset = 1

offset = "bubba".indexOf("b",1) // offset = 2

offset = "bubba".indexOf("b",3) // offset = 3

offset = "bubba".indexOf("ubb") // offset = 1

offset = "bubba".indexOf("a")    // offset = 4

offset = "bubba".indexOf("x")    // offset = -1

offset = "bubba".indexOf("starr")    // offset = -1


offset = "bubba".lastIndexOf("b") // offset = 3

offset = "bubba".lastIndexOf("u") // offset = 1

// in the next two statements, work from index back to front.

offset = "bubba".lastIndexOf("b",1) // offset = 0

offset = "bubba".lastIndexOf("b",2) // offset = 2

offset = "bubba".lastIndexOf("ubb") // offset = 1

offset = "bubba".lastIndexOf("a")    // offset = 4

offset = "bubba".lastIndexOf("x")    // offset = -1

offset = "bubba".lastIndexOf("starr")    // offset = -1
```

To get a character at a given index, call the method:

```
stringObject.charAt(index)
```

An empty string is returned if the index is too high. For example, see some statements used on strings:

```
x = "grok".charAt(0)   // x = "g"

x = "grok".charAt(1)   // x = "r"

x = "grok".charAt(2)   // x = "o"

x = "grok".charAt(3)   // x = "k"

x = "grok".charAt(4)   // x = "" empty string.
```

To get a substring instead of just one character, use this method:

```
stringObject.substring(startIndex, stopIndex)
```

Here are a few examples:

```
clip = "NT vs UNIX".substring(0,2) // clip = "NT"

clip = "NT vs UNIX".substring(2,2) // clip = "vs"

clip = "NT vs UNIX".substring(6,4) // clip = "UNIX"

clip = "NT vs UNIX".substring(0,0) // clip = ""
```

String objects are very helpful when creating HTML documents. Methods on string objects let you encapsulate strings between tags when printed out. The HTML-specific functions are as follows:

anchor("anchorName")
big()
blink()
bold()
fixed()
fontcolor(colorValue)
fontsize(size)
italics()
link(URL)
small()
strike()
sub()
sup()

The functions without any parameters simply produce a string with the HTML tags around them. For example, the statement

```
"Bugs Bunny".bold()
```

will produce the following string:

```
"<B>Bugs Bunny</B>"
```

The `string.anchor()` method will produce an anchor surrounded by <A> and </A> tags, as follows:

```
"Bugs Bunny".anchor("hero")
```

will produce the anchor tags:

```
<A NAME="hero">Bugs Bunny</A>
```

The `string.link` method will create HREF tags for you. For example, the following statement:

```
"Mrs Wabbit".link("theWife.htm")
```

will evaluate to this:

```
<A HREF="theWife.htm">Mrs Wabbit</A>
```

Finally, there's really nothing preventing you from constructing HTML tags around strings yourself. For example, you can just as easily use the statement:

```
myName = "<B>" + myName + "</B>"
```

instead of `myName.bold()` for a string. The methods simply make the operation consistent and prevent you from forgetting to include trailing HTML tags. For example, you will get a lot of BOLD text if you forget to append a </B> tag to a string variable. You would use these methods when you create HTML documents on-the-fly and use strings to create HTML tags. See Chapter 7, "JavaScript Documents," for more information on creating documents.

Tip JavaScript has functions that let you create ASCII codes for easier processing in CGI scripts. For example, in CGI scripts, space characters (" ") are replaced with %20. So "Bugs Bunny" looks like "Al%20Bundy". To do this replacement automatically, use the escape() method. To make the string more human readable, use the unescape() method. See the example below:

```
a = escape("Bugs Bunny") // a = "Al%20Bundy"

b = unescape(a) // b = "Bugs Bunny"
```

Operator Precedence

Operator precedence is the priority in which operators between variables are evaluated. Consider the following expression:

```
y = 3 + 2 * 4;
```

The value of y is 11 (i.e., 2 times 4 plus 3) because the multiplication operator is of a higher precedence than the addition operator. Operators with the highest precedence in an expression are evaluated first. Precedence evaluation for operators with the same precedence is done from left to right just like in other languages, such as Java or C++. The order of precedence evaluation from highest to lowest is listed in Table 3.5.

Table 3.5 Operator Precedence

Operator	Type of Function
--------	----------------
() [] .	Parantheses, Brackets, members.
! ~ - ++ --	Negation (boolean and bitwise) Increment, Decrement
* / %	Multiply Divide Modulo
+ -	Addition/subtraction
shift <<	
>> >>>	Bitwise shifts.
< <= > >=	Less than, less than or equal to
	Greater than, greater than or equal to
== !=	Equal to, not equal to
&	Bitwise AND
^	Bitwise XOR
		Bitwise OR
&&	Boolean AND
||	Boolean OR
?:	Tertiary
= += -= *= /=	
%= <<= >>= >>>=	
&= ^= |=	Assignment statements
,	Comma operator

Parentheses can be used to override any natural order of precedence. In our example, if you wanted to evaluate the addition before the multiplication, you would write the statement as:

```
y = (3 + 2) * 4;
```

Adding parentheses (even at times when not necessary) is sometimes quite useful in making the code easier to read. Parentheses can be nested to ensure the order of execution. The inner-most parentheses are always executed first, proceeding to the next outer level, and so on to the out-most set of parentheses. For example, consider what happens when evaluating the following expression:

```
y = ((((x +2) * 4) + 7) * 3.141);
```

First, 2 is added to the value of x, the result is multiplied by 4, then 7 is added, it is multiplied by 3.141, and finally the result is assigned to y.

> **Tip** Be sure to match the number of open and closed parentheses in any expression to avoid syntax errors. Even if you match parentheses, it's up to you to ensure that the real meaning of what you intend is well defined.

Flow and Loop Control Segments

JavaScript supports conditional and loop control statements for program flow control. The following flow control statements are supported:

- *if...else*
- *for*
- *while*
- *break (for breaking out of a loop)*
- *continue (for continuing a loop)*
- *for...in (for looping in members of a function)*

The if ... else Statement

The *if ... else* statement is useful for performing one sets of statements or another given the value of a conditional statement. The *else* clause is optional, as shown in square brackets in the following syntax:

```
if (condition) {

            statements to execute if condition is true }
[else {

            statements to execute if condition is false}]
```

The *condition* in the above syntax can be any JavaScript expression that evaluates to either a true or a false value. More than one statement in either the true or false statements portion have to be enclosed between curly braces. It's better to make the code readable and less ambiguous by using curly braces whenever possible.

Several *if* statements can be nested as long as the nesting order is defined by the judicious use of curly braces. For example, in the following code, if x is less than 10, then the value of y will never be checked.

```
if (x > 10) {

        if (y > 10) {

        msg = " both x and y are greater than 10";

        }

        else {

        msg = " x is greater than 10 but y is not";

        }

}

else

{

msg = " x is greater than 10";

}
```

It's a good idea to use braces to remove ambiguity and make the code more readable. The style you choose is, or course, up to you.

For and While Looping Constructs

Statements with looping structures are executed until a specified condition is false. Two looping structures are provided in JavaScript: the *for* loop and the *while* loop. Loops can be broken with the use of the "break" statement, or started with a new index item with the "continue" statement, which we'll discuss in the next section.
A `for` loop repeats a loop until the specified condition in the loop evaluates to false. The syntax for the `for` loop is shown below and should be familiar to C programmers:

```
for ([start-expression;] [stop-condition;] [at-every-
iteration]) {

        enclosed-statements

}
```

There are three statements in the `for` loop declaration: the *start-expression*, the *stop-condition*, and the expression *at-every-iteration*. The statements between the curly braces (*enclosed-statements*) are executed each time through the loop.

When a `for` loop is about to be started, JavaScript interpreters execute the *start-expression*. The *at-every-iteration* is performed at the end of every loop. The statements are executed as long as the *condition* evaluates to true. The *stop-condition* expression is evaluated at the start of every loop (even before the very first time) and terminates if the stop-condition returns a true value. The first statement in the *enclosed-statement* group is executed every time through the loop as long as the *stop-condition* returns a false value.

As an example, look at the following statement:

```
for (x=4,i=0,y=0; i< x; i++) {

        y += (x << i)

}
```

Note how the values of `i`, `x`, and `y` are set in the initial condition by using the comma operator. Also, note that there is no semi-colon terminating the assignment to `y` in the enclosed statement. This is because there is only one statement in there.

A `while` statement looks as follows:

```
while (condition) {

    statements

}
```

The statements within the curly braces will be executed as long as the *condition* is true. At the end of each loop (after execution the set of statements), the `while` loop condition is checked and, if false, the control will be passed to the statement following the `while` loop. The condition is therefore tested after each iteration in the loop. **There is no "do .. until" or "do .. while" loop.** If you want to make your code between the braces execute at least once, then use the following style:

```
resp =      makeSomething()

while( resp)  {

        resp = makeSomething()

}
```

where the `makeSomething()` function will return a Boolean value indicating whether or not to continue with the loop. The body of the function `makeSomething()` is what you would have placed in a `while` loop. The contents of the "do...until" loop would be the same code as shown in the previous example except that the condition would be the logical reverse of what was being checked in the `while` loop. (That is, it would check if something is false instead of true.)

The Break and Continue Statements

It's possible to have infinite loops with the condition set to "true;" however, you do need to break out of the loop with a break condition. The break statement ends a for or while loop and then passes program control to the statement just after the terminated loop.

A break statement within a while loop will look like:

```
while (true) {

        if (some_condition) break;

        else {

                do something here ...

                }

        }
```

A continue statement is analogous to the break statement in that it terminates a while or for loop; however, it does not pass program control to the next statement outside the loop. Instead, program control is passed to the top of the loop to process the next iteration. In a while loop, the program control jumps back to the condition at the top of the loop; in a for loop, program control is passed to the at-every-iteration expression.

For example, to add only those numbers less than 100 but divisible by 7, you would use the following lines in a function. (We'll cover functions in a later section.)

```
function addSevens(count) {

i = 0

sum = 0

while (i < count) {

    i++

    if (i % 7)      //exactly divisible by 7? if not,

        continue    // jump up to the top of the loop

    sum += I // okay add it;

}

return sum
```

The for...in Statement

The *for...in* statement is used to traverse members of objects. There is no need for a counter, a test for a condition, or initialization of anything. The `for...in` loop simply goes step by step through each member item one at a time. The syntax for using this special loop is:

```
for ( item in object )  {

        // statements using item.

}
```

As an example, given an object "builders", you can go through and list each of its members using the following loop:

```
sellers = ""

for ( maker in builders ) {

        sellers += builders[count] + " "

}
```

After the loop is over, the values of the member items in the builder object will be listed in the sellers string. We will cover the object model in Chapter 5, "The History, Link, Anchor, and Location Objects."

Functions

A *function* in JavaScript behaves pretty much the same way as a function would in C or any other language. The syntax for declaring a function is as follows:

```
function name([param] [, param] [..., param]...]]) {

    statements

}
```

Parameters into a function could be strings, numbers, or objects. (We will cover objects in detail the next chapter; here, we'll stick with the basics of the language.)

Functions whose return values are used in a JavaScript statement may return a value. Functions do not have to return a value if they are not used in a place where their return value may be used. It's up to the calling program to use the returned value from a function.

All values passed into a function are passed *by value* and not *by reference*. In other words, functions cannot change the value of a variable by changing a parameter that's been passed into it. Passing by value makes sense if you keep in mind that you do not have the equivalent of C language *pointers* to anything in JavaScript.

Functions are declared at the global level outside of any curly braces. In other words, they are available to the rest of the code in the file. Also, functions cannot be nested within other functions.

You just saw an example in the previous section where numbers not divisible by seven were added together. Here's another function that calculates a y coordinate given an x coordinate.

```
function square( x ) {

    var y = 0;

    var t

    if (x == 0) return y

    t = 3.14159265358 / x

    y = x * x;

    return y

}
```

Note the use of the *var statement* in the above example. A var keyword is used to declare a variable that is not visible to the rest of the world. This variable is called a local variable because it's scope of influence is localized to the block of code in which it's declared. The scope of a variable declared with a var statement is therefore within the current function. Using the var variable outside a function's curly braces makes no sense because the declared variables will be visible to all the rest of the functions anyway.

The syntax for declaring such variables is as follows:

```
var varname [= value] [..., varname [= value] ]
```

The *value* in the above definition is what you want to initialize a variable to.

A Small Example of Using Functions

Let's take a look at a small example of how to use JavaScript code. Don't worry if you do not understand some of the objects being used in this example. We will be covering objects, properties, and methods in Chapter 4, "The JavaScript Object Model."

The line numbers are added in the code for the benefit of illustration only and must not be present in the final code.

First, create a file as shown in Program 3.1. The code in the example will cycle through all the items in a selection box, use local variables, and interact with HTML forms. Again, just look at the syntax of how statements were used in the code, not what this script actually does, which is to show what the user selected from a selection list. By the time you finish this chapter, this code will make sense to you.

Program 3.1: Using JavaScript: A simple example.

```
1 <HTML><HEAD><TITLE>Text Home Page </TITLE>

2 <SCRIPT>

3

4 <!---

5 function getMon(selectObject) {

6

7 //

8 //   Declare a local variable called str

9 //

10        var str = ""
```

(continued)

```
11 for (i=0; i < selectObject.options.length; i++) {
12 if (selectObject.options[i].selected==true) {
13 if (selectObject.options[i].text =="March") str += " c1"
14 if (selectObject.options[i].text =="May") str += " c2"
15 if (selectObject.options[i].text =="July") str = " c3"
16 if (selectObject.options[i].text =="September") str = " c4"
17 if (selectObject.options[i].text =="December") str =  " c5"
18 }
19 }
20 //
21 // Return a string back to the caller
22 //
23 return str;
24 }
25 //
26 // Don't write any more comments in JavaScript after
        next line
27 //
28 <!-- End of script hiding comments -->
29
30 </SCRIPT>
31 </HEAD>
32 <FORM NAME="crbIndex">
33 <P><B>Delivery Month For CRB Index:</B>
34 <BR><SELECT NAME="delMon" MULTIPLE>
35     <OPTION> March
36     <OPTION> May
37     <OPTION SELECTED> July
38     <OPTION> September
```

(continued)

```
39      <OPTION> December

40 </SELECT>

41 <P><INPUT TYPE="button" VALUE="Month Number"

42  onClick="alert ('Code for Months Selected: '

        + getMon(document.crbIndex.delMon))">

43 </FORM>
44 </HTML>
```

Let's look at the output of the JavaScripted page on two different platforms. Figure 3.1 shows the output on a Linux machine using *fvwm* as the window manager and Figure 3.2 shows the output on a Windows 95 machine. Both machines are using Navigator 3.0 as the browser. If you are using a different browser, such as the Internet Explorer 3.0 from Microsoft you'll probably get different results.

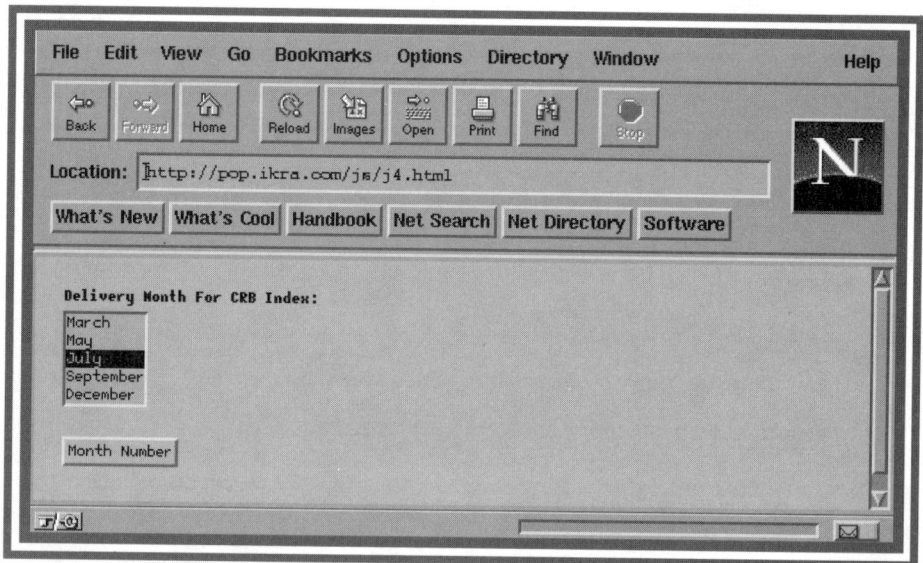

Figure 3.1 Using Navigator on UNIX-like machines

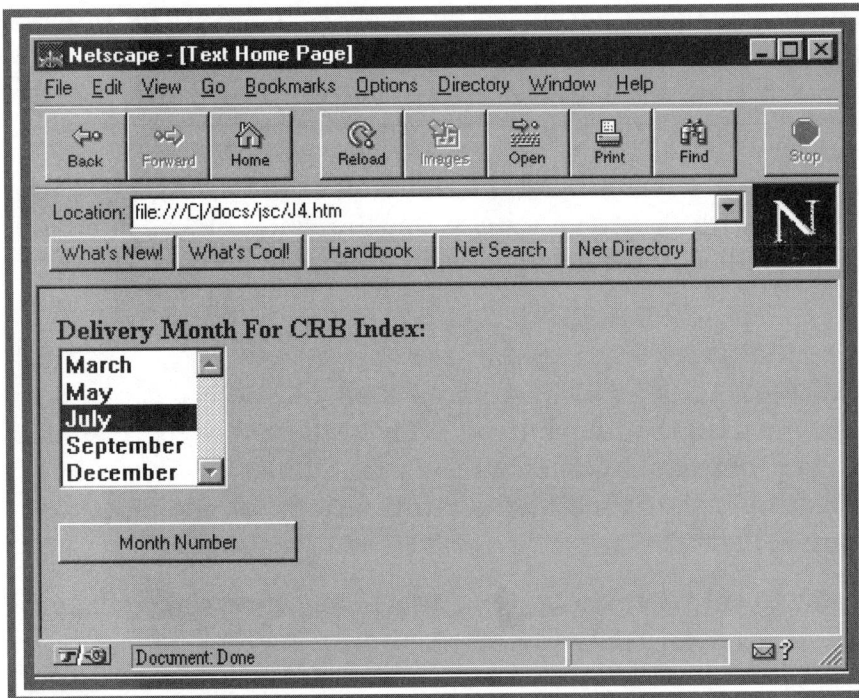

Figure 3.2 Using Navigator on Windows 95 machines

Let's now examine how the lines are used in the same script in Program 3.1. Line 4 begins a comment for all browsers and basically tells the browsers not to echo the text until the end of comment (at line 28). At Line 5, you see the declaration of a function `getMon`, which takes one parameter, `selectObject`. Note that the script did not really specify the type of the object we are sending. Line 6 declares a local variable, `i`, in the function with the `var i` statement. This means that `i` will not be seen outside the function. Lines 7 through 9 are comments only.

It is important to note: JavaScript code does not have to exist in between the <HEAD> and </HEAD> tags. The code can go in between <BODY> and </BODY> tags as well. Code in between HEAD tags is defined before there is any chance of it being called from within the BODY tags. The text between HEAD tags is defined before the body of the document is loaded. Defining a function in between BODY tags creates the risk that your function may be called before it's defined.

Line 10 declares a variable `str` that is local to the function `getMon`. As with the local variable, *i*, the local variable `str` will not be accessible from code outside the function. Note also that the script initializes the value of `str` to an empty string.

A `for` loop is shown in line 11. Note that the starting expression is to start *i* with 0. At every iteration, the value of *i* is compared with the length of the object (i.e., the number of items in the object passed in to the function). The value of *i* is incremented at the end of every loop.

The passed object will have more than one selected item. The variable *i* is used to index into an array of these objects. The index is specified between square brackets (see Lines 13 through 17). Note also how the value of the string in `str` is appended to as items are collected.

The function returns a copy of the string back to the caller at line 23. The script itself is terminated on Line 30. The Header is terminated in Line 31.

The remaining code involves using an HTML form to set and display a list and two buttons. We will cover how to do this in the rest of the book. However, since you are learning about JavaScript syntax, this example will show how your Java-Script coexists with it's HTML file.

Pay close attention to Line 42, which shows the call to the `get-Mon()` function from an INPUT button. The caption of the button is "Month Number." The alert box shown in Figure 3.3 is simply a dialog box with an OK button and some text on it. The alert box is displayed when the button "Month Number" is pressed.

Note also how the string is created within the parentheses by concatenating the values of the first string with the values returned from the call to `getMon()`. The concatenated string is then sent to the alert function call. The whole thing is set in motion when the button is clicked because the callback function is registered for the `onClick` method.

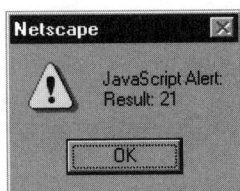

Figure 3.3   The alert box in Navigator

Built-in Functions and Objects

JavaScript has four built-in objects, which are used as building blocks for its programs. There are four objects that you will find useful when scripting JavaScript programs: Array, String, Math, and Date. These objects are built into JavaScript and have their own functions (mostly referred to as *methods*). We will briefly introduce these objects and their methods in this chapter, and the rest of the book will offer several sections and examples on how to use objects and methods. For a complete list of methods and objects, please refer to Appendix A.

String Object

You have seen some usage of the string object in the example in the previous section, "Functions." Basically, a string object is a variable with a string literal in it. The methods defined in a string object allow a programmer to work on the string. For example, using a method such as UpperCase() on a string will return an upper-cased string, and a method such as italics() will return the string encased in <I> and </I> tags, which makes the string suitable for use in an HTML page.

Array Object

The JavaScript Array object is new in Navigator 3.0. You can create new objects using the new method. The length of an Array is set when the Array object is populated. Array objects are not aprase and resize themselves to a size equal to the highest index value plus one. Elements within an array are indexed from 0 and up. The size of the array is readable from the *length* member of an Array object. Arrays can be initialized to a size by passing in the size as one and only one argument to the *new Array* call. For example, to create a array of 52 elements, you would make the following call:

```
var cards = new Array (52)
```

Passing more than one parameter to the new call will create an array with each passed item in each element of the array. For example, to create an array with items starting in sequence from index, you could use the following statements:

```
var suits = new Array ("clubs", "hearts", "spades", "dia-
monds")
```

The `suits` array would be four elements long, so it's length would be set to four.

JavaScript applications cannot decrease the size of an Array, nor can they explicitly set the `length` member of an array. However, by indexing into the highest value of an array, a program can increase the size of the Array.

```
var myarray = new Array()

myarray[1] = 'hello'

if (myarray.length != 2) alert( "Whoa major Bug!");

myarray[25] = 2

alert(" Array size is " + myarray.length);
```

This Array will not be sparse and space will be allocated for 26 items. Space for elements 0 and 2 through 24 will be allocated, but the array item itself shall be empty.

Math Object

JavaScript has a Math object for common mathematical constants and functions. For example, the `Math.PI` property is the value of pi to a reasonably good number of digits, and `Math.isNaN(variable)` returns whether something is a number or not. The Math object also includes the simple trigonometric, logarithmic, exponential, and other math functions. Just remember to use radians when working with any of the trigonometric methods that you use.

> **Tip** Navigator 3.0 supports a Math.random() method that is based on the current time. Earlier versions of JavaScript and Navigator 2.0 did not have a random method.

The `with` statement is useful for reducing the typing you have to do. (Pascal programmers will find this somewhat familiar.) Use the `with(object)` statement and place all the items between curly braces. Shown below are two ways of doing a calculation to get a value of vx and vy. One method explicitly calls out a Math object, the other method uses a "with" statement to imply the Math object within the curly braces:

```
a = Math.sqrt(x * x + y * y)

s = Math.sqrt(x * x + y * y + z * z)

vx = s * Math.cos(phi)

vy = a * Math.cos(phi)
```

The shorter version of accomplishing the same thing with the `with` statement is:

```
        with (Math) {

a = sqrt(x * x + y * y)

s = sqrt(x * x + y * y + z * z)

vx = s*cos(phi)

vy = a*cos(phi)

        } // end of working with Math module
```

Functions that are available for use with Math objects are listed in Table 3.6. All methods listed in the table have to be used either with the `with` statement or as `mathObject.method()`.

Table 3.6   Math Functions

abs(v)	absolute value
acos(v)	arc cosine
asin(v)	arc sine
atan(v)	arc tangent
ceil(v)	next integer greater than v
cos(v)	cosine
exp(v)	returns e to the power of v
floor(v)	next integer less than value
log(v)	natural log of value
max(v1,v2)	greater of v1 or v2
min(v1,v2)	lesser of v1 or v2
pow(v1,v2)	returns v1 to the power of v2
random()	returns a random number between 0 and 1
round(v)	if fractional part >= 0.5, return ceil(),else floor()
sin(v)	sine
sqrt(v)	square root
tan(v)	tangent

The math object has some well-known, predefined constants as well, which are listed in Table 3.7. Use these constants instead of devising your own values. Of course, the accuracy of these numbers will be up to about 14 digits on most platforms and will not be suitable for very accurate results. For most users, these constants will be great.

Table 3.7   Math constants

Math.E	Euler's constant
Math.LN2	Natural log of 2
Math.LN10	Natural log of 10
Math.LOG2E	Log base 2 of E
Math.Log10E	Log base 10 of E
Math.PI	Pi
Math.SQRT2	Square root of 2
Math.SQRT1_	2 square root of 0.5

Date Object

To compensate for its lack of a Date type, JavaScript offers a Date object. The Date object has many methods for setting, getting, and manipulating different dates. Internally, JavaScript store dates as an unsigned integer of the number of milliseconds since January 1, 1970 00:00:00.

To create a new object, called `myDateObject`, use the following statement:

```
myDateObject = new Date(parameters)
```

The parameters for the Date constructor can be any of the following:

- *Nothing to create today's date and time.*

- *Raw numbers for the month, day, and year. (Be careful if you are from the UK.)*

- *Raw numbers for the month, day, year, hours, minutes, and seconds. Also, be aware of the fact that this is a 24-hour clock, so there is no AM or PM to pass in.*

- *A date in the form of a string "Month Day, Year Hours:minutes:seconds".*

Some examples of setting dates are:

```
var   review = new Date("April 14,96, 23:59:45)

var   taxTime = new Date(3,15,96,22,0,0)

var   taxday = new Date(3,15,96)
```

The parameters passed into the Date object are indexed from 0 and up. So, January is 0 and December is 11, midnight is 0 and noon is 11. The only exception to the zero index rule is the day of month, which is indexed from 1 to 31 inclusive.

Date objects have several methods to get and set values for each individual component of the date separately. This way, you can work with seconds, minutes, hours, days, months, and years individually. The day of the week is automatically calculated when a Date object is modified, and you can get it using the getDay() function.

Time comparison is accomplished by using the getTime() function on two Date objects. The getTime() function returns the number of milliseconds since 1/1/70 0:0:0. The number of milliseconds per hour is 60 * 60 * 1000 and is a useful constant to have when calculating time differences. The getTime and setTime methods are useful for comparing dates. The getTime method returns the number of milliseconds since the epoch for a date object. An example of it's usage is as follows:

```
atStart = new Date()         // Get starting time

reply = doSomething()          // Take a long time to do something

atStop = new Date()            // Get stopping time

timeTaken = (atStop.getTime() - atStart.getTime()) / 1000;

timeTaken = Math.round(daysLeft) // Get an integer back.

document.write("Time Taken to chew up CPU power = " + timeTaken
+ " seconds");
```

Converting Strings to Integers or Floating-Point Numbers

The `parseInt()` and `parseFloat()` functions return an integer or floating-point number when given a string as an input argument. They both return NaN (not a number) if the input string cannot be parsed. Numbers are defined to have digits [0-9], + or – sign, exponents (e), and decimal point. Parsing stops as soon as the first unacceptable character, such as a space, is reached.

The `parseInt` function takes a string as input as in `parseFloat()`; however, it also takes an optional second parameter that specifies the radix to use. The default radix is 10, and you have to specify 8 for octal, 2 for binary, 16 for hex.

The eval( ) Function

JavaScript allows you to evaluate strings as code with the use of the `eval` function. The word *eval* is short for "evaluate." The `eval` function takes a single string as its argument. The input string can be any string representing a JavaScript expression, statement, or even a sequence of statements including variables and properties of existing objects. The scope of the variables is the same as the calling function.

> **Tip**
> On some browsers, clicking the Reload button in Navigator does not re-load in the HTML page with it's JavaScript application; instead, a previously cached file is loaded. So, if you make changes to an HTML page with some JavaScript code in it, the HTML page may not reflect those changes. Try going through the File menu selection and use the Open file instead, which will reopen the file and re-load it.

One very common use of the eval function is therefore to construct run-time JavaScript statements and execute them. For example, consider the code in Program 3.2, which takes a mathematical expression and returns the result in an alert box.

Program 3.2: Using the date object and the eval function

```
1  <HTML>

2  <HEAD> <TITLE>Test Eval Function</TITLE>

3  <SCRIPT>

4  function computeMe(obj) {

5      t = new Date()

6      s = eval(obj.userText.value);

7      return s + t

8  }

9

10 </SCRIPT>

11 </HEAD>

12 <FORM NAME="myForm">

13 <P>Enter Code = <INPUT TYPE=text NAME="userText" size=35>

14 <BR>

15 <P><INPUT TYPE=button VALUE="Evaluate"

16   onClick="alert ('Result: ' + computeMe(document.myForm))">

17 </FORM>

18 </HTML>
```

This code shows a simple example of an expression evaluator, which is defined in Lines 4 through 7. The real work of evaluation is done at line 6, where the `eval()` function is called on the value of the "obj" objects' member called "userText". The call to do the evaluation is done on line 16.

Line 5 shows how a new Date object is created with the current date. The Date object will be destroyed after the call to the function. If you do not declare t as "var", you may leave dangling objects on some systems. After the call to the function, if "t" is not declared as "var", it will continue to exist in the global scope. The second call to create a new object and assign it to "t" may cause the previous Date() object to exist with no way of killing it until the browser exits.

The example shown in Program 3.2 can be enhanced to use a TEXTAREA object to display the result of the calculation instead of an alert box. The new program is shown in Program 3.3. The output is shown in Figure 3.4. Line 6 is really the different line in the function `computeMe`. In this case, we are setting the value of the TextArea (*mine*) on the form (*myForm*), which in turn is placed on a document. Each member of an object is referred to by a period (.) to get to the final value on the left-hand side.

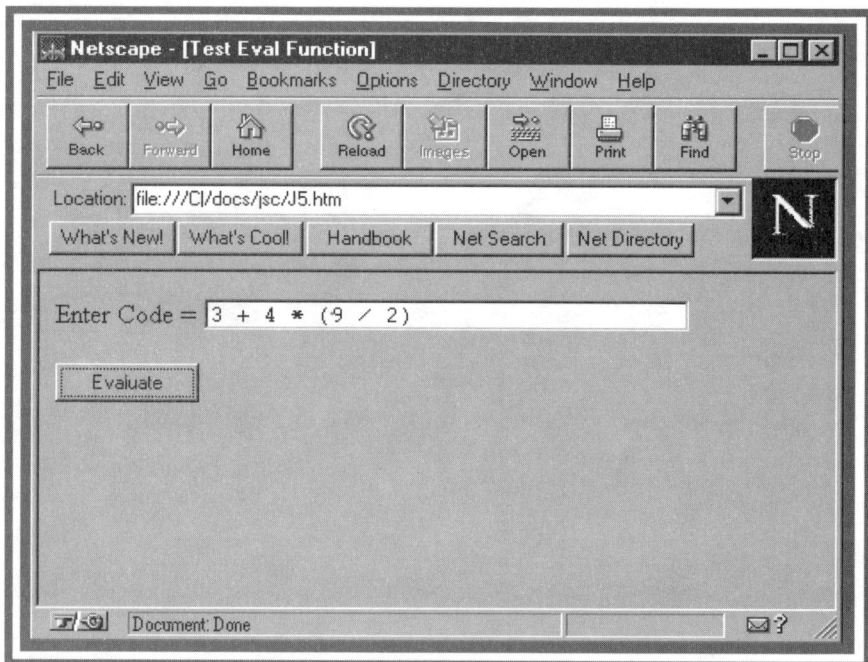

Figure 3.4 Using the date object and eval() function

Program 3.3: Using the date object and eval() function

```
1  <HTML>

2  <HEAD><TITLE>Test Eval Function</TITLE>

3  <SCRIPT>

4  function computeMe(obj) {

5      s = eval(obj.userText.value);  var t = new Date();

6      document.myForm.mine.value = s; // or try s + t

7      return s + t

8  }

9

10 </SCRIPT>

11 </HEAD>

12 <FORM NAME="myForm">

13 <P>Enter Code = <INPUT TYPE=text NAME="userText" size=35>

14 <BR>

15 <TEXTAREA NAME="mine" ROWS=2 COLS=15>

16 Help

17 </TEXTAREA>

18 <P><INPUT TYPE=button VALUE="Evaluate"

19  onClick="alert ('Result: ' +
    computeMe(document.myForm))">

20 </FORM>

21 </HTML>
```

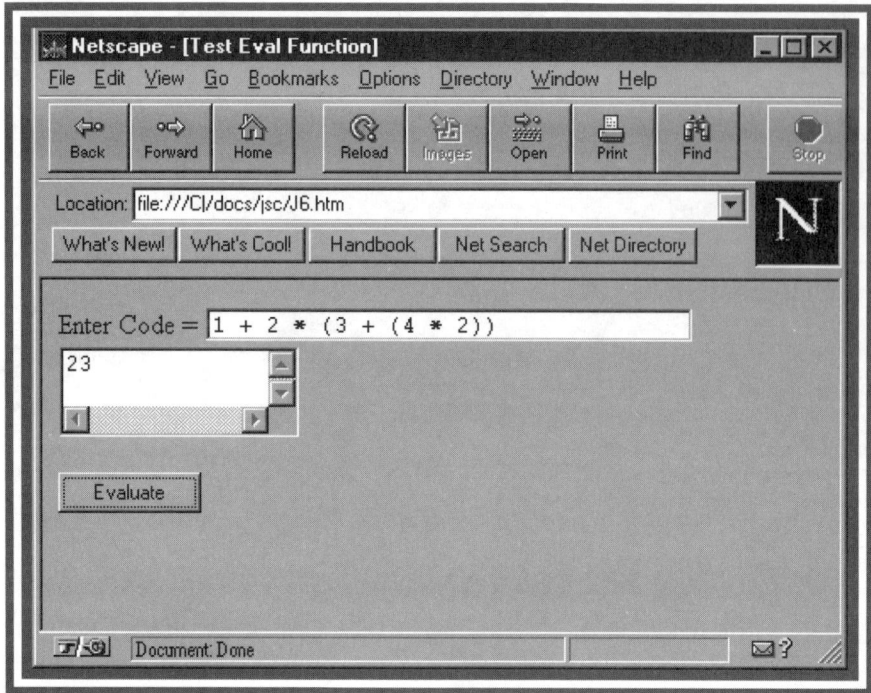

Figure 3.5 Using the eval() function

Summary

In this chapter, we have provided a very quick overview of some of the basics of writing JavaScript applications. We have also introduced some of the basics involved in writing JavaScript applications using objects. We will build on these basics as we go further into this book. A quick checklist of the JavaScript features we have learned include:

- *JavaScript supports three basic types of data: strings, number, and Boolean. A variable can be nothing as well.*

- *Variables come into existence when they are assigned to. Variables not in existence before they are used cause an error.*

- *Statements do not have to end with a semicolon. You can have more than one statement on a line by separating each statement with a semicolon.*

- *Looping statements can be controlled by one condition in a* while *loop or be stepped through using a* for *loop. Loops can be broken out of using a* break *statement or be forced to move to the next iteration with the* continue *statement.*

- *Built-in functions allow you to do math, time and date, and string manipulations operations.*

- *User-defined functions can be created. Nesting of functions is not permitted. Variables within a function can be limited to their scope with the* var *statement.*

- *JavaScript statements can be created and executed at run-time with the* eval() *statement.*

Coming Up

This chapter introduced you to programming with, and using some of the objects available such in JavaScript. In the next chapter we will cover other user interface JavaScript objects that you can use to build applications. The next chapter will also cover how to create and use your own JavaScript objects.

CHAPTER 4

JavaScript and Objects

- Using JavaScript Objects
- Methods & Properties
- Objects within Objects
- Built-in JavaScript Objects

The term *object-oriented programming* musters up different thoughts in different programmers—thoughts ranging from drooling fantasies to horrifying nightmares. While JavaScript does support objects, it is definitely not a full-blown object-oriented programming (OOP) language.

This chapter will not teach you about object-oriented programming. JavaScript does not offer all the functionality of an object-oriented programming language. If you are already familiar with OOP, be prepared to live without some of the OOP features you are so used to.

107

With JavaScript, there are no real inheritance, polymorphism, operator overloading, or data encapsulation that you would find in other object-oriented programming languages such as C++ or Ada. The JavaScript language is a simple language that lets you use items and attach functions to those items. The power of JavaScript comes from its simplicity and the use of objects. An object in JavaScript simply allows you to encapsulate information about an item in one place. Objects in JavaScript contain information in *members*. Each piece of information about an object is called a *property*. Members of an object contain specific information about each property of an object.

Each member could be a data type, such as a string, numeric, or Boolean variable. Each member could also be another object, such as a String, which is built-in to JavaScript, or a programmer-defined object. Objects also contain methods that allow a programmer to manipulate the object's methods. Methods are just functions that happen to know which object they are dealing with.

Two objects are considered to be of the same *class* if they have the same member variables and methods. A class is basically a type, or category. of an object. Many objects can be of the same class, but an object cannot be more than one class in object-oriented programming. A reference to an object contained in one object is referred to as being in a *subclass* of the class of the object in which it is contained. So, if object A is contained in object B, then object A is a subclass of object B. Also, object B is a superclass of object A. (This definition is stretching object oriented programming a bit, but serves its purpose.)

To be a bit more specific, a window is an object in JavaScript. Each window can contain information such as its location on the screen, its width, height, screen colors used, and similar attributes. All these items are the window's properties. Each window will have it's own methods, such as what action to take when loaded, on getting focus, and the like, and each action is a method that can be applied to the window.

Of course, more than one window can exist on a screen, each in a different location and with its own set of attributes. These windows have the same class of object and are therefore the same types of properties. However, the values of member variables in each window can be different, allowing the windows to have different sizes, locations on the screen, and colors.

Objects in JavaScript are really just variables that can hold more than one type of variable and its value all at the same time. Some objects can hold more than one type of value, but only one value at one time. A programmer has to be aware of what type of object they are dealing with.

Most properties of objects can be read by JavaScript, but there are some properties that cannot be modified at certain times. For example, the background and foreground colors of a window object in Java-Script can be read. They can both be set programmatically when the window's document is being laid out (More on this in Chapter 7, "Java-Script Documents"). However, once the page is laid out, only the background color property of a window can be modified; the foreground color property cannot be modified.

Note JavaScript does not purport to have all the fancy features of object-oriented programming. Yes, objects can contain other objects to provide a class-to-subclass hierarchy, but do not let this fool you. There is no inheritance, overrides, virtual functions, etc. JavaScript is not a fully structured way of programming, as you would expect from Ada, Lisp, or C++. If you want to do object-oriented programming, consider a different language that offers a bit more support in terms of object-oriented programming and is suited for the Internet.

Using Objects

A JavaScript object has properties associated with it, which you can access with the following simple notation:

```
objectName.propertyName
```

Both the object name and the property name are case sensitive, as are variable names. To assign values to members, use the following syntax:

```
objectName.propertyName = value
```

Creating Objects

Javascript objects are created with a function definition. This might be a bit uncomfortable for some programmers to work with because there is no `class` or `typedef` keyword to deal with.

To define a type of object, create a function for the object type that specifies its name, properties, and methods. For example, suppose you want to create an object type for houses. You want this type of object to be called `aHouse`, and you want it to have properties for bedrooms, baths, age, square-footage, and address. To create this type of object, you would write a function as follows:

```
function aHouse(beds,baths,age,sqft,addr) {

        this.beds = beds

        this.baths = baths

        this.age = age

        this.sqft = sqft

        this.addr = addr

}
```

The reserved word `this` refers to the object whose members you are defining. Note how the `this` reserved word is used to assign values to the object's properties based on the values passed to the function.

There are five properties in the `aHouse` object: beds, baths, age sqft and addr. Each property is assigned a value based on the input parameters passed into the function. It's not absolutely necessary to specify the incoming variable names as the names of the property member variables, but doing so makes the code more readable.

To create a new house, you would make a call to the new function with a call to the object function as follows:

```
myHome = new aHouse(4,2,4,3000,"1234 digit st.");
```

This would create an object `myHome` with beds=4, baths=2, age=4, and sqft=3000. The `addr` variable is assigned the string "1234 digit st.". You can create many houses using the `aHouse` object type. For example:

```
myHome = new aHouse(4,2,4,3000,"1234 digit st.");

myHut = new aHouse(1,1,12,700,"3141 pie av.");

myLodge = new aHouse(2,1,12,1700,"2828 Euler Blvd.");

myEstate = new aHouse(12,9,12,20000,"1 Ego St.");
```

Accessing the members of an object you create is easy. To get the number of bedrooms for `myHome`, for example, you would use a statement such as:

```
x = myHome.beds
```

To assign a value to a property, you can make the call as:

```
myEstate.addr = "111 Consumptia"
```

Member variables in a user-defined object can be read and written to, unlike some read-only properties in JavaScript objects. Actually, the member variables in a user-defined object are stored in an associative array. We covered arrays in Chapter 3, "JavaScript Language Basics," but here's a quick review with objects in mind.

An array is simply an ordered set of values associated with a single variable name. Items within this set can be addressed using a numeric index. The first item in an array is at index 0, the next at 1, and so on. An associate array is one in which items can be indexed using names. So, the first item can be at index "foo", the next at "bar", and so on.

> **Note** In earlier versions of Navigator, there was no array object with which to work.

This is important enough to repeat: In a JavaScript object, the properties of an object are stored in an associative array. You can address the properties of the aHouse object using the following statements:

```
myHouse["beds"] = 2

myHouse["baths"] = 1

myHouse["age"] = 111

myHouse["sqft"] = 2000

myHouse["addr"] = "321 Reverse st"
```

Each of these members can also be accessed by its index in the array. The order of these elements is based on the order in which they are declared in the function.

```
myHouse[0] = 2

myHouse[1] = 1

myHouse[2] = 111

myHouse[3] = 2000

myHouse[4] = "321 Reverse st"
```

It's a bit dangerous to use indices to address member variables because the indices are based purely on the order in which the members are declared. If you change the order of occurrence in the function, then you must also remember to change the indices where ever they are used. When possible, try to use member names instead of indices to avoid such problems. The really bad part about such a bug is that the swapping of indices will not even generate a bug unless the types of variables happen to be different. For example, in the aHouse example, if the beds and baths variables were to be swapped, your program will be using wrong variables for aHouse[0] and aHouse[1] if you expect beds to be the first variable all the time. Following is a small function to display all the properties of an object:

```
function showProperties(obj, objName) {

    var output = ""

    for (var i in obj)

        output += objName + "." + i + " = " + obj[i] + "\n"

    return output;

}
```

Note A member can be created either with an index (aHouse[0]="beds") or by name (aHouse["beds"] = 2). However, the catch is that these statements create two different members (i.e., the string "beds" is not equal to 0, so the array is indexed in two different locations). The exception to this rule is the document forms, elements, links, frames, images, and anchors array, which can be referred to by name and by index.

To use this function, you would use the HTML file shown in Program 4.1. The output of a sample run is shown in Figure 4.1.

Program 4.1: Displaying properties of an object

```
<HTML>

<HEAD><TITLE>Show Some Objects Properties</TITLE>

<SCRIPT>

<!---

function showProperties(obj,objName) {

        var output = "";

        for (var i in obj)

        output += objName + "." + i + " = " + obj[i] + "\n";

        alert(output);

}
```

(continued)

```
function aHouse(beds,baths,age,sqft,addr) {

        this.beds = beds

        this.baths = baths

        this.age = age

        this.sqft = sqft

        this.addr = addr

}


myHome = new aHouse(4,2,4,3000,"1234 digit st.");

myHut = new aHouse(1,1,12,700,"3141 pie av.");

myLodge = new aHouse(2,1,12,1700,"2828 Euler Blvd.");

myEstate = new aHouse(12,9,12,20000,"1 Ego St.");


function showMyHut() {

        showProperties(myHut,"myHut");

}


function showMyHome() {

        showProperties(myHome,"myHome");

}
```

(continued)

```
//

// Don't write any more comments in JavaScript after next line

//

<!-- End of script hiding comments -->


</SCRIPT>

</HEAD>

<FORM NAME="ShowItAll">

<HR>

<B>Show Properties</B>

<HR>

<P><INPUT TYPE="button" VALUE="Show myHome" onClick="showMy-
Home()">

<P><INPUT TYPE="button" VALUE="Show myHut" onClick="showMy-
Hut()">

<P><INPUT TYPE="button" VALUE="Show myLodge"

          onClick='showProperties(myLodge,"myLodge")'>

</FORM>

</HTML>
```

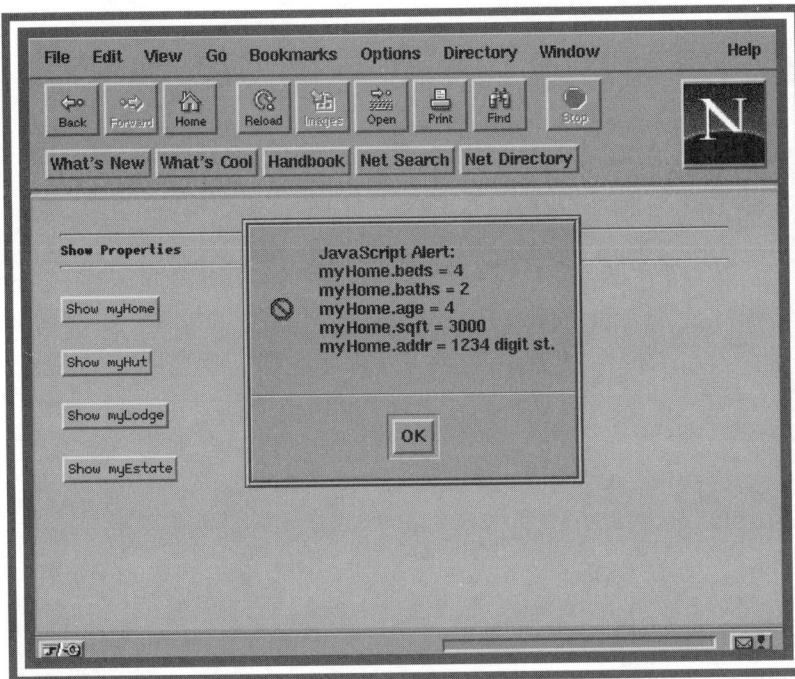

Figure 4.1 Displaying properties of objects

Note how the `showProperties` function is called both indirectly (for `myHouse` and `myHut`) and directly (for `myLodge`). You can construct variable and object names on-the-fly, too. You can even use the `eval()` function to evaluate a string to get a method!

For example, to show a button for `myEstate`, you can add a function that evaluates the name passed to it and use the returned value from eval as an object. See how the code in Program 4.1 is modified in Program 4.2 to handle the `myEstate` object from a string. The output is shown in Figure 4.2.

Program 4.2: Evaluating strings to get an object

```html
<HTML>

<HEAD><TITLE>Show Some Objects Properties</TITLE>

<SCRIPT>


<!---

function showProperties(obj,objName) {

        var output = "";

        for (var i in obj)

        output += objName + "." + i + " = " + obj[i] + "\n";

        alert(output);

}


function aHouse(beds,baths,age,sqft,addr) {

        this.beds = beds

        this.baths = baths

        this.age = age

        this.sqft = sqft

        this.addr = addr

}


myHome = new aHouse(4,2,4,3000,"1234 digit st.");

myHut = new aHouse(1,1,12,700,"3141 pie av.");

myLodge = new aHouse(2,1,12,1700,"2828 Euler Blvd.");

myEstate = new aHouse(12,9,12,20000,"1 Ego St.");
```

(continued)

```
function showMyHut() {

        showProperties(myHut,"myHut");

}


function showMyHome() {

        showProperties(myHome,"myHome");

}


function doEvaluation(name) {

        showProperties(eval(name),name);

}


//
// Don't write any more comments in JavaScript after next line
//
<!-- End of script hiding comments -->

</SCRIPT>
</HEAD>
<FORM NAME="ShowItAll">
<HR>
<B>Show Properties</B>
<HR>
<P><INPUT TYPE="button" VALUE="Show myHome" onClick="showMy-
Home()">
<P><INPUT TYPE="button" VALUE="Show myHut" onClick="showMy-
Hut()">
<P><INPUT TYPE="button" VALUE="Show myLodge"
```

(continued)

```
                    onClick='showProperties(myLodge,"myLodge")'>
<P><INPUT TYPE="button" VALUE="Show myEstate"
            onClick='doEvaluation("my" + "Estate")'>
</FORM>
</HTML>
```

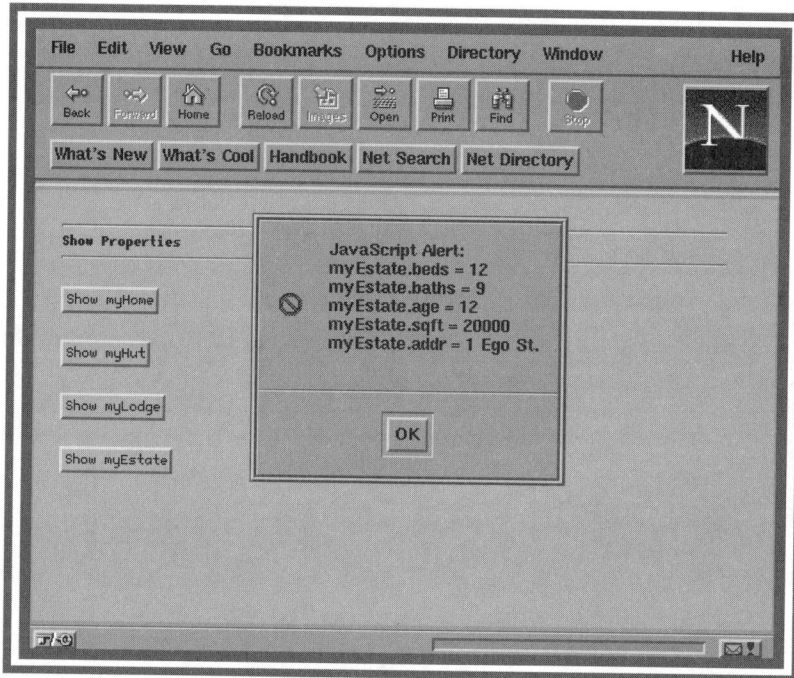

Figure 4.2 Evaluating strings to get an object

Note how the call to the function `doEvaluation` is made. The function takes one string as its argument. The call is made by concatenating the words "my" and "Estate" together. The word "myEstate" is passed to the `eval()` function, which returns an object. The code in Programs 4.1 and 4.2 shows that you can pass objects to functions just as easily as you would pass numbers or strings. The code shows how to manipulate these objects to derive objects and their properties.

One important point to keep in mind is that you do not create an object just by declaring a function for it. Just like functions, declaring a function makes the code declared for that function available. Calling the function makes the code in the function run. In the case of programmer-declared objects, an object is only created when the function for the object is sent with a call to *new()*.

More on Methods

A method is a function that is associated with an object. You define a method in the same way as you define a standard function. Methods can only be called by using an existing object. To call a method, use the following syntax:

```
object.methodName = functionForMethod(params)
```

where `object` is an existing object, `methodName` is the name you are assigning to the method, and `functionForMethod` is the name of the function. Methods do not have to take any parameters.

For example, to expand on the `aHouse` object, you can add a method that simply returns its address in a well-known format. Let's define the following function:

```
function showOffHouse() {

        var output=""

        output += "This house has " + this.beds  + "\n"

        output += " and " + this.baths + " bathrooms.\n"

        output += "It is " + this.age + " years old\n"

        output += "with " + this.sqft + " square feet of
space \n"

        output += "and is located at " + this.addr + "\n"

        alert(output);

}
```

Now, define the aHouse object as follows by adding a reference to this method:

```
function aHouse(beds,baths,age,sqft,addr) {

        this.beds = beds

        this.baths = baths

        this.age = age

        this.sqft = sqft

        this.addr = addr

        this.showMe = showOffHouse // LOOK here!!

}
```

By convention, the name of the function is kept the same as the member. This nomenclature is not a requirement of the language, though. To call the method in the myHome button's onclick handler, you would use the following statement:

```
myHome.showMe()
```

The complete listing of how to this method is shown appears in Program 4.3. Note how the name of the method is not the same as the function being called when looking at showMe and showOff-House(). Also note how two different local variables called "output" are being created and used in two separate functions. See the results in Figure 4.3.

Program 4.3: Using methods in objects

```
<HTML>

<HEAD><TITLE>Show Some Objects Properties</TITLE>

<SCRIPT>


<!---

function showOffHouse() {

        var output=""

        output += "This house has " + this.beds  + "\n"
```

(continued)

```javascript
 output += " and " + this.baths + " bathrooms.\n"

        output += "It is " + this.age + " years old\n"

        output += "with " + this.sqft + " square feet of space
\n"

        output += "and is located at " + this.addr + "\n"

        return(output);

}

function showProperties(obj,objName) {

        var output = "";

        for (var i in obj)

        {

        if (i + ""  == "showMe")  {

        output += objName + "." + i + " = " + obj.showMe(); }

        else  {

        output += objName + "." + i + " = " + obj[i] + "\n"; }

        }

        alert(output);

}

function aHouse(beds,baths,age,sqft,addr) {

        this.beds = beds

        this.baths = baths

        this.age = age

        this.sqft = sqft

        this.addr = addr

        this.showMe = showOffHouse

}
```

(continued)

```
myHome = new aHouse(4,2,4,3000,"1234 digit st.");

myHut = new aHouse(1,1,12,700,"3141 pie av.");

myLodge = new aHouse(2,1,12,1700,"2828 Euler Blvd.");

myEstate = new aHouse(12,9,12,20000,"1 Ego St.");


function showMyHut() {

        showProperties(myHut,"myHut");

}


function showMyHome() {

        showProperties(myHome,"myHome");

}

function doEvaluation(name) {

        showProperties(eval(name),name);

}
//
// Don't write any more comments in JavaScript after next line
//
<!-- End of script hiding comments -->
```

(continued)

Creating Objects

```
</SCRIPT>

</HEAD>

<FORM NAME="ShowItAll">

<HR>

<B>Show Properties</B>

<HR>

<P><INPUT TYPE="button" VALUE="Show myHome"
onClick="alert(myHome.showMe())">

<P><INPUT TYPE="button" VALUE="Show myHut" onClick=
"showMyHut()">

<P><INPUT TYPE="button" VALUE="Show myLodge"

        onClick='showProperties(myLodge,"myLodge")'>

<P><INPUT TYPE="button" VALUE="Show myEstate"

        onClick='doEvaluation("my" + "Estate")'>

</FORM>

</HTML>
```

Tip   It is possible code recursive functions in methods. The this keyword is passed to each successive call.

If more than one object with the same name is created, JavaScript will create an array with the same name, items of which will be all the synonymous objects.

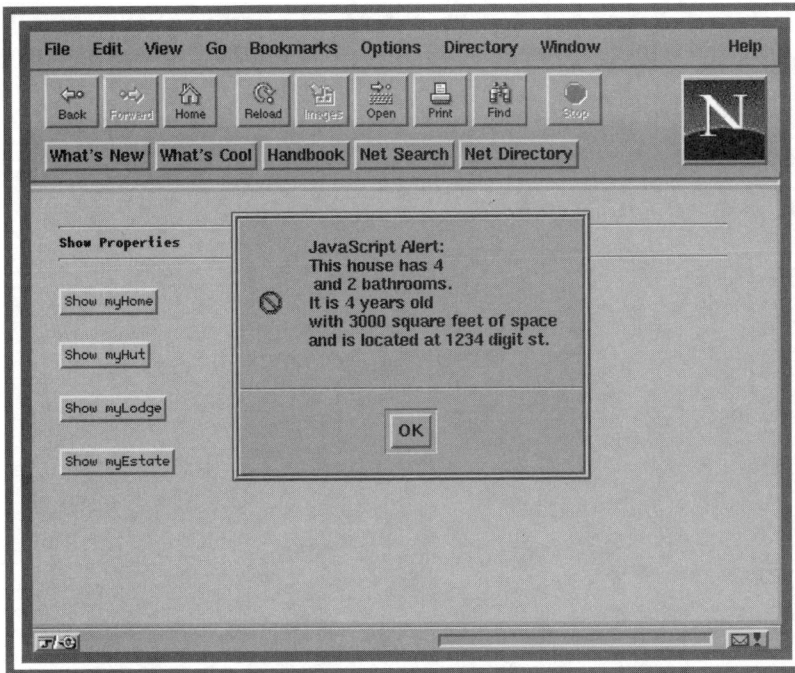

Figure 4.3 Using methods in objects

> **Note** JavaScript has a reserved word, *this*, that you can use to refer to the current object. When referring to items within an object, such as to get to the sqft item within the aHouse object, you use the *this* keyword.

Objects Within Objects

It's possible to define objects within objects in JavaScript. Let's define a new object of the type of loan on a house, aLoan. The loan object has one function that simply displays it's members. The returned value from its display function, showLoan(), can be used in an alert box or in conjuction with other strings. For example, the showMe()

function of the `aHouse` object now shows the loan information in addition to the information about the rest of the house (see Program 4.4, and the output in Figure 4.4).

Program 4.4: Objects within objects

```
<HTML>

<HEAD><TITLE>Show Some Objects Properties</TITLE>

<SCRIPT>


<!---


function showLoan() {

        var output=""

        output += "This is a " + this.terms + " loan \n"

        output += "with " + this.terms + " percent \n"

        output += "for " + this.len + " years.\n"

        return output

        }

function aLoan(terms,interest,len){

        this.terms = terms

        this.interest = interest

        this.len = len

        this.showLoan = showLoan

        }
```

(continued)

```
function showOffHouse() {

        var output=""

        output += "This house has " + this.beds  + "\n"

        output += " and " + this.baths + " bathrooms.\n"

        output += "It is " + this.age + " years old\n"

        output += "with " + this.sqft + " square feet of
space \n"

        output += "and is located at " + this.addr + "\n"

        if (this.loan != null)

        output += "Loan information = " +
this.loan.showLoan()


        alert(output);

}


function showProperties(obj,objName) {

        var output = "";

        for (var i in obj)

        output += objName + "." + i + " = " + obj[i] + "\n";

        alert(output);

}
```

(continued)

```
function aHouse(beds,baths,age,sqft,addr,loan) {

        this.beds = beds

        this.baths = baths

        this.age = age

        this.sqft = sqft

        this.addr = addr

        this.showMe = showOffHouse

        this.loan = loan

}


conventional = new aLoan("conventional",8,30)

assumeable = new aLoan("assumeable",8,30)

shortTerm = new aLoan("15 year",7,15)


myHome = new aHouse(4,2,4,3000,"1234 digit st.", conventional);

myHut = new aHouse(1,1,12,700,"3141 pie av.",assumeable);

myLodge = new aHouse(2,1,12,1700,"2828 Euler Blvd.",shortTerm);

myEstate = new aHouse(12,9,12,20000,"1 Ego St.",conventional);


function doEvaluation(name) {

        showProperties(eval(name),name);

}
```

(continued)

```
//

// Don't write any more comments in JavaScript after next line

//

<!-- End of script hiding comments -->


</SCRIPT>

</HEAD>

<FORM NAME="ShowItAll">

<HR>

<B>Show Properties</B>

<HR>

<P><INPUT TYPE="button" VALUE="Show myHome"
onClick="myHome.showMe()">

<P><INPUT TYPE="button" VALUE="Show Loan on Home"

          onClick="alert(myEstate.loan.showLoan())">

<P><INPUT TYPE="button" VALUE="Show myHut"
onClick="myHut.showMe()">

<P><INPUT TYPE="button" VALUE="Show myLodge"
onClick="myLodge.showMe()">

<P><INPUT TYPE="button" VALUE="Show myEstate"
onClick="myEstate.showMe()">

</FORM>

</HTML>
```

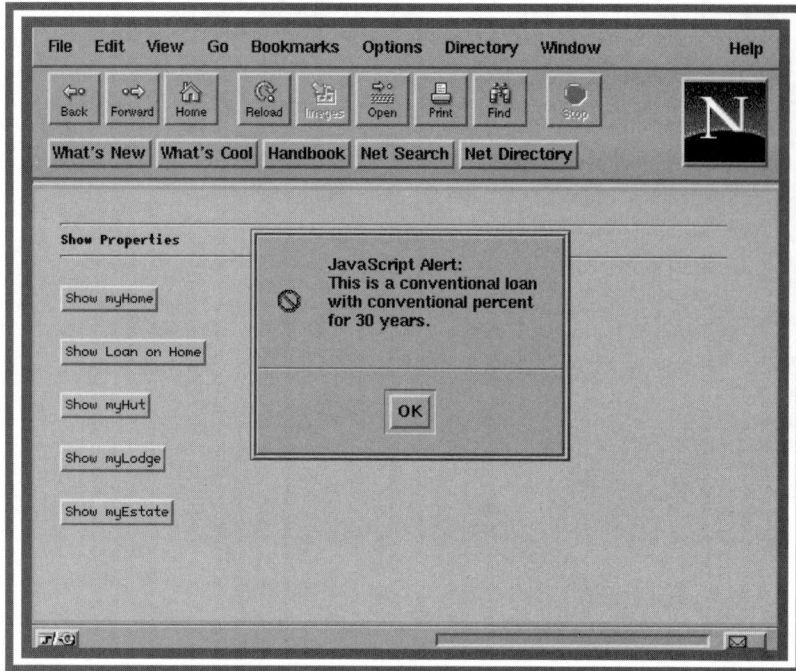

Figure 4.4 Using objects within objects

An `aLoan` object can be addressed in one of two ways: as a member of an existing `aHouse` object—for example, `myHome.loan`—or explicitly, using the word conventional as in the call to create `myHome`. The syntax to address subjects is:

```
object.containedObject.anotherObj.  .. and so on.
```

It's easy to get carried away and have object hierarchy trees in this manner. To access a member or method of an object, simply concatenate the names in the hierarchy to get to the member. For example, to call the function `showLoan` for `myHome`, you can use:

```
myHome.loan.showLoan()
```

Within the `myHome` object, the loan member has a reference to the object. So the `showLoan()` function is referred to as follows:

```
this.loan.showLoan()
```

The concept of hierarchy is an important one to understand if you are to understand the Javascript object model for the predefined objects with which Javascript supplies you.

Adding New Members

It's possible to add new members to existing objects with the use of the prototype member. The prototype member is used as follows to create a new member in the aHouse object type:

```
function aHouse(beds,baths,age,sqft,addr,loan) {

        this.beds = beds

        this.baths = baths

        this.age = age

        this.sqft = sqft

        this.addr = addr

        this.showMe = showOffHouse

        this.loan = loan

}



//Create the garage member

aHouse.prototype.garage = true
```

Now you can use the member function `garage` for all the objects of type `aHouse`.

JavaScript Object Model

The JavaScript Object Model is the hierarchy of objects that we are allowed to manipulate using JavaScript scripts. The Object Model consists of a handful of pre-defined objects and also allows developers to create their own objects using the new operator.

When you load a Web page into your Navigator browser, JavaScript fills in certain data structures with the contents of the Web page. These data structures are the objects that we can use in our scripts. Table 4.1 lists predefined objects available in JavaScript.

Table 4.1   Predefined Navigator Objects

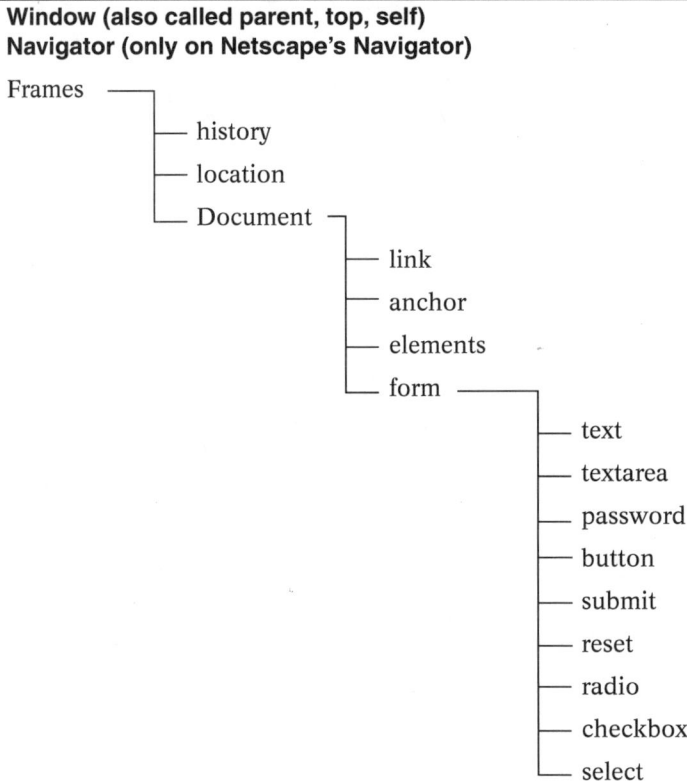

Window (also called parent, top, self)
Navigator (only on Netscape's Navigator)

```
Frames ──┐
         ├── history
         ├── location
         └── Document ──┐
                        ├── link
                        ├── anchor
                        ├── elements
                        └── form ──┐
                                   ├── text
                                   ├── textarea
                                   ├── password
                                   ├── button
                                   ├── submit
                                   ├── reset
                                   ├── radio
                                   ├── checkbox
                                   └── select
```

Each of the objects listed will be further discussed in the rest of the book. Basically, what you need to remember is the name of each object's method and how it fits in the entire hierarchy of JavaScript objects. For example, window and frame objects contain documents, history, and location objects. A document can contain links, anchors, and forms. Forms in turn can contain other HTML objects, such buttons, radio buttons, checkboxes, and the like. Each of these HTML objects contain their own methods and properties. Forms, links, and anchors are stored as arrays in the document and are in the order in which they are declared in the file.

One point to note is that the window object can be referred to as "top," "parent," or "self," depending on where you are in the document. To get to an object in a JavaScript application, you can refer to it relative of an object, or from the *top* object. For example, to get to a button on a form in a document, you can address it as:

```
top.document.form.buttonvalue.value
```

If you are processing from a function within an object already on the form, then you need just refer to the value as:

```
buttonName.value
```

During the call to event handlers, the `this` keyword refers to the calling object, not the called object. For example, in the following call for the `onClick` handler, the `this` refers to the button that is pressed.

```
<INPUT TYPE='button' VALUE="Help!" onClick="showName(this)">
```

Inside the `showName` event handler, the value of `this.value` will be "Help!". To send the form to the event handler, you will have defined the call to the `onClick` handler as:

```
<INPUT TYPE='button' VALUE="Help!"  NAME="kamran"
       onClick="showName(top.document.form[0])">
```

The `top.document.form[0]` will refer to the first form in the document. The top document can be replaced with the word "document." The button can be referred to by its index in the document's elements array, or by its name "kamran." So, if the button is the fifth HTML object declared, it can be referred to as `document.elements[4]`. The easier way to refer to the value of the above button is to just call it by name:

```
document.kamran.value
```

As you can see, you have a lot of flexibility in how you can refer to an object: by name, it's location in the hierarchy, or, in the case of an object contained in a document, its location in the elements array of a document.

A quick way to determine what element you are dealing with is to use the `typeof` method, which returns the type of the object being developed. Table 4.2 shows the returned values.

Table 4.2   Returned messages from type of method

Type of Object	Returned value as string
undefined item	"undefined"
function or method	"method"
user defined	
objects	"object"
integer or	
floating point	"number"
true or	
false	"boolean"
string objects	"string"

The methods and members of these objects are defined in Appendix A. In Chapter 3, "JavaScript Language Basics," we covered the use of the String, Date, and Math objects. Chapters 5 through 11 show the usage of each of the built-in JavaScript objects shown in Table 4.1.

There is one object that we have not mentioned in Table 4.1 and that is the Navigator object, which is used to provide the version number of the browser that is bringing up the document.

Remember that JavaScript objects are created in the order they are found in a document. User-defined objects have to be explicitly declared with a new statement.

To get the number of properties for an object you can write a function similar to the one shown below:

```
function listPropeties(myObject){

    var j = myObject.length;

    var list = ''

    for (var k = 1; k < = j; k++) {

    list += this[k] + "";     // give a space

    }

    return list;

}
```

The returned list will contain the names of the properties of the object for which the listProperties method is defined. The above function can be rewritten as a method to display the properties of an object:

```
function listPropeties(){

        var j = this.length;

        var list = ''

        for (var k = 1; k < = j; k++) {

        list += this[k] + "";       // give a space

        }

        return list;

}
```

Now the method is referring to the object whose properties are being listed by using the "this" keyword. Note how a reference to an object is not passed into the method. Don't forget to make the function a method by referring to it within the object as:

```
myObject.listProperties = listProperties
```

The three steps you have to take when converting an ordinary function to a method are:

1. *Don't pass the object as a parameter to the function.*

2. *Replace all references to the object within the function with the keyword "this".*

3. *Make the function a method of the object.*

On occasion, you will want to pass variable-length arguments to a method. Missing arguments to a function will then be defaulted to some predefined values. For example, in the case of a summing object in which you want to return the sum of all the arguments passed into the function, you want to do two things: First, determine the number of arguments passed in. Second, iterate over the arguments to sum them up. A function to do just that is shown here:

```
          function sumSeries(str_) {

var items = sumSeries.arguments.length;

var sum   = 0

var I


for (I = 0; I < items; I++) {

        sum += sumSeries[I];

}

return sum

}
```

Note how the `arguments.length` is applied to the `sumSeries` function to get the length and number of items passed into the function. Then, to get the arguments themselves, each item is indexed with the variable I. Basically, we are treating the function elaborate as an object and the "arguments" as an object within it.

In the example shown above, all the arguments are used to get their sum. To get a more elaborate function that defaults to known values, you can use something like this:

```
function elaborate( e ) {

        var items = elaborate.arguments.length;

        var j

        var name, addr, smoker, healthy


        if (items < 2) {

        response = "Must send at least two arguments"

        return response

        }

        name = elaborate.arguments[0]

        addr = elaborate.arguments[1]

        smoker = 0;

        healthy = 1;

        if (items >= 3) {

        smoker = elaborate.arguments[2]

        }

        if (items >= 4) {

        healthy = elaborate.arguments[3]

}

// more code here.

}
```

In this example, you are attempting to use at least two arguments for the elaborate function called. If the remaining two arguments are not supplied, a default value for each unspecified item is assumed. Coding a function or method in this fashion allows for great flexibility in passing parameters. The only catch is to remember to use defaulted parameters from the right-hand side of the argument list so that the mandatory arguments are always on the left side of the argument list. Because we process arguments from left to right in an argument list, it's easy to know when to stop. Skipping arguments in the middle is not possible because arguments are picked off by the order in which they appear.

A Word on the Navigator Object

The Navigator object is a built-in object in Navigator browsers from Netscape. It has several properties that can be utilized by JavaScript applications to determine the type of functionality to use. The properties for the Navigator object include:

- *appName—The official name of the browser application.*

- *appCodeName—Netscape's internal name of the browser application.*

- *appVersion—The version number of the browser.*

- *mimeTypes—an array of objects describing the types of mime headers supported by the browser.*

- *plugins—an array of objects describing the Plug-In objects in the browser.*

- *userAgent—The value of the USER_AGENT environment variable for the browser.*

The appCodeName, appName, and appVersion are useful when writing JavaScript applications that apply to a particular Navigator version. The userAgent property is not very useful unless you are writing a CGI script that relies on the value of USER_AGENT being set to a particular value.

The mimeTypes array contains objects, each of which has the following properties: type, description, suffixes, and enabledPlug-in. The number of items in the mimeTypes array can be read from navigator.mimeTypes.length. Here's a simple application to list the MIME types supported on a browser:

```
<HTML><HEAD><TITLE>List all the MIME types</TITLE>

</HEAD>

<BODY>


<SCRIPT LANGUAGE="JavaScript">


<!-- Hiding

var txt

var i

var ob

var len

// txt = "Mime types = " + navigator.mimeTypes.length + "<BR>";

len = navigator.mimeTypes.length

if (len > 20 ) { len = 20  }

for (i = 0; i < len; i++)
```

(continued)

```
              {

              txt = navigator.mimeTypes[i].type + ",";

              txt += navigator.mimeTypes[i].description + ",";

              txt += navigator.mimeTypes[i].suffixes + ",";

              txt += navigator.mimeTypes[i].enabledPlugin +
"<BR>";

              document.writeln(txt)

              }

// Uncomment the next few lines to see all properties.

// ob = navigator.mimeTypes[0];

// for (len in ob) {

        // txt += ' ' + len   + "</BR>"

// }

// -->

</SCRIPT>

</BODY>
```

Note how the output is limited to only the first 20 or so items in the array. If the length is not limited, the 3.0b5 version of Navigator crashes. So until this "feature" is fixed, limit the length to a small number of items to display at one time. The output you see will vary with the type of browser you happen to be running.

Also, the previous code shows some lines that are commented out. The lines that are commented out can be used to list the property names of the navigator object.

The plugins array contains objects that describe the properties of all the plug-ins loaded into a browser. The properties of each element in this array are listed as: name, filename, description, and length. The values of the properties can be displayed by using a simple program, as follows:

```
<HTML><HEAD><TITLE>MPS Inc. Home Page </TITLE>

</HEAD>

<BODY>

<SCRIPT LANGUAGE="JavaScript">

<!-- Hiding

var txt

var i

var ob

var len

txt = "<BR>"

ob = navigator.plugins[0];

for (len in ob) {

 txt += len  + ",";

 }
```

(continued)

```
document.writeln(txt)

txt += "<BR><P>"

len = navigator.plugins.length

if (len > 20 ) { len = 20  } // limit output

for (i = 0; i < len; i++)

        {

        txt = navigator.plugins[i].name + ",";

        txt = navigator.plugins[i].filename + ",";

        txt += navigator.plugins[i].description + ",";

        txt += navigator.plugins[i].length + "<P>";

        txt += "<HR>";

        document.writeln(txt)

        }

// start html again -->

</SCRIPT>

</BODY>
```

As you can see, there are some useful items built into the Navigator object that you can use to customize your application. Most applications will not use these features, but it's nice to know that these items are available to your JavaScript applications should the need arise. If you do use these values, it will be mostly for determining if your JavaScript application will run on the type of browser into which it has been loaded.

Summary

This chapter has provided a brief introduction on how to work with objects in JavaScript. Basically, we have covered the following points:

- *Objects have members that are properties and methods. Objects are declared with the `function()` statement and created with a call to a `new()` function.*

- *Member variables can be addressed with an `object-Name.memberName` statement, or by using the associative array of member names for that object.*

- *Methods are simply functions that happen to know to which object they belong.*

- *To make a function into a method, take these steps: make the method a property of the object, don't pass the object into the method, and change all references to the object to use the word 'this'. Objects can contain other objects to form a hierarchical tree of objects. The JavaScript object model is based on such a tree model. The window object contains other frames, documents, and HTML objects to form a cohesive structure for objects in a JavaScript application.*

- *Synonymous objects are inserted in the order they are found in an array of the same name.*

Coming Up

With the knowledge gained in this chapter, you can create your own objects as well as work with the objects supplied by JavaScript. This chapter and the others that make up the first part of this book will serve as the basis for discussion in Part II of the book, as we dive deeper into the methods and properties of each built-in JavaScript object.

PART TWO

The JavaScript Objects

Price

Futures
Price
in
cents :   5.0

| 7.50 |
| 7 |
| 6.50 |
| 6 |

Put
Price
in
cents: 4.5

| 5.50 |
| 5 |

Cost of
Put
Option   0.15
in
cents:

| 4.50 |
| 4 |
| 3.50 |
| 3 |

Tell Me

Part II explains in detail the major objects that are available to the JavaScript programmer. Understanding the definition and use of these objects, along with their methods and properties, is essential for developing useful, and interesting, JavaScript scripts.

Chapter 5, "The History, Location, Link, and Anchor Objects," introduces four basic, and related objects, History, Link, Anchor, and Location. All of these objects involve the use of URLs (Uniform Resource Locators) and they all are useful navigational tools in JavaScript scripts. JavaScript can add interactivity to Web pages using event handlers, which are introduced in Chapter 6, "Events, Input, and Output." Events are usually generated by a user clicking on HTML form fields or buttons. Chapter 6 shows how HTML forms can be used with JavaScript's event handlers to create more useful and interesting forms.

What's a document? It's only the most important object in the JavaScript arsenal. Chapter 7, "JavaScript Documents," introduces the document object and its myriad of properties. The document object is the Web page itself and Chapter 7 explains the importance of its properties. A typical use of JavaScript is for on-the-fly creation of HTML, and Chapter 7 offers good examples on how to do just that. While documents are the most important object, windows, especially subwindows or "frames," are the most useful.

Chapter 8, "Windows in JavaScript," outlines how to create and use frames and windows using JavaScript and includes several useful examples, including an implementation of put options in the futures (stock trading) market.

All the major JavaScript objects are in the can now, but there are still some important concepts we haven't discussed in detail. Chapter 9, "Applying JavaScript," talks about those concepts, which include cookies, the document.image object, JavaScript in client-side image maps, and creating your own objects.

CHAPTER 5

THE HISTORY, LOCATION, LINK, AND ANCHOR OBJECTS

Move Through the History List

Reference Special URL Protocols

Reference Links and Anchors in HTML Documents

The history, link, anchor, and location objects all help you deal with Uniform Resource Locators (URLs) in JavaScript. With these objects, you can use JavaScript scripts to find out where a document came from, where it's been, and to take a user to a document located elsewhere. In this chapter, we explain the nature of these objects and how you can use them to help a user navigate the Web using JavaScript. This chapter contains many small code examples. At the end of the chapter, we present a longer example that uses most of the objects discussed.

Links and anchors are properties of the document object. A link is a standard HTML hypertext link with the addition of optional JavaScript event handlers. Anchors are standard HTML anchors with the addition of a NAME attribute. JavaScript creates links and anchor arrays instantiated with all of the hypertext links and anchors in the current document. You can then reference these arrays in your scripts. The history object refers to the history list in the Navigator browser that you can view by pulling down the Window menu and selecting History. The history object always contains the current history list that can be referred to in your scripts. The location object is the location, or URL, of the document currently displayed in your browser window.

The History Object

The Netscape Navigator browser keeps track of all the pages you visit while your browser window is open. This list of pages is called the history list, and you can view the most recent 10 pages you've visited by pulling down Navigator's Go menu. By pulling down the Window menu and choosing History, you can see a list of all the pages you've visited during the current session.[1]

In JavaScript, the history list is yet another type of object (the history object) you can use to help users navigate Web pages. The history object is, as you might suspect, a linked list of URLs associated with a window or frame that contains the URLs of all the pages loaded into that window or frame. Because the history object is a list, let's just refer to is as the history list for the rest of this discussion.

History List Properties and Methods

The history list has only one property, called length, which is the number of URLs in the list. If you wanted to know the length of your window's history list, you would use:

```
mywindow.history.length
```

---

1. The history list is limited in length only by the memory available to Navigator. On Unix and Windows systems, you can set an environment variable, NS_HISTORY_LIMIT, to limit the size of the history list.

For a particular frame, such as `bigframe`, you would use:

```
bigframe.history.length
```

You can neither delete nor edit URLs in the history list, and the list persists until a frame or window is closed. When a new frame or window is created, such as with a `window.open()` call, its history list is empty (it has length zero) until you load a URL into the window.

To keep rogue scripts from accessing any private information you might have stored within the URLs of your history list, the actual data in the history list is not modifiable or directly accessible to Java-Script.[2] Because of this, there is no way to test the values of specific locations in the list, nor can you display the contents of the history list for a user. Also, there is no to way to determine what page you are currently at in the history list.

You can only access the history list using three methods: `go`, `back`, and `forward`. `Back` and `forward` are easy to understand because they serve the same functions as Navigator's `Back` and `Forward` directory buttons (if you don't see the `Back` and `Forward` buttons on your browser window, go to the Options menu and select Show Directory Buttons).

It's easy to create a button that takes you back to the previous page:

```
<FORM>

<INPUT TYPE="button"  VALUE="Go back in the history list"
onClick="self.history.back()">

</FORM>
```

If there is no page to go back to, which would happen if you've just opened a new browser window, then clicking on the button does nothing. The `go` method is more flexible than `back` or `forward`, and you will likely use it more often. `Go` takes either an integer or a string

2. In Navigator 3.0, this information can be accessed by using the taint() and untaint() functions. However, these functions were not working in the Beta version of Navigator 3.0 that we used.

as its argument. If the argument is a string, go searches your history list for the first URL matching the string and goes to that URL. Go does not search the titles you see when you pull down Navigator's Go menu. Instead, it searches the URLs associated with those titles. To see the list of URLs associated with each title, go to the Window menu and select History.

The following FORM has a text field for entering a search string and a button that, when clicked, searches the history list using the search string.

```
<FORM NAME="sform">

Enter a string to search for in the history list:

<INPUT  TYPE="text" NAME="sstring" SIZE="15">

<INPUT TYPE="button"  VALUE="GO using a string value"
NAME="goStrButton" onClick="history.go(sform.sstring.value)">

</FORM>
```

If no string is found matching a URL in the history list, nothing happens when the button is clicked. You can also use a positive or negative integer as an argument to go. A positive number moves ahead that many pages in the history list; a negative number goes back that many pages. The following FORM lets you enter a positive or negative integer in the text field and then uses the go method to move that many URLs forward or backward in the history list.

```
<FORM NAME="nform">

<INPUT  TYPE="text" NAME="nstring" SIZE="4">

<INPUT TYPE="button"  VALUE="GO using an integer value"
NAME="goIntButton" onClick="history.go
(eval(nform.nstring.value))">

</FORM>
```

If you specify an index that is too high or too low, go does nothing. Using zero as the argument reloads the current page.

The Back Button Problem

If you are using Navigator 2.x and you press the back button while viewing a page with frames, you may notice that the back button takes you back to the first page before the frames page is loaded. This happens regardless of how many pages may have been viewed in any individual frames on the page. This is an unfortunate 'feature' of the Navigator 2.0 browser that has been rethought in Navigator 3.0. What we'd like to have happen when the back button is pressed is have the last frame that was loaded move back one page in the history list.[3] To remedy this problem, many sites create their own buttons to help the user navigate frames without having to resort to the

3. Netscape does provide a mechanism for navigating frames, though few users are aware of it. If you press the right mouse button (or hold down the single mouse button on Macintosh) while your cursor is in a frame, a pop-up menu offers to take the frame back or forward in the history list.

back button on the Navigator browser. This is one place where the history list comes in handy. We can create buttons that will take the user backward and forward in another frame.

Figure 5.1 shows how those buttons might look in the bottom frame. The following form created those buttons.

```
<FORM NAME="nav">

<INPUT TYPE="button" VALUE="<<" onClick="parent.pets.
history.back()">

<INPUT TYPE="button" VALUE="Home Page" onClick="parent.
pets.location="home.htm">

<INPUT TYPE="button" VALUE=">>" onCLick="parent.pets.
history.forward()">

</FORM>
```

Consider using navigation buttons any time you want to guide a user through multi-frame windows such as this. We'll discuss frames further in Chapter 8, "Windows in JavaScript."

The Location Object

The location object is simply the URL that is currently loaded into a window. URLs are the strings that uniquely identify Web pages, files, and other resources on the Internet. The location object is useful for loading a specific document into the user's browser. We can make Netscape's home page immediately load into a user's browser by setting the `href` property of the location object as follows.

```
location.href='http://www.netscape.com/'
```

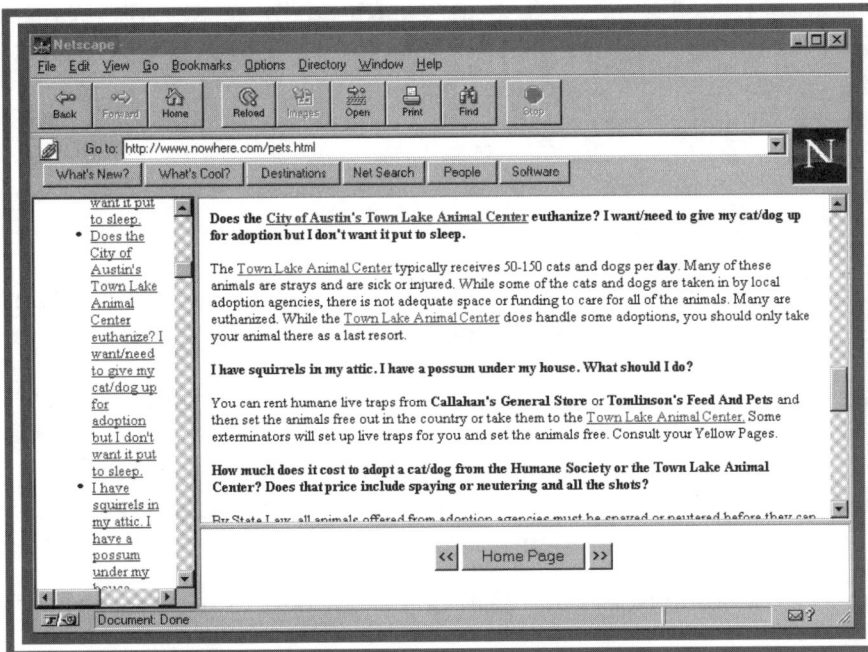

Figure 5.1 Buttons that manipulate the history list help overcome the problems with the Back button in Navigator 2.x

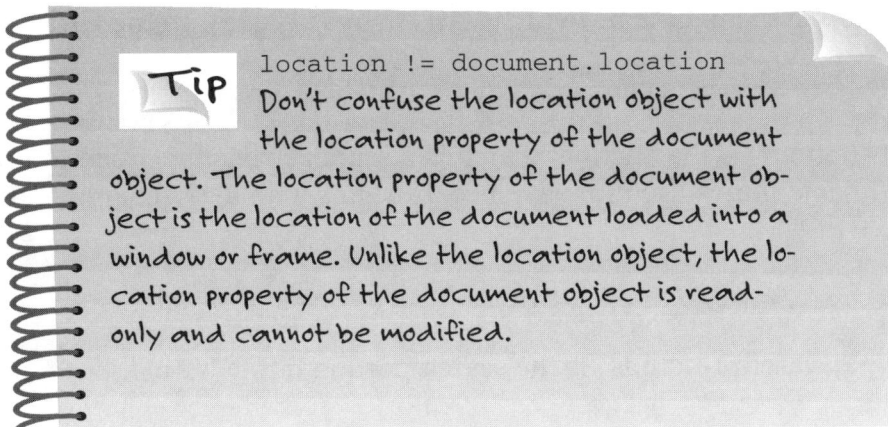

Tip `location != document.location`
Don't confuse the location object with the location property of the document object. The location property of the document object is the location of the document loaded into a window or frame. Unlike the location object, the location property of the document object is read-only and cannot be modified.

The way URLs are defined by JavaScript's location object is somewhat different from the Internet standard. Mostly, the difference is simply terminology, but JavaScript also extends the notion of URL to include some protocols that let you use the output of JavaScript functions as URLs. The next section clearly defines the differences between JavaScript's notion of URLs versus the Internet standard. It will be easier to understand the location object and its properties once these differences are clear.

URL Components

The Internet standard definition of a URL is in Request For Comments (RFC) 1738. It defines the components of the URL as:

```
[protocol]://[user]:[password]@[host]:[port]/[path]
```

The location object has properties that correspond to most of these components. Table 5.1 lists the properties of the Location object and their corresponding components.

Here is how some of the location object properties fit into the URL scheme:

```
[protocol]://[hostname]:[port]/[pathname][hash][search]
```

The properties hash, search, and target have no corresponding component in the RFC 1738 definition. Hash and search refer to strings that may be appended to the pathname. Hash is the anchor portion of the pathname, which starts with a "#" sign. In the URL

```
http://www.netscape.com/index.htm#bottom
```

"#bottom" is the anchor. Search is a search string appended to the pathname that is used for searches. It begins with a "?" character. In the URL

```
http://www.yahoo.com/bin/search?p=javascript+scripts
```

"p=javascript+scripts" is the search portion of the URL.

The target property is the name of the window or frame into which the URL is loaded. The name is usually assigned using the TARGET parameter of the link object (see the "Link Object" section, later in this chapter).

Table 5.1 Location Object Properties and Their Corresponding RFC 1738 Components

JavaScript Location Property	RFC 1738 URL component	Description
hash	n/a	The anchor portion of the pathname, which begins with the "#" character
host	host:port	The host:port portion of the URL
hostname	host	The host name or IP address of the URL
href	n/a	Refers to the entire URL
pathname	path	The file and directory pathname plus any anchor
port	port	The communications port that the server uses for communication
protocol	protocol	The protocol used to communicate the URL
search	n/a	The search string portion of the pathname, which begins with the "?" character
target	n/a	The window nameinto which the URL is loaded

URL Character Encoding

In your travels around the Net, you may have encountered URLs with percent signs (%) embedded in them, followed by two digits. That's an example of URL character encoding. It's used to embed special (generally non-printing or reserved) characters in your URLs. HTML URL character encoding has the form %nn, where nn is a hexadecimal representation of the character. URL encoding is a feature of HTML that you can use in your JavaScript URLs. In addition, there are two JavaScript functions, escape and unescape, that you can use to encode and decode characters in your URLs.

In the following example, we use the JavaScript unescape function to read the URL, BigLink, and translate the encoded : character (hexadecimal 3A). The : character is a reserved character for URLs that is used to separate the protocol field, in this case http, from the rest of the URL. However, in our example, we want to use the : character as part of the name of the Web page.

```
<SCRIPT Language="JavaScript">

var j=escape(":")

BigLink="http://www.movies.com/mission"+j+"impossible.htm"

document.writeln("This is BigLink: <B>"+BigLink+"</B><P>")

var i=unescape(BigLink)

document.writeln("This is BigLink after unescape: <B>"+i+"</B>")

</SCRIPT>
```

The encoded version of the URL, with the %3A, should be used in Web pages or within JavaScript scripts, otherwise an error may occur when the browser, or Web server, attempts to resolve the URL with two colons in it. The unescape function can be used in your scripts just before outputing the URL to a page, so that users can see the URL with the special characters. Figure 5.2 contains the output of this script, showing the effect of the escape and unescape functions.

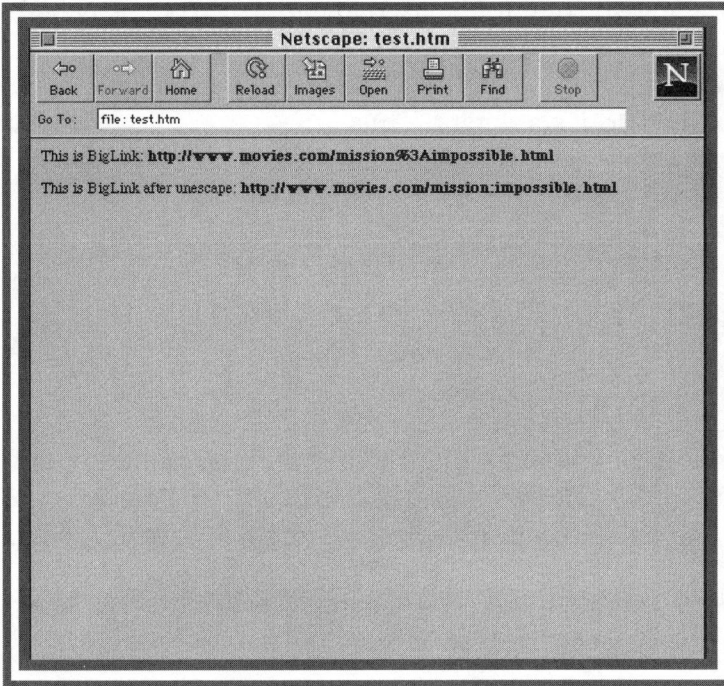

Figure 5.2 Using the JavaScript escape and unescape functions

Setting Location Properties

Setting location properties must be done with caution because any property assignments cause the Navigator browser to immediately attempt to resolve the new URL. For example, setting the port property to 80 (the default communications port for Web servers) causes Navigator to immediately attempt to load the ill-formed destination ":80" into the browser window.

```
<SCRIPT LANGUAGE="JavaScript">

location.port="80"

</SCRIPT>
```

In practice, the most commonly used location property is href, which refers to the entire URL string. Opening a new window or frame and then setting href to a URL is equivalent to including the URL in the `open.window` statement. Thus

```
MYWIN=window.open("")
```

```
MYWIN.location.href="http://www.netscape.com"
```

does the same thing as

```
MYWIN=window.open("http://www.netscape.com/")
```

You may be wondering how to add the user and password components of the RFC 1738 URL to a JavaScript location. The user and password components are often used to access ftp sites with a URL, such as:

```
ftp://Fred:Mypassword@ftp6.netscape.com/
```

That URL will attempt to log into the ftp site, `ftp6.netscape.com` with the username Fred and the password, Mypassword. You can use the user and password components of the RFC 1738 URL in your JavaScript URLs by assigning the entire string to the href property:

```
MYWIN.location.href="ftp://Fred:Mypassword@ftp6.netscape.com/"
```

Using the Location Object
for Backward Compatibility

One application of the location object is to provide backward compatibility between the JavaScript implementations in Navigator versions 2.0 and 3.0. Program 5.1 shows how we can provide backward compatibility with the SRC attribute of the <SCRIPT> tag (new in

Navigator 3.0). In the following script, the SRC attribute is ignored by Navigator 2.0 because the JavaScript implementation in Navigator 2.0 does not recognize it. Instead, Navigator 2.0 users execute the JavaScript statements between the <SCRIPT>...</SCRIPT> tags. Those statements use the location object to redirect Navigator 2.0 users to the HTML file in the directory "oldjs/". Navigator 3.0 browsers recognize the SRC attribute of the <SCRIPT> tag and execute the JavaScript statements contained in the file `date.js`. The JavaScript statements between the <SCRIPT>...</SCRIPT> tags are ignored by Navigator 3.0 users. An example HTML document and script is shown in Program 5.1.

```
<SCRIPT SRC="date.js">

<!-- Hide JavaScript with HTML comment

var p = location.pathname

location = "OLDJS/" + p.substring(p.lastIndexOf("/")+1,
p.length)

//    End of hiding   -->

</SCRIPT>
```

Program 5.1: We can make use of the location object to provide backward compatibility for the <SCRIPT> tag

```
<HTML>

<HEAD>

<TITLE>A Page With The Date And Time</TITLE>

<SCRIPT SRC="DATE.JS">

var p = location.pathname

location = "OLDJS/" + p.substring(p.lastIndexOf("/")+1,
p.length)

</SCRIPT>

</HEAD>


<BODY onLoad="FillDate()">

<FORM NAME="dform">

The current date and time is:

<INPUT TYPE="text" NAME="dateandtime" VALUE="You Do Not Have
JavaScript" SIZE=42>

</FORM>

<BR>

This page is brought to you by Prentice Hall. Thanks for
stopping by!

</BODY>


</HTML>
```

We could also use the location object to maintain separate pages for Navigator 2.x, 3.x, and 'other' browsers. All we'd have to do is change the script above to test for the version of Navigator and then send the user to the appropriate location. If the browser is not Java-Script-capable, then the <SCRIPT> tag is ignored and the rest of the page is read into the user's browser.

```
<SCRIPT>

<!-- Hide JavaScript with HTML comment

var p = location.pathname

var version=navigator.appVersion.charAt(0)

if (version == "2")

location = "navver2/" + p.substring(p.lastIndexOf("/")+1,
p.length)

else {

   if (version == "3")

 location = "navver3/" + p.substring(p.lastIndexOf("/")+1,
p.length)

}

//    End of hiding  -->

</SCRIPT>
```

Special Location Protocols

JavaScript defines three special protocols: about:, javascript:, and mocha:, that you can use in the protocol field of your URL to get information about Navigator, evaluate JavaScript expressions, or bring up a JavaScript expression interpreter. Table 5.2 lists the protocols and gives examples. These protocols only work inside the Navigator browser. Other browsers will return undefined results. Of the three protocols, only the javascript: protocol is really useful in scripts. The other two protocols are normally entered into the location field of your browser and are included here only for completeness.

Table 5.2 JavaScript Specific URL Protocols

Navigator and Javascript specific protocols	Explanation	Example
about:	Information about Navigator. about:cache returns information about the cache; about:plugins returns the list of MIME types supported by installed plugins; about: by itself returns the About Netscape information.	about:plugins
javascript:	Evaluates expression to the right of the colon and loads the string value returned by the expression. If no expression is entered to the right of the colon, it puts a command line on the page for entering javascript. An illegal expression causes an error alert box to spring up.	javascript:myFunc()
mocha:	Evaluates expression to the right of the colon and prints true or false in the window. If no expression is entered to the right of the colon, it puts a command line on the page for entering javascript. An illegal expression causes an error alert box to spring up.	mocha:document. write('hi')

Table 5.3 gives examples of typical protocols that are recognized by most Web browsers. You can use these protocols in your URLs to access various types of services on the Internet.

Table 5.3   Some URL Protocols Recognized by Navigator

URL Protocol	Explanation	Example
file:	Accesses local filesystem	file:///mydir/myfile.txt
ftp:	uses FTP protocol	ftp://ftp6.netscape.com/
gopher:	uses Gopher protocol	gopher://gopher.utexas.edu/
http:	uses HTTP protocol	http://www.netscape.com/
mailto:	uses SMTP protocol	mailto:fred@ibm.com
news:	uses NNTP procol	news://nntp.news.com/
snews:	uses secure NNTP protocol	snews://secnews.netscape.com/
https:	uses secure HTTP protocol	https://www.netscape.com/
telnet	uses telnet protocol	telnet://jason:pass-word@netscape.com
tn3270:	uses 3270 telnet protocol	tn3270://cs.utexas.edu

The javascript: protocol

The javascript: protocol has several uses in scripts and HTML page tags. It lets HTML tags with HREF or SRC attributes take action through JavaScript evaluation. You can use `"javascript:"` in the SRC portion of FRAME and IMG tags, as well as HREF. Table 5.4 offers some typical examples of `"javascript:"` protocol usage.

Table 5.4   Examples of the javascipt: Protocol

JavaScript Protocol Example	What it does
`<IMG SRC="javascript:genxbm()">`	Calls the function genxbm() which outputs a graphic image (in X bit-map format) that is used as the source for the <IMG> tag
`<A HREF="javascript:builddoc()">Click on me</A>`	Calls the function builddoc() whose output is used as the new document for this link
`<A HREF="javascript:history.go(-2)">Go back two clicks</A>`	Loads the URL that is two clicks back in Navigator's history list.
`<FRAME SRC="javascript:parent.builddoc('1')" NAME="navframe">`	Calls the function builddoc in the parent window with the string argument '1'. The output of builddoc is used as the SRC attribute for the FRAME.

JavaScript also offers a convenient way to load an HTML or text document that you've created on-the-fly. Here, the call to `builddoc()` is made when the user clicks on the hypertext link, which causes the current document to be replaced by the output of `builddoc()`.

```
<HEAD>

<SCRIPT LANGUAGE="JavaScript">

function builddoc()  {

var today= new Date()

var p="<HTML><BODY><h1>Welcome To My Page</h1><i>This document
was created on"+today+"</BODY></HTML>"

return p

}

</SCRIPT>

</HEAD>

<BODY>

<A HREF="javascript:builddoc()">Load a new  time-stamped
document</A>

</BODY>
```

In this example, if the string returned by p begins with a "<", then JavaScript assumes that it's of MIME type text/html. Otherwise, it assumes it's of type plain/text. We will discuss MIME types further in Chapter 10, "Working with Plug-Ins."

You can use the same technique to load a document into a FRAME using the SRC attribute (see Program 5.2), the results of which can be seen in Figure 5.3.

Program 5.2: ctest.htm loads a document into a FRAME using the SRC attribute

```
<HEAD>

<SCRIPT LANGUAGE="JavaScript">

function builddoc(n)  {

var today= new Date()

var p="<HTML><BODY><h1>Welcome To Frame Number "+n+"</
h1><i>This document was created on "+today+"</BODY></HTML>"

return p

}

</SCRIPT>

</HEAD>

<FRAMESET   ROWS="20%,80%">

<FRAME SRC="javascript:parent.builddoc('1')" NAME="navframe"
SCROLLING="auto" NORESIZE>

<FRAME SRC="javascript:parent.builddoc('2')" NAME="outframe"
SCROLLING="auto" NORESIZE>

</FRAMESET>
```

Note that because the SRC attribute is evaluated in the context of the FRAME, we refer to the JavaScript function `builddoc()` using `parent.builddoc()`.

In all cases, if the expression following `"javascript:"` evaluates to undefined, then no document is loaded.

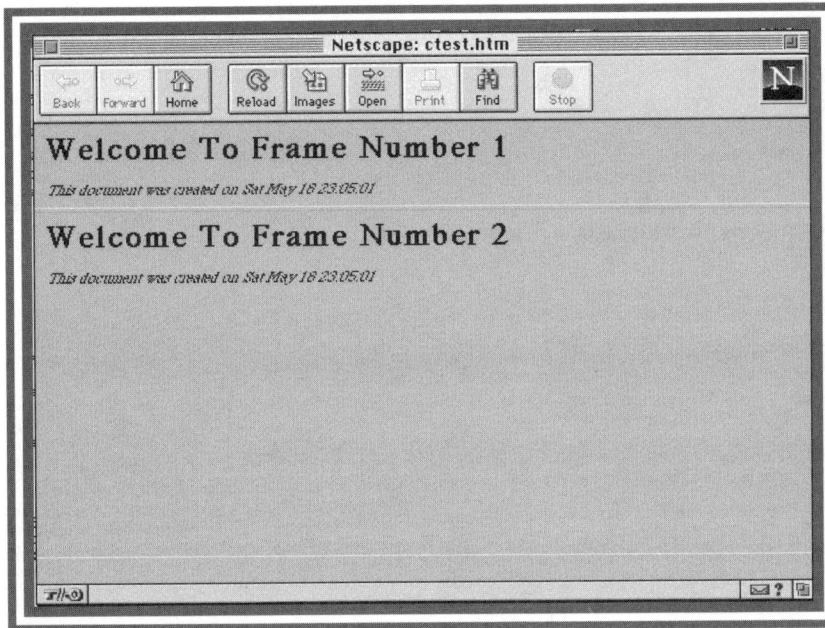

Figure 5.3 The Output of `ctest.htm`

The Link and Anchor Objects

Web documents frequently contain hypertcxt links and anchors. Java-Script offers a convenient way to access all of the hyptertext links in a document. For security reasons, however, JavaScript offers only limited access to the anchors in a document. When a new document is loaded into a window or frame, Navigator automatically creates an array of links and an array of anchors containing all of the links and anchors contained in the document. The format of the link and anchor objects is similar to the standard HTML links and anchors with the addition of several parameters. The format of the link object is as follows:

```
<A HREF=URL [NAME="anchorname"]   [TARGET="windowname"]
[onClick="handlertext"]   [onMouseOver="handlertext"]> Your
Link Text Here </A>
```

The format of the anchor object is as follows:

```
<A [HREF=URL] NAME="anchorname" [TARGET="windowName"]> Your
Anchor Text Here</A>
```

You can use JavaScript event handlers in your anchors and links. You can use the `onClick and onMouseOver handlers in your Web pages.`

If you use a NAME parameter in your link object, it is included in the anchors array as well as the links array. Similarly, if you use an HREF parameter in your anchors statement, it is included in the links array as well as the anchors array.

Unfortunately, though Navigator builds an anchors array, there is no way to access the values in the array for security reasons. All values in the anchors array are null when referenced from JavaScript. For example, the following statement prints null regardless of how many anchors are in the anchors array.

```
document.write(document.anchors[0])
```

The fact that the anchor values are inaccessible from JavaScript renders it useless for most practical purposes. But although the anchor values are inaccessible, you can still reference the anchor values indirectly using the anchors array. In order to load documents to a specific anchor, you must have prior knowledge of where the anchors are in the document and what they are named. In fact, the only information you can extract from the anchors array is the length property of the array.

In contrast, the link object is fairly useful because its array values are accessible. If you wanted to print the length of the anchors array, as well as the first and second links in your document, you could structure your page as in Program 5.3, linktest.htm, the output of which is shown in Figure 5.4.

Program 5.3: linktest.htm prints the anchor array length and the first two links in your page

```
<BODY>

<A NAME="TopAnchor">A SINGLE ANCHOR</a><p>

<A HREF="http://www.netscape.com/">The Netscape home page
link</A>

<BR>

<A HREF="http://www.ibm.com/">The IBM home page link</A>


<SCRIPT Language="JavaScript">

document.write("<p>The number of anchors in this document is:
"+document.anchors.length)

document.write("<p>Here is the first link: "+document.
links[0])

document.write("<p>Here is the second link: "+document.
links[1])

</SCRIPT>

</BODY>
```

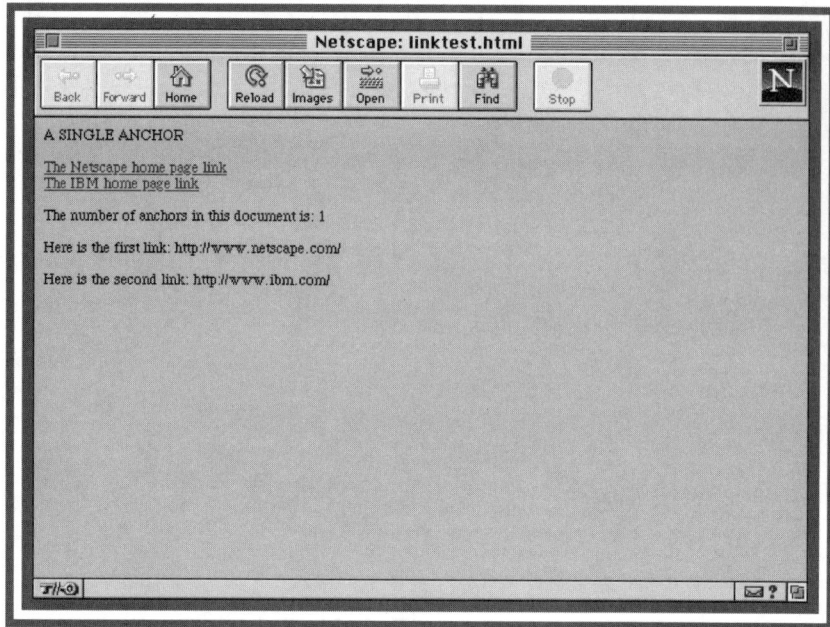

Figure 5.4 Output of `linktest.htm`

The Resource Toolbar Example

To demonstrate usage of the history list, links, and location objects, let's examine a somewhat more complex example, a resource toolbar. This example is implemented using multiple browser windows, though it could easily have been done using frames.

The resource toolbar, shown in Figure 5.5, is a window containing some buttons that you can use to navigate to various JavaScript resources available on the Internet. You can also use the history navigation buttons to move back and forth between various pages you have visited.

Netscape: RESOUf

JavaScript Resources

-> JavaScript Index

-> Gamelan

-> Java Links

-> JavaScript FAQ

-> Netscape Guide

Newsgroups

-> comp.lang.javascript

-> Live Software groups

-> Netscape groups

History Navigation

[Back] [Forward]
[Reload]

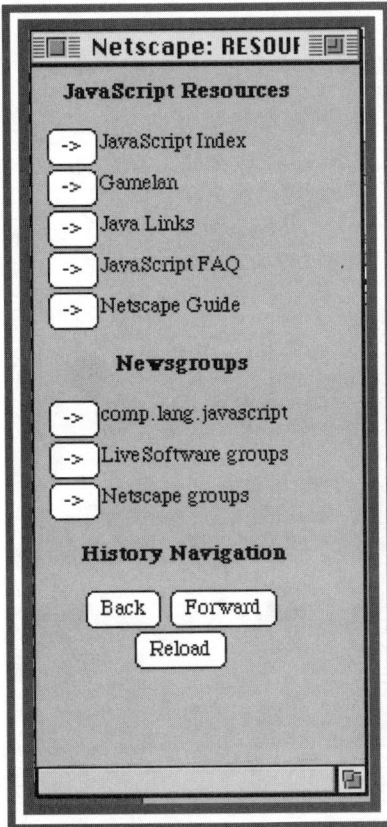

Figure 5.5 The resource toolbar: an example
using the history, link, and location objects

This example consists of two files, `openw.htm` (Program 5.4) and
`resource.htm` (Program 5.54). `openw.htm` is the file you load into
your browser. It creates a small window into which it loads the file
`resource.htm`, which creates the resource toolbar. You can continue to browse with your main browser window, or choose any of
the selections on the resource toolbar. When you want to go back or
forward on your history list, bring the navigation toolbar to the front
and click on the back and forward buttons.

Program 5.4: openw.htm creates the window into which it loads the toolbar, resource.htm

```
<HTML>

<SCRIPT LANGUAGE='JavaScript'>

<!-- Hide script from non-JavaScript browsers

//Open the toolbar window

var statwin = win-
dow.open("resource.htm","navwin","width=175,height=400,
scrollbars=yes,toolbar=no,directories=no,status=no,menubar=no,
location=no");

//Open window again (fix for Navigator 2.0 bug)

var statwin = win-
dow.open("resource.htm","navwin","width=175,height=400,
scrollbars=yes,toolbar=no,directories=no,status=no,menubar=no,
location=no");

//A trick that provides a way to reference this window

//from the window we just created.

statwin.workwin = self;

//  End hiding script  -->

</SCRIPT>

</HTML>
```

Program 5.5: `resource.htm creates the toolbar`

```
<HTML>

<HEAD>

<TITLE>RESOURCES!</TITLE>

<SCRIPT LANGUAGE="JavaScript">

//JavaScript index sites on the Internet

var dest1="http://www.c2.org/~andreww/javascript/"

var dest2="http://www.gamelan.com/noframe/Gamelan.
javascript.htm"

var dest3="http://dezines.com/dezines/javalinks.htm"

var dest4="http://www.freqgrafx.com/411/"

var dest5="http://home.netscape.com/eng/mozilla/3.0/handbook/
javascript/index.htm"

//JavaScript newsgroups

var news1="news:comp.lang.javascript"

var news2="news://news.livesoftware.com/livesoftware.
javascript.developer"

var news3="snews://secnews.netscape.com/netscape.
devs-javascript"

</SCRIPT>

</HEAD>

<BODY>

<CENTER>

<FORM>

<B>JavaScript Resources</B>
```

(continued)

```
</CENTER><BR>

<INPUT TYPE='button' VALUE='->' OnClick='self.workwin.
location=dest1' >JavaScript Index<BR>

<INPUT TYPE='button' VALUE='->' OnClick='self.workwin.
location=dest2' >Gamelan<BR>

<INPUT TYPE='button' VALUE='->' OnClick='self.workwin.
location=dest3' >Java Links<BR>

<INPUT TYPE='button' VALUE='->' OnClick='self.workwin.
location=dest4' >JavaScript FAQ<BR>

<INPUT TYPE='button' VALUE='->' OnClick='self.workwin.
location=dest5' >Netscape Guide<BR>

<BR><CENTER><B>Newsgroups</B></CENTER><BR>

<INPUT TYPE='button' VALUE='->' OnClick='self.workwin.
location=news1' >comp.lang.javascript<BR>

<INPUT TYPE='button' VALUE='->' OnClick='self.workwin.
location=news2' >LiveSoftware groups<BR>

<INPUT TYPE='button' VALUE='->' OnClick='self.workwin.
location=news3' >Netscape groups<BR>

<BR>

<CENTER><B>History Navigation</B></CENTER><BR>
```

(continued)

```
<CENTER>

<INPUT TYPE='button' VALUE='Back' OnClick='self.workwin.
history.back()'>

<INPUT TYPE='button' VALUE='Forward' OnClick='self.
workwin.history.forward()'>

<INPUT TYPE='button' VALUE='Reload' OnClick='self.workwin.
history.go(0)'>

</CENTER>

</FORM>

</CENTER>

</BODY>

</HTML>
```

Summary

This chapter has provided a detailed look at some basic, yet important, JavaScript objects that help users to navigate through Web pages:

- *The History object is a linked list of URLs associated with a window or frame it contains the URLs of all the pages loaded into that window or frame. It contains one property, length, and three methods,* `back()`*,* `forward()`*, and* `go()`*.*

- *The location object is the URL that is currently loaded into a window and its properties correspond to the components of a URL.*

- *JavaScript defines three location protocols: about:, javascript:, and mocha:. These protocols let you get information about Navigator, evaluate JavaScript expressions, or bring up a JavaScript expression interpreter.*

- *JavaScript offers an easy way to access all of the hyptertext links in a document, but only limited access to anchors. The format of the link and anchor objects is similar to the standard HTML links and anchors, with the addition of several parameters such as Name and Href.*

Coming Up

With the anchor, link, history, and location objects under our belts, it's time to move on to event handlers. Event handlers will help you tie JavaScript objects to user-initiated events, thus adding interactivity to Web pages.

CHAPTER

EVENTS, INPUT, AND OUTPUT

- Event Types

- Handling Events

- Writing Output

- I/O Objects

In this chapter, we cover events that occur as a user interacts with objects in a JavaScript application. We cover ways of recognizing and handling these events with JavaScript functions to provide feedback to the user, such as loading new pages, changing colors, or doing some calculations.

What are Events?

When creating a JavaScript-enabled page, you are placing objects and writing code to handle events in that page. The page is the document with which you are working and is also an object in itself. Objects include such items as buttons, text areas, and the like, which are then placed within the document. Objects in JavaScript are capable of handling events.

An event is a notification of something happening around an object at the user interface, which notification is sent to the object in your JavaScript program. JavaScript programming is really just event-driven programming. You write code, called *event handlers*, to handle each type of event. Each event is either handled by your code or by default event handlers built into JavaScript-enhanced browsers.

A quick note to those readers who want to get a head start.

The examples in this chapter show you how HTML components work in FORMs in a JavaScript document. In many cases, there are several ways presented to achieve the same results. No one way is the best way to write your own scripts, so learn from these scripts the various ways of performing certain functions. As you work with JavaScript, you will become more comfortable with taking shortcuts and will be better able to explore the various methods of doing so.

Each event in JavaScript is named after it's functionality. Following is a list of the events that can occur in a JavaScript application:

Click. This event happens when a button is clicked on an item in the window. The event handler for this event is called onClick.

Focus. The focus event occurs when your mouse pointer enters the area for the object you are concerned with or when a TAB entry moves the focus on to the object. The event handler for this event is called onFocus.

Blur. This event is the opposite of a focus event (you see a blur when you are not in focus, get it?). When a pointer is moved off an object or a TAB key moves the focus away, your object gets a blur event. The event handler for this event is called onBlur.

Change. The change event comes from an input area that the user has just modified. For a text input area, you would get these events only after the user has modified the input area and the object has lost focus. It is important to specify this distinction because you should not have to worry about getting these "change" events on each keystroke from a text input object. The event handler for this event is called onChange.

Load. The load occurs just before when an HTML page or a window is loaded. This event is useful to know about because you can use it to initialize items before your page is laid out for display by a browser. The event handler for this event is called onLoad.

MouseOver. The MouseOver event is caused when a pointer (it does not have to be a mouse!) moves over your object. The event handler for this event is called onMouseOver.

Select. The select event is reserved for use with text objects only when a section of text in the text object is selected. The event handler for this event is called onSelect.

Submit. This is used with FORMs on HTML pages. The event happens before your FORM makes the submission. This gives your script the chance to look over the FORM variables before you submit the actual transmission over the internet. The handler for this event returns true if you want to proceed with the submission and false if your handler found something that should prevent the submission. The event handler for this event is called onSubmit.

unLoad. The unload event happens when a window or a document is removed so that you may do some clean up. The event handler for this event is called onUnload.

We will be covering these events and their handlers in greater detail in the following sections.

The onMouseOver Event Handler

Let's start with the `onMouseOver` event handler. This event is used with the `<A>` and `</A>` (anchor) tags in HTML, which are used to specify a link. To refresh your memory, the following is an example of the anchor tags in use in an HTML document:

```
<A HREF="http://ikra.com/index.htm">My Home Page</A>
```

The text "My Home Page" will be shown in a different color than the main text in the browser window where this text is displayed. Clicking on this text in the browser will cause a jump to the location in the HREF attribute. By default, the location you will be sent to is shown in the status bar of your browser window.

If, for some reason, you wanted to provide a different message in the status bar, you can use the `onMouseOver` event handler to change the default and provide your own message when the pointer is passed over this link. An example of alternate text in the status bar could be a comment about something on the page over which the mouse moves. For example, if the mouse moves over a link called "Coffee," the status bar could display the message "Something that should really be taken intravenously." The syntax is:

```
<A HREF="url-to-whereever" onMouseOver="yourFunction">
Text to show</A>
```

The text shown in the *url-to-whereever* could be just the empty string if all you want to do is highlight some text. An example is shown below in Program 6.1. The two keywords used here are sugar and coffee. They should appear highlighted in the text shown at the browser. If you pass the mouse on top of and away from each of the words. Just passing it to and not removing the mouse will only display the URL the link is supposed to go to. Look at Figure 6.1 for what the display will look like.

Program 6.1: Using the onMouseOver Event.

```
<HTML>

<HEAD><TITLE>Test Some Display Objects</TITLE>

<SCRIPT LANGUAGE="JavaScript">



<!-- Hide stuff from older browsers with this start of comment



function showSugar(a,b){

     window.status = "Sugar is sweet";

     return true

}

function showCoffee(a,b){

     window.status = "Coffee wakes me up";

     return true

}



//

// Don't write any more comments in JavaScript after next line

//
// End of script hiding comments -->
```

(continued)

```
</SCRIPT>

</HEAD>

<HR>

<B>Some Terms  to test onMouseOver</B>

<HR>

This is some sample text to show you something about mouseOver

events. Let's see if we can add some

<A HREF="" onMouseOver="showSugar()">sugar </a>

to your cup of

<A HREF="" onMouseOver="showCoffee()">coffee?</a>

<HR>

</HTML>
```

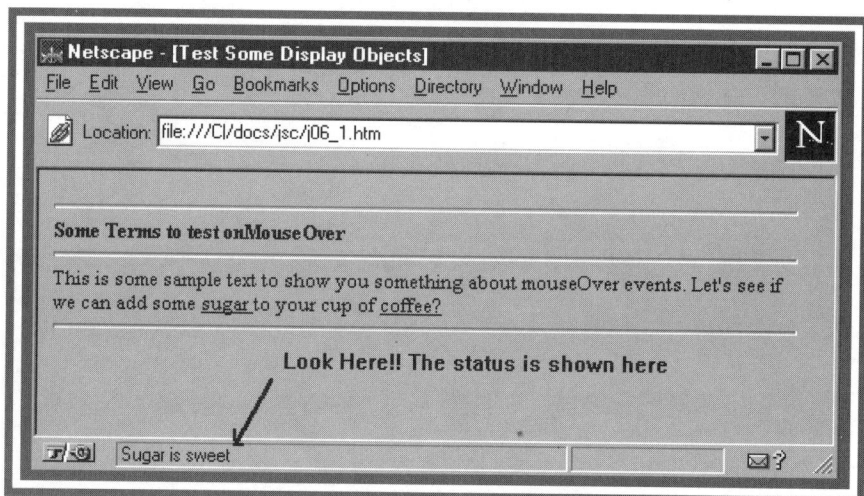

Figure 6.1 Using the onMouseOver event

Note how the last text message remains in the status bar, even after you have moved the pointer away. In the next section, we will cover how to turn this message off after a short time.

A click event occurs when the user clicks on an object in a form. The onClick event handler is called to handle this event. This function is called for the following objects: *pushbutton*, *checkbox*, *radio*, *link*, *reset*, and *submit* buttons.

Let's look at an example of how to use the onClick event handler with a link, a radio, and a checkbox button, as shown in Program 6.2. You can derive similar uses with reset and submit buttons.

Program 6.2: Using the onClick event handler

```
<HTML>

<HEAD><TITLE>Test Some Display Objects</TITLE>

<SCRIPT LANGUAGE="JavaScript">


<!-- Hide stuff


function creamClick(a){

     if (a)

     window.status = "You want cream!";

     else

     window.status = "You do not want cream!?";

     return true

}

function buttonClick(a){

     this.status = "You want " + a + " cubes of sugar!";

     return true

}
```

(continued)

```
function linkPass(){

     alert( "Coffee wakes me up.   I must have coffee
later!");

     return true

}

//

// Don't write any more comments in JavaScript after next line

//

// End of script hiding comments -->



</SCRIPT>

</HEAD>

<HR>

<B>Some Terms  to test Events: </B>

This is some sample text to show you something about mouseOver

events. Let's see if we can add some

<A HREF="" onMouseOver="linkPass()">sugar </a>

to your cup of coffee. How many cubes?  Passing the mouse over
the word sugar will create an alert box!
```

(continued)

```
<FORM>

<INPUT TYPE="checkbox" NAME="mst"

    onClick="if (this.checked) creamClick(0);

      else creamClick(1)">Cream<BR>

<INPUT TYPE="radio" NAME="cubes" onClick="buttonClick(0)">
none  <BR>

<INPUT TYPE="radio" NAME="cubes" onClick="buttonClick(1)">
one   <BR>

<INPUT TYPE="radio" NAME="cubes" onClick="buttonClick(2)">
two     <BR>


</FORM>

<HR>

</HTML>
```

First, the function `creamClick` takes one value and examines it to set the text on the windows status bar. Note how the function is called with some JavaScript in between double quotes. The special variable called "this" refers to the checkbox itself. The `if` statement checks the value of the checkbutton and calls `creamClick` based on the setting of the checkbox.

Now look at the function `buttonClick()`, which is called when any of the radio buttons are pressed. The value of the passed parameter of each button is sent in at the time it's pressed. As with the `creamClick()` function, we set the `window.status` bar, except that we make a call to using the "this" variable.

The `linkPass()` function is designed to bring up an alert box indicating, in this case, my frame of mind at the moment. The call to generate the alert box is triggered with the `onMouseOver` button. Note how we bring up a dialog box without the user having to click on anything.

The `this` pointer is a handy shortcut for substituting the name of an object instead of it's entire hierarchy. Please refer to Chapter 4 where we cover objects and the `this` variable in more detail.

> **Tip**
>
> Here's a friendly reminder for those readers who skipped Chapter 4. The "this" operator is used within JavaScript objects to refer to themselves. Within methods for an object, the this.member construct refers to the member of the instance of the object whose method is being called.
>
> The this shortcut is only available from inside a FORM.

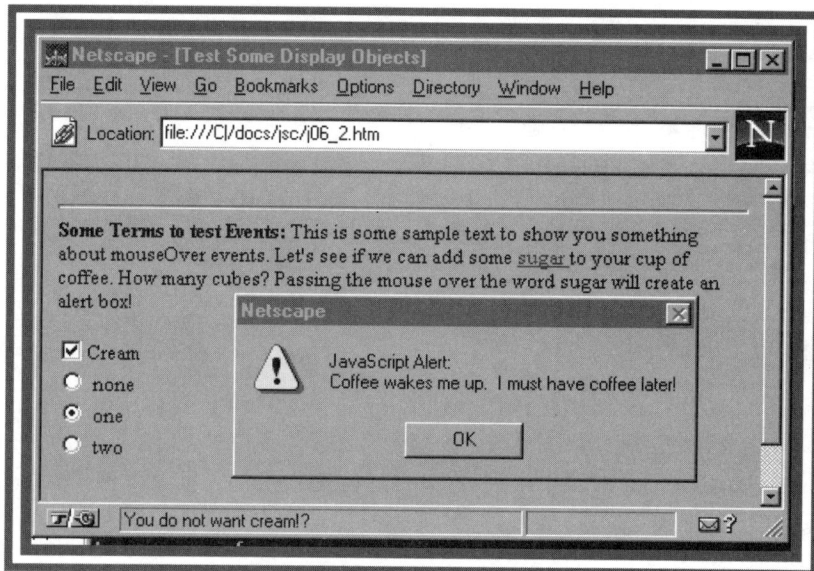

Figure 6.2 Using the `onClick` event

The `this` keyword does not always work in all JavaScript enhanced HTML pages. In the event that the code 'looks right' but the `this` keyword just doesn't work, try explicitly addressing the object using the `document.form[index]` method shown in Chapter 4.

The OnChange, OnFocus, OnBlur Event Handlers

The example shown in this section covers three event types: `onEvent`, `onFocus`, and `onBlur`. Rather than give three fragmented sets of examples, we show you how handlers for different types of events all fit together.

The example in Program 6.3 also covers the means to take input from various FORM elements and process it. We will be covering FORM handling in more detail in Chapter 7, "The document object" and in Chapter 9 "Applying Javascript," but this example will provide a good example of where to start on how to write code handle some events generated in FORMs. If you are new to HTML, this example will show you one way to create HTML FORMs to collect user input. See Figure 6.3 for a sample run of this file.

The `onFocus` and `onBlur` event handlers apply to windows as well as other objects. There is no `onClick` handler for windows. The `onFocus` handler for a window is called when the window (or frame) receives focus, such as being brought to the top of the window manager. For example, if you click on a window that is hidden by other windows, the window will become fully visible since the focus is now on this window. If there is an `onFocus` event handler, it will be called. Clicking on another window will cause the currently in-focus window to lose focus, that is, it's now a "blur". The `onBlur` event handler, if any is defined, is called when a window (or frame) loses focus.

Program 6.3: Using the onBlur and onFocus events.

```
<HTML>

<HEAD><TITLE>Test Some Display Objects</TITLE>

<SCRIPT LANGUAGE="JavaScript">


<!-- Hide stuff


//

// This function will be developed in the next example

//

function buttonClick(a){

        window.status = "You want insurance!";

        return true

}



//

// Clear the text in the window status bar.

//

function erase() {

        window.status= ""

        }
```

(continued)

```
//
// Check the age of the car for specific ranges.
//
function ckAgeOfCar(a) {
        if (a=="") return // You do not really need this
info?

        if (a < 0)
         alert ("let's make the car first shall we?")
        if (a > 15)
        { alert ("We do not insure antiques"); }

}


function jestAboutAge(a) {
        if (a == 25)
        {
        window.status = "Quarter century old!?"
        setTimeout("erase()", 5000);
        }
        if (a == 7)
        {
        window.status = "Feet reach the pedals??"
        setTimeout("erase()", 5000);
        }
        if (a == 40)
        {
        window.status = "Over the hill already?"
        setTimeout("erase()", 5000);
        }
}
```

(continued)

```
//

// Verifies that the user is between 1 and 100 years old

//

function getAge(a) {

        if ((a < 1) || ( a > 100))

        alert ("Get a Life and enter your correct age!")

}


//

// Return state name based on zip code, simple version

//

function makeZip(frm,val) {

        frm.region.value = "MO"

        if ((val >= 77000) && (val < 80000))

        frm.region.value = "TX"

        else if (val == 10001) frm.region.value = "NY"

        else if (val == 07458) frm.region.value = "NJ"

}
// ------------------------------------------------------------

// Don't write any more comments in JavaScript after next line

// End of script hiding comments -->
```

(continued)

```
</SCRIPT>

</HEAD>

<HR>

<B>V RIP U Insurance Application</B>

A sample questionaire to see how much we can get from you

for car insurance. Answer questions truthfully.

<HR>

<FORM>

First Name<INPUT TYPE="text" NAME="fname" SIZE=30

        onChange="this.value = this.value.toUpperCase()">


Age <INPUT TYPE="text" NAME="age" SIZE=5

        onBlur="jestAboutAge(this.value)"

        onChange="getAge(this.value)"><BR>


Last  Name<INPUT TYPE="text" NAME="lname" SIZE=30

        onChange="this.value = this.value.toUpperCase()">


State <INPUT TYPE="text" NAME="region" SIZE=2><BR>


City  Name<INPUT TYPE="text" NAME="city" SIZE=30

        onFocus="this.value = this.value.toLowerCase()">


ZIP <INPUT TYPE="text" NAME="zip" SIZE=5

        onBlur="makeZip(this.form,this.value)"> <BR>
```

(continued)

```
Model / Make <INPUT TYPE="text" NAME="cartype" SIZE=30

         onChange="this.value = this.value.toUpper-
Case()"><BR>


Age of Car<INPUT TYPE="text" NAME="carAge" SIZE=4

         onChange="ckAgeOfCar(this.value)"><BR>


Manufacturer <INPUT TYPE="text" NAME="carModel" SIZE=30

         onChange="this.value = this.value.toUpper-
Case()"><BR>


Complaints<TEXTAREA NAME="comments" ROWS=2 COLS=20

         onBlur="this.value = this.value.toUpperCase()">
</TEXTAREA>


<INPUT TYPE="button" NAME="cubes" VALUE="Tell me"

         onClick="buttonClick(this.form)" ><BR>


</FORM>

<HR>

</HTML>
```

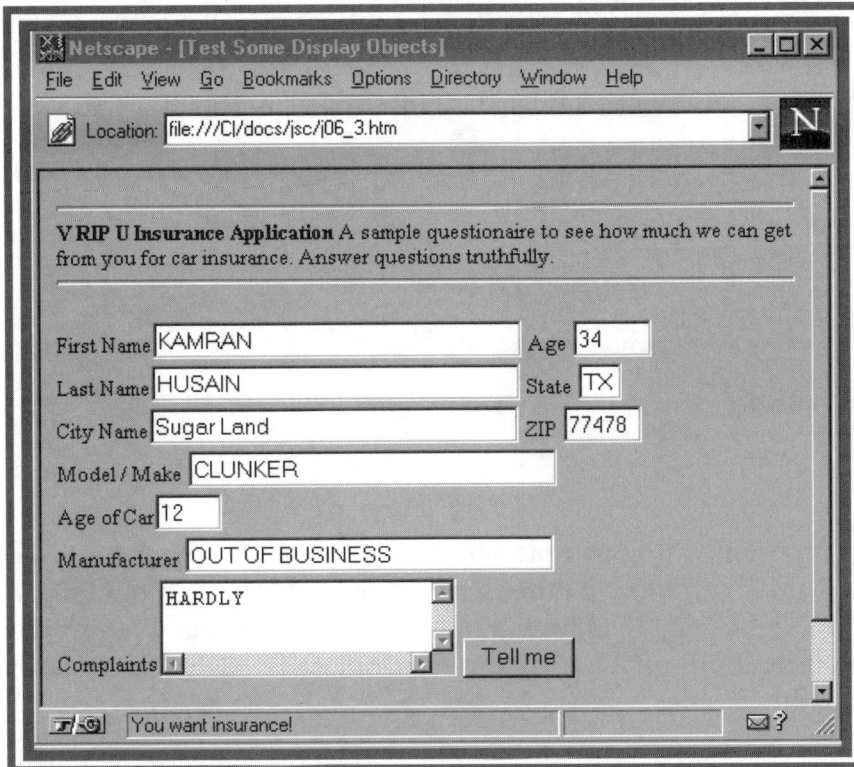

Figure 6.3 Using `onBlur`, `onFocus`, and `onClick`

The script in Program 6.3 uses several event handlers. Consider the call to convert the first name to all uppercase characters after the name is typed in:

```
First Name<INPUT TYPE="text" NAME="fname" SIZE=30
                onChange="this.value = this.value.toUpperCase()">
```

The `this` keyword is used to access the object called `fname`. The code in the double quotes is a JavaScript statement that converts the text in the field for `fname` into all uppercase characters. The returned result from the `toUpperCase` call is assigned back to the value of the fname object. The call is made only after the focus in the text area has been lost with a TAB press or click elsewhere on the page.

Notice how input regarding age is collected from the user and verified in this code fragment:

```
Age <INPUT TYPE="text" NAME="age" SIZE=5

    onBlur="jestAboutAge(this.value)"

    onChange="getAge(this.value)"><BR>
```

One important thing to note about this fragment is that both the onBlur and onChange handlers are defined here. The onChange event handler is called before the onBlur event, regardless of which event you define first. The value of the object is passed in to each event handler.

You must be very careful here not to change the value of the object in between function calls to event handlers. If you modify the value in one event handler, then the event handlers called will be working with a different value. For example, the following is not a good idea unless you can confirm the calling order of event handlers:

```
Age <INPUT TYPE="text" NAME="age" SIZE=5

    onBlur="jestAboutAge(this.value)"

    onChange="this.value = normalizeAge(this.value)"><BR>
```

Which function is called first, the onChange or onBlur? A good way to be sure is to use an alert function call in each function, then change the value of the object in the last function called. Obviously, if you want the value to be modified before the call to the second function, do it as shown above.

Note also in the above example that the onChange function is not called unless the text has changed. That is, if the text is not modified by the user, your onChange function will not be called. If you were relying on the call being made and doing some other operation, then your code may not work under all circumstances.

> **Tip**
>
> When defining more than one event handler for an object, it's a good idea to put alert() function calls in event handlers and then see the order in which the handlers are called. Be very careful of coding functions where event handler calling sequence is important and avoid such code unless absolutely necessary.
>
> Returning false from an onClick event handler normally cancels any action that would have been taken. For example, if the click action would have loaded a URL, a return value of false from the onClick handler will cancel any attempt to load the URL.

More than one parameter can be passed to a function by listing each argument at the time of the call. Look at the function call in the code snippet below:

```
ZIP <INPUT TYPE="text" NAME="zip" SIZE=5

        onBlur="makeZip(this.form,this.value)"> <BR>
```

In the `makeZip` function, the code will have access to the entire form as well as the value entered in the zip code field. Notice how the passed form is used to update one particular object (form.region.value) from the data in another object (form.region.zip) on the same form. In later examples in this chapter, you will see how values of variables on other forms can be modified by accessing them with the top-level document and the forms array.

Timed Events

We used a trick in Listing 6.3 to implement timeouts. In the function `jestAboutAge()`, the code places some text in the status bar that we don't want displayed all the time. When you place some code in the status bar, it stays there unless there is an event to modify it. If the user does not move the pointer around or do something else on the page, the text in the status bar will stay around. The text will not be removed until the user explicitly takes some action, such as load a new document, which will modify the text in the status bar.

This is where the timeout call comes in handy. JavaScript let's you set a timer that will call a function or execute code after it expires. The call to set up a timeout is:

```
setTimeout("Code", milliseconds);
```

The first argument to the `setTimeOut` function is the code to execute; the second argument is the number of milliseconds to wait. The timer in these calls is not terribly accurate, so don't think about using this for real time events, but you will get pretty darn close to it. The value returned from the `setTimeout()` function can be used to store an identifier for the timer. The identifier is useful if you want to clear a timer before it matures.

```
timerId = setTimeout("myCode()",100000);



.... some code here ...

if (bailout == true) clearTimeout(timerId);
```

Program 6.4 shows an example for a stopwatch using the status window. There are two functions in the example page: `startTimer` and `stopTimer`. They both use the global variables `timerId` and `counter` to hold the Id of the timer and the value of the time in seconds. Note how the value of the `timerId` is updated on every call to the timer function. See Figure 6.4 for what's shown at the end of the timed events.

Program 6.4 Using timeout events

```
<HTML>

<HEAD><TITLE>Test Some Display Objects</TITLE>

<SCRIPT LANGUAGE="JavaScript">



<!-- Hide stuff from old browsers



var counter;  // The value in seconds

var timerId;// The id for the counter
```

(continued)

```
//
// This function counts down
//
function countDown() {
        counter--;                // Decrement counter
        window.status= "Time:" + counter;
        if (BeginTimer > 0)
        timerId = setTimeout("countDown()", 1000);
        else
        alert ("Yo! Time's up !!")
        }


function startTimer(v) { // start the timer
        counter = v;
        timerId = setTimeout("countDown()", 1000);
        }


function clearTimer() {  // stop the timer
        if (timerId) clearTimeout(timerId);
```

(continued)

```
        }


// ------------------------------------------------------------

// Don't write any more comments in JavaScript after next line

// End of script hiding comments -->

</SCRIPT>

</HEAD>

<HR>

<B>Stop Watch Application</B>

<FORM>

Timer Value<INPUT TYPE="text" NAME="count" SIZE=5>


<INPUT TYPE="button" NAME="startMe" VALUE="Start Timer"

          onClick="startTimer(this.form.count.value)" >

<INPUT TYPE="button" NAME="stopMe" VALUE="Stop Timer"

          onClick="clearTimer(this.form.count.value)" ><BR>

</FORM>

<HR>

</HTML>
```

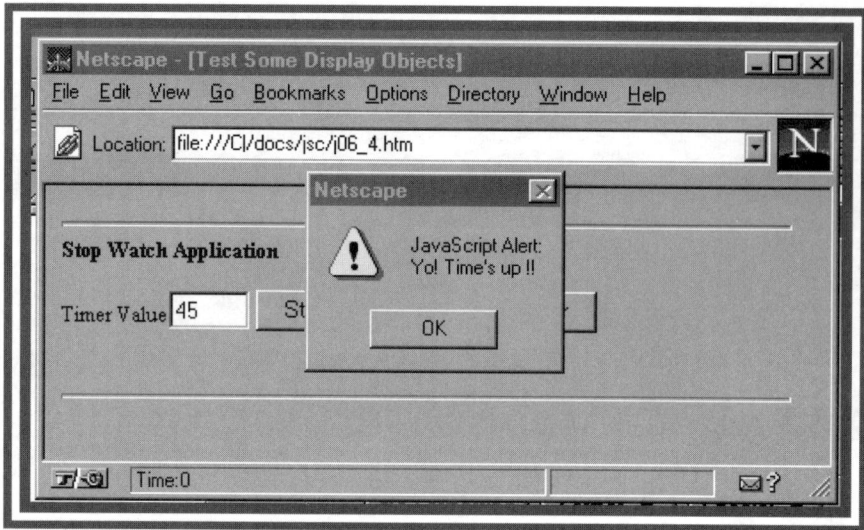

Figure 6.4 Using timed events

The OnLoad and OnUnload Events

The OnLoad event occurs when a document containing JavaScript code is loaded in for the first time. The OnUnload event is called when a the document exits. The two event handlers are placed in the <BODY> tags of an HTML document. If you are using <FRAMES> (which we really haven't covered yet, but be patient, we will in Chapter 8, "Windows in JavaScript"), then you can place the OnLoad and OnUnload event handlers in the <FRAME> tags. A point to remember is this: Event handlers in the FRAME are called after the event handlers in the BODY tags.

The onLoad and onUnload handlers are called once when a page is loaded and unloaded. Remember to initialize all variables in the onLoad handler. If you do not do so, there may be some residual values left in variables from a previous load. In some browsers, the onLoad handler is not called when a page is reloaded.

The code shown in Program 6.4 can be modified to accommodate the onLoad and onUnload event handlers by adding the <BODY> and </BODY> tags. Place the </BODY> tag just before the </HTML> tag. Add the <BODY> tag after the </SCRIPT> tag as follows:

```
<BODY onLoad="startTimer(20)" onUnload="clearTimer">
```

This code has set up a timer to start for 20 seconds when the page loads up. If, during those 20 seconds, the page is unloaded, it would be great to clear the timer out. That's where the onUnload function call would be called to clear the timer.

The complete listing of using the Load and Unload handlers is shown in Program 6.5.

Program 6.5: Using the Load and Unload Event Handlers

```
<HTML>

<HEAD><TITLE>Test Some Display Objects</TITLE>

<SCRIPT LANGUAGE="JavaScript">


<!-- Hide stuff from old browsers


var counter;   // The value in seconds

var timerId;   // The id for the countDown


//

// This function counts down

//

function countDown() {

        counter--;      // Decrement countDown

                window.status= "Time:" + counter;

        if (counter > 0)

                timerId = setTimeout("countDown()", 1000);

        else

                alert ("Yo! Time's up !!")

        }
```

(continued)

```
function StartTimer(v) { // start the timer

        counter = v;

        timerId = setTimeout("countDown()", 1000);

        }


function clearTimer() {  // stop the timer

        if (timerId) clearTimeout(timerId);

        }


// -------------------------------------------------------------

// Don't write any more comments in JavaScript after next line

// End of script hiding comments -->



</SCRIPT>


<BODY onLoad="StartTimer(4)"  onUnload="clearTimer()">

</HEAD>

<HR>

<B>Stop Watch Application</B>

<FORM>

Timer Value<INPUT TYPE="text" NAME="countDown" SIZE=5>
```

(continued)

```
<INPUT TYPE="button" NAME="startMe" VALUE="Start Timer"

        onClick="StartTimer(this.form.countDown.value)" >

<INPUT TYPE="button" NAME="stopMe" VALUE="Stop Timer"

        onClick="clearTimer(this.form.countDown.value)"
><BR>

</FORM>

<HR>

</BODY>

</HTML>
```

Multiple FORMS on One Page

More than one FORM can be used to check the value of another FORM. Check out the code in Program 6.6, where there are two FORMs in the listing. The first FORM is addressed using the array element document.forms[0] and the other document.forms[1]. The order of the FORMs is the other in which they appear in the *document.forms* array.

The second form processes the values entered in the first form. The checkInput() function progressively searches each element in the FORMs array to see if the values have been entered correctly. If any values are not entered, an alert box is created.

Program 6.6: Using more than one FORM

```
<HTML>
<TITLE>More than one FORM</TITLE>
<SCRIPT>
function checkInput() {
        var isOk = true
        var count = document.forms[0].elements.length
        var i = 0
        for (i = 0; i < count; i++) {
        if (document.forms[0].elements[i].value == "")
        isOk = false
        }
        if (isOk == false)
        alert (" Please fill in all responses ")
        return isOk
}
</SCRIPT>
<BODY>
<H1> Check it out</H1>
<FORM>
Your Full Name<INPUT TYPE="text" NAME="yname" ><BR>
Email Address.<INPUT TYPE="text" NAME="email" ><BR>
Postal Address<INPUT TYPE="text" NAME="email" ><BR>
</FORM>
<HR>
<BR>
The second form begins here <BR>
<HR>
<FORM>
<INPUT TYPE="button" NAME="doit" VALUE="Check Values"
onClick="checkInput()">
</FORM>
</BODY>
</HTML>
```

The onSubmit event handler is used to do FORM validation at the client side. Generally, the input entered at the client side is collected, packaged into a URL string, and then verified by a CGI script at the server side. To cut down the traffic time and verification load at the server, it's often easier to verify all the input at the client side using some JavaScript code.

The onSubmit event handler is called when a user submits a FORM. To use the handler, put a return statement at the end of the function. Return a value of true if you are sure that the user values are correct. Not putting the return statement will default to a return of true. If your JavaScript code finds obvious errors in the user input, flag the errors using an alert box and return a value of false.

The onSubmit() handler for a FORM is called when the input type of button called onSubmit is called. Consider the example in Program 6.7, which sends a mail message to the author of the HTML page only if all the input fields are filled. Examine the code for two ways of checking input.

Program 6.7: Using onSubmit() handlers

```
<HTML>

<TITLE>Check on the onSubmit handler</TITLE>

<SCRIPT>

function checkInput() {

        var isOk = true

        var count = document.forms[0].elements.length

        var i = 0

        for (i = 0; i < count; i++) {
```

(continued)

```
                    if (document.forms[0].elements[i].value == "")

                        isOk = false

            }

        if (isOk == false)

                alert (" Please fill in all responses ")

        else

                document.forms[0].submit();

}

</SCRIPT>

<BODY>

<H1> Check it out</H1>

<FORM METHOD="POST" ACTION="http://www.ikra.com/cgi-bin/
query.pl">

Your Full Name <INPUT TYPE="text" NAME="yname" ><BR>

Email Address. <INPUT TYPE="text" NAME="email" ><BR>

Postal Address <INPUT TYPE="text" NAME="email" ><BR>

<INPUT TYPE="SUBMIT" VALUE="Inquire">

</FORM>


<FORM>

<INPUT TYPE="button" NAME="doit" VALUE="Check Values"
onClick="checkInput()">

</FORM>

</BODY>

</HTML>
```

In this program, the function checkInput() checks the input as it did in Program 6.6. However, now the function submit() is also called for the first FORM if all the values entered are not null. The value of the variable isOk is checked to see if it's true before the submit() function is called in these lines:

```
if (isOk == false)

        alert (" Please fill in all responses ")

else

        document.forms[0].submit();
```

Notice also that the first FORM has a SUBMIT type of input box. We can also do the same type of checking with the onSubmit() handler in the first FORM. The modified code is shown in Program 6.8. The value of the onSubmit handler is checked to see if it's true or not before the form is submitted to the server. A return value of false will cause the client to not submit the data to the server.

Program 6.8: Using the onSubmit handler and submit()

```
<HTML>

<TITLE>Try it both ways!</TITLE>

<SCRIPT>

function sisterCheck() {

        var isOk = true

        var count = document.forms[0].elements.length
```

(continued)

```
            var i = 0
            for (i = 0; i < count; i++) {
            if (document.forms[0].elements[i].value == "")
            isOk = false
            }
            return isOk
}

function checkInput() {
            var tt = sisterCheck()
            if (tt == false)
            alert (" Please fill in all responses ")
            else
            document.forms[0].submit();
}
</SCRIPT>
<BODY>
<H1> Check it out</H1>
<FORM METHOD="POST" ACTION="http://www.ikra.com/cgi-bin/
query.pl"
            onSubmit="return sisterCheck()" >
Your Full Name <INPUT TYPE="text" NAME="yname" ><BR>
Email Address. <INPUT TYPE="text" NAME="email" ><BR>
Postal Address <INPUT TYPE="text" NAME="email" ><BR>
<INPUT TYPE="SUBMIT" VALUE="Inquire">
</FORM>
```

(continued)

```
<FORM>

<INPUT TYPE="button" NAME="doit" VALUE="Check Values"
onClick="checkInput()">

</FORM>

</BODY>

</HTML>
```

Calling Event Handlers Explicitly

You have just seen two ways of handling client input data: using the onSubmit handler or by calling the submit function explicitly in Program 6.8.

Event handlers can be called explicitly instead of resulting from some user interaction. To call an event handler for an object, simply call the function by name. For example, the onClick handler for an object is called "click." The naming of functions is quite consistent, as the list of handlers in Table 6.1 shows.

Table 6.1   Event Handlers and Their Description

Event	Description of Event
onclick()	onClick event handler. Valid for button, checkbox, radio, reset, and submit buttons.
onblur()	onBlur event handler. Valid for password, select, window, text, and textarea objects.
onfocus()	onFocus event handler. Valid for password, select, window, text, and textarea objects.
onselect()	onSelect event handler (when it works!). Valid for textarea objects.
onsubmit()	onSubmit event handler for Submit buttons.

Lets look at some examples of how this code could be used to simulate user action. See Program 6.9, where two buttons each have a handler. The first button explicitly calls the handler for the second button with a call to the onclick function. Pressing the first button will give you two alert boxes. Pressing the second button will only give you one alert box.

Program 6.9: Using the onclick handler

```
<HTML>

<TITLE>Check Submit Function</TITLE>

<SCRIPT>

function buttonOne() {

        alert ("button 1");

        document.forms[0].elements[1].onclick()

        }


function buttonTwo() {

        alert ("button 2");

        }


</SCRIPT>

<BODY>

<H1> Check me out</H1>

<FORM>

Button 1 <INPUT TYPE="button" NAME="btn1"
onClick="buttonOne()"><BR>

Button 2 <INPUT TYPE="button" NAME="btn2"
onClick="buttonTwo()"><BR>

</BODY>

</HTML>
```

Other event handlers could be handled the same way as the onClick handler. For example, the onBlur handler would be called in addition to the other handlers when the first button is pressed using the code shown in Program 6.10. You can use the other event handlers explicitly along with the examples shown here as a reference.

> Be careful when calling event handlers explicitly. Do not accidentally force one handler to be called recursively. For example, fun1() calls fun2(), which calls fun1() which calls fun2() and so on! This will cause a crash or lock your workstation up.

Program 6.10: Using the onblur handler

```
<HTML>

<TITLE>Check Submit Function</TITLE>

<SCRIPT>

function buttonOne() {

        alert ("button 1");

        document.forms[0].elements[1].onclick()

        document.forms[0].elements[2].onblur()

        }


function buttonTwo() {

        alert ("button 2");

        }
```

(continued)

```
function textOne() {

        alert ("text 1");

        }


</SCRIPT>

<BODY>

<H1> Check me out</H1>

<FORM>

Button 1 <INPUT TYPE="button" NAME="btn1" onClick="button-
One()"><BR>

Button 2 <INPUT TYPE="button" NAME="btn2" onClick="but-
tonTwo()"><BR>

Text 1 <INPUT TYPE="text" NAME="txt1" onBlur="textOne()"><BR>

</BODY>

</HTML>
```

Event handlers can be reassigned dynamically. For example, consider the code in Program 6.11, where the onclick handler for the button is reassigned a value. There are some important points to note about this code.

The first point is that it will only work with Windows 95/NT versions of Navigator. The second point is that the name of the function is used and not the function name followed by parentheses. Had the parentheses been used (i.e., textOne() instead of textOne), the results of the return from the function would be assigned to the value of onclick and not the function itself!

Note that all the function you are reassigning have to be declared in the head and not the body of the function. The functions that actually do the assignments must be declared in the body at the moment.

Program 6.11: Reassigning event handlers

```
<HTML>

<TITLE>Check Submit Function</TITLE>

<SCRIPT>

function textNone() {

        alert ("None");

        }


function textOne() {

        alert ("button 1");

        }


function textTwo() {

        alert ("button 2");

        }


</SCRIPT>

<BODY>

<H1> Check me out</H1>

<FORM NAME="Hello">
```

(continued)

```
<SCRIPT>

function setButtonOne() {

        document.Hello.btn0.onclick=textOne

        }


function setButtonTwo() {

        document.Hello.btn0.onclick=textTwo

        }


</SCRIPT>

Button 0 <INPUT TYPE="button" NAME="btn0"
onClick="textNone()"><BR>

Button 1 <INPUT TYPE="button" NAME="btn1"
onClick="setButtonOne()"><BR>

Button 2 <INPUT TYPE="button" NAME="btn2"
onClick="setButtonTwo()"><BR>

</BODY>

</HTML>
```

Summary

In this chapter, we have introduced you to events and event handlers in JavaScript. Programming in JavaScript really involves the coding of event handling functions. There are specific event types associated with each object on a screen. Each event can have a handler for it. A default event handler is called if the user specifies no handler. Care has to be taken before modifying values of objects in between successive calls to event handlers for the same object. Some default handlers will not be called or simply not work for some objects, so be prepareed to test these instances thoroughly.

There are a few points that you should be careful of when writing event handlers:

- *Events are usually the result of a user action. However, you can call the event handler explicitly, say at the end of timer.*
- *All objects do not have all types of events. You will not get an error if you define a handler for an object that it does not support.*
- *Be careful when calling one event handler from another. If two event handlers call each other, your JavaScript application will crash a browser.*
- *The order in which event handlers are called should not be important: however, it's good idea to write test handlers with alert boxes to see which handler is called first.*
- *The onLoad() Event handlers in a FRAME are called after the event handlers in the BODY tags.*

Coming Up

Now that you have learned about handling JavaScript events, let's move on to the next chapter, in which we cover how to use JavaScript documents. A JavaScript document contains objects, each of which can handle its own events. In the next chapter, you will see how to put together applications in a document using objects each handling it's own events.

CHAPTER 7

- What's a Document

- Properties of Documents

- Using Documents

- Manipulating Properties

In Chapter 6, we discussed how to handle JavaScript events as they occur when a user interacts with objects in a JavaScript application. A JavaScript document contains objects, each of which can handle it's own events. This chapter will cover the basics of using JavaScript documents. We'll discuss the properties of a document and the methods used to manipulate the behavior of documents, as well as how to put together applications in a document using objects, each of which handles it's own events.

What's a Document?

A document is simply an HTML file that is loaded as a Web page into a browser window. A document in a JavaScript application is an object with its own properties and methods. You can manipulate a document's appearance and contents by using methods and addressing properties in JavaScript statements.

Use the following syntax to create a JavaScript object within <BODY> and </BODY> tags in an HTML file:

```
<BODY

        BACKGROUND="color"

        FOREGROUND="color"

        TEXT="textColor"

        LINK="untraversedColor"

        ALINK="activeLinkColor"

        VLINK="visitedLinkColor"

        onLoad="onloadHandler Code"

        onUnload="onUnloadHandler Code" >

This is where you can address the document in your scripts.

</BODY>
```

Your attribute names are not case sensitive because the <BODY> and </BODY> tag is an HTML tag. The attributes are optional and may be specified in any order. Color values are specified either as triple bytes of raw RGB values or as color values. For example, you can define a <BODY> tag as either of the following two lines to show a white page with black text:

```
<BODY bgcolor="#FFFFFF" fgcolor="#000000" >

or

<BODY bgcolor="white" fgcolor="black">
```

Properties of Documents

A JavaScript document has *properties* that match the attributes used to create it. You can manipulate each of these properties and hence override the attribute value using *methods*. The properties and matching attributes (where available) for a document are as follows:

- *alinkColor (for ALINK attribute)*
- *anchors*
- *bgColor (for BACKGROUND attribute)*
- *cookie*
- *fgColor (for FOREGROUND attribute)*
- *forms*
- *lastModified*
- *linkColor (for LINK attribute)*
- *links*
- *location*
- *referrer*
- *title*
- *vlinkColor for VLINK attribute*

We will cover each of these properties in greater details in the rest of this book.

The way to access a property in a given document is in the form:

```
document.propertyName
```

where the `propertyName` is one of the properties previously listed.

Some of the document attributes are matched with document property member variables. For example, BACKGROUND is matched with the property `bgColor`, for FOREGROUND. Some properties do not have matching attributes, such as `forms`, `links`, and `location`.

Let's see what each property means in a document and how each is used. The first type of property we'll look at is the type that modifies the colors in a document.

Color Properties

The default background color of a JavaScript document can be changed using the `bgColor` property. The foreground color is the default color that is used to display text in a document and is set with the `fgColor` property. The `linkColor` property is the color for an HTML link that the browser sees as not visited. The `vlinkColor` property is the color for a link that has been visited. The `alinkColor` property specifies the color of an active link in a document. This is the color that a link turns when a mouse clicks it, before the mouse is released.

> **Tip** Colors in JavaScript can be specified one of two ways: either as triple byte values of RGB colors or as a name specified in the colors table in Appendix D, "Colors in JavaScript".

You can set the background color either at the time when the text is loaded or dynamically after the document has been loaded. Dynamically changing the background color is helpful when you want to show certain changes in context. For example, you may wish to change the background color to green when you are about to display information on grass-related items, or blue when you are about to display information on water. Sometimes, just subtly changing the shade of the background in a timer loop will bring out great special effects. For example, every time the user presses a button to reload the page, you can make the background get slightly lighter. Unfortunately, only the background color can be set dynamically. The rest of the colors have to be set when the page is loaded and cannot be changed once the page has been laid out. Therefore, you must set the value of these properties either in the body tag or in the onLoad handler when the page is first loaded.

The onLoad handler is called before the page is laid out, so you can affect the colors with this function. The catch is that the onLoad handler has to be declared outside the <BODY> tags for the color assignment to work.

For example, consider the alinkColor property, which is set using the ALINK attribute of the <BODY> tag. The value to set the tag is either a triplet RGB value or a known color. For example, to set the value of the alinkColor to brown, you could use either of the following two statements:

```
<BODY ALINK="brown">
```

or

```
<BODY ALINK="A52A2A">
```

Because the alinkColor has to be set before the layout is complete, you can set the value of the property in the function called during loading. For example, the following snippet of code form will set the alinkColor to white:

```
<!--

function loadMe(){

        document.alinkColor="white"

        }

--->



<BODY onLoad="loadMe()">
```

You can write similar examples for the `fgColor`, `linkColor` and `vlinkColor` attributes.

For the background color, you can set the value of the background color using a simple HTML page. The value of the background color is set as shown in Program 7.1.

Program 7.1: Setting the background

```
<HTML>

<HEAD><TITLE>Test Some Display Objects</TITLE>

<SCRIPT LANGUAGE="JavaScript">


<!-- Hide stuff

function setBGcolor(a){

        if (a != null) document.bgColor=a

}
```

(continued)

```
// Don't write any more comments in JavaScript after next line

//

// End of script hiding comments -->

</SCRIPT>

</HEAD>

<BODY ALINK="black" >

<B>Some Color testing ability</B>

<HR>

<FORM>

Test color setting ability. <BR>Fore

<INPUT TYPE="text" NAME="bgc" SIZE=20>

<INPUT TYPE="button" NAME="setBGColor"  VALUE="Back"

            onClick="setBGcolor(this.form.bgc.value)"><BR>

</FORM>

<HR>

</HTML>
```

The output from the program shown in Program 7.1 is shown in Figure 7.1.

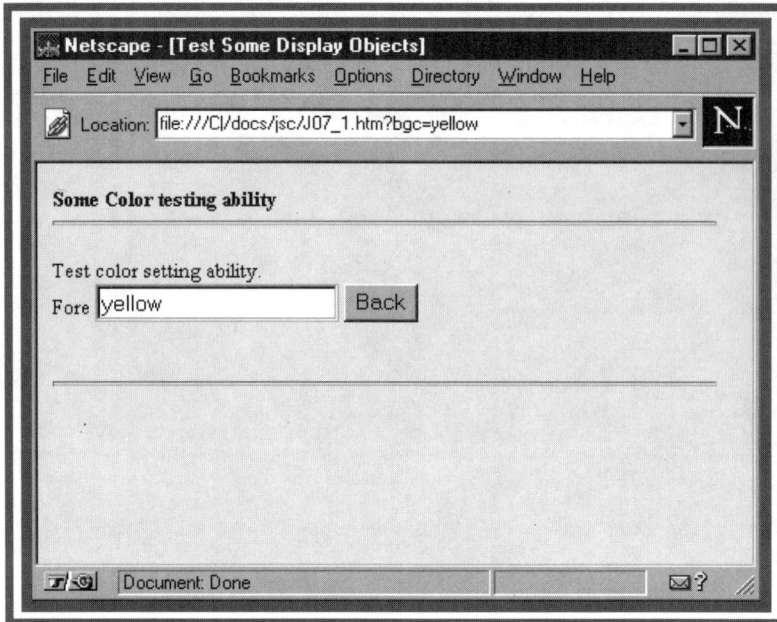

Figure 7.1 A simple HTML page lets you set the value of the background color

The UNIX version of Navigator 3.0 sets the entire window to the background color. To get the program shown in Program 7.1 for the UNIX platform, you have to use the "canned" version shown in Program 7.2. We will discuss how to write to documents later in this chapter, so just glance at this listing for now.

Program 7.2: Modified version of Listing 7.1 for UNIX

```
<HTML>

<HEAD><TITLE>Test Some Display Objects</TITLE>

<SCRIPT LANGUAGE="JavaScript">

<!-- Hide stuff


function setBGcolor(a){
```

(continued)

```
            document.close();

            document.open();

            document.write(' ');

            var x = '<FORM>' +

            ' Test color setting ability. <BR>Fore  ' +

            ' <INPUT TYPE="text" NAME="bgc" SIZE=20> ' +

            ' <INPUT TYPE="button" NAME="setBGColor"
VALUE="Back" ' +

            ' onClick="setBGcolor(this.form.bgc.value)"><BR> ';

            document.bgColor=a

            document.write(x)

}



// Don't write any more comments in JavaScript after next line

//

// End of script hiding comments -->
```

(continued)

```
</SCRIPT>

</HEAD>

<BODY ALINK="black" >

<B>Some Color testing ability</B>

<HR>

<FORM>

Test color setting ability. <BR>Fore

<INPUT TYPE="text" NAME="bgc" SIZE=20>

<INPUT TYPE="button" NAME="setBGColor"  VALUE="Back"

        onClick="setBGcolor(this.form.bgc.value)"><BR>

</FORM>

<HR>

</HTML>
```

In Program 7.2, the background color and the FORM to collect the user input has to be recreated. Another bug to work around is in the `document.clear()` call, which has to be replaced with a `document.close()` and a `document.open()` call. In addition, a blank line has to be written after the `open()` call to get the document to come up correctly.

Here's another example, in Program 7.3, which will use the timer function to update the background color dynamically. The choice of colors to use is entirely up to you, of course, but you can get an idea of how to set up colors without much user intervention. The timer function is started in the `onLoad` event handler. Each call to the timer resets the timer to start again after half a second (500 milliseconds).

In Program 7.3, the counter stops the kaleidoscope effect by not resetting the timer after 10 shifts (you can set it for any amount of shifts) through some weird colors.

Program 7.3: Using the timer to set background colors

```
<HTML><HEAD><TITLE>MPS Inc. Home Page </TITLE>

</HEAD>

<SCRIPT LANGUAGE="LiveScript">

<!-- Hiding

var bg = 0;

var counter = 1;


        function doit() {

    bg += 0x020202

    bg &= 0x1F1f1f

    document.bgColor= bg + ""

    counter += 1;

    if (counter < 100) {

        setTimeout("doit()",500);

        }

        window.status = "Color = " + bg;

        }

        function setMyTimer() {

        setTimeout("doit()",500);

        }
```

(continued)

```
// -->

</SCRIPT>

<BODY onLoad="setMyTimer()">

<P>

<A HREF="http://ikra.com/jindex.htm" >Click here if you are
using a JAVA enabled Browser</A>

<p>

<H1>Test Background Color</H1>

<IMG SRC="pirate.gif"> <B>Onward Ho!</B><P>

<address>e-mail-->Kamran Husain,  khusain@pop.ikra.com</
address>

<a href="mailto:khusain@ikra.com">khusain@ikra.com</a>
```

The `document.clear()` function does not work correctly. As a work around, use `document.close()` to complete the layout and let Navigator do the clearing for you. The `document.clear()` function has been known to crash browsers.

In both listings, the `onClick()` handler calls the function `setBGcolor()` to set the background to the color typed in the text box. The simple example shown here does not check for bogus strings typed in the text box and simply takes the value for granted. In other stricter environments, you might want to check if the length of the input color is at least one, and if the color is valid.

The Anchors and Links Properties

The *anchors* property in a document is really an array of anchor objects. Each anchor in a document is simply a link. Using this anchors property, you can access all the anchors in a given document. To define an anchor in an HTML document, use the following syntax with a pair of <A> and </A> tags:

```
<A HREF=locationURL   NAME="thisName"

        TARGET="WindowName"

        onClick="code" onMouseOver="code">

        text describing this window </A>
```

The HREF attribute declares this anchor to be a link to another document. The TARGET attribute is used to load the document specified by the HREF location into a window. If the HREF attribute is not defined, the TARGET attribute is ignored. We covered the `onClick` and `onMouseOver` attributes in Chapter 6, "Events, Input, and Output."

The NAME attribute makes the location of this anchor available in the same document. You can define links to this document using links of the form:

```
DocumentName#AnchorName.
```

The name of the document can be left out if the anchor is in the same document. So, if you have an anchor called `install` in the file `setup.htm`, the link to the anchor from points in the setup file would be:

```
<A HREF="#install> Go to Install </A>
```

To refer to this anchor from other documents, the link would be written as:

```
<A HREF="setup.htm#install"> Installation </A>
```

The *anchors* array property is a list of all the anchors specified by NAME within a document. Anchors without a NAME attribute are not listed in this array. The order of occurrence in the document is the order of items in the array. So, the first anchor in a document is `document.anchors[0]`, followed by `document.anchors[1]`, and so on. The total number of anchors within a document will be in the `document.anchors.length` property. The highest index with an anchor will be `(document.anchors.length - 1)`.

Just as with anchors, a document tracks all of it's links with the *links* property array.

> **Tip** If the link happens to be anchor as well, it will be listed in both the **links** and **anchors** property array.

Other Read-Only Properties

A document's *referrer* property contains the URL of the HTML document from which you jumped into the current document. The most common use of the *referrer* property is to jump back into the previous document without resorting to going to the history list. (History objects were covered in much more detail in Chapter 5, "The

History, Link, Anchor, and Location Objects.") An empty value in the referrer object simply means that either the current document is the first document loaded or the browser you came in from did not furnish this information, or it's just a bug in your browser. The referrer is a read-only property.

The *location* property in a document is a read-only string with the complete URL of the document. The location property has nothing to do with links. To use this property, you would use statements of the form:

```
var a = "You are here: " + document.location
```

The *lastModified* property is a read-only value of the date and time the current document was modified. Usually, you will set it up in a JavaScript application as

```
var a = "Last mangled on " + document.lastModified
```

See Program 7.4 for a simple use of the lastModified and location properties of a document. The output of this program is shown in Figure 7.2 for a Windows 95 display and in Figure 7.3 for a UNIX version of the browser.

The values in the last <TITLE> and </TITLE> tags are found in the read-only *title* property of a document. An empty value in title means that no title was specified.

The Forms Property

HTML forms are required to process the user input in JavaScript objects. Each FORM on an HTML page has a *form* object. All form objects in a document are stored in the `forms` property. The order of form object entries in the `forms` property is the same as the order in

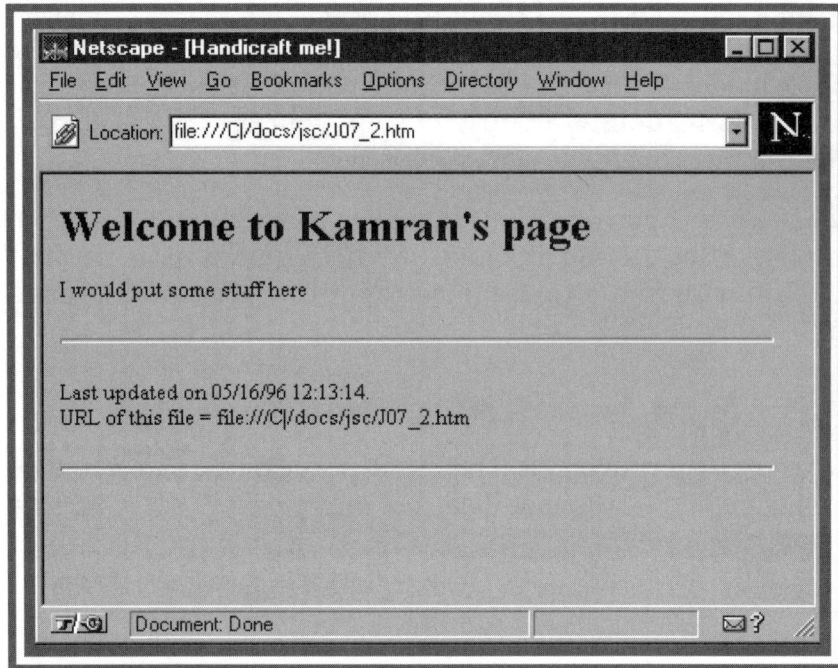

Figure 7.2 Using the lastModified and location properties in a document, as viewed in a Windows 95 browser

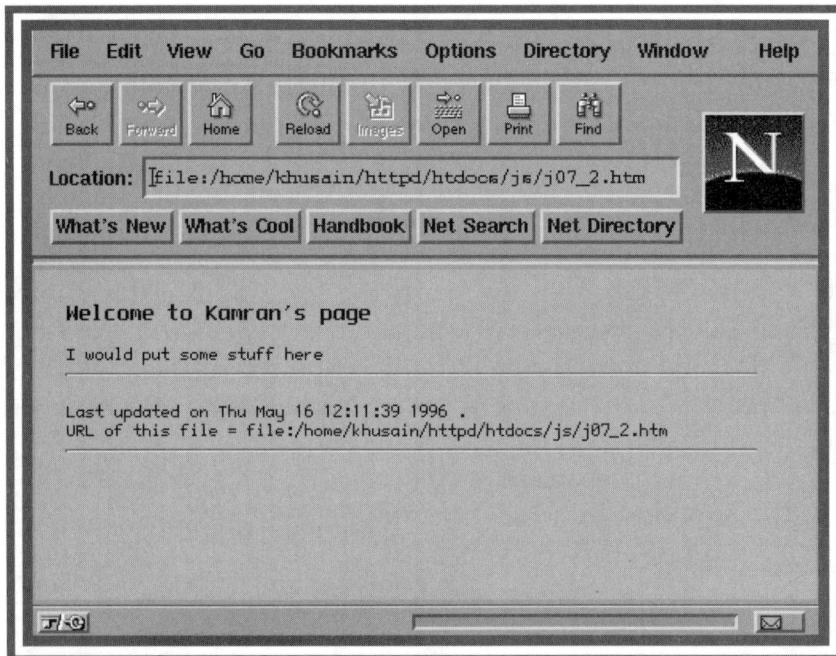

Figure 7.3 Using the lastModified and location properties in a document, as viewed in a UNIX browser

```
<HTML>

<TITLE>Handicraft me!</TITLE>

<H1> Welcome to Kamran's page </H1>

<BODY>

<P>

I would put some stuff here <BR>

<SCRIPT LANGUAGE="JavaScript">

var a = "<HR><BR>" +

          "Last updated on " + document.lastModified +
".<BR>" +

          "URL of this file = " + document.location +
"<BR><HR>";

document.writeln(a)

</SCRIPT>

</BODY>

</HTML>
```

which FORMs are found in the document. The total number of forms within a document will be in the `document.forms.length` property. The highest index with a form will be `(document.forms.length - 1)`.

To access a FORM in a document, you can access it either by it's index value in the `forms` array or by using the name of the FORM. Thus, for the second form called `grok` you can use either of the following two statements to get the property "propertyName" of a FORM:

```
document.forms[1].propertyName

 or

document.grok.propertyName

An HTML form is defined as:

<FORM NAME="nameOfForm" TARGET="window" ACTION="serverURL"

        METHOD=GET or POST

        ENCTYPE="typeOfEncoding"

        onSubmit=handlerText>

        ... Other objects to process user input go here ...

</FORM>
```

The <FORM> tag must be terminated with a </FORM> tag. The NAME attribute is used to name a FORM. The NAME is not required since you can always get a FORM via the `forms` array. The TARGET window is the name of the window from which the FORM will respond to input. (We will cover TARGETs in Chapter 8, "Windows in JavaScript," along with our discussion of FRAMEs.) The ACTION attribute specifies the URL to the server where the request shall be sent. The encoding type is the MIME type of data (e.g., text, GIF, audio,) being sent. The METHOD attribute can contain either a GET or POST value. The GET value sends the collected user input in an environment variable QUERY_STRING to the CGI script handling this FORM. The POST sends the collected user input into the CGI script by way of its standard input and sets the length of the input in CONTENT_LENGTH.

> **Tip** The name of a form in some browsers does not work when used as an argument to a function. You should try using the `document.form[index]` method of addressing the form in this case.

The `onSubmit` handler is the code to process FORM input data and does not have to be specified. When specified, an `onSubmit` handler must either return either a *true* or a *false* value. A return value of true will let the browser force the data to be submitted to the server whose URL is specified in the ACTION attribute. A return value of false will force the browser not to submit the collected input to the server.

Now let's look at the properties of a form object:

1. *action*

2. *elements*

3. *encoding*

4. *length*

5. *method*

6. *target*

The `action`, `method`, `encoding`, and `target` properties of a form is the read-only value specified in the ACTION, METHOD, ENCTYPE, and TARGET attributes, respectively. The `elements` property is a read-only array of all the elements on a FORM. The number of items in the `elements` property is in the `form.length` property for the form.

The Cookie Property

"Cookies" are used by a server to store information about a client. The client passes the cookie to the server during a transaction. The server determines the state of the client by reading the information in the cookie. JavaScript documents on the client side can keep this cookie in their `document.cookie` property.

Common uses for cookies include storing information such as a validation number or expiration date. For example, a stock quote server will validate a client once every four hours and not every time a client requests a stock quote. It would be extremely annoying for a user to have to enter their name and password every time they request a quote. By validating the user, their site and time of day, a server will simply honor any incoming request with an up-to-date cookie. Older cookies, such as those with a time of creation greater than four hours, would be regarded as old and the server would ask the user to register again. Other schemes would include updating the creation time of the cookie to that of the last request. So, only stale cookies (i.e., those that have not been used for more than four hours) would be rejected. Using cookies with CGI scripts is discussed in Chapter 9, "Applying JavaScript."

Using cookies does open up your server side to some security risks if you are not careful. It's not too difficult to masquerade a client's state using cookies. A rogue user can easily concoct their own cookie and trick a CGI server into divulging information to an unregistered client.

The document object is manipulated by calling its methods, which are listed below:

1. *clear*

2. *close*

3. *open*

4. *write*

5. *writeln*

Think of the document as an open canvas that you can write to. By using the above methods, you can create documents on-the-fly. You already saw a brief example of how to write to a document window in Program 7.2.

Using Documents and Forms

Let's look at an example of a situation where we put some on-line document for a tome we want to sell. The code for advertising this work of literature is in Program 7.5.

```
<HTML>

<HEAD>

<TITLE>Experiences in Cooking</TITLE>

<SCRIPT>

<!--

//
```

(continued)

```
 // This function will display some section headings

 // for a given chapter in an on-line section of a book

 //

function chapter(number) {

        var chapterNumber = "chapter" + number

        var xyz = top.beginBlurb + eval(chapterNumber) + end-
ingBlurb;

        document.write(xyz);

        return;

}

//

// Always print this out.

//


var beginBlurb= '<HTML>' +

        '<body bgcolor="#FFFFFF">' +

        '<font Color="Blue"><font size=6>Chapter Sections' +

        '</font></font><BR>' + "\n"   ;


var endingBlurb =

'<HR><A HREF="order.htm"> Order this book </A>' +

'<BR><HR> ' +
```

(continued)

```
                '</BODY></HTML>';


var chapter1= '<BL>' +

        '<LI> What is a fish'   +

        '<LI> What is a lake'   +

        '<LI> What is a fishing pole'   +

        '<LI> Summary ' +

        '<BL>' ;


var chapter2= '<BL> ' +

        '<LI> This is not a diner' +

        '<LI> Fish swim really fast' +

        '<LI> All about spears' +

        '<LI> Summary  ' +

        '<BL>' ;


var chapter3= '<BL> ' +

        '<LI> What is a scale?' +

        '<LI> Fishes and swimming' +

        '<LI> All about spears' +

        '<LI> Nets 101' +
```

(continued)

```
                    '<LI> Olfactory issues' +

                    '<LI> Summary' +

                    '<BL>' ;


var chapter4= '<BL> ' +

         '<LI> Why bother'  +

         '<LI> Home delivery' +

         '<LI> Why not to avoid nature'  +

         '<LI> Summary '  +

         '<BL>' ;


         // -->


</SCRIPT>
</HEAD>
<BODY>
<P>
<HR>
<H1>Finding, cooking eating and fish for city dwellers </H1>
<FORM>
<INPUT TYPE="button" VALUE="Chapter 1" ONCLICK="chapter(1)">
<INPUT TYPE="button" VALUE="Chapter 2" ONCLICK="chapter(2)">
<INPUT TYPE="button" VALUE="Chapter 3" ONCLICK="chapter(3)">
<INPUT TYPE="button" VALUE="Chapter 4" ONCLICK="chapter(4)">
</FORM>
</BODY>
</HTML>
```

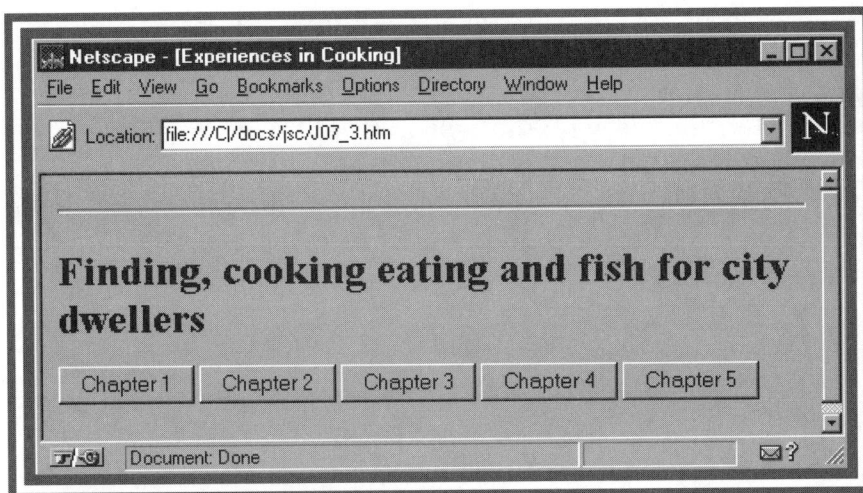

Figure 7.4 Initial output of Program 7.5

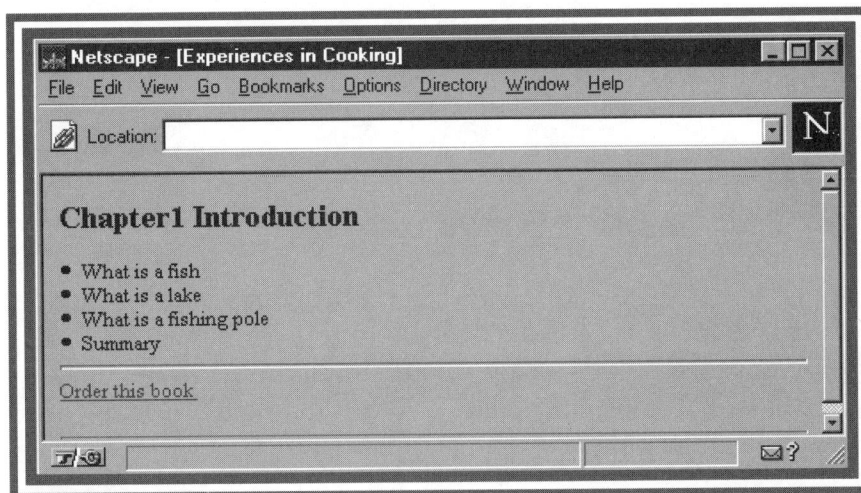

Figure 7.5 Output of Program 7.5 after clicking the "Chapter 1" button

The output from the code in Program 7.5 is shown in Figure 7.4. The output of the window changes when button "Chapter 1" is pressed, as shown in Figure 7.5.

Using the `document.write()` and `document.writeln()` functions let you create documents on-the-fly to programmatically take the user through various steps. By designing your pages carefully, you can take the client through pages based on their responses and not have to deal with many files on disk.

You must close a document you are writing to for the layout to be complete. If you do not call the `document.close()` function, the next `document.open()` call will begin appending to the current document. The text in the window will not appear correctly until the close function is called for the document. Likewise, images will not be shown correctly if the document you are writing to is not closed correctly. A good indicator to look for is the "Document Done" message in the status bar.

> **Tip** If you see a flash on your screen when writing to a document, and then some parts of your HTML document disappear, it's probably because you have not closed the document prior to writing to it again.

A Short Point About Focus

It's important to have your FORM input programs be user-friendly by directing the focus of the next user input to a known element. For example, when a user loads a page, focus should be set to the first text entry called *sname* with their name. You can define a function called `setFocus()` as follows:

```
function setFocus() {

document.form[0].sname.focus()

}
```

This `setFocus()` function could be called in the body tag so as to set the focus at the time the page is loaded. The encoding would be set as:

```
<BODY onLoad="setFocus()">
```

> **Tip**
> If you do not see the last line of text from a `document.write()` operation to create an HTML page, try putting a `<BR>` tag after the last line output.
>
> Output generated by the functions `document.write()` and `document.writeln()` only modifies the on-screen image. Any text generated by these two functions will not be printed in a hard copy.

Each line in your HTML file does not have to be written out with its own `writeln` or `write` function call. It's a whole lot easier to use a string to contain all the common code and just write the entire string to disk. Look at Program 7.5 and compare it with the code shown in Program 7.6.

The first change you will see in Listing 7.6 will be the minimal use of the `document.writeln()` function. The code is easier to read because it's not cluttered with lots of these write statements.

Secondly, each chapter has pretty much the same standard layout. The headers do not have to be repeated every time in each function for a chapter. One function can be written to write a standard header, another to write the trailer of an HTML document. The internal elements can be changed on a per-chapter basis.

Next, we use <font> tags to define the colors for text in a file. See Line 24 in Program 7.6. The colors defined here in the <font> tags are the same as those document colors. It's a good idea to use colors to highlight portions of text on your page. Be careful though not to over-use colors, as this will make the page hard to read.

Finally, the contents of each chapter are collected together in one location in one string. The string itself could be the result of a command or could be passed into a string for further processing.

Program 7.6: Using variables for HTML tags

```
1 <HTML>

2 <HEAD>

3 <TITLE>Experiences in Cooking</TITLE>

4 <SCRIPT>

5 <!--

6

7 //

8 // This function will display some section headings

9 // for a given chapter in an on-line section of a book

10 //

11 function chapter(number) {

12       var chapterNumber = "chapter" + number

13       document.write(beginBlurb);    // always at start

14       document.write(eval(chapterNumber)) // for given
chapter

15       document.write(endingBlurb);    // always at ending

16 }
```

(continued)

```
17
18 //
19 // Always print this out.
20 //
21
22 var beginBlurb= '<HTML>' +
23        '<body bgcolor="#FFFFFF">' +
24        '<font Color="Blue"><font size=6>Chapter 1' +
25        '</font></font><BR>' ;
26
27 var endingBlurb = '<BR>' +
28 '<HR><A HREF="order.htm"> Order this book </A>' +
29 '<BR><HR> ' +
30        '</BODY></HTML>';
31
32
33 var chapter1= '<BL>' +
34        '<LI> What is a fish'  +
35        '<LI> What is a lake'  +
36        '<LI> What is a fishing pole'  +
37        '<LI> Summary ' +
38        '<BL>' ;
39
```

(continued)

```
40 var chapter2= '<BL> ' +

41         '<LI> This is not a diner' +

42         '<LI> Fish swim really fast' +

43         '<LI> All about spears' +

44         '<LI> Summary  ' +

45         '<BL>' ;

46

47

48 var chapter3= '<BL> ' +

49         '<LI> What is a scale?' +

50         '<LI> Fishes and swimming' +

51         '<LI> All about spears' +

52         '<LI> Nets 101' +

53         '<LI> Olfactory issues' +

54         '<LI> Summary' +

55         '<BL>' ;

56   .

57

58 var chapter4= '<BL> ' +

59         '<LI> Why bother'  +

60         '<LI> Home delivery' +

61         '<LI> Why not to avoid nature'  +

62         '<LI> Summary  '  +

63         '<BL>' ;

64         // -->

65
```

(continued)

```
66 </SCRIPT>

67 </HEAD>

68 <BODY>

69 <P>

70 <HR>

71 <H1>Finding, cooking eating and fish for city dwellers </
H1>

72 <FORM>

73 <INPUT TYPE="button" VALUE="Chapter 1" ONCLICK="
chapter(1)">

74 <INPUT TYPE="button" VALUE="Chapter 2" ONCLICK="
chapter(2)">

75 <INPUT TYPE="button" VALUE="Chapter 3" ONCLICK="
chapter(3)">

76 <INPUT TYPE="button" VALUE="Chapter 4" ONCLICK="
chapter(4)">

77 </FORM>

78

79 </BODY>

80 </HTML>
```

Summary

In this chapter, we covered JavaScript documents. The main things you should have learned from this chapter are:

- *A JavaScript document is used to group objects on a page.*

- *A document can have several properties to set the colors and track other objects (such as forms or arrays that it holds), as well as methods that can be called to manipulate the behavior of a document.*

- *Documents do not necessarily have to reside in files and can be created using JavaScript variables. By using variables to create documents, you can maintain several documents in one source file.*

- *By creating documents dynamically, it's possible to customize the contents of an HTML page, such as changing the background color or redrawing the page, in response to user-interface actions.*

- *It's also possible to use different colors for displaying text, links, and other elements in a document, but these changes only take effect when a page is loaded and do not affect the display once the page is loaded.*

Coming Up

In this chapter we worked with one document in one window. In the next chapter, we will cover how to work with several documents on one page using Frames.

CHAPTER 8
WINDOWS IN JAVASCRIPT

- Windows and Frames

- Properties of Windows

- Input/Output with Windows

In the previous chapter, we covered how to place and work with Java-Script documents, using only one page at a time in a window. Now, let's work with multiple pages in one window, called *Frames*. One way that multiple-frame windows can add further functionality to a Web page is by creating one frame in which you can solicit input from your user and another in which you can display the results of that input, all in the same window. We will see several examples of using frames in the code examples in this chapter.

Window Objects

A JavaScript document is shown in a browser *window*. A window is a JavaScript object that allows you to display your HTML pages, provides a status bar in which to display some activity, space for a toolbar, and scrollbars. Internally, the Window object is the top-level container to the rest of the history, document, and location objects. Generally, there is one document per window with the document referred to by it's URL, but with newer browsers, more than one document can be stored on the same window through the use of Frame objects, each window with its own URL.

Creating a Window

A window object is created with the following command:

```
windowId = window.open("URL", "nameOfWindow"

         [,"feature" [,"feature"] ... ] );
```

The returned value from the open command will be an ID with which you can refer to the window, just like other objects. The call to open a window is nothing spectacular, as all it does is open an empty page for you to write in.

The real work is done by way of the of the optional features in the call to window.open function. Using these options, you can dictate the kinds of features a window can have, such as a toolbar, a location, and others. Most of these options are set to a value of true or false, but two are set to a numeric value:

- *toolbar*

- *location*

- *directories*

- *status*

- *menubar*

- *scrollbars*

- *resizeable*

- *width*

- *height*

The *height* and *width* correspond to the size of the new window in pixels. (You can only set the size; the location of the new window is left for your window manager to decide.) The rest of the optional features take a value of either 0 or 1.

Don't rely on these optional features to be set to 0 or 1 as a default value. Set them explicitly to whatever value you want. On some versions of Netscape, these values are defaulted to zero, which brings up an empty frame when an open call specifies no optional features. To turn an optional feature on, set its value to 1 before loading it or you can specify it by itself. More than one optional feature must be separated by a comma.

A very important point to note is that there should be no spaces between features. For some reason, inserting spaces between the comma and another feature does not let the window work correctly on Netscape. So "toolbar,resizeable" will work but "toolbar, resizeable" will not work.

Let's look at the call to open a window in Program 8.1.

Program 8.1: Using the `window.open` call

```
<HTML>

<HEAD>

<TITLE>Test Some Display Objects</TITLE>

<SCRIPT>

<!---

function newBrowser() {

yes = 1

wid = window.open("http://www.ikra.com","mine",

        "toolbar=yes,status=yes,directories,
location=yes,menubar,scollbars,width=200,height=300"

        )

}

//

// Don't write any more comments after next line

//

<!-- End of script hiding comments -->

</SCRIPT>

</HEAD>

<FORM NAME="Test Window">

<HR>

<B>Test a window</B>

<HR>

<P><INPUT TYPE="button" VALUE="New window"

 onClick="newBrowser()">

</FORM> </HTML>
```

Note that in Program 8.1, the code specifies the windows optional features as either "option" or as "option=1". The "=1" portion of an optional feature is implied if the "=1" is left out.

Windows can be addressed with either the word *window* or the word *self*. Therefore, `window.open()` is the same as `self.open()`. An `open()` call by itself would be referring to `document.open()` and not `window.open()`. This distinction of what `open()` function applies to which object is very important in a JavaScript application.

Note that the new window in Program 8.1 is created from within an event handler. The default action of an `open()` call in the event handler would be to the `open()` function in the current document. To explicitly create a new window, we have to call the `window.open()` function.

Window objects in a document exist in a tree hierarchy very similar to the file system on a UNIX or DOS machine. The root node in this tree is the *top* window object. Every window in an application has one *top* window and a *parent* window. The top window's parent is itself.

The *defaultStatus* property contains the default string displayed in the status bar. The status property can be set to change the text in the status bar of a browser with the command: `window.status = "string"` method.

The *name* property is a read-only value that is set to the name of the window object when it is first created. The value is set with NAME attribute in the `window.open` function call.

The *opener* property contains a reference to the document that called the `open()` method for that window. The opener property is unaffected even if the document is unloaded. Use the opener property to determine which document loaded you in the first place.

The `window.open` function is great for creating your own windows. Let's see how to create popup windows in Program 8.2.

Program8.2: Using popup windows

```
<HTML>

<HEAD>

<TITLE>Test Window Examples</TITLE>

<SCRIPT LANGUAGE="JavaScript">

var newWin = null

function showColor(f) {

        selectedColor=

(f.colList.options[f.colList.selectedIndex].value)

        if (newWin == null)

        {

        newWin = window.open("","","HEIGHT=200,WIDTH=200")

        }

        newWin.document.writeln("<HTML><BODY BGCOLOR=" +
selectedColor + ">")

        newWin.document.writeln("<H1>Test Color" +
selectedColor + "</H1>")

        newWin.document.writeln("</BODY></HTML>")

        newWin.document.close();

        }

</SCRIPT>

</HEAD>

<BODY>

<HR>

<FORM>
```

(continued)

```
Select a color: <BR>

<SELECT NAME="colList" onChange="showColor(this.form)">

        <OPTION SELECTED VALUE="red">Red

        <OPTION SELECTED VALUE="White">White

        <OPTION SELECTED VALUE="Blue">Blue

        <OPTION SELECTED VALUE="green">Green

        <OPTION SELECTED VALUE="gray">Gray

</SELECT>


</FORM>

</BODY>

</HTML>
```

Windows Methods

Once you have a windows object, you can interact with the user using its methods. The following methods exist in a window object:

- *alert*

- *close*

- *confirm*

- *prompt*

- *setTimeout*

- *clearTimeout*

You've already seen the alert object in practice in previous chapters to print out error messages and warn the user about things. We covered the functions related to timeouts (`setTimeout` and `clearTimeout`) in "Chapter 6: Events, Input, and Output," in the section called "Timeouts" and in Program 6.4.

The `close()` method in a window object closes the current window. Be careful when calling the `close()` method for a window. If the `close()` method is called from within a method, the context of the current document is assumed and the current document is closed. To specify that you want to close the current window, place the call as `window.close()` or `self.close()` to remove any ambiguity.

The `window.confirm()` method is called when you want the user to confirm a task. Calling the confirm method presents a dialog box, as shown in Figure 8.1. A sample call is shown below. The modification is done to the code shown in Program 8.1 to confirm the call to `newBrowser()` before proceeding.

```
onClick="if (confirm('Do you really want to do this?'))
newBrowser()">
```

Figure 8.1 A confirm box results from calling the confirm method

In some cases, however, a simple *yes* or *no* response will not do the trick. For example, you may want the user to enter in their name as a response to a query. Look at the example below, which asks for a location to jump to and then jumps to it. The dialog you get from a call to the prompt dialog may be different based on the type of platform on which your script is running. Look at the two different dialogs in Figure 8.2 for a Windows 95 version and in Figure 8.3 for a UNIX version of Navigator. As is the case with HTML documents, the presentation of a dialog using JavaScript is dependent on the browser on which the code happens to run. See Program 8.3 for a simple usage of the prompt dialog.

Figure 8.2 Prompt in a Windows 95 version

Figure 8.3 Prompt in a UNIX version

Program 8.3: Using the prompt method

```
<HTML>

<HEAD><TITLE>Test Some Display Objects</TITLE>

<SCRIPT>


<!---

function newLocation() {

        gohere = prompt("Enter the location to go to",
"http://www.ikra.com")

        top.location.href = gohere;

}

//

// Don't write any more comments in JavaScript after next line

//

<!-- End of script hiding comments -->

</SCRIPT>

</HEAD>

<FORM NAME="Test Window">

<HR>

<B>Test a window</B>

<HR>

<P>

<INPUT TYPE="button" VALUE="Go here" onClick="newLocation()">

</FORM>

</HTML>
```

The format for the prompt is:

```
prompt (message, [default string])
```

The *default string* is shown in the text entry box for the prompt dialog presented to the user. Specifying no default value will present either an empty text entry box or the string *<undefined>* to the user. The returned value from the call will be *null* if the user clicks on *cancel* or will be the value last entered in the text box if the user clicks on *OK*.

Declaring Frames

Frames allow you to slice the viewable window area into several scrollable areas. Each scrollable area is a frame object with it's own URL. By using frames, you are able to display more than one HTML document on a window. More than one frame can point to the same URL. A frame itself can be the target of a URL.

Use the <FRAMESET> and </FRAMESET> tags to declare frame objects. The syntax for this command is:

```
<FRAMESET>

ROWS="rows"

COLS="cols"

[onLoad='onLoadHandler']

[onUnload="onUnloadHandler"]

[ <FRAME SRC="url" NAME="nameOfFrame"]

        [ <NOFRAMES>

        [ HTML tags etc.

            for browsers that do not support frames ]

        </NOFRAMES> ]

<FRAMESET>
```

Window Objects

The NOFRAMES tag is used to house HTML tags for the Java-Script-challenged browsers, such as older versions of Mosaic. If you do not use the NOFRAMES tag, a user without a JavaScript-enhanced browser will not see anything on their page.

Let's look at an example. The code shown in Program 8.4 will create two frames on the window of your browser, one for a table of contents and the other for the contents of the chapter itself. The left-most window can have an index.

Program 8.4: Simple Frame setup

```
<HTML>

<HEAD>

<TITLE> My book </TITLE>

</HEAD>

<FRAMESET COLS="20%,80%">

        <FRAME NAME="ndx" SRC="toc.htm">

        <FRAME NAME="doc" SRC="intro.htm">

        <NOFRAMES>

        <H1> So sorry!.... </H1>

        <p>

        Please mosey on down to Netscape and upgrade your

        browser<BR>

        <A HREF="http://www.netscape.com"> Get it NOW!</A>

        </NOFRAMES>

</FRAMESET>
```

The window on your screen will be sliced into two parts with a divider in the middle. The area taken up by the left area will be about 20 percent of the screen and can be referred to as "ndx". The right size is called "doc" and takes about 80 percent of the screen space.

> **Tip** The "this" and "self" reserved words in JavaScript are synonyms for the current window. When used in a call, the "this" word implies the calling object, not the called object. For example, in the line onClick="doIt(this.thing)" the "this" implies the current object, not the called object. Whereas, in the function doIt() the "this" implies the current instance of the object to which the function is tied.

Using frames is relatively easy as long as you remember what target frames you are using. The target of a URL is specified with the use of the TARGET attribute. See Figure 8.4 for the output of the source file in Program 8.5.

Program 8.5: FRAMEs and TARGETs

```
<HTML><HEAD><TITLE>My books</TITLE></HEAD>


<FRAMESET cols="30%,70%">

        <FRAME NAME="whoCares" SRC="books.htm">

        <FRAME NAME="bookInfo" SRC="doc1.htm">

        <NOFRAMES>

        </NOFRAMES>

</FRAMESET>
```

The `books.htm` file is placed on the left-hand side and the `doc1.htm` for a sample book is placed on the right side. The `books.htm` file is really an index into the rest of the book. See Program 8.6 for the contents of `books.htm`. The important portion to look at is the TARGET attribute in each <A> tag for the books to display information about.

Program 8.6: Contents of `books.htm`

```
<HTML>

<HEAD>

<TITLE> Books </TITLE>

<SCRIPT LANGUAGE="JavaScript">


<!---

mailman="mailman.htm"

fishing="doc1.htm"

function goFish(loc) {

        alert( "Location = " + loc);

        top.bookInfo.location.href=loc;

}

//

// Don't write any more comments in JavaScript after next line

//

<!-- End of script hiding comments -->
```

(continued)

```
</SCRIPT>

<H1> Books to come </H1>

<FORM>

<HR>

<BL>

<LI> <font COLOR="#003F00">"Boring Others"</font>by Fulov
Zelf.

<LI> <font COLOR="Green">"Revenge made easy"</font> by Remm
Amber

<LI> <font COLOR="Green">"Hating Friends"</font> by Parah Noyd

        <A HREF="postman.htm" TARGET="bookInfo"> See it </
A>

<LI> <font COLOR="GREEN">"Mailman's Guide to Dawgs"</
font>,anon

        <A HREF="mailman.htm" TARGET="bookInfo"> Look  </A>

<LI> <font COLOR="GREEN">"Fishing for urbanites"</font>,

        <A HREF="fishing.htm" TARGET="bookInfo" > Go to it
</A>

<BL>

</FORM>

</HEAD>

</HTML>
```

Example 1: Using Frames With JavaScript

Let's start with a relatively easy example at first, one in which we can see how the TARGET attribute can be used to update data in another FRAME. Listing 8.7 is a simple application that puts together a URL for a free stock chart service on the Web. (The service itself is put together and is copyrighted by Mark Torrance at **stockmaster@stockmaster.com**.) We can use it freely to get end-of-day prices. The URL to get a graph of a stock's price from this site is of the form:

```
http://www.stockmaster.com/sm/g/LETTER/SYMBOL.htm
```

where LETTER is the first letter of the stock symbol. The SYMBOL is the all uppercase stock symbol. For example, for Intel, the stock symbol is INTC, and the URL will be

```
http://www.stockmaster.com/sm/g/I/INTC.htm
```

The JavaScript application to create a look-up based on a user-entered stock symbol is constructed in four HTML files: `stock.htm`, `stock1.htm`, `stock2.htm`, and `advert.htm`. The `stock.htm` page constructs two frames: one for getting the user input and one for constructing the URL using a JavaScript application contained in `stock1.htm`. The file `stock2.htm` is a placeholder for placing the returned results and is really shown here for the purpose of illustration. We will cover how to get rid of this file in a moment. For now, let's see how frames work with each other. See Program 8.7 for a stock market charting program.

Program 8.7: The `stock.htm` file

```
<HTML><HEAD>

<TITLE>stock.htm --  Simple stocking algorithm</TITLE>

</HEAD>

<FRAMESET  ROWS="10%,*">

<FRAME SRC="stock1.htm" NAME="askframe" SCROLLING="no"
NORESIZE>

<FRAME SRC="stock2.htm" NAME="outframe" SCROLLING="auto"

NORESIZE>

<FRAME SRC="advert.htm" NAME="crass" SCROLLING="auto"
NORESIZE>

</FRAMESET>

</HTML>
```

In Program 8.7, note the use of the asterisk in the ROWS declaration. The asterisk simply means "whatever is left." So, 10 percent of the top portion of the window is set to the first frame, the bottom portion to another frame, with the rest left for the last frame. The `advert.htm` is used for crass commercial messages (as referred to by Mr. G. Gordon Liddy!). Note that by using the NORESIZE tag, you prevent the user from getting rid of the advertising and user-input area. Scrollbars have been turned on in the frames to allow scrolling should the screen not be large enough to accomodate the entire input. See Figure 8.4 for a sample run of Program 8.6 with Navigator 3.0 on a Windows 95 machine.

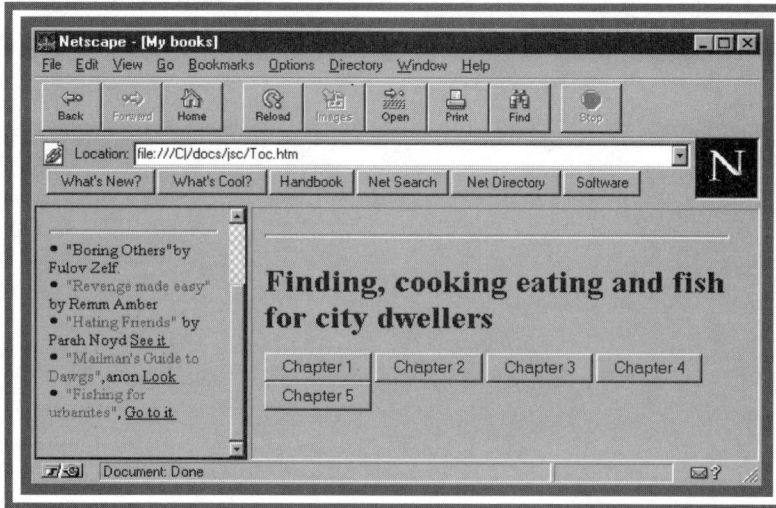

Figure 8.4 Using FRAMEs for displaying documents

The user input is collected and processed in `stock1.htm`, which is listed below in Program 8.8. Look carefully at the method that is called to create the URL. The output is shown in Figure 8.5.

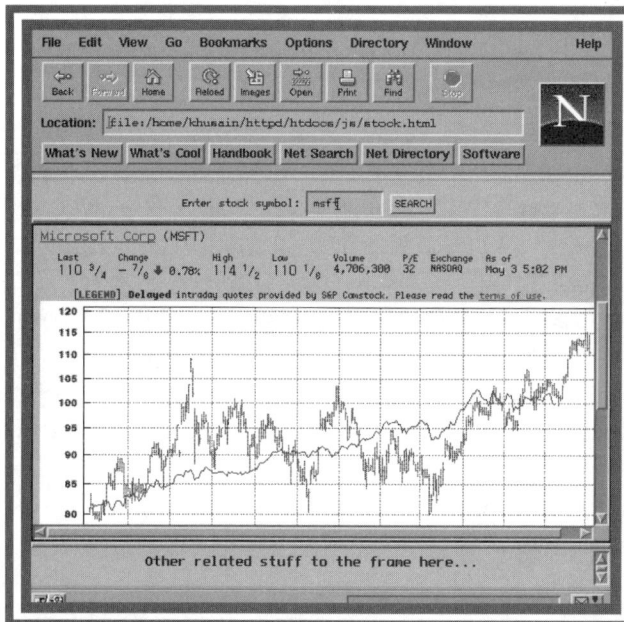

Figure 8.5 Using the `stock1.htm` file to collect and process user input

Program 8.8: The stock1.htm file

```
<HTML>

<HEAD>

<TITLE>stock1.htm -- Graph of Stock Prices from MIT</TITLE>


<SCRIPT LANGUAGE="JavaScript">

<!-- Hide this script from old browsers


//

// Get stock symbol

//

function stockMaster(stock)  {

var str = new String(stock)

stock = str.toUpperCase()

//

// "Straight forward use of print statements seems a heckuvalot

// easier to use than trying to arm wrestle with a debugger."

//

// alert("stock = " + stock + " 1st ltr = " + stock.charAt(0));

//

// Construct URL of the form:

//          "http://www.stockmaster/sm/g/N/NSCP.htm"
```

(continued)

```
//

top.outframe.location.href="http://www.stockmaster.com/sm/g/"

          + stock.charAt(0)

          + "/" + stock + ".htm"

}


function getStock(tform) {

//

//Check to make sure the user entered a stock symbol

//

if (tform.stockName.value == "") {

          alert("Enter a ticker symbol!")

          return

    }

var sname=tform.stockName.value

//  When debugging your app, try alert (sname);

stockMaster(sname);

}


<!-- End of script hiding comments -->

</SCRIPT>

</HEAD>

<BODY>
```

(continued)

```
<FORM  NAME="sform" onLoad="initMe()">

<CENTER>

Enter stock symbol:

<INPUT  TYPE="text" NAME="stockName" onChange="get-
Stock(this.form)" SIZE="10">

<INPUT TYPE="button" NAME="sbutton"  VALUE="SEARCH"
onClick="getStock(this.form)">

</FORM>

</BODY>

</HTML>
```

In this listing, the user input in *stock* is made all uppercase before being sent to the stockmaster server. Also, the stock graphs are kept in subdirectories named after the first letter of a stock symbol. This is where the `charAt(index)` function is used to extract the first letter.

The target frame is `top.outframe.location` in the function. The `href` property is set to the URL that's constructed and the browser gets the file into the target frame. For the sake of completeness, the `stock2.htm` is shown here, but is really not used. If you leave the URL for the second frame empty, you will get a directory listing of the current directory. Having this simple file keeps from listing your current directory out to world!

Here's the `stock2.htm` file in its entirety, shown in Program 8.9.

Program 8.9: The `stock2.htm` file

```
<HTML>

<HEAD>

<TITLE>stock2.htm -- Dummy file </TITLE>

</HEAD>

<BODY>

<CENTER><h1>Enter Symbol above</h1></CENTER>

</BODY>

</HTML>
```

Using a file to do this clearing seems like such a waste of disk resources. Also, should you move the HTML files to another machine, you have to remember to tag along this really useless file. The `advert.htm` file may not be that tedious to drag around because it will contain your commercial messages, which you would probably want to share with other HTML files. However, the empty file `stock2.htm` is really not required.

Why not let JavaScript handle this for you? Here's a new listing for `stock.htm` thatwill create an empty page with a white background. The code is shown in Program 8.10.

Program 8.10: Using JavaScript to create empty frames

```
<HTML>

<HEAD>

<TITLE> Improved stock graph application</TITLE>
```

(continued)

```
<SCRIPT LANGUAGE="JavaScript">

//

// This string variable

var DefaultFrame='<html><title>Default</title>' +

            '<body bgcolor="#FFFFFF"></body></html>';


function initme() {

            self.outframe.location ="javascript:parent.
DefaultFrame"

}


</SCRIPT>

</HEAD>


<FRAMESET  ROWS="10%,*,10%">

<FRAME SRC="stock1.htm" NAME="askframe" SCROLLING="no" RESIZE>

<FRAME SRC="javascript:parent.DefaultFrame" NAME="outframe"
SCROLLING="auto" RESIZE>

<FRAME SRC="advert.htm" NAME="advert" SCROLLING="auto" RESIZE>

</FRAMESET>

</HTML>
```

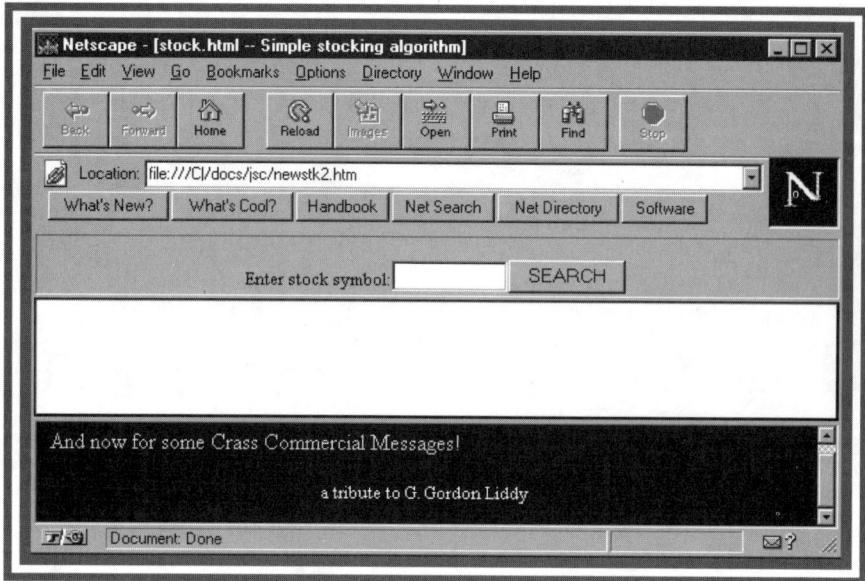

Figure 8.6 Using JavaScript:: directives instead of files

Look carefully at this statement, which sets the `DefaultDFrame` variable to HTML tags. The output for the `defaultFrame` is a blank page, as shown in Figure 8.6. Remember that we are within the comments and SCRIPT tags here, so the contents of this string shall be ignored by an old browser. The `DefaultFrame` simply creates a white page with nothing in it.

```
var DefaultFrame='<html><title>Default</title>' +

        '<body bgcolor="#FFFFFF"></body></html>';
```

To get JavaScript to call and use this variable instead of a temporary file on disk, you have to use the following syntax:

```
frameObject.location=javascript:object.property
```

The `frameObject` is the frame being targeted with the contents of the variable on the right-hand side of the equal sign. The HTML tags within the `javascript:object.property` string may not support all HTML 3.0 features, such as the <font> tag. However, you can set code up to call JavaScript methods in the parent script. So, to use the contents of the `DefaultFrame` variable, you will use the following statement:

```
function initme() {

         self.outframe.location ="javascript:parent.
DefaultFrame"

}
```

Note that word *parent* in the above example could also be replaced by the word *top* since the top-level window is the parent to both frames. Therefore, the following line will work too:

```
self.outframe.location ="javascript:top.DefaultFrame"
```

Just remember to explicitly state which variable of which object when specifying a variable to set the location. A wrong variable will show something unexpected on the screen. A null variable in the SRC attribute will show your current directory listing to the remote user.

Tip The BORDERCOLOR attribute can be set in the FRAMESET or FRAME tags to define the color of the border of the Frame being used. When the BORDERCOLOR attribute is set for a FRAMESET, it sets the default color for borders for Frames in that set. Individual Frames can override this value by setting their own BORDERCOLOR attribute. Conflicts in border color between two Frames sharing the same border are resolved by using the color of the innermost Frame or, if at equal nesting level, the color used by the Frame that is loaded last.

Example 2: Using Variables for HTML

The previous example, shown in Program 8.9, eliminated one source file. How about letting JavaScript handle the other source files too? It's possible to do all this in one file. Let's look at the new version of the stock charting file to see how we can accumulate the entire application in one source file. The single file is shown in Program 8.11.

Program 8.11: Using one file instead of three

```
<HTML>

<HEAD>

<TITLE>stock.htm --  Simple stocking algorithm</TITLE>

<SCRIPT LANGUAGE="JavaScript">


//

// This string variable

var DefaultFrame='<html><title>Default</title>' +

        '<body bgcolor="#FFFFFF"></body></html>';


var AdvertFrame= '<HTML>' +

        '<body bgcolor="#000000">' +

        '<font Color="yellow"><font size=4> And now for
some Crass Commercial Messages!' +

        '</font></font><BR>' +
```

(continued)

```
        '<CENTER><font Color="White">a tribute to G. Gordon
Liddy</font></CENTER>' +

        '</BODY></HTML>';


var AskingFrame= '<HTML>' +

        '<BODY>' +

        '<FORM  NAME="sform">' +

        '<CENTER>' +

        'Enter stock symbol:' +

        '<INPUT  TYPE="text" NAME="stockName"' +

        'onChange="getStock(this.form)" SIZE="10">' +

        '<INPUT TYPE="button" NAME="sbutton"  ' +

        '       VALUE="SEARCH" onClick="getStock(this.form)">' +

        '</FORM>' +

        '</BODY>' +

        '</HTML>'


function  stockMaster(stock)  {

var str = new String(stock)

stock = str.toUpperCase()

//

// Construct URL of the form: "http://www.stockmaster/sm/g/M/
NSCP.htm"
```

(continued)

```
//

top.outframe.location.href="http://www.stockmaster.com/sm/g/"

        + stock.charAt(0)

        + "/" + stock + ".htm"

}


function getStock(tform) {

//

//Check to make sure the user entered a stock symbol

//

if (tform.stockName.value == "") {

        alert("Enter a ticker symbol!")

        return

    }


var sname=tform.stockName.value

stockMaster(sname);

}

</SCRIPT>

</HEAD>
```

(continued)

```
<FRAMESET  ROWS="22%,*,10%">

<FRAME SRC="javascript:top.AskingFrame" NAME="askframe"
SCROLLING="no" RESIZE>

<FRAME SRC="javascript:top.DefaultFrame" NAME="outframe"
SCROLLING="auto" RESIZE>

<FRAME SRC="javascript:top.AdvertFrame" NAME="advert" SCROLL-
ING="auto" RESIZE>

</FRAMESET>

</HTML>
```

Example 3: Using FRAMEs and TABLEs

Now let's look at a more involved example using FRAMEs. In the example shown in Program 8.12, you will see several different ways of handling FRAMEs and their objects. For convenience, the lines in this program are numbered.

If you are already a player in the stock and commodities options market, skip this text over onto the text after the listing. The rest of this chapter is an incomplete introduction to the futures market with just enough information to make the example a little easier to understand.

A *futures contract* is simply a promise to purchase a certain amount of a commodity at a given price on or before a certain date. In Program 8.12, the commodity we use is the Sugar 11 futures contract. See the sidebar, "A brief lesson on futures contracts," for specifics on how the math is calculated for a futures contract.

The program in Listing 8.12 illustrates the use of tables to display calculated information. Although the example is slanted to displaying calculations for a futures contract, you can easily extend the idea for other applications.

The key point to remember is that it takes three steps to generate the tables. First, declare the header for the table, including all the captions for the columns. Second, iterate with <TR> tags for all rows in the table and calculate the values for each column at that row. You cannot go back up a row, so think of doing all the calculations as proceeding from the top left-hand corner to the bottom right-hand corner of the table. Envisioning this operation in this manner will help you organize the entries for the rows and columns so that they follow the order of calculations. Finally, do not forget to end the table with a </TABLE> tag.

A brief lesson on futures contracts

This information about futures contracts is very brief and definitely incomplete. We have ignored the time value of options, future margin calls, expiration months, and various other concepts that do not relate to our example. This book is about JavaScript and not about throwing money away at the futures market. For more information on trading options and futures, I recommend the book "Winning in the Futures Market" by George Angell, Probus Publishing Co., ISBN 1-55738-146-1.

Prices in the sugar commodity industry are listed in cents per $1120 worth of sugar. Let's say that you get one sugar contract with a purchase price of 3.50 cents. The value of the contract is $3.50 × 1120 = $392,000. You are required to deposit a minimum amount to cover a certain amount as determined by your broker and the commodities exchange. (By the way, Commission costs are ignored in this example.)

(continued)

If the price of sugar goes up one cent to 3.51, you are given $1120 in your account at the end of the day. If the price drops one cent to 3.49 cents, you lose $1120 at the end of the day. Each one-cent fluctuation in price of sugar causes a gain or loss of $1120. Your account is kept up-to-date at the end of the trading day, and if you run out of funds, your broker will close your account automatically. Therefore, it's important to track your account and know what your risks are. Futures markets can expose you to tremendous risk of loss.

Losses can be limited through the use of options. A futures option is the right to purchase a contract at a given price within a certain time. You do not have to exercise your right if you do not want to. The real difference between an option and a futures contract is that with a futures contract, you are obligated to make up the shortfall or get the gains at the end of the day. With an option, you decide whether or not to exercise the right to purchase. The money paid for an option is not redeemable at the end of the contract. However, with an option, your loss is limited to the price of the option. Both futures and options contracts have a time limit, after which they must be exercised or expired.

In Listing 8.11, the futures contract we are working with is a long one. A long contract is a promise to purchase one contract of sugar at a given price. (A short contract is a promise to sell at a given price.) To save ourselves from a sudden drop in the market price, it's advisable to purchase a "put" option (i.e., the ability to sell a sugar futures contract at a given price). (A "call" option is the right to purchase a contract at a given price.) The program here calculates the maximum possible risk you take with this type of long/put position on a sugar futures contract.

Now let's see how this basic futures calculation is done in Java-Script. Let's examine the code in Program 8.12. The output is shown in Figure 8.7.

Program 8.12: Using a put option in the futures market

```
1

2 <HTML>

3 <HEAD>

4 <TITLE>Futures Markets

5 </TITLE>

6 <SCRIPT>

7 <!--

8 var defaultFrame = "<html><title>Sample</title>" +

9        '<body bgcolor="#FFFFFF"> </body></html>';

10

11 // Format the number "n" to decimal points in "pts"

12 //

13 function fmtNumber(n,pts) {

14   var s = "" + n

15   var decimal = s.indexOf(".")  // get the decimal point
```

(continued)

```
16     if ( decimal == -1) return s   // if none, return amount

17     decimal += (pts + 1)               // Do not forget the
                                           decimal point

18     return (s.substring(0,decimal));

19 }

20

21 var tblHdr = "<TABLE BORDER> " +

22     "<TH>Price</TH> " +

23     "<TH COLSPAN=2>Futures</TH> " +

24     "<TH COLSPAN=3>Put Option</TH> " +

25     "<TH>Total</TH> " +

26     "<TR><TD>" +

27     "<TD>Value<TD>Profit" +

28     "<TD>Price<TD>Value<TD>Profit" +

29     "</TR> " ;

30

31 //

32 // callPrice in cents

33 // putPrice  in cents

34 // costOfOption in cents

35 // ptValues dollars per cent

36 //

37 function analyze(callPrice,putPrice,costOfOption,ptValue) {

38 var basePrice
```

(continued)

```
39 var putCost   // dollar value

40 var i

41 var hi

42 var lo

43 var cv // current value

44 var fv // futures value

45 var fp // futures profit

46 var pp // put price

47 var pv // put value

48 var pf // put profit

49 var tp // total profit

50 var tblRow

51 var count

52

53    basePrice  = Math.round(callPrice)

54    cv = callPrice * ptValue

55    putCost = costOfOption * ptValue

56    doDoc(callPrice,putCost,ptValue)

57    parent.results.document.writeln(tblHdr)

58

59    k = 0.5

60    //

61    // Determine extents to use.

62    //

63    hi = basePrice + (5 * k)
```

(continued)

```
64      lo = basePrice - (5 * k)

65      if (lo < 0.0) lo = 0.0

66      count = 0

67      for (i = hi; i > lo ; i -= k) {

68          if (count > 20) break

69          fv = i * ptValue   // Contract Value

70          fp = fv - cv       // Profit in cents

71

72          pp = putPrice - i // put price difference

73          if ( pp < 0.0 ) pp = 0.0   // only if exercised

74          pv = pp * ptValue   // value of put option

75          pf = pv - putCost

76          tf = fp + pf

77          tblRow = "<TR><TD>" + fmtNumber(i,2) + "</TD>" +

78      "<TD>" + fmtNumber(fv,2)   + "</TD>" +

79      "<TD>" + fmtNumber(fp,2)   + "</TD>" +

80      "<TD>" + fmtNumber(pp,2)   + "</TD>" +

81      "<TD>" + fmtNumber(pv,2)   + "</TD>" +

82      "<TD>" + fmtNumber(pf,2)   + "</TD>" +

83      "<TD>" + fmtNumber(tf,2)   + "</TD>" +

84      "</TR>" ;
```

(continued)

```
85              parent.results.document.writeln(tblRow)

86     }

87

88     parent.results.document.writeln("</TABLE><BR><HR>")

89     parent.results.document.close();

90

91 }

92   Rewrite the

93 function doDoc(value,base,pts) {

94 parent.results.document.writeln("<H2> Option Analysis</
H2>")

95 parent.results.document.writeln("<b>Future Price = </b>" +
fmtNumber(value,2) + "<BR>")

96 parent.results.document.writeln("<b>Put Price  = </b>" +
fmtNumber(base,2) + "<BR>")

97 parent.results.document.writeln("<b>Dollar value of 1 cent
move  = </b>" + fmtNumber(pts,2) + "<BR>")

98 parent.results.document.writeln("<br><HR>");

99

100 }

101   get base prices from user

102 function getInput(iForm) {

103

104   if (iForm.callPrice.value == "")
```

(continued)

```
105    {

106    alert("Enter a call price!")

107    return;

108    }

109    if (iForm.putPrice.value == "")

110    {

111    alert("Enter a put option price in cents!")

112    return;

113    }

114    if (iForm.putCost.value == "")

115    {

116    alert("Enter a value for the cost of the option!")

117    return;

118    }

119

120    analyze(iForm.callPrice.value,iForm.putPrice.
       value,iForm.putCost.value,1120);

121    }

122

123    var askingFrame =

124      '<H1>Sugar Futures Contract Example</H1>' +

125      '<P>' +
```

(continued)

```
126      'Analysis of using a Put option with a futures
contract.' +

127      '<FORM>' +

128      '<TABLE> ' +

129      '<TR>' +

130      '<TD> Futures Price in cents :</TD>  ' +

131      '<TD> <INPUT TYPE="text" NAME="callPrice" >' +

132      '</TR>' +

133      '<TR>' +

134      '<TD> Put Price in cents:</TD>  ' +

135      '<TD> <INPUT TYPE="text" NAME="putPrice" >' +

136      '</TR>' +

137      '<TR>' +

138      '<TD> Cost of Put Option in cents:</TD>   ' +

139      '<TD> <INPUT TYPE="text" NAME="putCost" >' +

140      '</TR>' +

141      '</TABLE> ' +

142      '' +

143      '<INPUT TYPE="button" VALUE="Tell me" ' +

144      '      ONCLICK="top.getInput(document.forms[0])">' +

145  '</FORM> ';
```

(continued)

```
146

147  // -->

148  </SCRIPT>

149  </HEAD>

150  <FRAMESET COLS="40%,*">

151  <FRAME SRC="javascript:top.askingFrame" NAME="askFrame"
RESIZE>

152  <FRAME SRC="javascript:top.defaultFrame" NAME="results"
RESIZE>

153  </FRAMESET>

154  </HTML>
```

Let's examine this code shown in Program 8.12 and look at the important lines. Lines 8 and 9 simply define a blank white frame.

Lines 13 through 19 define a number formatting function called fmtNumber. By using this function, you can write numbers out to the precision defined in the *pts* parameter. JavaScript prints floating-point numbers to 14 decimal places and it's not really very pleasant to look. What the fmtNumber() function does is to find the decimal point and print out all the digits to the right of the decimal point. If no decimal point is found, the entire number is printed. We truncate digits in this function and do not round up or down.

Lines 21 through 29 store the text for the table header that's output for the results of the calculation.

Line 37 starts the calculator function, which does the analysis for us. Note the use of the "var" keyword to declare local variables in the analyze() function. At line 53, we round the value of the price passed into the function.

Note how the results FRAME is addressed at line 57 to write the table header out to. The parent object is used to get the correct FRAME whose document is written to.

The `hi` and `lo` variables are then setup to provide a reasonable number of prices that can happen during the life of the contact. At line 65, the value of the put option is set to zero if it's not in the money (i.e., we will not exercise the right to sell if the selling price is lower than what we can buy the commodity for). Lines 68 through 76 calculate the values for the columns to use in the table for the results.

At line 77, we create one row to display in the table. This row is output to the correct document by explicating using the `parent. frame` prefix. At line 93, we use the same indirection to address the correct document from the parent object.

The `getInput` function is declared from line 102. It's addressed from the table in the variable `askingFrame` by indirecting with the `top.` prefix. See Line 144 for the call to `getInput()`. If you do not use the top. prefix, JavaScript will complain about the function not being found.

The output from the Program 8.12 example is shown in Figure 8.7. I made the prices up to be a long contract price for 5.0 cents and the put option at 0.15 cents. By looking at the right-most column, you can see that the maximum amount at risk is $728, whereas the profit potential is not limited. Be careful though when dealing in the futures market because the market can move in very erratic ways and past performance is not a guarantee of the future. Also, there is no guarantee with this program; risk your money with your own calculator.

And one final note: When processing numbers typed in at a text object, it's sometimes necessary to see if numbers were correctly entered or not. Here's a simple function to check if a number was entered correctly:

```
function isNumber(n) {

        for (var i=0; i< n.length; i++) {

        var ch = n.substring(i,i+1)

        if (!(((ch > "0") && (ch < "9")) || (ch == ".")))

        return false

        }

        return true

}
```

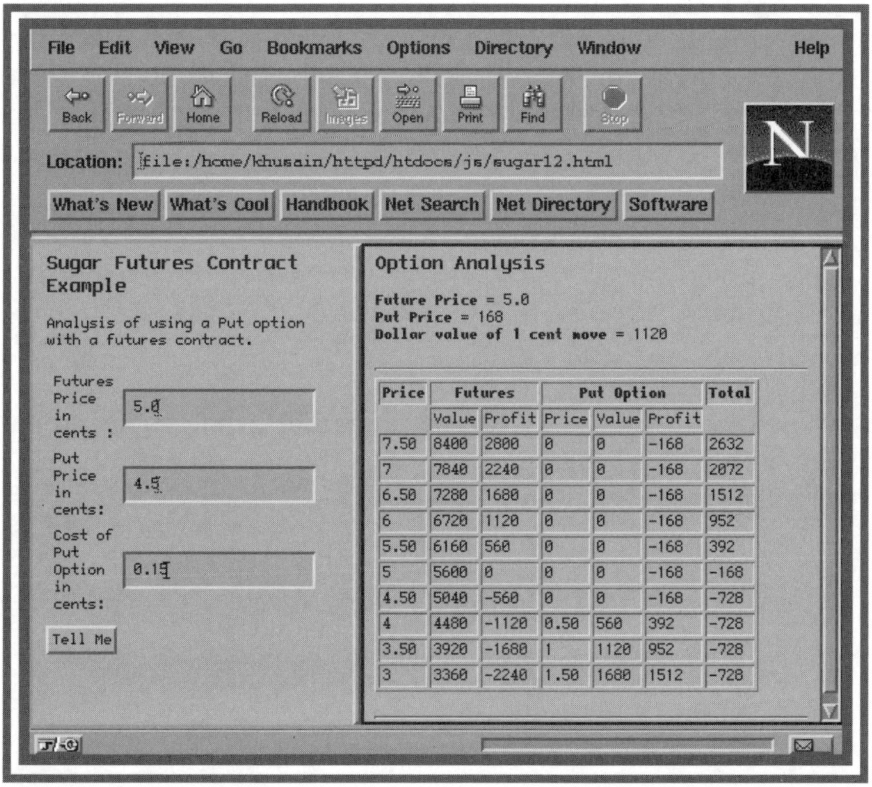

Figure 8.7 A basic futures calculation as done with Java-Script.

Note how the variables i and ch are declared within the for loop. The previous example can be modified to include plus, minus, or handle hex numbers too.

Colored Tables

Another new feature in Navigator 3.0b4 and later is the use of color in table elements. Only the background color can be set at this time. You use the bgcolor attribute for the TR, TH, TD, and TABLE tags to set the background color for the element. For example, the statement,

```
<TABLE bgcolor=#00FF00>
```

will set the default color of all elements in the table to Green. To set the color in a row, set the bgcolor in the <TR> tag as follows:

```
<TR bgcolor=#0000FF>
```

The background color for a header can be set with the <TH> tag. This feature is great for creating colorful tables and jazzing up a returned report. For example, in Program 8.12, you can replace line 82, which looks like this

```
"<TD>" + fmtNumber(pf,2)   + "</TD>" +
```

with this line

```
profitColor + + fmtNumber(pf,2)   + "</TD>"
```

The value of profitColor can be set earlier in the code (probably just at line 76 in Program 8.12) with the use of the following statements:

```
if (pf < 0)  {

profitColor = "<TD bgColor=#FF0000>"

}

else {

profitColor =  "<TD bgColor=#00FF00>"

}
```

Now, if the profit is greater than zero, the background color of the cell showing the profit will be green. If the profit is less than zero (i.e., a loss) the background color the cell showing the value will be red. Just remember that this is a new feature in Navigator 3.0 and may not work with older browsers.

Tainted Documents

Navigator 3.0 has fixed a security hole in Navigator versions 2.1 and earlier. The security hole allowed one window to view the contents of a document in another window. Some JavaScript applications actually relied on this "feature" to put complex applications together. To upgrade such applications in the future, you can use the `taint()` and `untaint()` properties of a document. Now, when a JavaScript application attempts to use data from another window, (referred to as the "tainted window") and send it to a server, a dialog is brought up to confirm the transaction. The user of the browser at the client side can then allow or cancel the attempted transaction. Note that this dialog is presented only when data from the tainted window is being sent outside the computer on which the browser happens to reside.

Programmatically, typing in the following line of code:

```
reply = untaint(document.form1.myName)
```

will make the contents and properties of the variable `document.form1.myName` available for use by other forms in the application. The "reply" variable contains a reference to the variable or its property being tainted.

You remove the taint property of an object to allow its items to be used by other windows. You apply the taint property to disallow the use of properties of an object by other windows. For example to disallow the use of the `Name` property of the `myName` object used earlier, you would use the following statement:

```
reply = taint(document.form1.myName.value)
```

To enable the tainting features, you have to set the environment variable NS_ENABLE_TAINT to a non-zero value on UNIX and Windows systems. On a Macintosh, edit the "envi" resource and the number 128 in the Netscape application by removing the dual backslashes (//) in front of the NS_ENABLE_TAINT word. The idea of tainted objects came about as the result of fixes to security holes in having more than one window in an application. This feature protects a user at browser from unwittingly disclosing sensitive information in one Netscape window to another window. A rogue JavaScript application may be able to take password or other sensitive information entered in another window and pass this information off to a server. Be sure that this feature will not adversely affect security at your site before enabling NS_ENABLE_TAINT.

Summary

In this chapter, we have introduced you to handling Frames and windows in JavaScript. A JavaScript application lets you create new windows and set the contents and colors in a Frame.

A Frame is simply a sliced portion of the window with it's own writeable space. This chapter has covered the following topics:

- *You can create new windows to start a new thread of processing for a new browser. The properties of each window, such as a toolbar, a location, and so on, can be set at the time the window is created. By using Frames, more than one document can be displayed in separate sections of windows.*

- *The use of variables to create documents dynamically can be used with Frames as well the use of one file to manage several documents.*

- *The use of* bgcolor *attributes in TABLE, TR, TH and TD tags in a table can be used to create very nice, colorful tables.*

- *The* taint() *and* untaint() *functions can be used to allow or disallow, respectively, the use of documents and variables in one window by another window.*

Coming Up

The next chapter will cover how to use images, mapping the mouse to images and objects in documents and Frames. By using these features and the knowledge gained in this chapter, you will be able to create snazzy applications in no time.

CHAPTER 9

APPLYING JAVASCRIPT

- Handling Images

- Properties of Images

- Objects and Windows

This chapter will cover details of how to load images into a document using JavaScript. We will also cover how to do image mapping in order to produce user interfaces that let a user click on a image to call a JavaScript function. We will put the knowledge gained in the last eight chapters to use here for some applications.

Handling Images

An HTML image is usually a GIF or JPEG file. In most cases, you will find GIF images on a Web site. JPEG files are smaller in size than an equivalent GIF image, but tend to lose some contents of the original

299

image when they are created. GIF images can be recreated without any loss of data and tend to be the preferred choice for Web sites.

An image in JavaScript is declared with the IMG tags. Each image defined in a FORM with IMG tags is a JavaScript object in the document. All images in a document can be addressed using the built-in *images* array. The first image in a document is `document.images[0]`, the next image is `document.images[1]`, and so forth. The number of images in a document is listed in the property `document.images.length`.

Eight properties of IMG objects are available to your JavaScript application, only two of which are writeable. The properties are:

- *border—set to BORDER attribute of image (width in pixels)*
- *height—set to HEIGHT attribute of image in pixels*
- *width—set to WIDTH attribute of image in pixels*
- *vspace—set to VSPACE attribute*
- *hspace—set to HSPACE attribute*
- *complete—Boolean value set to true when image is complete*
- *lowsrc—low resolution image file URL*
- *src—URL of the image file*

Only the `lowsrc` and `src` properties can be set by your application. The rest are read-only. In addition, the `lowsrc` property must be set before you set the `src` property. When setting the URL, you do not have to worry about setting the height and width of the incoming image because the image will be scaled to fit.

Three event handlers are also supported in images:

- *onload—called when the image is loaded*
- *onerror—called when an error occurs while an image is being loaded*
- *onabort—called if the user prevents the image from being loaded.*

Program 9.1 provides an application to test how the loading of images works with GIF files and IMG objects. The five buttons below are listed in Program 9.1 with names equal to the GIF images. You do not have to do this, and will probably have a function for each button to load its own image. The image object is addressed by its ordinal index in the `documents.images` array.

The output of Program 9.1 is shown in Figure 9.1. You will need the six GIF images listed in the source file, or you could substitute your own. The first image is a 50×50 image called "`blue1.gif`". When the page is first loaded into a browser and laid out, a 50×50 space will be set aside for `blue1.gif` and the contents of the image will be displayed in it. The rest of the five images (`red.gif`, `blue.gif`, `green.gif`, `yellow.gif`, and `magenta.gif`) are 10×10 images. As each button is pressed, one of these images will be loaded into the viewing area set aside originally for `blue1.gif`. Because the incoming image is not the same size as the original image, the incoming image will be sized to fit the viewing area.

There is one caveat to this resizing. Images scaled up or down into a viewing area may be distorted or blurry owing to differences in the aspect ratio. The images in this example were contrived to be of different sizes just to point out this resize effect. In the real world, you might want to keep image sizes the same to avoid the scaling problem. There may be an occasion where you want to present "thumb-nail" representations of an image where the resize may help in scaling down a large image to allow a user to preview it. You have to examine these features on a case-by-case basis and then decide whether to keep all images the same size or use a consistent fixed size display area for all images of varying sizes.

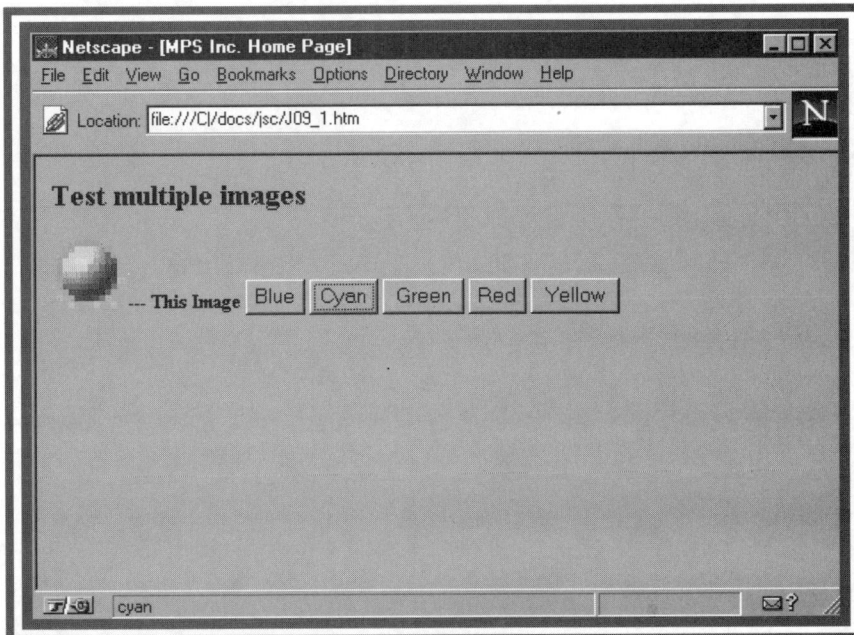

Figure 9.1 Using the image SRC attribute

The linux and UNIX versions of Program 9.1 doesn't work even, with the NS_ENABLE_MOJA environment variable turned on. Only the Windows 95 and Windows NT version work.

Program 9.1: Using image objects

```
<HTML><HEAD><TITLE>MPS Inc. Home Page </TITLE>

</HEAD>

<SCRIPT LANGUAGE="LiveScript">

<!-- Hiding


//

// Set the image to something

//

function setSource(t) {

        document.images[0].src = 'file:///C|/docs/jsc/' +
t.name + '.gif'

        window.status = t.name

}

// -->

</SCRIPT>

<BODY>

<P>

<p>

<H2>Test multiple images </H2>
```

(continued)

```
<P>

<FORM NAME="bta">

<IMG SRC="blue1.gif" BORDER > <B>--- This Image</B> <R>

<INPUT TYPE="button" NAME="blue"    VALUE="Blue"   onClick="
setSource(this)">

<INPUT TYPE="button" NAME="cyan"    VALUE="Cyan"   onClick="
setSource(this)">

<INPUT TYPE="button" NAME="green"   VALUE="Green"
onClick="setSource(this)">

<INPUT TYPE="button" NAME="red"       VALUE="Red" onClick="
setSource(this)">

<INPUT TYPE="button" NAME="yellow"   VALUE="Yellow"
onClick="setSource(this)">

</FORM>

</HTML>
```

The advantages of being able to load images by simply modifying the SRC attribute of an image are too many to list here. For example, you can create very simple, yet visually effective and pleasing, user manuals, or photo shots of houses based on user responses... with minimal CGI network overhead. Instead of having a server-side CGI application do your image processing for you, the JavaScript application can handle this processing.

You can save coding time and effort by creating simple animations with the GIF89 format. The GIF89 format is suitable for creating animations in your Web pages. Do not scoff at this seemingly simple way of creating animation in an image. Choosing the GIF89 format for animation has the advantage of not being affected by network traffic as each frame is displayed on the browser. The downside is that all the frames have to be loaded before animation can begin. Also, the color palette for all frames must remain the same. Changing the palette between images can lead to very strange color schemes for your images. There are several utilities for Windows and Macintosh machines for creating images ranging in price from free to several hundred dollars. Two notable mentions are the GIF Construction Set from Alchemy Mindworks (www.mindworks.com) and the GIF Builder (member.aol.com/royalef/toolbox.htm).

Tip There are a few points to keep in mind when designing animated GIF files. First, the first image will remain static while the rest of the image loads and the last image in the frame will be what the user sees when the animation stops. Fade-out images are easy to do with a spray paint tool in a paint program. Fade-in images are simply the reversed sequence of the spray painted image. In Navigator 3.0, you can have finite loops but, once started, a loop cannot be stopped. In Navigator 2.0, loops are infinite but stoppable with the use of the STOP button.

> A GIF89 animated loop will cause the onLoad event handler to be called each time it goes through the loop.

Some graphics animation is possible using timers, Frames, and the image attribute. There is a price to be paid with this option and you must be aware of this price: you will cause a lot of traffic on the network on which you reside. It is important to remember this point as you read further so the point is repeated: *you will cause a lot of traffic on the network on which you reside.* If you want to use some graphics that require speed, use the GIF file format itself. Where the GIF format fails is in flexibility because, once the images for the animation are created, their content and order cannot be modified.

There are times when you just want to view something on a remote site every so often. For example, a Web site may be updating the current weather map every 10 minutes. You have the option of clicking the URL for the Web site every time you want to look at the weather conditions. In most cases, a eb browser can just sit idle on a display. Why not let it update itself with the weather report every 10 minutes? JavaScript will let you do this quite easily. See the code in Program 9.2 for a simple JavaScript application that loads in a GIF image from a Web site every 10 minutes.

One more thing about this process. The update time between successive loading of images must be kept long enough to allow for network delays and the time required to render large images. Then there is virtually no synchronization between the browser and occasionally the browser may attempt to pick up an image that is not complete on the server side or is in the process of being rewritten and therefore just not be displayed. The process is by no means a fool-proof one, but it will work for the casual user. For more sophisticated, real-time updates, you will probably be better off writing your own dedicated application.

Program 9.2: Updating images periodically

```
<HTML>

<HEAD>

<TITLE>Test crude animation</TITLE>

</HEAD>


<SCRIPT LANGUAGE="LiveScript">

<!-- Hiding

var counter = 1;



//

// Redraw the lower frame.

//

function setSource(iFrame) {

        iFrame.document.writeln(showFrame);

        iFrame.document.close();

        }


//

//   Lower frame with GIF file
```

(continued)

```
//

var showFrame = "<html><title>Sample</title>" +

          '<body bgcolor="#FFFFFF">' +

          ' <IMG SRC="http://204.251.103.1/t.gif"> <B>Onward
Ho!</B><P> ' +

          ' </body></html>';

//

// User interface buttons

//

var askFrame  = "<html><title>Sample</title>" +

          ' <H1>This is not a fast process!</H1> ' +

          ' <FORM name="bta"> ' +

          ' <INPUT TYPE="button" NAME="Again"  VALUE="Again"
onClick="top.setSource(parent.showMe)"> ' +

          ' <INPUT TYPE="button" NAME="Again"  VALUE="Start"
onClick="top.setMyTimer()"> ' +

          ' </FORM> ' ;



//

// Canned routine to stop updating after 10 tries

// each try attempted after 10 minutes.
```

(continued)

```
// You might want to let this run forever, just bear

// in mind that you are loading the network down.

//

function doit() {

        top.setSource(parent.showMe);

        counter++

        window.status = "Timer = " + counter + " " ;

        if ( counter < 10) {

        setTimeout("doit()",10000);

        }

}



//

// Start the animation process

// NOTE: this will not work if called from within onLoad().

//

function setMyTimer() {

        counter = 0

        setTimeout("doit()",3000);

        window.status = "counter = " + counter + " " +
document.images.length
```

(continued)

```
            }

// -->

</SCRIPT>


<FRAMESET ROWS="50%,*">

<FRAME SRC="javascript:top.askFrame" NAME="askMen"  RESIZE>

<FRAME SRC="javascript:top.showFrame" NAME="showMe" RESIZE>

</FRAMESET>
```

The setTimer function calls a function that writes a new document to a Frame, called *showFrame*. Part of the document written to showFrame is an IMG tag pointing to the server-based GIF file. On every timer tick, the image is collected from the server and the document redrawn. Simply resetting the "src" for the IMG tag will not work because there is no clear way to override the internal caching in the browser. That is, if you just set the IMG tag, the browser will pick up it's cached version and not the image from the server. Flushing the cache or setting the value of the cache memory size to zero does not help either.

The server-side script for this example is a Perl script and is shown Program 9.3. If you are not familiar with Perl, don't worry; you can write the GIF file out in whatever language you prefer. The only reason for using Perl is that it's the de facto language of choice for Web servers and is therefore quite popular with WebMasters the world over.

Program 9.3: Server-side Perl script to send images back

```perl
#!/usr/bin/perl

#

# Sample perl server to generate images.

#


$updateTime = 60;    # up to the minute reporting


while (1)

    {

    #

    # You would write your own news page generator here.

    #

    `date > usage`;

    `pbmtext < usage | ppmtogif > t.gif 2>&1`;

    sleep $updateTime;

    }
```

The $updateTime variable is set to 60 seconds so that the image on the server side is updated every minute. The time was set to a short interval; you might have requirements that allow a longer time.

The while loop does three things. First, it creates a text file with the date and time at the server side. You will probably want to write a different function to create your own file. The backticks (`) in the `date > usage`; command run the date program in UNIX and store the results in a file called usage. The next line executes a series of commands to convert the text file into a GIF using the freely available Portable Bitmap Tools pbmplus library. The pbmtext program converts a text file into a PBM file and the ppmtogif program converts the PBM file into a GIF file. (PBM is a subset of PPM file formats.) The results are stored in a file called t.gif. The "2>&1" construct redirects any output from standard error stdout. The last thing it does is sleep for the predetermined time in $updateTime.

At the risk of being redundant, the method just shown is good for the occasional user. Collecting images every minute from a Web site may ruffle the feathers of the most friendliest of system administrators. You have to carefully weigh how often you want to display the images and what sizes the images can have. Be very careful not to overload your network.

Using XBM Files

Netscape Navigator 2.0 and 3.0 let you display XBM files just as they do GIF files. The reason why XBM files are not very popular is because images in the XBM format are always black and white only. Secondly, they are very slow to load into a browser because it's an ASCII format. On the other hand, because it is ASCII, an XBM file can be used in JavaScript to provide some sort of crude drawing ability.

An XBM file is generally created with the bitmap program in X windows. The format is straightforward and is C code. Two lines define the height and width of the image, followed by a declaration of array of bits in the image. For example, for a given image, the XBM file looks like:

```
#define red_width 6

#define red_height 5

static char red_bits[] = {

0x04,0x1a,0x3a,0x36,0x1e,0x1e};
```

By writing JavaScript, you can write your own graphic lines in a image. The process will be slow and painful and the results may not be as spectacular as you would expect, but it can be done. Drawing a point on the screen would involve taking the following steps:

- *Create a new document.*
- *Write a height and width definition to it.*
- *Create the bits for the image to display in memory.*
- *Write the bits of the image out to the document.*
- *Close the document.*

During the drawing process, you will be manipulating bits in a character array. JavaScript does have bit-manipulation operators, but again, this is certainly not the most effective way to use JavaScript.

Using Image Maps

Navigator lets you use images within an HTML document without the need for a server-side *imagemap* executeable program. With Java-Script code, you can perform some basic functions at the client side instead of the server side. The advantage of this approach is the faster response time to the user and less overhead on the server side. Plus, the coordinates for the map are stored in the HTML file itself instead of another file at the server with *httpd* servers.

The steps to take when using JavaScript to perform basic mapping functions are:

- *Get all the coordinates for the image hotspots.*

- *Define coordinates in <MAP> attributes.*

- *Declare the image in <FORM>.*

- *Write the JavaScript handler functions for each hot spot.*

The first step in taking coordinates is to get the top left-hand corner pixels and the bottom right-hand side coordinates. You can load the image into a picture editor and do this by clicking the cursor at various spots and writing the coordinates down. Do not overlap any hot spot areas.

To use image maps within Netscape, use the <MAP> tags to define a mapping. Use the name attribute to uniquely identify the mapped area. The syntax for using the type of <MAP> tag that we are concerned with is as follows:

```
<map NAME="name">

<area coords="x1,y1,x2,y2", href="url">

<area coords="x1,y1,x2,y2", href="url">

<area coords="x1,y1,x2,y2", href="url">



. . .



</map>
```

More than one area may be defined for use with hotspots. Just remember not to overlap them. The areas we'll use for modifying the TOC.HTM file are shown in Program 9.4. The TOC.HTM file was used in Chapters 7 and 8 to provide links into other HTML documents. Let's modify the files used in those chapters to use an image map instead of links and buttons.

Program 9.4: The TOC.HTM

```
<HTML>

<HEAD>

<TITLE>Table of Contents</TITLE>

</HEAD>

<FRAMESET rows="33%,*">

        <FRAME NAME="ButtonFrame" SRC="doc0.htm">

        <FRAMESET cols="30%,*">

        <FRAME NAME="bookInfo" SRC="doc1.htm">

        <FRAME NAME="dontcare" SRC="books.htm">

        </FRAMESET>

</FRAMESET>
```

Then `btn.htm` file is going to the URL referred to in the IMG tag's `href` attribute is the Javascript function to call. The output of Programs 9.4 and 9.5 are shown in Figure 9.2.

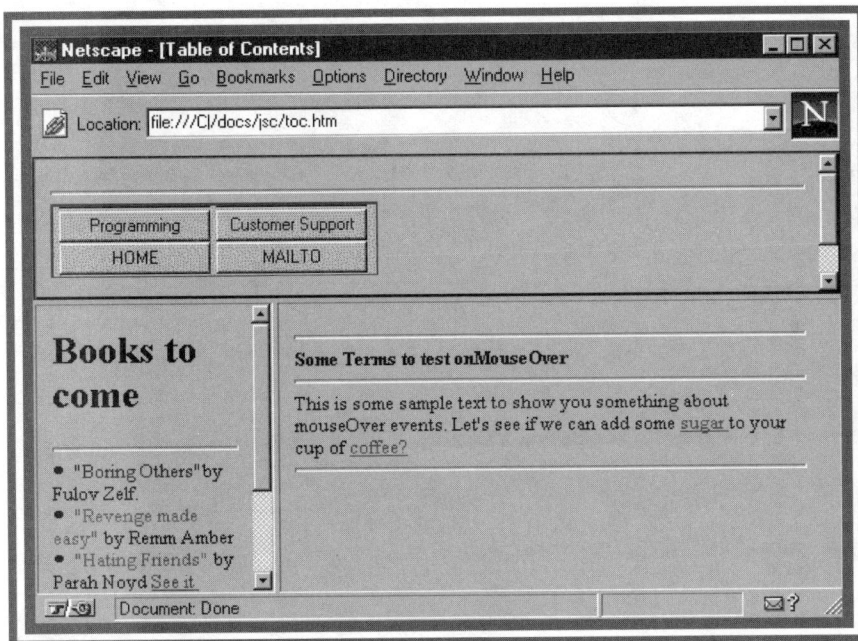

Figure 9.2 Using Image maps

Program 9.5: Using Image Maps in `doc0.htm`

```
<HTML>

<HEAD>

<TITLE> Use image maps </TITLE>

<SCRIPT LANGUAGE="JavaScript">
```

(continued)

```
<!---

//

// .... Set the location based on button number ....

//

function setFile(i) {

    if ( i == 1) {

            top.location.href = "compass.htm";

            return;

            }

    if ( i == 2) {

            top.location.href = "mailman.htm";

            return;

            }

    if ( i == 3) {

            top.location.href = "fishing.htm";

            return;

            }

    if ( i == 4) {

            top.location.href = "postman.htm";

            return;

            }

}
```

(continued)

```
//

// Don't write any more comments in JavaScript after next line

//

<!-- End of script hiding comments -->


</SCRIPT>

</HEAD>

<BODY>

<map name="mitems">

<area coords="2,1,104,20" href="javascript:setFile(1)" >

<area coords="2,22,104,42" href="javascript:setFile(2)" >

<area coords="105,1,209,20" href="javascript:setFile(3)" >

<area coords="105,22,209,42" href="javascript:setFile(4)" >

</map>

<FORM>

<HR>

<IMG SRC="buttons.gif" usemap="#mitems"><BR>

</FORM>

</body>

</HTML>
```

The `books.htm` file referenced in this program is shown in Program 9.6. The contents of the file show how to set the HREF attribute to set the contents of a window.

Program 9.6: The `books.htm` file

```
<HTML>

<HEAD>

<TITLE> Books </TITLE>

<SCRIPT LANGUAGE="JavaScript">


<!---

//

// Declare some "global" variables here

//

mailman="mailman.htm"

fishing="doc1.htm"


function goFish(loc) {

    alert( "Location = " + loc);

    top.bookInfo.location.href=loc;

}


//

// Don't write any more comments in JavaScript after next line

//

<!-- End of script hiding comments -->
```

(continued)

```
</SCRIPT>

</HEAD>

<BODY>

<H1> Books to come </H1>

<body>

<FORM>

<HR>

<BL>

<LI> <font COLOR="#003F00">"Boring Others"</font>by Fulov
Zelf.

<LI> <font COLOR="Green">"Revenge made easy"</font> by Remm
Amber

<LI> <font COLOR="Green">"Hating Friends"</font> by Parah Noyd

     <A HREF="postman.htm" TARGET="bookInfo"> See it </A>

<LI> <font COLOR="GREEN">"Mailman's Guide to Dawgs"</
font>,anon

     <A HREF="mailman.htm" TARGET="bookInfo"> Look  </A>

<LI> <font COLOR="GREEN">"Fishing for urbanites"</font>,

     <A HREF="books.htm" TARGET="bookInfo" > Go to it </A>

<BL>

</FORM>

</body>

</HTML>
```

The listing shown in Program 9.5 shows how to create image maps with the <MAP> tag. Each area on the display being mapped outlined a button on the display screen. There is a function associated with this button. When a mouse is clicked within this area, it's as if the button is "pressed". Visually, the area around the "button" is not depressed but the function mapped to the area is called. This is a technique to make your own "buttons" or other spots on a display come alive with buttons.

Using Objects and Frames

As we learned in Chapter 4, "JavaScript and Objects", JavaScript lets you create objects for your own use. Let's examine a very simple example of creating and using objects along with Frames. The sample code is shown in Program 9.7. This example creates two frames and displays some text in one frame based on a selection box in the other. This example defines a bunch of commodities and collects information about them. The commodity object defined in this example encapsulates the major common components of futures commodities. Another example for such a set up would be to collect information about a loan, such as amount, interest rate, and months to pay, in one Frame and then create an amortization table in the other Frame based on responses in the first frame.

It's always possible to create your own objects and stack them using arrays. Objects in JavaScript are created with the use of a *function* call. The special reserved word this refers to the object being referred to in the function. Methods are added the same way as assigning members. Please refer to Chapter 4 again if this object creation seems unfamiliar.

The Chicago Board of Trade defines months in a strange numbering sequence: F for January, G for Feburary, etc. (It's actually necessary to do this to list contracts on tickers.) The showMonths() function translates these codes into more meaningful month names.

Program 9.7: Using objects

```
<HTML>

<HEAD>

<TITLE>Types of commodities</TITLE>


<SCRIPT>

<!--

var defaultFrame = "<html><title>Sample</title>" +

            '<body bgcolor="#FFFFFF"> </body></html>';


var askFrame = '<H1> Futures Contract Example</H1>' +

    '<P>' +

    '<FORM>' +

    '<SELECT NAME="contracts">' +

    '<OPTION> Corn' +

    '<OPTION> Oats' +

    '<OPTION SELECTED> Soybeans' +

    '<OPTION> Wheat' +

    '<OPTION> Cotton' +

    '</SELECT>' +
```

(continued)

```
                '<INPUT TYPE="button" VALUE="Tell Me About It" ' +

                '       ONCLICK="top.getInput(document.forms[0])">' +

                '</FORM>';


function getInput(iForm) {

        var i = iForm.contracts.selectedIndex

        eval(iForm.contracts.options[i].text + ".showIt
(parent.results)");

        }



//

// Make sure you have the right number entered

//

function isNumber(n) {

        for (var i=0; i<n.length; i++) {

        var ch = n.substring(i,i+1)

            if (!(((ch > "0") && (ch < "9")) || (ch == ".")))

                    return false

        }

return true

}
```

(continued)

```
//

// Format the number "n" to decimal points in "pts"

//

function fmtNumber(n,pts) {

    var s = "" + n

    var decimal = s.indexOf(".")   // get the decimal point

    if ( decimal == -1) return s   // if none, return amount

    decimal += (pts + 1) // Do not forget the demical point

    return (s.substring(0,decimal));

}




// ---------------------------------------------------------

// Method of commodity "class"

// Write to a specific document in the iFrame

// object that's passed in.

// ---------------------------------------------------------

function showIt(iFrame) {

    var info = "The commodity <B>" + this.name +

        "</B> trades in " + this.size + " units of " +
```

(continued)

```
                    this.units + " each." +

            "<BR>Each one cent move is worth $" + fmtNum-
    ber(this.ptValue) +

            ". The limit move is " + fmtNumber(this.ilimit) +

            "<BR> The month code for " + this.name +

            " is " + this.months + ". " + this.showMonths()

            "." ;



    iFrame.document.writeln(info);

    iFrame.document.close();

    // -------------------------------------------------------

    // Yes, you can be explicit and use these lines

    // instead of the two lines shown above.

    //      parent.results.document.writeln(info);

    //      parent.results.document.close();

    // -------------------------------------------------------

}



// -------------------------------------------------------------

// Method of commodity "class"

// Convert bizarre Commodities month codes into more
```

(continued)

```
// meaningful names for display

// -----------------------------------------------------

function showMonths() {

    var txt = ""

    var len = this.months.length

    for (var i = 0; i < len; i++) {

        var ch = this.months.charAt(i)

        if (ch == "F") txt += "January "

        if (ch == "G") txt += "February "

        if (ch == "H") txt += "March "

        if (ch == "J") txt += "April "

        if (ch == "K") txt += "May "

        if (ch == "M") txt += "June "

        if (ch == "N") txt += "July "

        if (ch == "Q") txt += "August "

        if (ch == "U") txt += "September "

        if (ch == "V") txt += "October "

        if (ch == "X") txt += "November "

        if (ch == "N") txt += "December "

    }

    return (txt.bold())

}
```

(continued)

Using Objects and Frames

```
                    this.units + " each." +

                    "<BR>Each one cent move is worth $" +
fmtNumber(this.ptValue) +

                    ". The limit move is " + fmtNumber(this.ilimit) +

                    "<BR> The month code for " + this.name +

                    " is " + this.months + ". " + this.showMonths()

                    "." ;


        iFrame.document.writeln(info);

        iFrame.document.close();

        // -----------------------------------------------------

        // Yes, you can be explicit and use these lines

        // instead of the two lines shown above.

        //     parent.results.document.writeln(info);

        //     parent.results.document.close();

        // -----------------------------------------------------

}



// -----------------------------------------------------

// Method of commodity "class"

// Convert bizarre Commodities month codes into more
```

(continued)

```
// --------------------------------------------------------
// define the class here with it's initialiation function
// --------------------------------------------------------
function commodity(name,size,units,months,ptValue,ilimit) {


    //
    // Initialize the member values.
    //
    this.name = name

    this.size = size

    this.units = units

    this.months = months

    this.ptValue = ptValue

    this.ilimit = ilimit


    //
    //  assign function to object for use as method
    //
    this.showIt = showIt

    this.showMonths = showMonths

}
```

(continued)

```
//------------------------------------------------------

// Create all the objects for use with the application here.

// -------------------------------------------------------------


 Corn = new commodity("Corn",5000,"Bushels","HKNUZ",50,10);

 Oats = new commodity("Oats",5000,"Bushels","HKNUZ",50,10);

 Soybeans = new commodity("Soybeans",5000,"Bush-
els","FHKNUQX",50,30);

 Wheat = new commodity("Wheat",5000,"Bushels","HKNUZ",50,20);

 Cotton = new commodity("Cotton",50000,"Lbs","HKNVZ",500,2);

 Sugar = new commodity("Sugar",112000,"Lbs","HKNV",1120,2);


// -->

</SCRIPT>

</HEAD>

<FRAMESET ROWS="30%,*">
```

The example in Program 9.7 shows how to use arrays of objects and how to connect these arrays to objects on the screen. The idea is to map user interface objects onto objects within JavaScript code. This way, changes or actions made by the user through the user interface are reflected immediately in the underlying objects. The reverse could be true as well for objects that reflect their value back to the display, such as values set by timers being reflected back to the user.

Objects in JavaScript reside in one tree off the top-level node. All objects are accessible from using the "top" or "parent" objects. For example, all documents are available through the `top.documents` array, and variables in the application through the parent object. Therefore, the internal user-defined objects can always be mapped in one way or another to a user interface object. The mapped object can contain more information about a user interface object. In the example presented here, the drop-down selection list only contain the name of the commodity that the user can select. It was the underlying object with the commodity name that contained more information given a commodity name. We used this information to print out readable information in another JavaScript Frame.

Using Cookies

Cookies are used by CGI servers to store state information about client applications. A CGI server can send state information back to the client along with HTML objects. The cookie's state information includes a range of URLs, machine, and user for which it is valid. When the client makes more requests with the same cookie, the server can advance them through a state machine. The current state simply advances to the next state based on the responses from a user.

Several avenues are possible for use with cookies. You can walk through rooms in a virtual house and track which rooms have been visited. Shopping programs can track objects for purchase in a client's shopping cart. Fee-based services can register a client once and not have to ask them for a password during session.

The following is an example of a maze program called "Dork," a very simple tribute to the famous text-based game: Zork. The example shown here illustrates the use of cookies to maintain the state of a user as they walk around a little house. See Figure 9.3 for a mental image of our imaginary house. The demo uses three files: `maze.htm`, `layout.htm`, and `compass.htm`, which files are shown in Programs 9.8, 9.9, and 9.10, respectively.

The present state of the document is indicates which room that the user happens to be in. More elaborate information—a photograph, for example-- is possible by adding more cookies to the document, such as a URL of an image of the room. Each room is an object with information in it on how to get to connecting rooms (see Figures 9.4 and 9.5 for examples of what the player sees). The rooms are assigned direction and items if any in the following lines of code.

```
var rooms= new Array(7)

rooms[0] = new room(0,"foyer",-1,3,1,-1,"none");

rooms[1] = new room(1,"living",-1,4,2,0,"none");

rooms[2] = new room(2,"bedroom",-1,6,-1,1,"none");

rooms[3] = new room(3,"kitchen",0,-1,4,-1,"knife");

rooms[4] = new room(4,"Dining",1,-1,5,3,"none");

rooms[5] = new room(5,"bathroom",-1,-1,6,4,"wrench");

rooms[6] = new room(6,"closet",2,-1,-1,5,"none");
```

Figure 9.3 The maze to walk through in Dork

The `displayCurrentRoom()` function is used to create the text that is displayed for each room. The layout form is used to print this state information about each room and it's connections. See Program 9.9 for the `layout.htm` file.

Embedded in the script for `maze.htm` are these lines:

```
if (getCurrentRoom() == null)  {

        initializeRooms()

}
```

It's easy to confuse these lines as a function declaration and not realize that this code is executed before the page is laid out. This code initiliazes the cookies for the document when the document is loaded. Subsequents loads of the same page will not destroy it's cookie state. Closing the document and reopening a new document will create a fresh cookie and cause a reinitialization.

Moving around in the rooms is done with the `compass.htm` file shown in Program 9.10. Note the use of the borderless table to layout buttons. By default, HTML buttons are laid out in a ragged fashion when displayed by a browser. Using a table, you can lay these buttons out in a slightly more organized manner. The size of the button, alas, will vary depending on the text you place in them. Just try to ensure that the verbiage in buttons value is of the same length.

The code to implement the structure of the Dork game is surprisingly small. It's easy to reduce the lines of code and make it even smaller. The cost would be to make the code a bit more difficult to understand. However, you should be able to see how to apply the concepts illustrated here to create your own walk-through for client applications.

More Information on JavaScript and Cookies

Web sites with good information about cookies are Bill Dortch's site at http://www.hidaho.com/cookies and Danny Goodman's Web site www.dannyg.com. Bill is a recognized Javascript author and has graciously placed code for handling cookies in the public domain, which we've used in Program 9.9. Danny Goodman is THE well-known authority on scripting languages and has a ton of good information on Javascript authoring at his Web site. The strongly recommended example with using cookies is Danny Goodman's Decision Helper program. Finally, you can check out information on more Javascript applications and uses at the repository in www.gamelan.com.

Program 9.8: The maze.htm file

```
<HTML>

<HEAD>

<TITLE>Check it out</TITLE>
```

(continued)

```
<SCRIPT>

<!--

var defaultFrame = "<html><title>Sample</title>" +

            '<body bgcolor="#FFFFFF"> </body></html>';


var StatusMessage = 'Messages Here!' ;



function makeMessage(msg) {

        return ( '<font color="#00FFFF"><font size=4>' +

            msg +

            '</font></font> ');

}



var blueFrame = showStatus(makeMessage(StatusMessage));


function showStatus(msg) {

var str = "<html><title>Sample</title>" +

            '<body bgcolor="#FFFFFF" fgcolor="#000000">' +

            "<center>" +
```

(continued)

Using Cookies

```
                    msg +

                "</center>" +

                '</body></html>';


        return str

}



// ------------------------------------------------------------

// From Danny's Goodman's Web site.

// ------------------------------------------------------------

function getCookieVal (offset) {

  var endstr = document.cookie.indexOf (";", offset)

  if (("" + endstr) == "" || endstr == -1)

    endstr = document.cookie.length

  return unescape(document.cookie.substring(offset, endstr))

}



// ------------------------------------------------------------

// From Danny's Goodman's Web site.

// ------------------------------------------------------------
```

(continued)

```
function getCookie (name) {

  var arg = name + "=";

  var alen = arg.length;

  var clen = document.cookie.length;

  var i = 0;

  while (i < clen) {

    var j = i + alen;

    if (document.cookie.substring(i, j) == arg)

      return getCookieVal (j);

    i = document.cookie.indexOf(" ", i) + 1;

    if (i == 0) break;

  }

  return null;

}



// ------------------------------------------------------

// From Danny's Goodman's Web site.

// ------------------------------------------------------

function setCookie (name, value) {

  document.cookie = name + "=" + escape (value) + ";"

}
```

(continued)

```
function room(ndx,name,n,s,e,w,prize) {

    this.ndx=ndx

    this.name = name

    this.n = n

    this.s = s

    this.e = e

    this.w = w

    this.prize = prize

}



// ------------------------------------------------

//  See figure for  layout of rooms

// ------------------------------------------------


var rooms= new Array(7)

rooms[0] = new room(0,"foyer",-1,3,1,-1,"none");

rooms[1] = new room(1,"living",-1,4,2,0,"none");

rooms[2] = new room(2,"bedroom",-1,6,-1,1,"none");

rooms[3] = new room(3,"kitchen",0,-1,4,-1,"knife");

rooms[4] = new room(4,"Dining",1,-1,5,3,"none");
```

(continued)

```
rooms[5] = new room(5,"bathroom",-1,-1,6,4,"wrench");

rooms[6] = new room(6,"closet",2,-1,-1,5,"none");


function getCurrentRoom() {

    return getCookie("currentRoom")

    }

// Show current status (note the use of semicolons!)

function displayCurrentRoom() {

    var i = getCookie("currentRoom");

    var msg = "Room " + i;

    if (i != -1 )

        {

        msg += "<BR>"

        msg += "You are now in the " + rooms[i].name  + "<BR>"


        if (rooms[i].prize != "none")

            {

            msg += "This has a weapon ["

            msg += '<font color="red">'

            msg += rooms[i].prize + "]</font><BR>"

            }
```

(continued)

```
msg += "You can now go in these directions <BR> "

k = rooms[i].n

if (k != -1)

    {

    msg += "North to " + rooms[k].name + " (" + k + ")<BR>"

    }

k = rooms[i].s

if (k != -1)

    {

    msg += "South to " + rooms[k].name + " (" + k + ")<BR>"

    }

k = rooms[i].e

if (k != -1)

    {

    msg += "East to " + rooms[k].name + " (" + k + ")<BR>"

    }

k = rooms[i].w

if (k != -1)

    {

    msg += "West to " + rooms[k].name + " (" + k + ")<BR>"

    }
```

(continued)

```
            }

        parent.layoutFrame.document.write(showStatus(msg));

        parent.layoutFrame.document.close()

        }

// Initialize all the cookies

function initializeRooms() {

        setCookie("currentRoom", 0)

        setCookie("wrench", 0)

        setCookie("knife", 0)

}


if (getCurrentRoom() == null)  {

        initializeRooms()

}

//  Control user's movements

function moveMe(dir) {

        var i =  getCookie("currentRoom");

        if (dir == 0) i = rooms[i].n

        if (dir == 2) i = rooms[i].s

        if (dir == 3) i = rooms[i].e

        if (dir == 1) i = rooms[i].w
```

(continued)

```
            if (i == -1)

                {

                showStatus("Cannot go to " + makeMessage(dir))

                }

        else

                {

                setCookie("currentRoom",i)

                }

        displayCurrentRoom()

}


// -->

</SCRIPT>

</HEAD>

<FRAMESET ROWS="40%,*">

        <FRAMESET COLS="20%,*">

        <FRAME SRC="compass.htm" NAME="compassFrame" RESIZE>

        <FRAME SRC="javascript:top.defaultFrame"  NAME="status-
Frame" RESIZE>

        </FRAMESET>

<FRAME SRC="layout.htm" NAME="layoutFrame" onload="displayCur-
rentRoom()" RESIZE>

</FRAMESET>
```

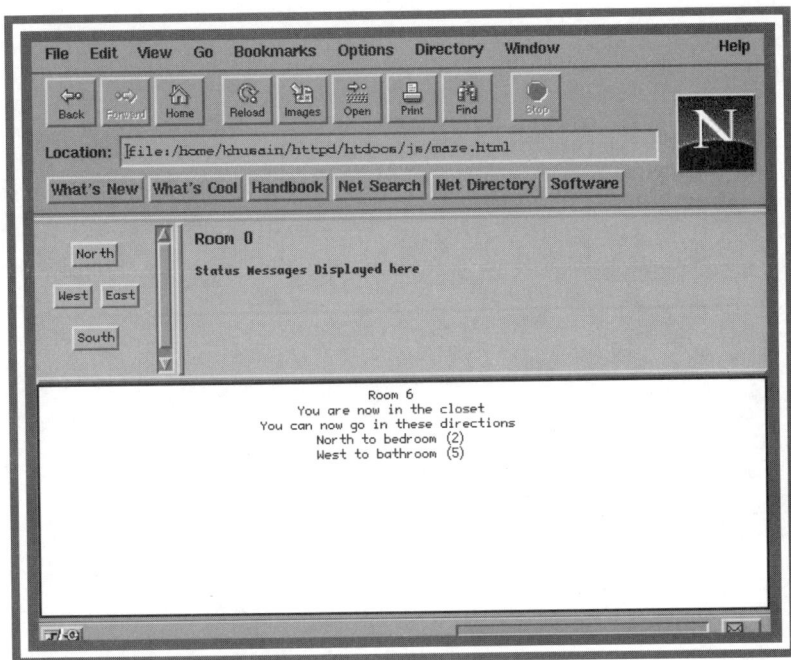

Figure 9.4 Using `maze.htm` in UNIX

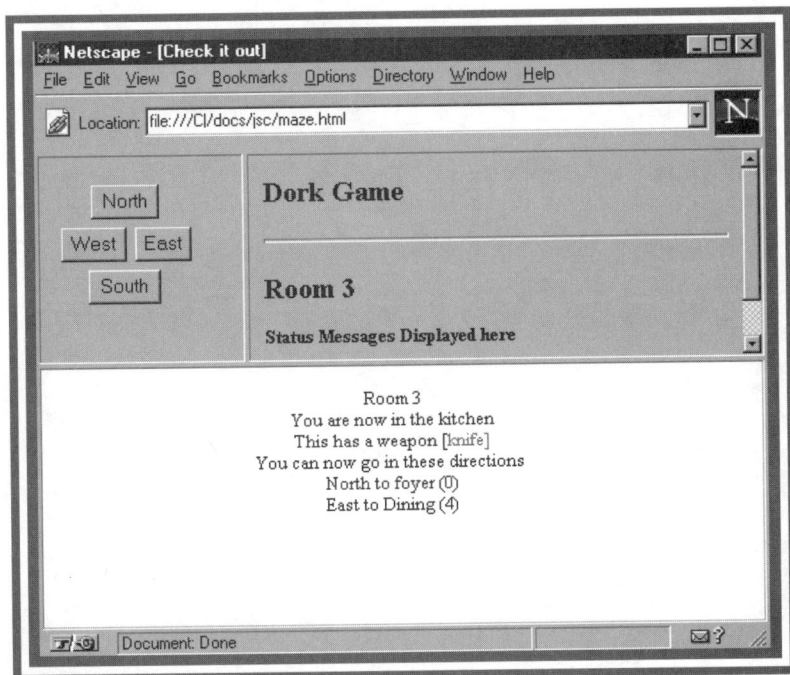

Figure 9.5 Using `maze.htm` in Windows

Program 9.9: The `layout.htm` file

```html
<HTML>

<BODY>

<H2>Dork Game</H2>

<HR>

<SCRIPT>

<!--

function doit() {

iFrame = parent.statusFrame

iFrame.document.writeln("<H2>" + "Room " +  parent.
getCurrentRoom() + "</H2>")

iFrame.document.writeln("<H4> Status Messages Displayed here
</H2>")

iFrame.document.writeln(parent.displayCurrentRoom());

iFrame.document.close();

}


doit();

//-->

</SCRIPT>

</BODY>

</HTML>
```

Program 9.10: The compass.htm file

```
<html>

<head>

<title>compass</title>

</head>

<body>

<form NAME="toto">

<table>

<td colspan=2 align=center>

      <INPUT TYPE="button" VALUE="North" NAME="North"

          onClick="parent.moveMe(0)"></td><tr>

<td align=left ><INPUT TYPE="button" VALUE="West" NAME="West"

          onClick="parent.moveMe(1)"></td>

<td align=right><INPUT TYPE="button" VALUE="East" NAME="East"

          onClick="parent.moveMe(3)"></td><tr>

<td colspan=2 align=center><INPUT TYPE="button" VALUE="South"
NAME="South"

          onClick="parent.moveMe(2)"></td><tr>

</table>

</form>

</body>

</html>
```

Program 9.11: Bill Dortch's public domain cookie functions.

```
<xmp>

<html>

<head>

<title>Cookie Functions</title>

</head>

<body>

<script language="javascript">

<!-- begin script

//

//   Cookie Functions -- "Toss Your Cookies" Version (22-Mar-96)

//

//   Written by:  Bill Dortch, hIdaho Design <bdortch@hidaho.com>

//   The following functions are released to the public domain.

//

//   This version modifies the DeleteCookie function to handle

//   the Mac date bug. The fix method was proposed by Brendan Eich

//   of Netscape.

//

// Background: A bug in the Macintosh version of Netscape Navigator
```

(continued)

```
//    versions 2.0 and 2.01 causes dates returned by the Date
object to

//    be off (ahead) by a day. Because the DeleteCookie function
deletes

//    cookies by setting the expiration date to one millisecond
prior to

//    the current time, cookies were not being deleted until a
day after

//    DeleteCookie was called on Mac platforms.

//

//    The fix code for DeleteCookie recalibrates the date prior
to

//    deleting the cookie.

//

//    ***** HERE IS THE FIX FUNCTION.   DO NOT DELETE IT!!! *****


function FixCookieDate (date) {

  var base = new Date(0);

  var skew = base.getTime(); // dawn of (Unix) time - should be
0

  if (skew > 0)  // Except on the Mac - ahead of its time

    date.setTime (date.getTime() - skew);

}


//    ***** END OF FIX FUNCTION *****
```

(continued)

```
//

// *IMPORTANT NOTE: The same bug that afflicted DeleteCookie
will also

//  affect dates you pass to SetCookie (see discussion below).
I have

//  included, but commented out, a line of code in SetCookie to
call the

//  function above. This line is commented out in SetCookie
because many

//  users of the cookie functions have already adjusted for
this bug

//  elsewhere in their code. If you would like SetCookie to
automatically

//  correct dates for you, just uncomment the call (remove the
//).

//

//  Note that the FixCookieDate() function could be used for
dates

//  elsewhere in your program as well -- not just in cookies.
However,

//  be very careful not to call it more than once for a given
Date object.

//

//
*********************************************************
*******
```

(continued)

```
//

//   Cookie Functions - Second Helping  (21-Jan-96)

//

//   The Second Helping version of the cookie functions dis-
penses with

//   my encode and decode functions, in favor of JavaScript's
new built-in

//   escape and unescape functions, which do more complete
encoding, and

//   which are probably much faster.

//

//   The new version also extends the SetCookie function, though
in

//   a backward-compatible manner, so if you used the First
Helping of

//   cookie functions as they were written, you will not need to
change any

//   code, unless you want to take advantage of the new capabil-
ities.

//

//   The following changes were made to SetCookie:

//

//   1.  The expires parameter is now optional - that is, you
can omit

//   it instead of passing it null to expire the cookie at the
end
```

(continued)

```
//          of the current session.

//

//    2.  An optional path parameter has been added.

//

//    3.  An optional domain parameter has been added.

//

//    4.  An optional secure parameter has been added.

//

//  For information on the significance of these parameters, and

//  and on cookies in general, please refer to the official cookie

//  spec, at:

//

//        http://www.netscape.com/newsref/std/cookie_spec.htm

//

//

//  "Internal" function to return the decoded value of a cookie

//

function getCookieVal (offset) {

  var endstr = document.cookie.indexOf (";", offset);
```

(continued)

```
if (endstr == -1)

    endstr = document.cookie.length;

  return unescape(document.cookie.substring(offset, endstr));

}


//

//  Function to return the value of the cookie specified by
"name".

//    name - String object containing the cookie name.

//    returns - String object containing the cookie value, or
null if

//      the cookie does not exist.

//

function GetCookie (name) {

  var arg = name + "=";

  var alen = arg.length;

  var clen = document.cookie.length;

  var i = 0;

  while (i < clen) {

    var j = i + alen;

    if (document.cookie.substring(i, j) == arg)

      return getCookieVal (j);
```

(continued)

```
        i = document.cookie.indexOf(" ", i) + 1;

        if (i == 0) break;

    }

    return null;

}



//

//   Function to create or update a cookie.

//      name - String object containing the cookie name.

//      value - String object containing the cookie value.
May contain

//         any valid string characters.

//      [expires] - Date object containing the expiration data
of the cookie.  If

//         omitted or null, expires the cookie at the end of the
current session.

//      [path] - String object indicating the path for which the
cookie is valid.

//         If omitted or null, uses the path of the calling
document.

//      [domain] - String object indicating the domain for which
the cookie is

//         valid.  If omitted or null, uses the domain of the
calling document.
```

(continued)

```
//     [secure] - Boolean (true/false) value indicating whether
cookie transmission

//        requires a secure channel (HTTPS).

//

//   The first two parameters are required.  The others, if
supplied, must

//   be passed in the order listed above.  To omit an unused
optional field,

//   use null as a place holder.  For example, to call SetCookie
using name,

//   value and path, you would code:

//

//        SetCookie ("myCookieName", "myCookieValue", null, "/");

//

//   Note that trailing omitted parameters do not require a
placeholder.

//

//   To set a secure cookie for path "/myPath", that expires
after the

//   current session, you might code:

//

//        SetCookie (myCookieVar, cookieValueVar, null, "/
myPath", null, true);

//
```

(continued)

```javascript
function SetCookie (name, value) {

  var argv = SetCookie.arguments;

  var argc = SetCookie.arguments.length;

  var expires = (argc > 2) ? argv[2] : null;

  var path = (argc > 3) ? argv[3] : null;

  var domain = (argc > 4) ? argv[4] : null;

  var secure = (argc > 5) ? argv[5] : false;

//if (expires!=null) FixCookieDate(expires); //*** Uncomment
this line for automatic date correction (see above)

  document.cookie = name + "=" + escape (value) +

    ((expires == null) ? "" : ("; expires=" + expires.
toGMTString())) +

    ((path == null) ? "" : ("; path=" + path)) +

    ((domain == null) ? "" : ("; domain=" + domain)) +

    ((secure == true) ? "; secure" : "");

}



//  Function to delete a cookie. (Sets expiration date to
current date/time)

//    name - String object containing the cookie name
```

(continued)

```
//

function DeleteCookie (name) {

  var exp = new Date();

  FixCookieDate (exp); // Correct for Mac bug

  exp.setTime (exp.getTime() - 1);  // This cookie is history

  var cval = GetCookie (name);

  if (cval != null)

    document.cookie = name + "=" + cval + "; expires=" +
exp.toGMTString();

}


//

//  Example

//

var expdate = new Date ();

expdate.setTime (expdate.getTime() + (24 * 60 * 60 * 1000)); /
/ 24 hrs from now (mod Mac bug)

SetCookie ("ccpath", "http://www.hidaho.com/colorcenter/",
expdate);

SetCookie ("ccname", "hIdaho Design ColorCenter", expdate);

SetCookie ("tempvar", "This is a temporary cookie.");
```

(continued)

```
SetCookie ("ubiquitous", "This cookie will work anywhere in
this domain",null,"/");

SetCookie ("paranoid", "This cookie requires secure
communications",expdate,"/",null,true);

SetCookie ("goner", "This cookie must die!");

document.write (document.cookie + "<br>");

DeleteCookie ("goner");

document.write ("ccpath = " + GetCookie("ccpath") + "<br>");

document.write ("ccname = " + GetCookie("ccname") + "<br>");

document.write ("tempvar = " + GetCookie("tempvar") + "<br>");

// end script -->

</script>

</body>

</html>

</xmp>
```

For more information on cookies and how to use them, check out the Web page at http://www.hidaho.com.

Summary

This chapter has covered a lot of ground. Keep the following in mind as we leave this chapter:

- *Loading images in JavaScript is possible with the IMG tag. JavaScript is capable of loading GIF, JPEG, and even XBM files.*

- *The GIF image offers the most flexible way to create images and animation flows. The speed has a price in that the sequence and contents of images are fixed within the GIF image.*

- *By periodically querying the server for successive frames in an animation sequence, you can do some crude animation. The cost of this process is a high load on the network as well as subjecting the animation to delays of the network.*

- *Locations on images can be mapped to call JavaScript functions using an image mapping tag <MAP>. Using the <MAP> tags lets you define "hot spots" on an image that, when clicked on by a mouse, call a JavaScript function.*

- *Cookies in a JavaScript document allow the JavaScript application to retain the state of a specific client. By using freely available cookie management functions, you can create powerful applications to store state information about a client in between successive pages.*

Coming Up

In the next chapter, we will cover JavaScript plug-ins that further enhance your Netscape browser.

PART THREE

Advanced JavaScript:
Using LiveConnect and LiveWire

Mastering JavaScript hasn't been all that difficult. Once you understand the built-in objects and what they can do, the rest is just programming. But the real power of JavaScript lies in its ability to connect the disparate elements of Netscape's Internet Application Architecture to create Internet applications that offer far greater capabilities than JavaScript alone can provide. Part III introduces Livewire, Netscape's Web server management tool and server-side JavaScript development environment, and LiveConnect, which is the umbrella term that describes communication between Netscape plug-ins, Java applets, and JavaScript scripts in Navigator 3.0.

In Chapter 10, "Working with Plug-Ins," we go through a number of examples illustrating ways you can control and manipulate plug-ins using JavaScript, including a complete example of how to access the exposed properties of LiveConnect-enabled plug-ins.

Chapter 11, "JavaScript and Java," looks at communication with Java applets. Again, exposed properties of applets are available to JavaScript scripts, and the combination allows Web pages that can communicate more information to users, and permit more flexibility in the user interface.

Finally, Chapter 12, "An Introduction to Server-Side JavaScript and LiveWire," offers a brief look at Livewire, a fairly extensive Web server management tool, which includes a server-side JavaScript implementation. A complete Livewire example using server-side JavaScript is included, and although it clearly shows how easy it is to use your existing client-side JavaScript knowledge to create end-to-end Internet applications using Livewire, a complete discussion of Livewire is beyond the scope of this book. Chapter 12, however, offers ample motivation, if you should choose to pursue Livewire further.

CHAPTER

10

WORKING WITH PLUG-INS

- Manipulate Plug-Ins Using the <EMBED> Tag

- Detect Plug-Ins Using JavaScript

- Control LiveConnect-Enabled Plug-Ins

JavaScript examples in this chapter only work with either Navigator 2.x or Navigator 3.0, as indicated by the chapter subheading. None of the examples in this chapter work with Microsoft's Internet Explorer. Examples in the section "Using LiveConnect To Control Plug-Ins" only work with Navigator 3.0 or Navigator Gold 3.0 because it contains Netscape's LiveConnect Feature.

Starting with Navigator 2.0, Netscape introduced their plug-in API, which lets third-party developers extend the capabilities of the Navigator browser. Plug-ins are dynamic code modules that are loaded when Navigator starts up and become a functional part of the Navigator execution environment. Plug-ins extend Navigator's architecture by supporting new Multimedia Internet Mail Extension (MIME) types and network protocols.

Developers have embraced the plug-in API because it lets them add support for their existing products quickly and effectively. Such companies as Adobe, Apple, Farrallon, and RealAudio have created plug-ins for Navigator that offer native support for their proprietary document formats or network protocols.

Unlike Java Applets, which are compiled into a platform-neutral format that lets them run on any platform running Navigator, plug-ins must be developed separately for each platform. Thus, some plug-ins may only be available for certain platforms. Plug-ins can take advantage of platform-specific features, such as the Macintosh Speech Manager under MacOS or the Windows Registry under Microsoft Windows 95 and NT.

The plug-in API is an open standard that Netscape has made available to other browser developers. Microsoft supports the Netscape plug-in API on some versions of their Internet Explorer browser.[1]

This chapter describes how to access plug-ins and will discuss the topics presented above. JavaScript under Navigator 2.0 allows limited access to plug-ins, but there are a few useful techniques we will explore in this chapter. JavaScript under Navigator 3.0, on the other hand, has plug-in and MIME-type objects, which are properties of the Navigator object. We can use these objects to determine whether a particular MIME type is supported. Also, using the LiveConnect feature of Navigator 3.0, JavaScript scripts can directly access plug-in routines through Java public classes defined in the plug-in code.

The <EMBED> Tag

There are two ways to reference foreign file types from within Web pages. One way is to simply place the file in a hypertext link, as follows:

---

1. As of this book's publication, only the Macintosh version of Internet Explorer 2.x and the Windows 95 version of Internet Explorer 3.0 supports the Netscape plug-in API

```
<a href="http://www.prenhall.com/magazine.pdf">Click
here to view this Acrobat PDF file</a>
```

The other, more flexible, method is to use the <EMBED> tag. The <EMBED> tag was devised by Netscape so that users could reference other types of content from within HTML pages. The attributes of the <EMBED> tag are shown in Table 10.1. You use the SRC attribute of the <EMBED> tag to reference files that are recognized by your installed plug-ins. If we wanted to load a document in Acrobat's PDF (Portable Document Format) to be read by Adobe's Amber plug-in, for example, we could use the following <EMBED> tag:

```
<EMBED SRC="magazine.pdf">
```

When a user downloads a Web page containing an <EMBED> tag, the file pointed to by the SRC attribute is automatically downloaded to the user's Web browser.

Table 10.1   <EMBED> Tag Attributes

<EMBED> tag attribute	Description	Example
NAME = any string (Navigator 3.0 only)	Used by JavaScript to reference Java public classes defined in the plug-in.	<EMBED NAME='big-movie' SRC='big-movie.avi'>
HIDDEN = value (Navigator 3.0 only)	Indicates whether the plug-in is visible on the page. The value can be either true (the default) or false. A value of true overrides the values of HEIGHT and WIDTH, making the plug-in zero-sized.	<EMBED SRC='big-movie.avi' HIDDEN='true'>
PALETTE = value	indicates the mode of the plug-in's color palette. The value can be either foreground or background (the default). The palette mode is only relevant on the Windows platform.	<EMBED SRC='big-movie.avi' PALETTE='foreground'>

(continued)

The <EMBED> Tag

<EMBED> tag attribute	Description	Example
PLUGINSPAGE= URL (Navigator 3.0 only)	indicates the location of instructions on installing the plug-in. The URL is used by the assisted installation process if the plug-in registered for the MIME type of this EMBED tag is not found.	<EMBED SRC='big-movie.avi' PLUGIN-SPAGE='http://www.netscape.com'>
SRC = URL	The URL of the source document.	<EMBED SRC='http://www.nowhere.com/big-movie.avi'>
TYPE = mime type	optionally indicates the MIME type of the EMBED tag, which in turn determines which plug-in is loaded to handle this EMBED tag. Either the SRC attribute or the TYPE attribute is required in an EMBED tag. Use TYPE instead of SRC for plug-ins that require no data (for example, a plug-in that draws an analog clock) or plug-ins that fetch all their data dynamically.	<EMBED TYPE='application/clock'>
WIDTH = size in pixels HEIGHT = size in pixels	specifies the width and heigth of the embedded document, in pixels.	<EMBED SRC='big-movie.avi' WIDTH=200 HEIGHT=250>
UNITS = units	defines the measurement unit used by the HEIGHT and WIDTH attributes. The value can be either pixels (the default) or en (half the point size).	<EMBED SRC='big-movie.avi' WIDTH=200 HEIGHT=250 UNITS='en'>
PARAMETER_NAME = PARAMETER_VALUE	Optional, vendor specified, parameters to send to plug-ins. Unrecognized parameters are ignored.	<EMBED SRC='big-movie.avi' loop=yes interpolate=no controls=no>

Unlike simple links, the <EMBED> tag lets you specify optional parameters to control the plug-in. These parameters are vendor-specific, so you'll have to consult your vendor documentation to find out what parameters work with your plug-in.

A reference to an ASAP WebShow file referenced in a Web page might look like this:

```
<EMBED SRC="http:/www.mysite.com/mystuff.asp" WIDTH=400
HEIGHT=300  AutoAdvance=on LoopBack=on>
```

Here we have set two of ASAP's parameters, AutoAdvance and LoopBack, to "on." This will make the ASAP WebShow presentation, `mystuff.asp`, loop continuously.

MIME Types and Plug-Ins

Plug-ins extend the functionality of Navigator by supporting types other than the default types supported by Navigator. When files are downloaded to the Navigator browser from Web servers using Hyper-Text Transport Protocol (HTTP), the Web server sends along the MIME type to identify the contents of the `file`.[2] Your Web browser determines how to display the file based on the MIME type sent by the Web browser. Table 10.2 shows the MIME types of some common file formats.

The Netscape Navigator browser has two mechanisms for displaying files that it cannot display natively: plug-ins and Helper applications. Navigator itself can only handle a few types of files natively (i.e., without using plug-ins or Helper applications). They are HTML files, plain text files, GIF images, JPEG images, JavaScript scripts, Java applets, and X-Window bitmap images.

After Navigator receives the MIME type of the file being downloaded, it checks to see if it's a MIME type that it can handle natively. If it is, the file is displayed in the browser. If it isn't a MIME type Nav-

---

2. NOTE: If you use a protocol such as FTP, instead of HTTP, no MIME information is sent from the Web server. In that case, Navigator will use the file extension to determine which plug-in to use.

igator handles natively, it checks to see if it is handled by an installed plug-in and hands the file to the plug-in. If none of the installed plug-ins handle the file, it checks to see if a Helper application is configured to handle the MIME type. If a Helper application is configured, Navigator launches the Helper application and hands the file to it.

Finally, if the file has a MIME type that isn't supported natively or by an installed plug-in or configured Helper application, Navigator displays a dialog box that lets the user choose to either save the document to disk or hand the document off to another application installed on his/her computer.

Table 10.2 lists some common MIME types. A complete, up-to-date list is available on the Internet at the Internet Assigned Numbers Authority web site.

```
http://www.iana.org/
```

Table 10.2   Some common MIME types

File type	File extension(s)	MIME type
Web page	.htm, .html	text/html
JavaScript script	.js	application/x-javascript
plain text	.txt, .text	text/plain
JPEG image	.jpg, .jpeg	image/jpeg
Microsoft Word document	.doc	application/msword
GIF image	.gif	image/gif
WAV audio	.wav	audio/wav

Plug-Ins in Navigator 2.0

Navigator 2.0 offers limited communication between JavaScript and plug-ins, though there are a few tricks worth noting. The next few sections will discuss ways you can access and query the plug-ins installed in your Navigator 2.0 browser.

Listing Your Installed Plug-ins

We'll start by using the `about:` protocol to list the plug-ins (if any) currently installed in Navigator. Type:

```
about:plugins
```

into the Location: window of your Navigator browser and Navigator will create a document listing the MIME types supported by your installed plug-in modules.

Alternatively, you can use the following HTML statement:

```
<A HREF="about:plugins">List plug-ins</A>
```

Because there is no way for JavaScript to grab hold of any of the information in the document created by `about:plugins`, you can't do anything further with the information offered by the `about:plugins` statement.

Using JavaScript to Pass Parameters to an <EMBED> Tag

Because an <EMBED> tag is part of your Web pages, you can use JavaScript to create it dynamically from within a JavaScript script. This can be useful if you want to offer the user the opportunity to configure plug-in options or to use JavaScript to calculate a parameter to pass to a plug-in.

In order to demonstrate passing parameters to plug-ins, we'll use a plug-in called mBED. It is developed and sold by mBED Software of San Francisco, California and is available for download from their web site, `http://www.mbed.com/`. The mBED plug-in lets developers add multimedia capabilities to web pages through the use of mBED scripts, called `mbedlets`.

Some plug-ins let you pass parameters using the <EMBED> tag, others don't.[3] The mBED plug-in does allow it, so we'll use it for our example. In the <EMBED> tag example listed in Program 10.1, the variable DSTR is set to the current date and then passed to mbedlet contained in the file example.mbd, which is shown in Figure 10.1.

Program 10.1: Passing parameters to the mbedlet contained in the file example.mbd using the <EMBED> tag

```
<SCRIPT LANGUAGE='JavaScript'>

today=new Date()

document.write('<EMBED SRC="example.mbd" WIDTH=402 HEIGHT=52
DSTR=\"'+today+'\">')

</SCRIPT>
```

Figure 10.1: example.mbd

```
<mbedlet version=1.0>

        <SLOTS>

                DSTR="PASS ME A VALUE!"

        </SLOTS>

        <PLAYERS>

                <TEXT NAME=HELLO>

                        <PROPERTIES>

                                VISIBLE
```

(continued)

3. Passing parameters with the <EMBED> tag only works if the plug-in supports parameter passing with the <EMBED> tag. Consult the plug-in vendors' documentation for details.

```
            VALUE=$DSTR

            RECT=0,0,400,50

            SMOOTH

            JUSTIFY=CENTER

            SIZE=24

        </PROPERTIES>

        <HANDLERS>

            <MOUSEENTER>

            HELLO HIDE

            </MOUSEENTER>

            <MOUSELEAVE>

            HELLO SHOW

            </MOUSELEAVE>

        </HANDLERS>

      </TEXT>

    </PLAYERS>

  </MBEDLET>
```

Opening a Stream to a Plug-in

In Navigator 2.0, JavaScript offers a way to open a direct stream to a plug-in using the open method of the document object. The format is:

```
document.open('[MIME type]')
```

If you have mBED's plug-in loaded, you can open up a stream to it using the `document.open` method:

```
document.open("application/mbedlet")
```

`application/mbedlet` is the MIME type handled by the mBED plug-in.

The `document.open` call opens a stream to the mBED plug-in. Subsequent write calls will write directly to the plug-in. In the example in Program 10.2, we write an `mbedlet` script directly to the mBED plug-in. It is executed as soon as the `mywin.document.close()` statement is executed.

Program 10.2: This JavaScript script writes an mbedlet directly to the mBED plug-in

```
<script language='javascript'>

mywin=window.open("","mbed","width=302,height=52,tool-
bar=0,menubar=0")

mywin.document.open("application/mbedlet")

mywin.document.writeln("<mbedlet version=1.0>")

mywin.document.writeln("<PLAYERS>")

mywin.document.writeln("<TEXT NAME=HELLO>")

mywin.document.writeln("<PROPERTIES>")

mywin.document.writeln("VISIBLE")

mywin.document.writeln("VALUE=HELLO WORLD")

mywin.document.writeln("RECT=0,0,300,50")

mywin.document.writeln("SMOOTH")
```

(continued)

```
mywin.document.writeln("JUSTIFY=CENTER")

mywin.document.writeln("SIZE=24")

mywin.document.writeln("</PROPERTIES>")

mywin.document.writeln("<HANDLERS>")

mywin.document.writeln("<MOUSEENTER>")

mywin.document.writeln("HELLO HIDE")

mywin.document.writeln("</MOUSEENTER>")

mywin.document.writeln("<MOUSELEAVE>")

mywin.document.writeln("HELLO SHOW")

mywin.document.writeln("</MOUSELEAVE>")

mywin.document.writeln("</HANDLERS>")

mywin.document.writeln("</TEXT>")

mywin.document.writeln("</PLAYERS>")

mywin.document.writeln("</MBEDLET>")

mywin.document.close()

 </script>
```

Testing for Plug-ins Using JavaScript

Our previous examples work fine if the user is using Navigator 2.0 and has the mBED plug-in loaded on their machine. But what happens if the user doesn't have the appropriate plug-in installed? Ideally, we would like to use JavaScript to first test to see if the user has a particular plug-in installed. Unfortunately, in Navigator 2.0, there is no clean way of telling whether a user has a particular plug-in installed.

Netscape's documentation recommends using the following function to test for the existence of a plug-in. The following routine tests for the existence of Macromedia's Shockwave plug-in. If it isn't found, we display the GIF file `plugpic.gif`.

```
<SCRIPT Language='JavaScript'>

function probePlugIn(mimeType) {

    var havePlugIn = false

    var tiny = window.open("", "teensy", "width=1,height=1")

    if (tiny != null) {

        if (tiny.document.open(mimeType) != null)

            havePlugIn = true

        tiny.close()

    }

    return havePlugIn

}



var haveShockWavePlugIn = probePlugIn("application/x-director")

if (!haveShockWavePlugIn)

    document.write('<IMG SRC="plugpic.gif">')

</SCRIPT>
```

This script causes an annoying dialog box to appear if the user doesn't have the tested plug-in loaded (see Figure 10.2). There is no workaround but, as we'll see in the next section, the problem is fixed in Navigator 3.0.

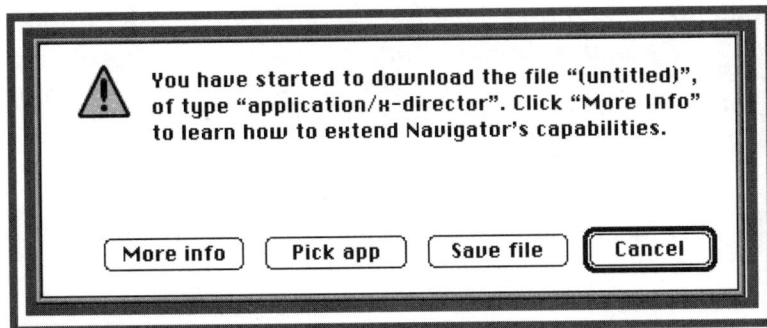

You have started to download the file "(untitled)", of type "application/x-director". Click "More Info" to learn how to extend Navigator's capabilities.

More info   Pick app   Save file   Cancel

Figure 10.1 An annoying dialog box alerting users that a plug-in referenced by an <EMBED> tag is not installed on their machine

Plug-Ins in Navigator 3.0

Working with plug-ins is much easier in Navigator 3.0 than in Navigator 2.0. However, you can still use all the previous Navigator 2.0 scripts with Navigator 3.0. Navigator 3.0 introduces two new objects that are properties of the navigator object, mimeTypes and plugins.

The mimeTypes and Plugins Objects

We can use these two new objects to determine whether a particular plug-in is installed and what MIME type(s) it handles. We can then use that knowledge to decide whether to download a particular file, such as a WAV sound file.

The new mimeTypes object is an array of mimeTypes. The array can be indexed by either an integer index or the type property. The mimeTypes object has the following properties:

1. *length—number of elements in the array*

2. *type—the name of the MIME type, for example: video/ mpeg, audio/x-wav*

3. *description—Description of the type*

4. *suffixes—String listing possible file suffixes (also known as filename extensions) for the MIME type. This property*

is a string consisting of each valid suffix, typically three letters long, separated by commas.

5. *enabledPlugin—a reference to the plugins object that handles the MIME type*

The new plugins object is an array of plugins and has the following properties:

1. *length—Number of elements in the array*

2. *name—Name of the plug-in*

3. *filename—Name of the plug-in file on disk*

4. *description—Description supplied by the plug-in itself*

5. *[...]—Array of mimeType objects, indexed by number or type, that plug-in can handle*

The plugins array can be indexed by either an integer index or the name property. The mimeTypes and Plugins arrays are filled by Navigator with lists of all the mimeTypes and Plugins currently installed.

The Refresh Method

The plugins object also has a method, called `refresh`, that causes Navigator to look for any newly installed plug-ins and update itself accordingly (normally, you'd have to quit Navigator and restart it to use a new plug-in). Using `true` as the argument to refresh:

```
navigator.plugins.refresh(true)
```

will also cause Navigator to reload any page that might change as a result of a new plug-in being installed. A call to refresh without any argument will not reload any page.

The refresh method enables you to guide the user through the installation of a plug-in and then call this method at the end to make the plug-in active, without requiring the user to quit and re-start Navigator. You can also use this method to verify that plug-in installation was successful: a script could assign `navigator.plugins` to a local variable, call `navigator.plugins.refresh`, and then compare the current `navigator.plugins` with the saved copy to see if it changed in the appropriate ways.

Listing Your Installed Plug-ins

We'll start off by writing a script that displays the names of all your installed plug-ins and all the MIME types supported. The MIME types listing includes all the MIME types supported internally by Navigator, all the MIME types supported by your installed plug-ins, and all the MIME types supported by your various configured Helper applications. The list of all your currently supported MIME types can also be found in Navigator's Helper configuration window, which you can view by pulling down your Options menu, selecting General Preferences, and clicking on the Helpers tab. In Navigator 2.0x, the Helpers tab does not necessarily show all the MIME types supported by your installed plug-ins.

```
<SCRIPT Language="JavaScript">

document.write("<h3>Installed Plugins</h3>")

for (var i=0; i < navigator.plugins.length; i++)  {

        document.write(navigator.plugins[i].name+"<BR>")

}

document.write("<h3>MIME types supported internally and by
Plugins and Helper apps</h3>")

for (var i=0; i < navigator.mimeTypes.length; i++)  {

        document.write(navigator.mimeTypes[i].type+"<BR>")

}

</SCRIPT>
```

The list of all supported MIME types includes those that are listed on the Helpers tab as "Unknown: Prompt User". That means that there is no helper application or plug-in configured to handle the

MIME type. Unfortunately, that means that if we search the complete list of mimeTypes for a particular MIME type, we can't be certain that the MIME type will be handled by an installed plug-in or Helper application.

The list of supported MIME types only tells us what MIME types our browser will recognize, but it doesn't tell us what the browser will do with the MIME type. It might hand it off to a plug-in, a helper application, or return an error message. To find out what the browser will do with a particular MIME type, we need to use the enabledPlugin property of the mimeTypes object.

Determining What Plug-Ins are Enabled

The list of all supported MIME types tells us what MIME types are supported by a browser. The list of installed plug-ins tells us what plug-ins are installed. However, neither of these lists tells us which plug-ins are enabled. The enabled plug-ins are the ones that will actually be launched by Navigator to handle embedded documents.

Installed Plug-Ins are not Necessarily Enabled

Just because a plug-in is installed in your browser does not mean that it will automatically be launched to handle the MIME types it supports. The plug-in must first be enabled. By default, Navigator will enable plug-ins in alphabetical order when you start your browser. So, if two plug-ins handle the same MIME type, the first one that Navigator loads, alphabetically, will be enabled to handle the plug-in. In the Macintosh version of Navigator 3.0, you can change which plug-in is enabled by going to the Options menu, selecting General Preferences, and selecting the Helpers tab. The easiest way to find out whether a plug-in is enabled is to select the About Plugins menu on your Navigator browser.

To determine what plug-in is enabled to handle a particular MIME type, we use the enabledPlugin property of the mimeTypes array. The following test returns true if the LiveAudio plug-in is enabled to handle WAVE audio files:

```
plugenabled = (navigator.mimeTypes["audio/wav"].
enabledPlugin.name == "LiveAudio")
```

If we simply wanted to check to find out if there is some plug-in enabled to take care of WAVE files, but we don't care what plug-in, we could use:

```
plugenabled = (navigator.mimeTypes["audio/wav"].
enabledPlugin != null)
```

The enabledPlugin property is the only way you can test for an enabled plug-in. Unfortunately, a bug in Navigator 3.0 (all platforms) causes taint errors when the enabledPlugin property is used when subsequent statements reference the plug-in. As this book goes to press, there is no workaround.

In Navigator 3.0, using the enabledPlugins property causes taint to accumulate. Any subsequent references to the plug-in in your script causes a "tainted JavaScript datum" error to occur.

Determining What Plug-Ins are Installed

Although testing with the enabledPlugin property is the only way to guarantee that a particular plug-in will be launched for a MIME type, there may be times when you only needto know that a plug-in is installed, especially if the plug-in is unique and is therefore unlikely to duplicate the capabilities of other installed plug-ins. The following script demonstrates three tests which you can use to determine if a plug-in is installed. They do not tell you if the installed plug-in is enabled.

```
<SCRIPT Language="JavaScript">

var hasplugin = navigator.plugins["maczilla"]

var hasmimetype = navigator.mimeTypes["application/mbedlet"]

var plughasmime = navigator.plugins["LiveAudio"]["audio/wav"]

if (hasplugin)

    document.writeln("<EMBED SRC='jungle.mov'>")

if (hasmimetype)

    document.writeln("<EMBED SRC='forest.mbd'>")

if (plughasmime)

    document.writeln("<EMBED SRC='sounds.wav'>")

</SCRIPT>
```

The script shows the Quicktime movie, jungle.mov, only if you have the maczilla plug-in installed. It shows the mbedlet, forest.mbd, only if you have a helper app or plug-in supporting the MIME type application/mbedlet. It plays the WAV sound file, sounds.wav, only if you have the LiveAudio plug-in installed and it supports the MIME type audio/wav.

Plug-Ins and Browsers Without JavaScript

There is currently no good general way to test browsers to see if they support plug-ins. We recommend simply asking the user whether they have a particular plug-in installed before they click on a link corresponding to a download for a plug-in.

It is interesting to note that there are already browsers appearing, such as Microsoft's Internet Explorer 2.x for Macintosh, that don't support JavaScript, yet they do support plug-ins.

For browsers that don't support plug-ins or the <EMBED> tag, there is still one possible solution. The <NOEMBED>...</NOEMBED> tag was originally designed to contain HTML statements to be intepreted by a browser that doesn't have the appropriate plug-in or that can't understand the <EMBED> tag. Unfortunately, in practice, some browsers ignore the <NOEMBED> tag. All browsers that support plug-ins disregard the <NOEMBED> tag, even if they don't have the proper plug-in loaded. However, for browsers that don't recognize the <EMBED> tag, <NOEMBED> may still work. Here is an example of a page using the <NOEMBED> tag:

```
<EMBED SRC="mystuff.asp"  WIDTH=400 HEIGHT=300  AutoAdvance=
on LoopBack=on>

<NOEMBED>

You don't have the ASAP WebShow plug-in for Navigator! Try this

<a href="htmlver.html">HTML version of the show</a>.

</NOEMBED>
```

Because there are many types of Web browsers in use, each with somewhat different feature sets, it's difficult for a developer to work around them all. However, using a combination of JavaScript, the <NOEMBED> tag, and instructional text should adequately support most users.

Using LiveConnect to Control Plug-Ins

With the introduction of Navigator 3.0 and it's LiveConnect capabilities, Netscape gave plug-in developers the tools to let their plug-ins communicate with Java applets and JavaScript scripts. Netscape implemented the Java Runtime Interface (JRI), which lets developers define Java classes in their C++ code, and added the JRI to their plug-in API. This new Netscape plug-in API lets plug-ins include public Java classes that can be referenced from JavaScript scripts as well as Java Applets. Nearly all plug-in developers have rewritten their plug-ins with the new Netscape plug-in API, which means that these new plug-ins can be referenced from JavaScript scripts and Java Applets.

LiveConnect Can Be Turned On or Off

The LiveConnect capability of the Navigator 3.0 browser is turned on when both the "Enable Java" and "Enable Java-Script" check boxes are checked under the Options menu, in the Network Preferences selection, on the Languages tab. If either box is unchecked, LiveConnect is turned off.

How Plug-in Routines are Accessed Using JavaScript

Accessing plug-in routines from JavaScript is straightforward. Plug-in files become JavaScript properties of the current document when you use the NAME attribute with your <EMBED> tag. For example, the following <EMBED> tag creates a document property named smoothsnd.

```
<EMBED NAME=smoothsnd SRC="http://www.soundlab.com/
jazz.wav">
```

This <EMBED> tag will cause a plug-in to load the Windows WAVE sound file `jazz.wav`. We can then use `smoothsnd` as a property of the current document to control the plug-in handling this sound.

If we know that the user has a LiveConnect-enabled plug-in, and that plug-in supports a function named play that plays the sound, we can use play as a method for our sound. We could then play the sound by using the following in our scripts: This statement will cause the plug-in to play the sound file jazz.wav.

```
document.smoothsnd.play()
```

In practice, we would first make sure that our plug-in is LiveConnect aware before accessing the function play. To do this, we test to see if the smoothsnd property has any methods.

```
if (document.smoothsnd != null)

    document.smoothsnd.play()
```

We might also go a step further and test to see whether the play method exists:

```
if (document.smoothsnd != null) {

    if (document.smoothsnd.play != null)

        document.smoothsnd.play()

}
```

Unfortunately, we must first embed the sound with the <EMBED> tag using the NAME attribute in order to do the accesibility test above. If we choose to delay the <EMBED>, say, by putting it in a document.write statement, we have no way to test whether the plug-in is LiveConnect aware. Another problem is that, even if the plug-in is LiveConnect aware, any JavaScript accessible functions are vendor specific. So, for example, the function play() might be used by one plug-in vendor to start playing a sound, while another plug-in vendor might name the function start().

Consult Vendor Docs for LiveConnect-
accessible Functions

When writing scripts for LiveConnect aware plug-ins, you
must consult the vendor's documentation to determine the
names and usage of any accessible plug-in functions.

Two Examples: Controlling LiveAudio

Netscape bundles a plug-in with Navigator 3.0, called LiveAudio,
that is LiveConnect aware. As you might imagine, LiveAudio plays
back audio files, Netscape has defined Java public methods in
LiveAudio that lets you control it from JavaScript scripts and Java
applets. In this section, we demonstrate using JavaScript to control
the LiveAudio plug-in. LiveAudio offers up an impressive array of
accessible functions which are listed in Table 10.3. We can use all of
these functions in our JavaScript scripts.

Table 10.3 Functions available to control a loaded LiveAudio
plug-in

Functions	Purpose
Control functions	
play('TRUE | FALSE', 'URL of sound')	Using TRUE as the argument causes the sound to begin playing when it's finished loading. The default is FALSE. A second, optional, argument can be the URL of a sound file you want to load.
stop()	Stops playing the sound.
pause()	Pauses a currently playing sound.

(continued)

Functions	Purpose
start_time(int seconds)	This integer value tells LiveAudio to start playing the EMBEDed sound at a particular point (i.e., if you'd like a sound to start thirty seconds into piece, set this value to 30).
end_time(int seconds)	This integer value tells LiveAudio to stop playing the EMBEDed sound at a particular point (i.e., if you'd like a sound to stop thirty seconds into piece, set this value to 30).
setvol(int percent)	This value should be a number between 0 and 100 (0-100%). This sets the volume for the sound that is playing. The default volume level is the current system volume.
fade_to(int to_percent)	This value should be a number between 0 and 100 (0-100%). This fades the current volume for the sound which is playing to the specified volume percentage.
fade_from_to(int from_percent,int to_percent)	Values should be numbers between 0 and 100 (0-100%). Fades the current volume for the sound which is playing from the from_percent volume to the to_percent volume.
start_at_beginning()	Starts playing the sound at the beginining of the sound (overrides a start_time()).
stop_at_end()	Stops playing the sound at the endof the sound (overrides an end_time()).

State Indicators

IsReady()	Returns TRUE if the plug-in instance has completed loading
IsPlaying()	Returns TRUE if the sound is currently playing
IsPaused()	Returns TRUE if the sound is currently paused
GetVolume()	Returns the current volume as a percent

The LiveAudio <EMBED> Tag Has Other Options

For Navigator 2.0 browsers, and other non-LiveConnect aware browsers, the LiveAudio <EMBED> tag offers alternatives to the functions in Table 10.3. For example, for these browsers, we can implement a play button using the LiveAudio <EMBED> tag option, PLAYBUTTON. Consult Netscape's LiveAudio documentation for details.

```
<HTML>

<HEAD>

<SCRIPT LANGUAGE="JavaScript">

<!-- Begin hiding JavaScript

// BUTTON.HTM -- A simple example of LiveConnect.

// This script requires Navigator 3.0 and the LiveAudio
plug-in

//

function playsound ()  {

if (document.smoothsnd == null)
```

(continued)

```
        alert("The plug-in handling WAV files is not LiveConnect
aware.")

    else {

        if (document.smoothsnd.play == null)

            alert("This script assumes the LiveAudio plug-in
is handling WAV files.")

        else  {

                document.smoothsnd.play(false)

            }

        }

}

//   End hiding JavaScript -->

</SCRIPT>

</HEAD>

<BODY>

<h1>PLAY A JAZZY SOUND</h1>

<EMBED name='smoothsnd' SRC='JAZZ.WAV' HIDDEN=TRUE
AUTOSTART=FALSE MASTERSOUND>

<form>

<input type=button  onclick="playsound()" value="PLAY SOUND">

</form>

</BODY>

</HTML>
```

The LiveConnect aspect of BUTTON.HTM is straightforward. We first use the <EMBED> tag to embed the sound and attach a name property, smoothsnd, to the current document.

```
<EMBED name='smoothsnd' SRC='JAZZ.WAV' HIDDEN=TRUE
AUTOSTART=FALSE MASTERSOUND>



We then cause the sound to play when the following statement is
executed:

document.smoothsnd.play(false)
```

Let's now look at another, much more involved program using JavaScript and the LiveAudio plug-in. This program, called speech.htm and shown in Program 10.4, embeds two sounds files, speech.aif and applause.wav, that are loaded by the LiveAudio plug-in. We then use JavaScript to control the plug-in. This program presents the user with three selectable speech segments, which all happen to be portions of the speech.aif soundfile. By selecting one of the three radio buttons, the user can select which portion of the sound file is played. The user can also select the volume at which the sound file is played. Finally, when the user exits the page, the applause sound, called applause.wav, is played and fades out.

Study the comments in Program 10.4 to see what each statement accomplishes. Figure 10.3 shows what the program looks like running. Note that this program only works in Navigator 3.0 and requires the LiveAudio plug-in. It will load into Navigator 2.0, but will return errors when you click on a speech button.

Program 10.4: SPEECH.HTM, a speech player

```
<HTML>

<HEAD>

<SCRIPT language="Javascript">

<!-- Hide the JavaScript from other browsers

//

// SPEECH.HTM

// This program requires Navigator 3.0 and the LiveAudio plug-
in.

// It uses the LiveConnect feature of Navigator 3.0, so, under
your Options

// menu,  you must have both  Java and JavaScript enabled in
the Languages

// tab of your Network Preferences.

//

// Note: In rare cases, your LiveAudio plug-in may not be
configured to

// handle AIFF and WAV sound files. If that is the case, you
will

// need to change the settings for AIFF and WAV to LiveAudio
under the Options

// menu, by selecting General Preferences and configuring AIFF
and WAV under

// the Helpers tab.

//

//
```

(continued)

```
// Generic function to make arrays with index starting at zero

function MakeArray(n) {

for (var i=0; i<=n; i++) {

   this[i]=0

      }

   return this

}



// Plays a portion of the speech based on input on the form
spform

function speech_play(spf)  {

document.speech.stop()  // Stop any speech currently playing

// Find which speech was checked

   for (var i=0; i <  spf.choice.length;  i++)  {

       if (spf.choice[i].checked) {

               // Start the speech at startt[i]

            docu-
ment.speech.start_time(parseInt(startt[i],10))

               // End the speech at startt[i] +
spf.choice.value

  docu-
ment.speech.end_time(parseInt(startt[i],10)+parseInt(spf.
choice[i].value,10))
```

(continued)

```
                    // Set the volume of the speech

                        for (var i=0; i < spf.vol.length;  i++)
{

                                if (spf.vol[i].checked)

                    document.speech.set-
vol(parseInt(spf.vol[i].value,10))

                        }

                    // Play the speech

                        document.speech.play(false)

            }

        }

}


function  fade_cheers() {

    // Set the cheers at maximum volume

    document.clap.setvol(100)

    // Play the cheers

    document.clap.play(false)

    // Fade the volume of the cheers out for 4000 milliseconds

    window.setTimeout('document.clap.fade_from_to(100,0)',
4000)

}

// Create an array of start times for the speechs

// The first selection starts at the beginning (0 seconds)
```

(continued)

```
// The second selection starts at 11 seconds into the speech

startt= new MakeArray(3)

startt[0]=0

startt[1]=11

startt[2]=19

// End hiding JavaScript from other browsers -->

</SCRIPT>

</HEAD>

<BODY onLoad="fade_cheers()">

<h2>Harry S. Truman talks about dropping the bomb on
Hiroshima</h2>

<embed name="speech"  SRC="SPEECH.AIF" HIDDEN=TRUE
AUTOSTART=FALSE  MASTERSOUND>

<embed name="clap" SRC="APPLAUSE.WAV" HIDDEN=TRUE
AUTOSTART=FALSE  MASTERSOUND>

<FORM NAME="spform">

Topics:<BR><BR>

<!-- The VALUES in the buttons below are the length  -->

<!-- (in seconds) each speech lasts.  -->

<input type="radio" NAME="choice"  VALUE="7"
onclick="speech_play(spform)">The world will note that....

<input type="radio" NAME="choice"  VALUE="7"
onclick="speech_play(spform)">We have used it in order to
shorten....
```

(continued)

```
<input type="radio" NAME="choice"  VALUE="6"
onclick="speech_play(spform)">We shall continue to use it....


<BR><BR><BR>

Speech volume:

<input type="radio" NAME="vol"  VALUE="100" >Loud

<input type="radio" NAME="vol"   VALUE="75"  CHECKED>Medium

<input type="radio" NAME="vol"   VALUE="50" >Soft

</BODY>

</HTML>
```

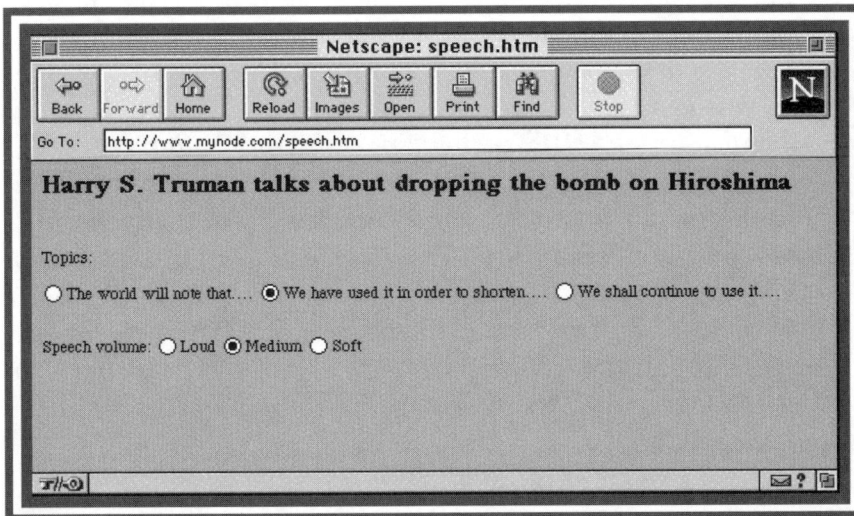

Figure 10.2 speech.htm lets users select which portion of the speech they want to hear and at what volume

Summary

This chapter has shown how to address plug-ins in both Navigator 2.0 and 3.0. In Navigator 2.0, access to plug-ins is extremely limited though we showed how to send parameters to plug-ins via the <EMBED> tag and open a stream to a plug-in. In Navigator 3.0, a plug-in object is introduced in the JavaScript implementation which facilitates plug-in manipulation. Also, the addition of LiveConnect in Navigator 3.0 lets us directly communicate with plug-in functions. In summary, remember the following points when working with plug-ins:

- *The <EMBED> tag lets users reference other types of content from within HTML pages and manipulate plug-ins. Refer to Table 10.1 for attributes of the <EMBED> tag.*
- *While there are routines that will let you test for installed plug-ins in Navigator 2.0, there is no clean way to do it. In Navigator 3.0, however, with its mimeType and plugins objects, makes it much easier to do so. Navigator 3.0 also lets you test which plug-ins are enabled.*
- *Because an <EMBED> tag is part of your Web pages, you can use JavaScript to create it dynamically from within a JavaScript script, which can be useful if you want to offer the user the opportunity to configure plug-in options or to use JavaScript to calculate a parameter to pass to a plug-in.*
- *Unfortunately, you can't test to see if a MIME type has a helper application configured. However, you can check to see if a certain MIME type is going to be handled by an installed plug-in.*
- *You can use LiveConnect to control plug-ins with JavaScript. Accessing plug-in routines from JavaScript is straightforward--plug-in files become JavaScript properties of the current document when you use the NAME attribute with your <EMBED> tag.*

Coming Up

In the next chapter, we'll take LiveConnect further and show how we can use it to control Java Applets with JavaScript.

CHAPTER 11
JavaScript
and Java

- Exporting Variables in Java applets

- Calling Applet Methods from within JavaScript

- Functions to use with JavaScript and Java

⚠️ **Warning** JavaScript examples in this chapter take advantage of Netscape's LiveConnect feature which is only available in the Navigator 3.0 or Navigator Gold 3.0 browser. Examples in this chapter will not work with Navigator 2.x or Microsoft's Internet Explorer.

The Java Programming Language is an object-oriented programming language that is very similar to, but much simpler than, C++. Programmers can create their own objects as classes in source code files.

A Java *Applet* is the result of running a Java compiler on Java source code. A Java applet can consist of several classes defined in

391

one or more source files. Each class is a series of byte codes produced by the Java compiler, **javac**. The series of byte codes is referred to as "Applets". Applets reside on servers and are downloaded to clients when referenced by a URL on the Web. Applets execute on remote sites under the auspices of the browser that downloaded them. The address space and code execution is modeled under a process known as the Java Virtual Machine (JVM). The JVM describes how to implement Java applet code and addresses issues regarding the ways to parse the bytes codes in an applet. Java is designed to be secure and robust enough to not allow any instruction in an applets byte codes to compromise the client machine's system integrity. By using the JVM model, byte codes can be verified by javac to ensure that the resulting applet will not compromise system integrity. In almost all cases, unless explicitly stated otherwise, Java applets tend to hide their variables from being modified by other programs.

Also, the influence of applets on the display of a browser is limited to the screen space set aside for them. Once placed on an HTML page, Java applets are then restricted to drawing within the confines of this space. More than one applet can exist in one display screen, with each displaying it's own data in it's own space.

JavaScript applications tend to control the layout of the HTML page and can use applets to build an application using several applets. To control the display of the contents within applets, a JavaScript application would require some means of communicating from within a JavaScript application to a Java applet.

The latest release of Navigator 3.0 will support communication between Java applets and JavaScript applications. This feature will let programmers have tremendous leverage in scripting together Web applications using Java applets as building blocks and using Java-Script to "glue" them together. For Microsoft's visual basic programmers, such a development would be akin to scripting visual basic applications using VBX and OCX tools.

Tip The communication feature is still in beta release mode at the time this book goes to print. The official release will be out "very soon." Some of the details and bugs forewarned about here may be eliminated by the time this book gets in your hands.

Java code can be integrated with Javascript using either plug-ins or by directly calling members and methods within these applets. The communication will be bi-directional. JavaScript applications can access any public Java variables and methods. Conversely, Java packages, classes, and objects are available to Javascript applications as objects.

JavaScript can also manipulate Java applet objects, which are accessible through document.applets. By importing the Netscape packages, Java code can access JavaScript methods and properties. Setting parameters in the applet would be done with the <PARAM> tags or through JavaScript code. This enables HTML elements with associated JavaScript code to manipulate applets and gives applets access to some data structures exposed through JavaScript, such as HTML reflections. The possibilities are endless. With the flexibility of JavaScript and and the power of Java and plug-ins, programmers can add depth to HTML pages.

Before We Begin

If you are not already working with Navigator 3.0, then the features discussed in this chapter will not work. Even with the pre-release 4 software, you have to explicitly turn the communication feature on, as it is turned off by default. To enable the communication, your browser must be started with the environment variable NS_ENABLE_MOJA set to 1. On UNIX systems and look-alikes, use the following commands:

For Korn, Bourne, bash, and look-alike shells:

NS_ENABLE_MOJA=1

export NS_ENABLE_MOJA

For csh, use the **setenv NS_ENABLE_MOJA=1** command. In Windows NT, use the Control/system panel to set the variable. On Windows 95, the fastest solution is to simply edit the autoexec.bat with the **set NS_ENABLE_MOJA=1** command and reboot. The variable is now set whenever you boot.

Sometimes opening an HTML file after dumping the cache in Navigator, or using reload, does not reload an applet! The only *Warning* workable solution is to "touch" the HTML, then recompile (not just "touch" to set a new date and time of modification) the Java applet code and then press the reload button. This guarantees that both the HTML file and the Java applet were reloaded. Hopefully, this will simply be a Windows 95 bug and will be removed by the time you read this.

Using Java Applets

JavaScript applications are able to access all public variables and methods of applets in an HTML document once the feature is enabled. Applets are included in an HTML document using the <APPLET> tags.

A sample usage for such an applet is shown below.

```
<applet code=Trader.class name=Trader width=200  height=300>

<param name="color" value="green">

<param name="sign" value="No Vacancy">

</applet>
```

More than one applet can be included in an HTML document. All the applets in a document are stored in an array called `document.applets`. The number of applets in the document is `document.applet.length`. The `documents.applet` array is indexed by the applet name. References to applets are in the order in which the applets appear in the document. Think of this applet array as behaving very much like the documents.forms array.

Each applet in a document can be referred to in one of two ways: either by index in the `documents.applets` array or by its name. So, for example, if the `Trader.class` applet is the first class in the system, you can address it in the document as either `document.Trader` or as `documents.applet["Trader"]`.

Accessing Applet Member Variables

All public variables declared in an applet (and its ancestor classes and packages) are available in JavaScript. A variable in a Java applet is not public by default; however, all Java applet static methods and properties are available to the loading JavaScript code as methods and properties of the applet object itself. You can get and set property values of an applet simply by referring to the variable within the applet that is defined for that property. For methods, you are limited to calling functions that return nothing or that return a value that Javascript will understand (i.e., only string, numeric, and Boolean values are allowed.) Numeric types in JavaScript are "doubles" (double precision numbers) in Java.

Let's look at a sample Java applet, as shown in Program 11.1, and an HTML file that has a JavaScript application to manipulate the Java applet's parameter (Program 11.2). The output is shown in Figure 11.1.

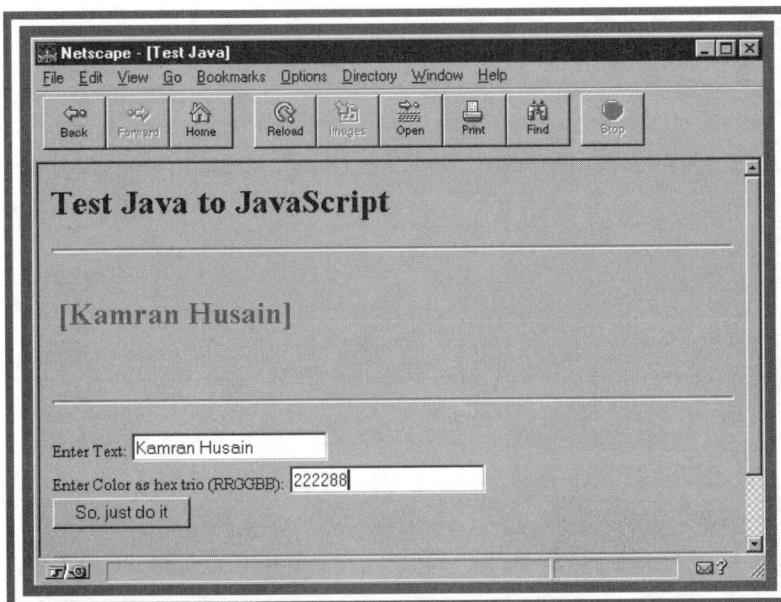

Figure 11.1 Using Java and JavaScript together

Program 11.1: The Java applet itself

```
import java.applet.*;

import java.awt.Graphics;

import java.awt.Font;

import java.awt.Color;


public class Ch11 extends java.applet.Applet {

    Font f = new Font ("TimesRoman", Font.BOLD, 24);

    public String neon;

    public String fgColor;

    public String inColor;

    Color foreground;


    public void init() {


    foreground =  Color.green;

    neon   = getParameter("neon");


    if (neon == null) // Don't let it be null

        neon = "Nothing";

    inColor = getParameter("ForeColor");

    if (inColor != null)
```

(continued)

```
        {

        foreground = getColorValue(inColor);

        }

else

        {

        foreground = new Color(0,100,0);

        }

}


public Color getColorValue(String name)  {

int iValue;

try {

    iValue = Integer.parseInt(name,16);

    }

catch (NumberFormatException e)

        {

        return new Color(0,0,0);

        }

return new Color(iValue);

}
```

(continued)

```
    public String getAppletInfo() { return "This is Version
1.0beta by Kamran Husain";

    }


    public void paint (Graphics g) {

    g.setFont(f);

    if (fgColor != null)

        {

        foreground = getColorValue(fgColor);

        }

    else

        {

        foreground = new Color(0,100,0);

        }

    g.setColor(foreground);

    String str;

    str = "[" + neon + "]";

    g.drawString(str,5,50);

    }

}
```

Program 11.2: Using the Java applet in an HTML document

```
<HTML>

<HEAD>

<BODY>

<TITLE>Test Java

</TITLE>

<SCRIPT>

<!--


function checkColor(c) {

     var alen = c.length

     c = c.toUpperCase()

     for (var i=0; i< alen; i++) {

          var ch = c.substring(i,i+1)

          if (!(((ch >= "0") && (ch <= "9")) ||

               ((ch >= "A") && ( ch <= "F"))))

               return false

          }

     return true;

     }

//

// Set java applet parameters

     //
```

(continued)

```
function doit(iform) {

    var txt = iform.sign.value;

    var color = iform.fColor.value;

    if (checkColor(color) == false) {

        color = "000000" // use default black

    }

    alert ("color = " + color);


    if (txt != null) {

        //alert ("About to assign " + txt)

        //alert ("Date to use   " + mydate)

        //alert ("Length to assign " + top.document.
applets.length)

        parent.document.myBeans.fgColor = color

        parent.document.myBeans.repaint()

        parent.document.myBeans.neon = txt

        parent.document.myBeans.repaint()

    }

}
```

(continued)

```
//-->

</SCRIPT>

</HEAD>

<H1>Test Java to JavaScript</H1>

<HR>

<APPLET code="Ch11.class" width=400 height=100 Name="myBeans">

<PARAM NAME="neon" VALUE="Kamran Husain" >

<PARAM NAME="ForeColor" VALUE="00FFFF" >

</APPLET>

<HR>

<FORM>

Enter Text: <INPUT TYPE="text" NAME="sign"><BR>

Enter Color as hex trio (RRGGBB):

        <INPUT TYPE="text" NAME="fColor" ><BR>

<INPUT TYPE="button" VALUE="So, just do it" onClick="doit
(document.forms[0])">

</FORM>

<HR>

<SCRIPT>

document.write("<H2>Applet version:");

document.write(parent.document.myBeans.getAppletInfo() +
"</H1>");
```

(continued)

```
var mydate = new java.util.Date()

document.write("<H2>Today's date: ");

document.write(mydate + "</H1>");

</SCRIPT>

</BODY>

</HTML>
```

The call in `index.htm` to get the applet version shows how to call Java methods. Here's the function that is called.

```
public String getAppletInfo() { return "This is Version
1.0beta by Kamran Husain";

}
```

The JavaScript statement to call the above function is shown here:

```
document.write("<H2>Applet version:");

document.write(parent.document.myBeans.getAppletInfo() + "</
H1>");
```

You can also call java library functions directly using the `java.library.function()` syntax. For example, to get the date from the Java library call, you could use the following statements, which print the return value in the current document:

```
var mydate = new java.util.Date()

document.write("<H2>Today's date: ");

document.write(mydate + "</H1>");
```

You can send debug messages to the console with the use of the `java.lang.System.err.println()` command in Java. To access the System package, you can use the following statements for debugging the application shown in Program 11.2:

```
var sysPkg = java.lang.System;

sysPkg.err.println("Text = " + neon + ", Color = " + fgColor);
```

The JavaScript application in Program 11.1 actually sets a variable with the text to display and another variable with a color value. Both the variables, fgColor and neon are declared as public variables in the Java applet. The JavaScript application calls the exported method `repaint()` to refresh the screen with the modifications.

Java code is distributed through *packages*. The top-level package for Java is referred to as "Packages" from within Javascript applications. Given references to class objects in a package, you can access fields and methods for that class using the same syntax that you would use in a Java applet.

> **Tip** The names java, sun, and netscape are synonyms for the Java
> `Packages.jav`, `Packages.sun`, and `Packages.netscape`, respectively. Your Java-Script application can refer to the main Java class `java.lang.System` as either the name of `Packages.java.lang.System` or `java.lang.System` with no loss in meaning.

Another Example

Here's another example of using Java applets with JavaScript applications. JavaScript does not support graphics. Some limited bar charts are available by using the IMG tag and sizing the image with a known graphic. The problem is that the size cannot be changed once the page is laid out. A gauge applet, as shown in Program 11.3, will let a user change the value and color automatically. The usage is shown in Program 11.4, with the results displayed in Figure 11.2.

The only important point to see is that new values are sent as strings, not as numbers. The conversion of strings is easy to follow. You could use the numeric type instead, but using strings make it easy to debug and this is not a real-time application requiring split-second adjustment, so speed is not an issue. Sending updates for real-time updates requires very precise timing and very optimized code. JavaScript, and in fact even Java, is not designed for such applications. Being interpretive, JavaScript makes the code slower and therefore unsuitable for such applications.

Program 11.3: The gauge applet

```java
import java.applet.*;

import java.awt.Graphics;

import java.awt.Font;

import java.awt.Color;


public class Gauge extends java.applet.Applet {


    public  String currentStr;
    public  String highStr;
    public  String lowStr;
    Font f = new Font ("TimesRoman", Font.BOLD, 10);


  int current;
    int high;
    int low;


    public void init() {
            String str;
            str  = getParameter("current");
            if (str == null)
            {
```

(continued)

```
            currentStr = "50";

        }

    else

            {

        currentStr = str;

        }


        str   = getParameter("high");

        if (str == null)

        {

        highStr = "50";

        }

    else

            {

        highStr = str;

        }


        str   = getParameter("low");

        if (str == null)

        {

        lowStr = "50";

        }
```

(continued)

```
        else

                {

            lowStr = str;

            }


    }


    public String getAppletInfo() { return "Gauge Bar Ver-
sion 1.0beta, Kamran Husain";

    }


    public void paint (Graphics g) {

    int w;


        try {

            current = Integer.parseInt(currentStr);

            }

            catch (NumberFormatException e)

            {

            current = 50;

            }


        try {

            high = Integer.parseInt(highStr);

            }
```

(continued)

```java
catch (NumberFormatException e)
             {
             high = 50;
             }


      try {
          low = Integer.parseInt(lowStr);
          }
          catch (NumberFormatException e)
          {
          low = 50;
          }


      if (current > 100) current = 100;
      if (high > 100) high = 100;
      if (low > 100) low = 100;
      if (current < 0) current = 0;
      if (high < 0) high = 0;
      if (low < 0) low = 0;


g.setColor(Color.green);
if (current > high) g.setColor(Color.red);
if (current < low) g.setColor(Color.blue);
```

(continued)

```
        w = (int) ((size().width) * current) / 100;

        g.fillRect(0,0,w,size().height);

        g.setColor(Color.black);

        g.setFont(f);

        g.drawString(current + "%",5,10);

    }

}
```

Program 11.4: Using the gauge applet in an HTML document

```
<HTML>

<HEAD>

<BODY>

<TITLE>Test Java Gauge

</TITLE>

<SCRIPT>

<!--
```

(continued)

```
function doit(iform) {

    var current = iform.icurrent.value;

    var high = iform.ihigh.value;

    var low = iform.ilow.value;

    if (low != null)

        parent.document.myGauge.lowStr = low

    if (current != null)

        parent.document.myGauge.currentStr = current

    if (high != null)

        parent.document.myGauge.highStr = high


    parent.document.myGauge.repaint()

    }



//-->

</SCRIPT>

</HEAD>

<H1>Test Java Gauge</H1>

<HR>

<APPLET code="Gauge.class" width=200 height=10 Name="myGauge">
```

(continued)

```
<PARAM NAME="current" VALUE="60" >

<PARAM NAME="high" VALUE="75" >

<PARAM NAME="low" VALUE="25" >

</APPLET>

<HR>

<FORM NAME="myform">

Enter New Value: <INPUT TYPE="text" NAME="icurrent"><BR>

Enter High Value: <INPUT TYPE="text" NAME="ihigh"><BR>

Enter Low Value: <INPUT TYPE="text" NAME="ilow"><BR>

<INPUT TYPE="button" VALUE="So, just do it" onClick="doit
(document.forms[0])">

</FORM>

<HR>

<SCRIPT>

document.write("<H2>Applet version:");

document.write(parent.document.myGauge.getAppletInfo() +
"</H2>");

</SCRIPT>

</BODY>

</HTML>
```

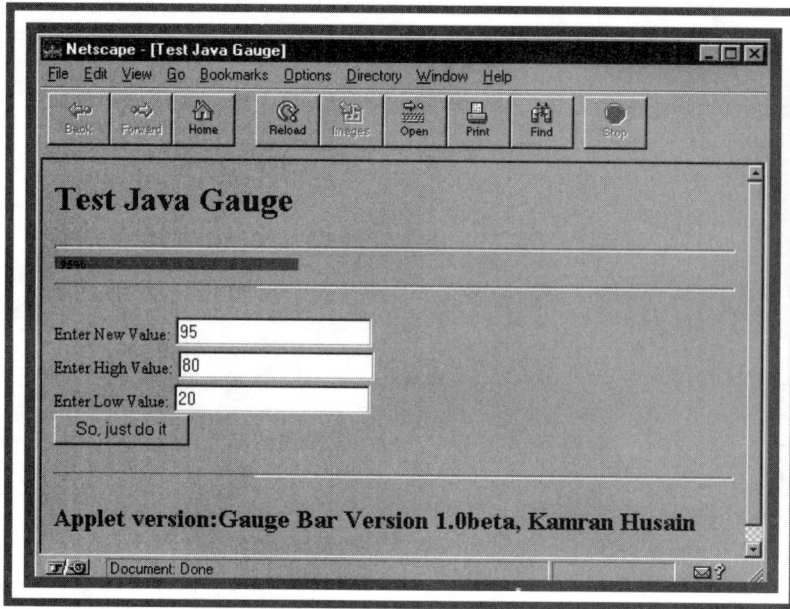

Figure 11.2 Using the gauge applet

For more information on writing Applets

Most of the applets on the you see now on the Net do not have public variables. After all, these applets were designed to hide variables in closed black-box objects. You will probably need to write your own applets to do custom programming. The topic on Java applet writing would require a book in itself. Consult the following books for more information on writing Java applets:

"Java Developer's Resource" by Elliotte Rusty Harold (Prentice Hall PTR, ISBN 0-13-570789-7, Aug. 1996).

"Java in a Nutshell" by David Flanagan (O'Reilly & Associates, ISBN 1-56592-183-6, Feb. 1996).

"Teach Yourself Java in 21 Days" by Laura Lemay and Charles Perkins (Sams Publications, ISBN 1-57521-030-4, Apr. 1996).

Summary

This chapter covered a few new feature of allowing communication between Java applets and JavaScript applications. The topic is new and the current version of JavaScript is being modified to accommodate new features. Stayed tuned to `developer.netscape.com` for details.

The main items you must remember when setting up Java to JavaScript communication are:

- *Java applets must declare the variables they want manipulated as public.*
- *Only string, boolean, or numeric types of variables are swapped between JavaScript and Java. Functions must return either one of these types of values or nothing.*
- *The MOJA_ENABLE environment variable must be set to 1 for this to work with Navigator 3.0. By default, the variable is not set.*

Coming Up

Thus far in this book, we have discussed those aspects of JavaScript that deal primarily with client-side implementation. But, as mentioned in the Introduction to this book, there's a whole other side to JavaScript, one that facilitates server-side implementation. In the next chapter we will introduce the concept using JavaScript on the server side to provide better control over client/server applications.

CHAPTER

12

AN INTRODUCTION TO SERVER-SIDE JAVASCRIPT AND LIVEWIRE

- Create and Deploy Server-Side Scripts

- Objects in Server-Side JavaScript

- Create and Manage Server-Side Applications Using LiveWire

Warning Examples in this chapter can only be tested using Netscape's LiveWire web management and development tool (http://www.netscape.com/comprod/products/tools/livewire_datasheet.html). You cannot test examples in this chapter by simply opening them with a web browser.

Until now, this book has focused on the client-side implementation of JavaScript, which is implemented inside the Navigator 2.0 and 3.0 browsers, as well as the Microsoft Internet Explorer 3.0 browser. However, Netscape also offers a server-side implementation of Java-

415

Script. We could easily write an entire book just about server-side JavaScript (and some people are doing just that!), so this chapter offers only a brief look at its capabilities.

Server-side JavaScript is a key component of Netscape's Internet Application Framework. Server-side JavaScript scripts replace Common Gateway Interface (CGI) scripts that you might deploy on your Web server. Server-side JavaScript also has special objects and methods for accessing SQL databases that conform to the Open DataBase Connectivity (ODBC) standard.

In order to develop and deploy server-side JavaScript applications, you need a special program called LiveWire, which is Netscape's Web site management and application development tool. LiveWire works in concert with Netscape's Web server to make server-side JavaScript applications available to browsers.

Although this chapter is, by no means, a complete introduction to LiveWire and server-side JavaScript, it does cover points that you will find useful, as well as present a working example of server-side JavaScript in action.

Server-Side Versus Client-Side

Server-side JavaScript and client-side JavaScript are syntactically and structurally identical. The two differences are the objects available to the programmer and the way that that the scripts are executed.

The available object hierarchy in server-side JavaScript is quite different from client-side JavaScript. On the client-side, the principal objects are windows, documents, and forms, and the "lifespan" of the objects depends on when a document is loaded and unloaded, or when a window is closed or opened. On the server-side, the principal objects are server, project, client, and request, and the "lifespan" of the objects depends on when software components (such as the Web server) are started up or when a browser makes a request for Web page. Figure 12.1 shows the primary objects of client-side and server-side JavaScript.

client-side   **server-side**

window

document

form

server

project

client

request

Figure 12.1 Primary objects in client-side Java-Script and server-side JavaScript

With client-side JavaScript, all scripts are executed using the Java-Script interpreter built-in to your browser. Scripts are referenced or contained using the <SCRIPT> tag. With server-side JavaScript, the LiveWire application executes scripts before the requested page is sent to the browser (see Figure 12.2). As with client-side scripts, server-side scripts can be placed inside HTML Web pages. Server-side scripts are contained using the <SERVER> tag, or they can reside in separate files that have the file extension `.js` .

Creating Scripts

In order to develop with server-side JavaScript, you need both LiveWire and a Netscape Web server (version 2.0 or higher). LiveWire includes a JavaScript compiler as well as tools for installing your application so that users can retrieve it from the Netscape server.

```
JavaScript          page              Netscape
script is       ← containing  ←        Server
executed          JavaScript
here
```

Navigator   Netscape
Browser   Server

CLIENT-SIDE JAVASCRIPT

```
                    Generated                   JavaScript
              ←     web       ←                  script is
                    page                         executed
                                                 here
```

Navigator   Netscape   Livewire
Browser   Server

SERVER-SIDE JAVASCRIPT

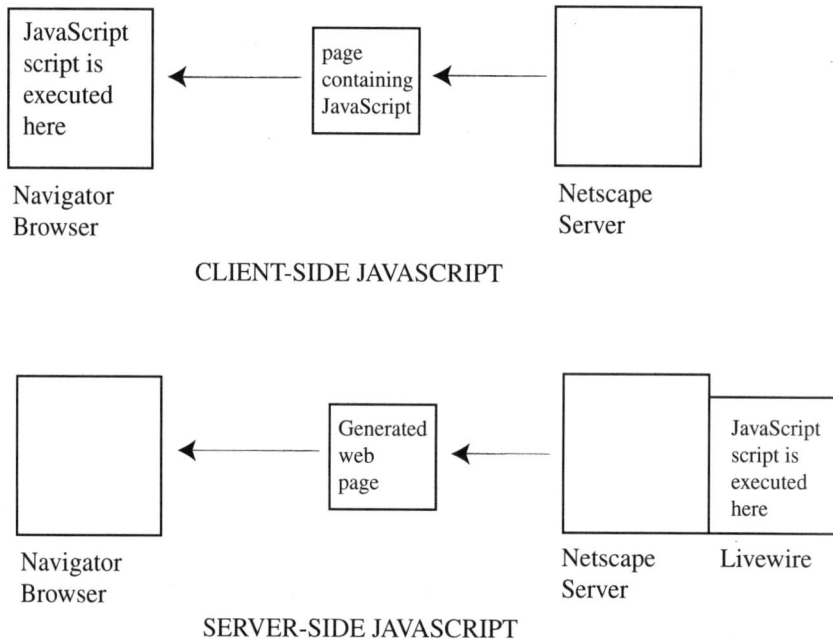

Figure 12.2 The execution flow of JavaScript scripts. Server-side scripts are executed by LiveWire. Client-side Javascript scripts are executed inside the Navigator web browser

Creating an application containing server-side JavaScript requires three basic steps:

1. *Create the source files. The source files can be any combination of: plain HTML files, HTML files with embedded server-side and/or client-side JavaScript,, and JavaScript only files (* `.js` *file extension).*

2. *Compile the source files using the LiveWire compiler. This creates the bytecode executable application, which has the file extension* `.web` *.*

3. *Install the application with the LiveWire Application Manager.*

Putting Scripts Into HTML Files

Server-side JavaScript scripts are placed within HTML pages using two methods:

1.   *<SERVER>...</SERVER> container tag, and*

2.   *Backquotes `....`*

The <SERVER> container tag serves the same purpose as the <SCRIPT> tag does in client-side JavaScript. The difference is that, because all code contained in the <SERVER> tag is executed on the server before it reaches your browser, you will never see the <SERVER> tag or server-side JavaScript code in your document source when you select "document source" from Navigator's View menu.

For example, the following server-side script creates a new variable, `project.total`, if it doesn't already exist. Then, it increments `project.total` by `request.amount`, and finally outputs HTML that gets sent to the user.

```
<SERVER>

if (project.total == null)

    project.total = 0

project.total = parseInt(project.total,10) +
parseInt(request.amount,10)

write("<h1>Total Pledge is: $</h1>"+project.total)

</SERVER>
```

You can use backquotes to embed server-side JavaScript within HTML tags. For example, you might want to choose an `onLoad` event handler for client-side JavaScript based on whether or not the user is running Navigator 2.0 or 3.0.

```
write('<BODY onLoad=\''+client.jsroutine+'\'>')
```

The LiveWire Object Framework

Server-side JavaScript shares most of the basic language features of client-side JavaScript, including flow-control statements, variables, and operators. However, other than the String, Math, and Date objects, they have no objects in common.

The LiveWire Object Framework is Netscape's name for the objects used in server-side JavaScript. Table 12.1 lists the JavaScript server-side objects.

Table 12.1   JavaScript's Server-Side Objects

Object	Description
server	Can contain global data available to all applications and clients.
project	Can contain data available to all clients.
client	Contains data available to a specific client. Client state maintained by cookies or URL encoding.
request	Contains data available to a specific request.
database	Created when a database is opened successfully with the `database.connect` method.
cursor	Database management objects created using the `database.cursor` method.
File	Lets an application manage a file located in the server's filesystem.
Date	Same as client-side Date.
Math	Same as client-side Math.
String	Same as client-side String.

Server-side JavaScript also has a number of useful built-in functions. Table 12.2 lists them.

Table 12.2   JavaScript's Server-Side Built-In Functions

Function	Description
flush()	LiveWire buffers write() calls. Use flush() to force all writes() to the client.
write(expression)	Writes the expression as HTML directly to the client
writeURL(variable)	Generates a URL suitable for use with client URL encoding or short URL encoding (see Communicating With the Client Object later in this chapter)
redirect(URL)	Redirects the client to the specified URL.
debug(expression)	Displays the value of an expression for debugging purposes.
registerCfunction(arg list)	Registers an external C function for use with a LiveWire application.
callC(arg list)	Calls an external C function.

Communication Between Client and Server

In LiveWire, communication between your browser client and your Web server is handled by using properties of the request, client, project, and server objects in the LiveWire Object Framework. Which object you use to communicate with is dependent largely on the lifespan of the object. Table 12.3 shows the lifespan of these four objects.

Request objects are typically used to transmit form fields to the LiveWire application. The client object is useful for temporarily identifying a particular user and carrying the user some state variable. The project object is good for storing data that needs to be accessible to all clients accessing an application, such as a function that returns unique userids. The server object is used for storing objects that may need to be shared by other applications running under LiveWire.

Table 12.3 Lifespan of Important Server-Side Objects

Object	Instantiated	Lifespan
request	When the user sends a URL request to the application.	Typically less than one second. Just enough time for a page to be parsed by LiveWire.
client	When the user runs the application for the first time.	Variable. Can be set with JavaScript or it will automatically be expired by LiveWire.
project	When the application is started with the LiveWire Application Manager.	Until the application is stopped by the LiveWire Application Manager.
server	When the Web server is started up.	Until the Web server is shut down.

Communicating With the Request Object

The LiveWire object framework makes it easy to send form values to a server-side JavaScript script for processing. Each input element in an HTML form corresponds to a property of the request object. The property name is specified by the NAME attribute of the form element.

For example, the following form field

```
<INPUT TYPE="text" NAME="name" VALUE="" MAXLENGTH="20">
```

when submitted, can be referenced in a sever-side script as a property of the current request object,

```
request.name.
```

We'll show a full example of how this can be accomplished at the end of the chapter.

You can also manually encode request properties into URLs by using the following syntax:

```
URL?varName=value[&varName=value...]
```

where URL is the base URL, varName is a variable name, and value is its value. This scheme requires following the base URL by a question mark (?), that is then followed by pairs of variable names and their values. Separate each pair with an ampersand (&). This creates a request property named varName for each variable listed.

For example, the following HTML defines a hyperlink to a page that instantiates the request properties i and j to 1 and 2, respectively. The JavaScript file refpage.htm can then reference these variables as request.i and request.j.

```
<A HREF="refpage.htm?i=1&j=2">Click Here</A>
```

Communicating With the Client Object

The client object is, perhaps, the most important object, since you use it to communicate client-specific data to and from the application. The client object has no predefined properties, but that's ok. You make up your own to fit your application. Each time the user accesses the application, they will have access to any properties of the client object that you have created. The following server-sde script assigns the value of request.total to a client property named client.savetotal that we created.

```
<SERVER>

client.savetotal=request.total

</SERVER>
```

You can use server-side JavaScript statements to save client values that are accessible during the duration of the user's execution of the application. LiveWire keeps track of user accesses with client state maintenance mechanisms.

What is client state?

The HTTP (HyperText Transport Protocol) used over the World Wide Web is a stateless protocol. That means that there is no information stored between connections to the Web server. Put simply, each time you request a Web page by clicking on a hypertext link or entering a URL, your Web browser establishes a connection to the Web server and the Web server sends the page. The Web server maintains no information about who you are or even what page you're viewing. If you click on a link in that downloaded page that comes from the same web server, a request is sent to the same Web server, the Web server doesn't know that you're currently viewing a document downloaded from its server. All it knows is that you're asking for another page. The Web server doesn't know about your previous *state*.

In order to develop interesting Web applications, however, we'd like to know something about what the user is doing at the Web site. We'd like to know what fields he or she filled into a form, whether he or she requested access to a database, or what kind of web browser he or she is using. We'd also like to maintain this information, this *state* information, over time. So, for example, if the user connects next week, we'll recognize who she is and what she did that last time she connected.

The usual way to maintain state between client and server is to use client Cookies, which we demonstrate in Chapter 9, "Applying Java-Script." Cookies work by putting small amounts of state information in a file on your computer, and using a custom CGI on the server side that stores corresponding information on the Web server's machine. Because CGI programming is required on the server-side to maintain anything other than trivial amounts of state information, cookies are cumbersome to work with.

Maintaining client state with LiveWire.

To maintain a user's *state* while a user executes a LiveWire application, LiveWire offers five kinds of client state maintenance mechanisms. You can choose the one that best fits your application's requirements. Table 12.4 summarizes the advantages and disadvantages of each approach.

Table 12.4 Types of Client State Maintenance Techniques Offered by LiveWire (this table was taken from the LiveWire documentation)

Technique	Description	Advantages	Disadvantages
Client Side Maintenance Techniques (state data is stored on client)			
client cookies	Uses Netscape cookie protocol (see example in Chapter 9)	Preserves properties after server restart.	Maximum of twenty properties per application, 4K per property. Modest increase in network traffic.
client URL encoding	Attach name/value pairs to URLs	Works with all clients. Preserves properties after server restart.	Lose client properties when submit a form. Cannot control client expiration. Requires using addClient for dynamic links or redirects. Largest increase in network traffic.

(continued)

Technique	Description	Advantages	Disadvantages
Server Side Maintenance Techniques (state data is stored on server)			
IP address	Server maintains state, indexed by user's IP address	Works with all clients. No increase in network traffic.	Does not support dynamic IP access providers, DHCP, or users behind proxy servers. Properties lost when server restarted. Consumes server disk space. All applications on one client machine share one client object
server (short) cookies	Server maintains state, cookie holds client identification	Little increase in network traffic.	Properties lost when server restarted. Consumes server disk space.
server URL encoding	Server maintains state. URL holds client identification	Works with all clients. Little increase in network traffic.	Lose client properties when submit a form. Requires using addClient for dynamic links or redirects. Properties lost when server restarted. Consumes server disk space.

Setting client state in your LiveWire application.

In order to maintain the various objects over their lifespan, LiveWire offers five kinds of built-in state maintenance mechanisms. You can choose which mechanism you want to use in your applications when you install your application with the LiveWire Application Manager. Figure 12.3 shows how easy it is to select your choice of client state maintenance using LiveWire.

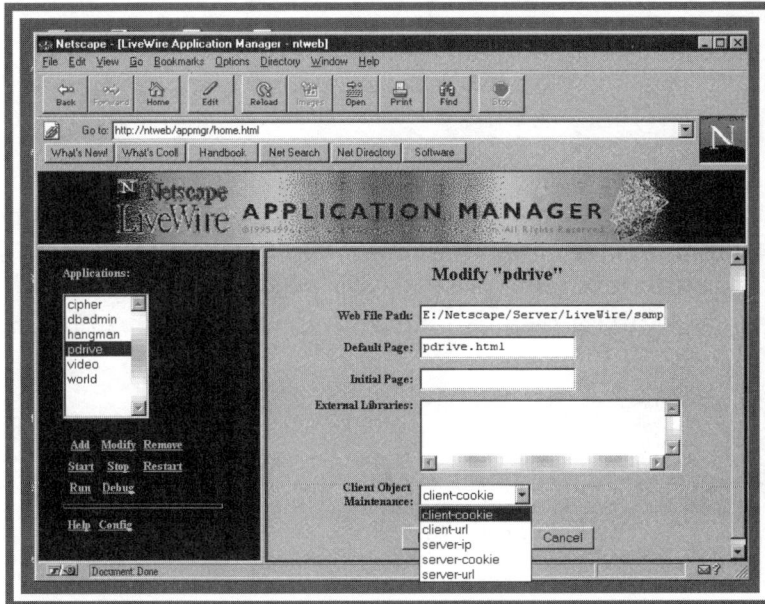

Figure 12.3 Selecting client state maintenance for your LiveWire application

Communicating With the Project and Server Objects

The project and server objects are both globally defined and have no properties. You can make up your own properites to share with other clients, in the case of the project object, and with all applications, in the case of the server object. Since these properties are globally accessible, always use the lock and unlock properties of the project and server objects before manipulating properties. In this example, we lock the project object before setting the project property `project.total`.

```
<SERVER>

project.lock()

project.total += request.amount

project.unlock()

</SERVER>
```

Executing Scripts

Now that we have an understanding of client/server communication using server-side JavaScript, we can take a look at the actual details of LiveWire application execution. LiveWire performs a predictable series of steps each time a page is requested from an application, as outlined in Table 12.5.

Table 12.5 LiveWire Execution Order

action	Details
1. Creates new request object	All built-in properties are initialized.
2. Creates client object	If the client object already exists, LiveWire retrieves it based on the specified client maintenance.
3. Saves client object properties	LiveWire saves client object properties immediately before outputting the page to the client.
4. Outputs HTML	LiveWire sends the page content to the client. For static pages, the server simply transfers the HTML to the client. For dynamic pages, LiveWire performs the application logic to create the HTML and then sends it to the client.
5. Saves or destroys client object	LiveWire saves or destroys the client object, created previously.
6. Destroys request object	LiveWire destroys the request object created previously

We've created an example, which we'll call the Pledge Drive example, that demonstrates some of the basic features of server-side JavaScript. We'll go through the entire development cycle, step by step, to show how quickly you can create Internet applications without CGI programming.

Our example application is fairly simple. It displays a form that users can complete to pledge money to a community radio station. The user fills out the form, including the amount pledged, and submits it. When the user submits the form, server-side JavaScript statements take the form fields and write them to a file on the server. Upon completion, a "thank you" page is sent back to the user.

The entire logic for the program, which includes both client-side and server-side JavaScript scripts, is contained in a single file named `pdrive.htm`.

The User Interface

HTML forms are the standard way of creating user interfaces on the Web. The user interface portion of `pdrive.htm` is a standard form in all respects and it will display in all forms-capable browsers. It also calls a simple client-side JavaScript routine to make sure the user enters something in the *name* and *phone number* fields. The client-side JavaScript runs fine in any Navigator 2.0 or 3.0 browser. If the user has a browser that doesn't support JavaScript, the user interface will still display properly, but the client-side JavaScript will be ignored. The server-side JavaScript, which we'll look at in a moment, will still be executed on the server, however. The following is the user interface portion of `pdrive.htm`.

```
<SCRIPT LANGUAGE="JavaScript">

<!--

function checkthis() {

if (document.pform.name.value == "") {

    alert("You must enter your name")

    return false

}

if (document.pform.phone.value == "") {

    alert("You must enter your phone number")

    return false

}

return true

//    -->

</SCRIPT>

</HEAD>

<BODY><h2>Community Radio Pledge Drive</h2>

<B>Current Online Pledge Total:
$<server>write(project.total)</server></B>

<FORM NAME="pform" ACTION="pdrive.htm" METHOD=POST onSubmit=
'return checkthis()'>

Name: <INPUT TYPE="text" NAME="name" VALUE="" MAXLENGTH="20">

<BR>Address: <INPUT TYPE="text" NAME="address" VALUE=""
SIZE="40" MAXLENGTH="40">
```

(continued)

```
<BR>Address: <INPUT TYPE="text" NAME="address2" VALUE=""
SIZE="40" MAXLENGTH="40">

<BR>City: <INPUT TYPE="text" NAME="city" VALUE="" SIZE="16"
MAXLENGTH="40">

State: <INPUT TYPE="text" NAME="state" VALUE="" SIZE="2"
MAXLENGTH="2">

<BR>Zip Code: <INPUT TYPE="text" NAME="zip" VALUE="" SIZE="10"
MAXLENGTH="10">

<BR>Phone Number: <INPUT TYPE="text" NAME="phone" VALUE=""
SIZE="15">

<P>Pledge Category:<BR>

<INPUT TYPE="radio" NAME="amount" VALUE="15">$15.00 student

<INPUT TYPE="radio" NAME="amount" VALUE="30" CHECKED>$30.00
regular

<INPUT TYPE="radio" NAME="amount" VALUE="50">$50.00 family

<INPUT TYPE="radio" NAME="amount" VALUE="100">$100.00 business

<INPUT TYPE="hidden" NAME="cmd" VALUE="putdata">

<P><INPUT TYPE=reset><INPUT TYPE=submit VALUE="Submit Pledge">

</FORM>

</BODY>
```

Note three unusual features of this form. First, notice the ACTION attribute of the <FORM> tag.

```
<FORM NAME="pform" ACTION="pdrive.htm" METHOD=POST onSub-
mit='return checkthis()'>
```

It is set to `pdrive.htm`. Surprise! That's the name of the file that contains our form! This means that when the user clicks the *submit* button in the form, the file `pdrive.htm` will again be requested from the server, except this time, all of the data associated with the form will be made available to the server-side JavaScript code in the file `pdrive.htm`.

The server-side JavaScript script in `pdrive.htm` looks at the value of the following hidden field to decide what to do. We set it to the value "putdata" before the form is submitted by the user. The server-side JavaScript script in `pdrive.htm` will use this value to determine that the user has submitted the form.

```
<INPUT TYPE="hidden" NAME="cmd" VALUE="putdata">
```

Finally, we display a running total of all current pledges with the line:

```
<server>write(project.total)</server>
```

Each time `pdrive.htm` is fetched, the current value of `project.total` will be fetched from the server and displayed.

Server-Side JavaScript

The entire logic for `pdrive.htm` is contained in this short server-side JavaScript script.

```
<SERVER>

if (request.cmd == "putdata") {

    pfile = new File("PLEDGES")

project.lock()

    result = pfile.open("a")

    if (!result) {

        project.unlock()

        redirect("error.htm")

    }

    pfile.writeln(request.name)

    pfile.writeln(request.address)

    pfile.writeln(request.address2)

    pfile.writeln(request.city+", "+request.state)

    pfile.writeln(request.zip)

    pfile.writeln(request.phone)

    pfile.writeln(request.amount)

    pfile.writeln("   ")

    pfile.flush()

    pfile.close()
```

(continued)

```
    project.total = parseInt(project.total,10) +
parseInt(request.amount,10)

project.unlock()

    redirect("thanks.htm")

} else {

if (project.total == null)

    project.total = 0

}

</SERVER>
```

Note that the entire script is wrapped in the statement:

```
if (request.cmd == "putdata")
```

The first time a user fetches pdrive.htm from the server, the value
of request.cmd will be null, so only the statement

```
if (project.total == null)
        project.total = 0
```

will be executed. This statement checks to see if the variable
project.total exists. If it doesn't exist, it is created and set to the
value 0. It then displays the form for the user and writes the value of
project.total. Later, when the user submits the form, the value of
request.cmd will be equal to "putdata" and this will cause our main
server-side JavaScript to execute.

The bulk of our server-side JavaScript does three basic things. It opens a file for writing, writes the form data into the file, and closes the file. The name of our file containing the Pledge Drive databases is "PLEDGES". To open PLEDGES, we first create a new file object we'll call pfile.

```
pfile = new File("PLEDGES")
```

Since multiple people might be submitting pledges at the same time, we need to lock the file access routines to avoid conflicts. The `project.lock()` statement gives us temporary exclusive access to the server-side JavaScript code immediately following it.

```
project.lock()
```

We open the file in append mode using the open method of the file object. If the open fails, we unlock the project and display the file `error.htm`, which simply tells the user an error occurred.

```
result = pfile.open("a")

    if (!result) {

        project.unlock()

        redirect("error.htm")

    }
```

If the open succeeds, we use the `writeln` method of the file object to write all the form fields to the PLEDGES file.

```
pfile.writeln(request.name)

    pfile.writeln(request.address)

    pfile.writeln(request.address2)

    pfile.writeln(request.city+", "+request.state)

    pfile.writeln(request.zip)

    pfile.writeln(request.phone)

    pfile.writeln(request.amount)
```

We write a blank line to make the file look nice. We then call the flush property of the file object to write the buffer cache to disk. Finally, we close the file.

```
pfile.writeln("  ")

    pfile.flush()

    pfile.close()
```

Before unlocking the project, we update our running total of the accumulated pledges with the pledge amount.

```
project.total = parseInt(project.total,10) +
parseInt(request.amount,10)

project.unlock()
```

Because everything succeeded, we display a "thank you" page for the user. The redirect statement jumps out of the execution context of our main file, `pdrive.htm`, which ensures that nothing else in `pdrive.htm` will be executed.

```
redirect("thanks.htm")
```

Program 12.1 contains the complete `pdrive.htm` file.

Program 12.1: The complete `pdrive.htm` file

```
<HTML>

<HEAD>

<TITLE>Pledge Drive</TITLE>

<SERVER>

if (request.cmd == "putdata") {

    pfile = new File("PLEDGES")

project.lock()

    result = pfile.open("a")

    if (!result) {

        project.unlock()

        redirect("error.htm")

    }
```

(continued)

```
    pfile.writeln(request.name)

    pfile.writeln(request.address)

    pfile.writeln(request.address2)

    pfile.writeln(request.city+", "+request.state)

    pfile.writeln(request.zip)

    pfile.writeln(request.phone)

    pfile.writeln(request.amount)

    pfile.writeln("  ")

    pfile.flush()

    pfile.close()

    project.total = parseInt(project.total,10) +
parseInt(request.amount,10)

project.unlock()

    redirect("thanks.htm")

} else {

if (project.total == null)

    project.total = 0

}

</SERVER>
```

(continued)

```
<SCRIPT LANGUAGE="JavaScript">

function checkthis() {

if (document.pform.name.value == "") {

   alert("You must enter your name")

   return false

}

if (document.pform.phone.value == "") {

   alert("You must enter your phone number")

   return false

}

return true

}

</SCRIPT>

</HEAD>

<BODY>

<h2>Community Radio Pledge Drive</h2>

<B>Current Online Pledge Total:
$<server>write(project.total)</server></B>

<FORM NAME="pform" ACTION="pdrive.htm" METHOD=POST onSubmit=
'return checkthis()'>

Name: <INPUT TYPE="text" NAME="name" VALUE="" MAXLENGTH="20">
```

(continued)

```
<BR>Address: <INPUT TYPE="text" NAME="address" VALUE=""
SIZE="40" MAXLENGTH="40">

<BR>Address: <INPUT TYPE="text" NAME="address2" VALUE=""
SIZE="40" MAXLENGTH="40">

<BR>City: <INPUT TYPE="text" NAME="city" VALUE="" SIZE="16"
MAXLENGTH="40">

State: <INPUT TYPE="text" NAME="state" VALUE="" SIZE="2" MAX-
LENGTH="2">

<BR>Zip Code: <INPUT TYPE="text" NAME="zip" VALUE="" SIZE="10"
MAXLENGTH="10">

<BR>Phone Number: <INPUT TYPE="text" NAME="phone" VALUE=""
SIZE="15">

<P>

Pledge Category:<BR>

<INPUT TYPE="radio" NAME="amount" VALUE="15">$15.00 student

<INPUT TYPE="radio" NAME="amount" VALUE="30" CHECKED>$30.00
regular

<INPUT TYPE="radio" NAME="amount" VALUE="50">$50.00 family

<INPUT TYPE="radio" NAME="amount" VALUE="100">$100.00 business


<INPUT TYPE="hidden" NAME="cmd" VALUE="putdata">

<P><INPUT TYPE=reset><INPUT TYPE=submit VALUE="Submit Pledge">

</FORM>

</BODY>

</HTML>
```

Our sample application refers to two other files, `thanks.htm` and `error.htm`, as shown in Programs 12.2 and 12.3, respectively. They are trivial files, but for completeness sake, we include them here.

Program 12.2: The `thanks.htm` file, thanking for pledges

```
<html>

<head> <title>Thanks!</title> </head>

<body>

<H2>Thanks For Your Pledge!</h2>

</body>

</html>
```

Program 12.3: The `error.htm` file alerts users of an error in opening the database

```
<html>

<head> <title>An Error Occured</title> </head>

<body>

<H3>An error occured when we tried to open the pledge database.
Try again later.</h3>

</body>

</html>
```

Compiling Our Project

Once we have the source files for our project, the next step is to compile them into a single pdrive.web project file using the LiveWire JavaScript compiler. The JavaScript compiler is called lwcomp. To create our pdrive.web file, we use the lwcomp command line:

```
lwcomp -v -o pdrive.Web pdrive.htm error.htm thanks.htm
```

It compiles the three files, pdrive.htm, error.htm, and thanks.htm into a byte code binary named pdrive.web. Figure 12.4 shows the output of lwcomp.

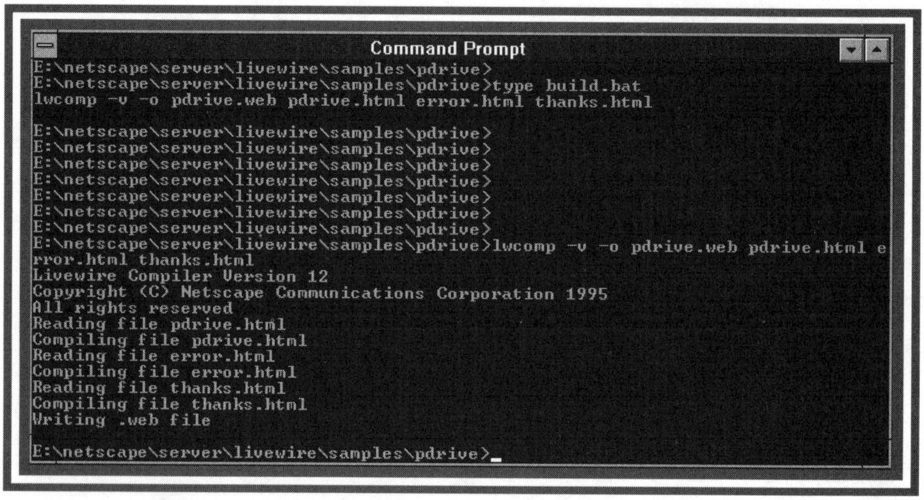

```
Command Prompt
E:\netscape\server\livewire\samples\pdrive>
E:\netscape\server\livewire\samples\pdrive>type build.bat
lwcomp -v -o pdrive.web pdrive.html error.html thanks.html

E:\netscape\server\livewire\samples\pdrive>
E:\netscape\server\livewire\samples\pdrive>
E:\netscape\server\livewire\samples\pdrive>
E:\netscape\server\livewire\samples\pdrive>
E:\netscape\server\livewire\samples\pdrive>
E:\netscape\server\livewire\samples\pdrive>
E:\netscape\server\livewire\samples\pdrive>
E:\netscape\server\livewire\samples\pdrive>lwcomp -v -o pdrive.web pdrive.html e
rror.html thanks.html
Livewire Compiler Version 12
Copyright (C) Netscape Communications Corporation 1995
All rights reserved
Reading file pdrive.html
Compiling file pdrive.html
Reading file error.html
Compiling file error.html
Reading file thanks.html
Compiling file thanks.html
Writing .web file

E:\netscape\server\livewire\samples\pdrive>_
```

Figure 12.4 Output of the lwcomp compiler

Any syntax errors lwcomp finds will be noted in the output, and the project file, pdrive.web will fail to be created.

Managing the Application With LiveWire

After initially creating our project file, we're ready to attach it to LiveWire using the LiveWire Application Manager (see Figure 12.5). We click on "add" to add our LiveWire application, which we call `pdrive`. The only two pieces of information we need to give it is the Web File Path, which is the location of the `.web` project file, and the default page, which we call `pdrive.htm`.

We select "start" to load `pdrive` into LiveWire, which advertises it to the Web server and makes it available for download. We can launch it ourselves by selecting "run," or if we want to see debugging information, we select "debug." If we want to make changes to `pdrive.htm`, `thanks.htm`, or `error.htm`, we need to recompile them using `lwcomp`, and select "restart" from the LiveWire Application Manager. Selecting "run" will then run the new version of pdrive.

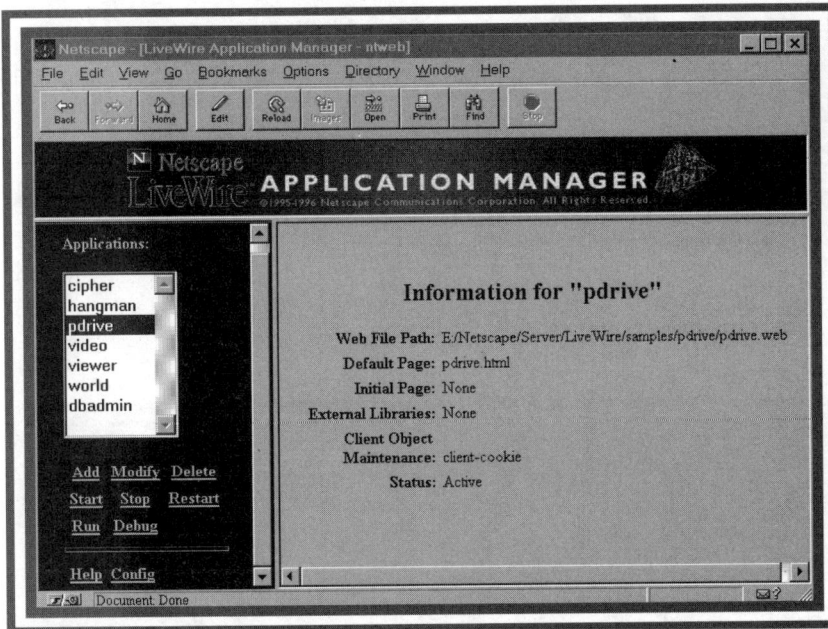

Figure 12.5 The LiveWire Application Manager

Selecting "run" yields the same output as a user will see when they reference the Web page over the Internet. Figure 12.6 shows the form displayed by `pdrive`. Note that several runs have been made and the pledge drive total is up to $100.

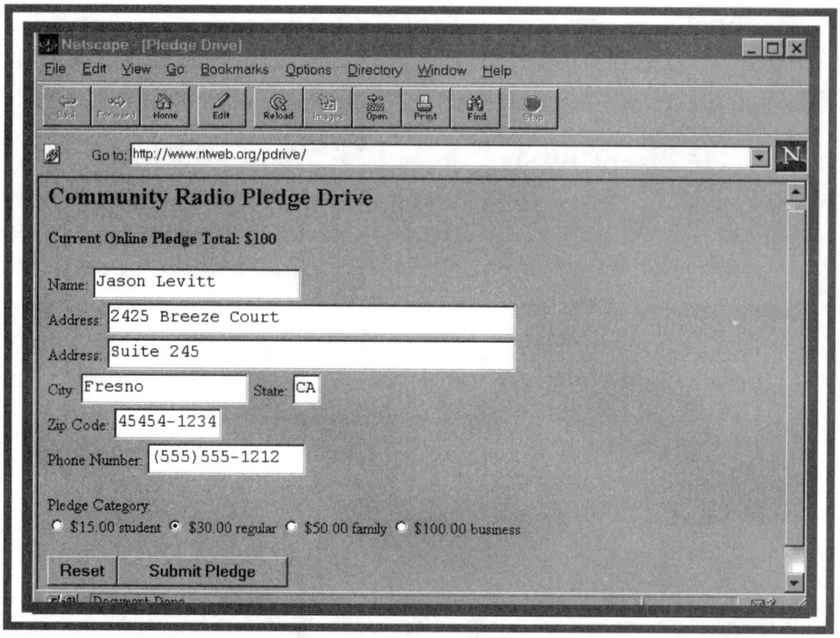

Figure 12.6 The form displayed by running pdrive

After the user presses the Submit Pledge button, `pdrive` returns the `thanks.htm` page, which displays as in Figure 12.7.

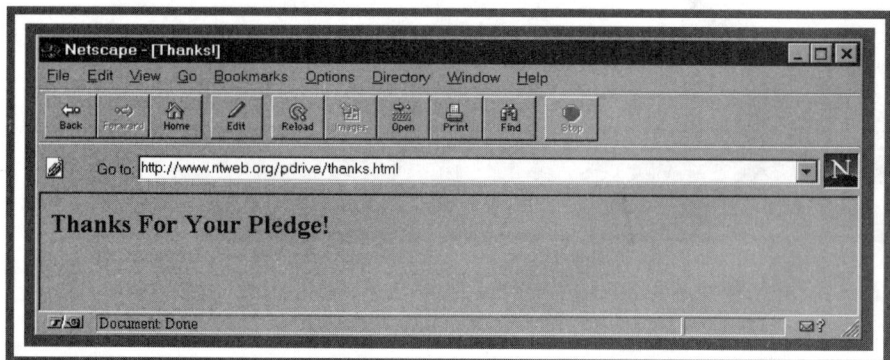

Figure 12.7 The "Thanks for Pledging" screen

As a result of pressing the Submit Pledge button, the fields in Figure 12.5 are appended to the file PLEDGES. The data written into the PLEDGES file for the form in Figure 12.6 is listed below in Figure 12.8.

```
Jason Levitt
2425 Breeze Court
Suite 245
Fresno, CA
45454-1234
(555)555-1212
30
```

Figure 12.8   The data written into the PLEDGES file from the form in Figure 12.6.

Using Databases With JavaScript

The pledge drive example works fine for small pledge drives, but if your pledge drive had, say, a hundred thousand pledges, and you later needed to maintain the pledge data in a database, the flat file used in the example would be impractical. Fortunately, server-side JavaScript includes a database object that you can use to connect to, and access, Open DataBase Connectivity (ODBC)-compliant SQL databases such as those offered by Microsoft, Sybase, Informix, and Oracle.

The LiveWire database access and management implementation was not fully functional as this book went to press, so we offer only a brief summary here to get you started.

The Database Object

To connect to a database from within a server-side JavaScipt script, you use the connect method of the database object. If our pledge drive database were kept in a Sybase database named PLEDGES, which resided on the machine `ntweb`, we could connect to the database using the connect method of the database object as illustrated in the following script. This example assumes I have access to the database using username `jason` and password `mypasswd`.

```
<SERVER>

database.connect(SYBASE, ntweb, jason, mypasswd, PLEDGES)

if (!database.connected())

    write("Error connecting to database")

<SERVER>
```

The database object has many other methods that are used to handle SQL transactions, create database cursors, and return error codes. Table 12.6 shows all the database methods available in server-side JavaScript.

There are two basic ways to structure database access for your LiveWire applications. You can have your initial application page open the database and then subsequently all clients that connect will share that same database connection. Or, you can set up your application so that each client establishes its own connection to the database.

Table 12.6   The Methods of the Database Object (this table is from the Netscape LiveWire documentation).

Method	Description	Parameters
beginTransaction	Begins a SQL transaction.	None.
commitTransaction	Commits the current transaction.	None.
connect	Connects application to a database and creates database object.	Database type, server name, user name, password, database name.
connected	Returns true if application is connected to a database.	None.
cursor	Creates a database cursor for the specified SQL SELECT statement.	String representing a SELECT statement, Boolean value indicating if cursor is updatable.
disconnect	Disconnects application from a database. After disconnecting, cannot use any other methods, except connect and connected.	None.
execute	Performs the specified SQL statement. Use for SQL statements other than queries.	String representing a SQL statement, such as INSERT, UPDATE, or DELETE.
rollbackTransaction	Rolls back the current transaction.	None.
SQLTable	Displays query results. Creates an HTML table for results of a SQL SELECT statement.	String representing a SELECT statement.
majorErrorCode	The major error code returned by the database server or ODBC.	None.
minorErrorCode	Secondary error code returned by vendor library.	None.
majorErrorMessage	The major error message returned by database server or ODBC.	None.
minorErrorMessage	Secondary message returned by vendor library.	None.

Other Database Features

As Table 12.6 shows, the database objects offers a rich set of methods for database transactions, SQL queries, binary large objects (blobs), and error diagnostics.

You can manage database transactions, which is a group of database actions that are performed together, with the following database methods:

```
database.beingTransaction()

database.rollbackTransaction()

database.commitTransaction()
```

You can attempt to perform all the actions using commitTransaction, and you can also roll back a transaction that you have not committed using the rollback method.

Server-side JavaScript has methods for making SQL (Structured Query Language) calls on databases. Those methods are:

```
database.cursor()

database.execute()

database.SQLTable()
```

Database queries return cursors, which are tables data returned by SQL calls. The cursor method of the database object lets you create cursors. You can execute SQL queries on a database with the execute method. Finally, the SQLTable method formats database data using HTML tables.

Server-side JavaScript has methods for data type conversion between database data types and JavaScript data types, support for blobs, and methods that return vendor-specific error diagnostics.

Summary

Server-side JavaScript, coupled with LiveWire, offers a powerful solution for Internet application developers. Most importantly, it means that developers can use JavaScript, on both client and server, as the basis for an end-to-end Internet solution. Now that Microsoft has committed to offering JavaScript in Internet Explorer 3.0, and presumably, future versions of Internet Explorer as well, developers can focus on using JavaScript as their primary Internet scripting language. Although it is fairly clear that Microsoft will not offer LiveWire and server-side JavaScript on their Web server platforms, it is possible that third-party vendors may offer it.

While, again, this chapter serves only as a quick introduction to server-side JavaScript, here are some final thoughts on the subject:

- *Structurally and syntactically, there's no difference between client-side and server-side Javascript. The main differences are in what objects are offered to the programmer and in how the two are executed. Also, LiveWire (which includes a JavaScript compiler) is needed along with a Netscape browser higher than 2.0 to develop server-side scripts.*

- *With server-side JavaScript, the principal objects are server, project, client, and request. The "lifespan" of the objects depends on when software components (such as the Web server) are started up or when a browser makes a request for Web page. The tables in this chapter contain more information about the objects used in server-side JavaScript.*

- *Server-side scripts are contained using the <SERVER> tag, or they can reside in separate files that have the file extension* `.js` *. As well, the LiveWire application executes scripts before the requested page is sent to the browser*

APPENDIX A

JavaScript Reference Manual

Here are a few notes about the information in this appendix. Keep these points in mind as you read this reference section:

- The items listed here are either Objects, Methods, Properties, or Functions. Methods and Properties are parts of objects. Functions can be called directly within JavaScript applications.

- If you express a color as a hexadecimal RGB triplet, you must use the format **rrggbb**. For example, the hexadecimal RGB values for red are red=FF, green=00, and blue=00, so the RGB triplet for red is "FF0000". You can specify color either as "red" or as "FF0000". These two statements are equivalent: document.bgColor="green" and document.bgColor="00FF00"

- Characters in a string are indexed from left to right, the first character is at index 0, the last at stringName.length – 1.

- In all the date-related functions, a year has a value greater than 1900. A month between 0–11 where 0 is january and 11 is december. The day of the month between 1–31, all hours are between 0–23, minutes between 0–59, and all seconds between 0–59. Time is measured as the number of milliseconds since January 1, 1970 00:00:00, Universal Coordinated Time (GMT).

- If multiple objects on the same form have the same name, JavaScript automatically creates an array with that name. Each element in the array is an individual form object with that name. Elements are added into this array as they are found in the document.

Function: about

Syntax:

```
about:[cache|plugins]
```

Use *about:* by itself is the same as choosing About Netscape from the Navigator's Help menu. The about:cache displays disk cache statistics and about:plug-ins displays information about plug-ins you have configured. This is the same as choosing About Plug-ins from the Navigator's Help menu.

Method: abs

Returns the absolute *value* of a number.

Syntax:

```
Math.abs(number)
```

where number is any numeric expression or the numeric *value* of a property of an existing object.

This method can be found in Math object.

Method: acos

Returns the arc cosine of a number.

Syntax:

```
Math.acos(number)
```

where number is a numeric expression between –1 and 1 or the property of an existing object. The *value* returned is in radians. If the input number is greater than 1 or less than –1, the function returns 0.

This method can be found in Math object.

See also: asin, atan, cos, sin, tan.

Property: action

This is a string indentifying a destination URL submitting FORM data to.

Syntax:

```
formName.action
```

where formName is either the *name* of a form or an element in the forms array. The action property is a reflection of the ACTION attribute of the <FORM> tag. Each section of a URL contains different information. See the location object for a description of the URL components.

This property is found in the form object.

See also: encoding, method, target properties

Method: alert

Display an Alert dialog box with a message and an OK button.

Syntax:

```
alert("message")
```

where the message is any string or a property of an existing object. This method can be found in the window object.

You normally use an alert box to show a message that does not require a user decision. Although alert is a method of the window object, you do not need to specify a windowReference when you call it. For example, windowReference.alert() is not necessary.

See also: confirm, prompt

Property: alinkColor

The color of an active link (between an mouse-button down and a mouse-button up).

Syntax:

```
document.alinkColor
```

This is a read only property of a document object. The alinkColor property is expressed as a hexadecimal RGB triplet or as one of the string literals listed in Color Values in Appendix D. Place all the code that sets this *value* before any BODY tags and do not use the ALINK attribute of the BODY tag. This property is same as the ALINK attribute of the <BODY> tag. For example, the two statement will both set the active link to green. You can use either of these two statements:

```
document.alinkColor="green"
```

```
document.alinkColor="00FF00"
```

See also: bgColor, fgColor, linkColor, and vlinkColor.

Method: anchor

Defines an HTML anchor for use as a hypertext reference.

Syntax:

```
text.anchor(nameOfAnchor)
```

where text is any string or a property of an existing object.

The *name*OfAnchor is any string or a property of an existing object and will be used in the <A> tag. The anchor will be added to the anchors array. Usually you will use the write function to create and display an anchor in a document.

This method can be found in the String objects. In HTML you have to use the following to define an anchor:

```
<A [HREF=locationOrURL]

    NAME="anchorName"

    [TARGET="windowName"]>

    anchorText

</A>
```

where HREF=locationOrURL identifies the destination URL. If this attribute is present, the anchor object is also a link object. The NAME attribute specifies a tag for hypertext target within the current document. The TARGET specifies the window that the link will be loaded into. This attribute is used only if HREF is present. The anchorText is displayed for the user to see.

Property: anchors

All anchor objects can be referred by the *anchors* array, which contains an entry for each <A> tag containing a NAME attribute in a document. Items in the anchor array are listed in the order they are found in the source. Two methods are used with the anchors array:

```
document.anchors[index]
```

```
document.anchors.length
```

The *index* is an integer ranging from 0 to 1. The length property is used to get the number of items in the array. All Elements in the anchors array are read-only.

Property: appCodeName

A read-only string specifying the code *name* of the browser.

Syntax:

```
navigator.appCodeName
```

This property is only found in the navigator object.

Property: appName

A read-only string specifying the *name* of the browser.

Syntax:

```
navigator.appName
```

This property is only found in the navigator object.

Property: appVersion

A read-only string specifying version information for Navigator.

Syntax:

```
navigator.appVersion
```

The format for the response is: releaseNumber (platform; country) where releaseNumber is the version number of the Navigator ("3.0b5") and the platform is the machine you running Navigator on ("Win32"). This property is only found in the navigator object.

Method: asin

Returns the arc sine of a number.

Syntax:

```
Math.asin(number)
```

Where number is a numeric expression between –1 and 1 or the property of an existing object. This method can be found in the Math object. The asin method returns a numeric *value* between –PI/2 and PI/2 radians. If the *value* of number is greater than 1 or less than –1, it returns 0.

See also: acos, atan, cos, sin, tan methods

Method: atan

Returns the arc tangent of a number.

Syntax:

```
Math.atan(number)
```

where number is either a numeric expression or the property of an existing object, with the *value* of the tangent of an angle. This is found in the Math object. The atan method returns a numeric *value* between $-PI/2$ and $PI/2$ radians.

See also: acos, asin, cos, sin, tan

Method: back

Go to the previous URL in a history list. This method performs the same action as a user choosing the Back button in Navigator. The back method is the same as history.go(-1). The following custom buttons let you go back and forth in the history <INPUT TYPE="button" VALUE="< Back"*onClick*="history.back()"> <P><INPUT TYPE="button" VALUE="> Forward" *onClick*="history.forward()">

Syntax:

```
history.back()
```

This method can be found in the history objects.

See also: forward, go

Property: bgColor

A string for the color of a background color, the bgColor property is defined as shown in Appendix D. This property is the same as the BGCOLOR attribute of the <BODY> tag. You can set the bgColor property at any time in Javascript code.

Syntax:

```
document.bgColor
```

This property is found in the document object.

See also: alinkColor, fgColor, linkColor, and vlinkColor.

Method: big

Puts <BIG> and </BIG> tags around text.

Syntax:

```
stringName.big()
```

where stringName is any string or a string property of an existing object. Use the big method with the write or writeln methods to format and display a string in a document. For example, the following statements are equivalent:

```
var worldString="Hello, world"

document.write(worldString.small())

document.write("<P>" + worldString.big())

document.write("<P>" + "Hello, World".big())
```

This method can be found in the String object.

See also: fontsize, small

Method: blink

Puts <BLINK> and </BLINK> tags around a string.

Syntax:

```
stringName.blink()
```

where stringName is any string or a property of an existing object. This method can be found in the string object.

See also: fontsize, small, bold, italics, strike

Method: blur

Removes focus from an object.

Syntax:

```
passwordName.blur()
```

where passwordName is either the *value* of the NAME attribute of a password object or an element in the elements array.

```
selectName.blur()
```

where selectName is either the *value* of the NAME attribute of a select object or an element in the elements array.

```
textName.blur()
```

where textName is either the *value* of the NAME attribute of a text object or an element in the elements array.

```
textareaName.blur()
```

where textareaName is either the *value* of the NAME attribute of a textarea object or an element in the elements array.

This method can be found in the password, select, text, and textarea objects.

See also: focus, select

Method: bold

Puts <B> and </B> bold tags around a string.

Syntax:

```
stringName.bold()
```

where stringName is any string or a property of an existing object.

For example, these lines:

```
var worldString="Hello, world"

document.write(worldString.blink())

document.write("<P>" + worldString.bold())
```

will produce this:

```
<BLINK>Hello, world</BLINK>

<P><B>Hello, world</B>
```

This method can be found in the string object.

See also: blink, italics, strike

Object: button

A pushbutton on an HTML form.

Syntax:

To define and use a button:

```
<INPUT

   TYPE="button"

   NAME="buttonName"

   VALUE="buttonText"

   [onClick="functionName"]>
```

where NAME is the *name* property of the button object and the VALUE is the *value* property, which is also the label to display for the button face. You can access buttons in one of several ways:

```
buttonName.propertyName

buttonName.methodName(parameters)

formName.elements[index].propertyName

formName.elements[index].methodName(parameters)
```

where buttonName is the *value* of the NAME attribute of a button object. The formName is either the *value* of the NAME attribute of a form object or an element in the forms array *index*ed by the *value* of *index*. The propertyName is one of the properties of the button object and methodName is one of the methods in the button object.

A button object is a form element and must be defined within a <FORM> tag. It has the following properties, methods, and event handlers:

Properties:

- name reflects the NAME attribute
- value reflects the VALUE attribute

Methods:

- click

Event Handlers:

- onClick

See also: form, reset, and submit objects

Method: ceil

Return the least integer greater than or equal to a number.

Syntax:

```
Math.ceil(number)
```

where number is any numeric expression or a property of an existing object.

For example, The ceil of 21.34 is 22.

This method can be found in the Math object.

See also: floor

Method: charAt

Returns the character at the specified *index* in a string.

Syntax:

```
stringName.charAt(index)
```

where stringName is any string or a property of an existing object and the *index* is any integer from 0 to stringName.length –1. If the *index* is greater than the length or negative, javascript returns an empty string.

This method can be found in the String object.

See also: *index*Of, lastIndexOf methods

Object: checkbox

This is a checkbox on an HTML form. A checkbox is really a switch to set a *value* on or off.

Syntax:

In HTML, use this syntax to define a checkbox and it's *onClick* event handler:

```
<INPUT

    TYPE="checkbox"

    NAME="checkboxName"

    VALUE="checkboxValue"

    [CHECKED]

    [onClick="function"]>

    textToDisplay
```

The NAME gives the *name* property of the checkbox object. The VALUE attribute specifies a *value* that is returned to the server when the checkbox is selected and the form is submitted. The default *value* is set to "ON" and can be set with the *value* property. The CHECKED attribute is set if the checkbox is displayed as checked and can be read from the defaultChecked property. The textToDisplay is the label to display next to the checkbox.

Here are the ways to access the properties in a checkbox:

```
checkboxName.propertyName

checkboxName.methodName(parameters)

formName.elements[index].propertyName

formName.elements[index].methodName(parameters)
```

The checkboxName is the *value* of the NAME attribute of a checkbox object. The formName is either the *value* of the NAME attribute of a form object or an element in the elements array. The *index* is an integer for the *index* a checkbox object in the forms array. The propertyName and Method Name are as listed here.

A checkbox object is a form element and must be defined within a <FORM> tag.

Properties:

- checked

This property lets you programatically check a checkbox; default-Checked reflects the *value* of the CHECKED attribute; *name* reflects the NAME attribute; *value* reflects the VALUE attribute

Methods:

- click

Event handlers:

- onClick

This property is found in a form object.

See also: form and radio

Property: checked

A Boolean *value* for the selection state of a checkbox or radio button object.

Syntax:

1. `checkboxName.checked`

2. `radioName[index].checked`

The checkboxName is either the *value* of the NAME attribute of a checkbox object or an element in the elements array. The radioName is the *value* of the NAME attribute of a radio object or an element in the elements array. The *index* is an integer representing a radio button in a radio object. If a checkbox or radio button is selected, the return *value* is true; otherwise it is false. You can set the checked property at any time. The display of the checkbox or radio button changes immediately when you set the checked property.

This property is found in the checkbox and radio objects.

See also: defaultChecked

Method: clear

Clears the document in a window.

Syntax:

```
document.clear()
```

The clear method empties the content of a window.

This method can be found in the document object.

See also: close, open, write, writeln

Method: clearTimeout

Stops a timeout previously set with the setTimeout method.

Syntax:

```
clearTimeout(timeoutID)
```

where timeoutID is a timeout setting is the *value* that was returned by a previous call to the setTimeout method.

This method can be found in the frame and window objects.

See also: setTimeout method

Method: *click*

Calls the *onClick* handler for an element.

Syntax:

```
1. buttonName.click()

2. radioName[index].click()

3. checkboxName.click()
```

where buttonName is either the *value* of the NAME attribute of a button, reset, checkbox, or submit object, or an element in the elements array. The radioName is the *value* of the NAME attribute of a radio object or an element in the elements array. The *index* is an integer representing a radio button in a radio object.

For button, reset, and submit, a call to this function performs the same action as *click*ing the button. For a radio, it selects a radio button at the *index*. For a checkbox, it checks the checkbox and sets its *value* to on.

This method can be found in the button, checkbox, radio, reset and submit objects.

Method: *close*

Closes a document or window and forces layout and display.

Syntax:

```
document.close()

windowReference.close()
```

The close method closes a stream opened with the document.open() method. It also stops any network access and displays "Document: Done" in the status bar. When applied to a window, it closes the specified window. If you call close without specifying a windowReference, JavaScript closes the current window. In event handlers, you must specify window.close() instead of simply using close(). A call to close() without specifying an object name is equivalent to document.close(). These three calls are equivalent:

```
window.close()
```

```
self.close()
```

```
close()
```

This method can be found in the document or window objects.

See also: clear, open, write and writeln

Method: confirm

Show a Confirm dialog box with a message as well as OK and Cancel buttons.

Syntax:

```
windowReference.confirm("msg")
```

```
confirm("msg")
```

where message is any string or a property of an existing object.

Use the confirm method when the user has to make a decision via an OK or a Cancel button. The msg argument is the message that is shown to the user. The confirm method returns true if the user chooses OK and false if the user chooses Cancel.

This method can be found in the window object.

See also: alert, prompt

Property: cookie

The string *value* of a cookie.

Syntax:

```
document.cookie
```

A cookie is a small piece of information stored by the Navigator in the cookies.txt file.

This property is found in the document object.

See also: hidden

Method: cos

Returns the cosine of a number.

Syntax:

```
Math.cos(number)
```

where number is a numeric expression for radians.

The cos method returns a numeric *value* between –1 and 1.

This method can be found in the Math object.

See also: acos, asin, atan, sin and tan

Object: Date

For use with time and date functions in JavaScript.

Syntax:

```
new Date()

new Date("month day, year hours:minutes:seconds")

new Date(year, month, day)

new Date(year, month, day, hours, minutes, seconds)
```

where dobj is either the *name* of a new object. The month, day, year, hours, minutes, and seconds are string *value*s or numeric *value*s. The Date object is a built-in JavaScript object. If you omit hours, minutes, or seconds they are interpreted as 0. Dates internally are the number of milliseconds since January 1, 1970 00:00:00. Negative dates aren't allowed.

Properties: None.

Methods:

- getDate
- getDay
- getHours
- getMinutes
- getMonth
- getSeconds
- getTime
- getTimezoneOffset
- getYear
- parse
- setDate
- setHours
- setMinutes
- setMonth
- setSeconds
- setTime
- setYear
- toGMTString
- toLocaleString
- UTC

Event handlers: None.

Property: defaultChecked

A Boolean *value* for the default selection state of a checkbox or radio button.

Syntax:

```
checkboxName.defaultChecked
```

```
radioName[index].defaultChecked
```

where checkboxName is either the *value* of the NAME of a checkbox or radio object or an element in the elements array. The *index* is an integer representing a radio button in a radio object.

This property is found in the checkbox and radio objects.

Property: defaultChecked

Initially reflects whether the CHECKED attribute is used within an <INPUT> tag; however, setting defaultChecked overrides the CHECKED attribute.

You can set the defaultChecked property at any time. The display of the checkbox or radio button does not update when you set the defaultChecked property, only when you set the checked property.

See also: checked property

Property: defaultSelected

A Boolean *value* for the default selection state of an option in a select object.

Syntax:

```
selectName.options[index].defaultSelected
```

where selectName is either the *value* of the NAME of a select object or an element in the elements array. The *index* is an integer for the option in a select object.

This property is found in the options array.

The *value* of the defaultSelected property is initially set to the SELECTED in an <OPTION> tag. Setting defaultSelected overrides the SELECTED attribute. You can set the defaultSelected property at any time. The display of the select object does not update when you set the defaultSelected property, only when you set the selected or selecte-d*Index* properties. A select object created without the MULTIPLE attribute can have only one option selected by default. When you set defaultSelected in such an object, any previous default selections are cleared. If you set defaultSelected in a select object created with the MULTIPLE attribute, previous default selections are not affected.

See also: *index*, selected and selected*Index*

Property: defaultStatus

Contains the default message in the status bar.

Syntax:

```
windowReference.defaultStatus
```

The windowReference is reference to a window object.

The defaultStatus message appears when nothing else is in the status bar.

This property is found in the window object.

See also: status property

Property: defaultValue

A string with the default *value* of a password, text, or textarea object.

Syntax:

```
passwordName.defaultValue

textName.defaultValue

textareaName.defaultValue
```

The passwordName is either the *value* of the NAME attribute of a password, text, or textArea object or an element in the elements array.

The initial *value* of defaultValue is set differently for each object: For text objects, it is set to the VALUE attribute, for textarea objects, it is set to text in between the the <TEXTAREA> and </TEXTAREA> tags. For password objects, it is null and ignores the VALUE attribute.

Setting defaultValue overrides the initial setting. You can set the defaultValue property at any time. However, the display of the related object update only when you set the *value* property.

This property is found in the password, text, and textarea objects.

See also: *value* property

Object: document

Container for methods and properties on current HTML document.

Syntax:

The HTML syntax to use the document uses the BODY tags:

```
<BODY

    BACKGROUND="backgroundImage"

    BGCOLOR="backgroundColor"

    TEXT="foregroundColor"

    LINK="unfollowedLinkColor"

    ALINK="activatedLinkColor"

    VLINK="followedLinkColor"

    [onLoad="handlerText"]

    [onUnload="handlerText"]>

</BODY>
```

The BACKGROUND specifies an image that fills the background of the document. BGCOLOR, TEXT, LINK, ALINK, and VLINK are color specifications expressed as a hexadecimal RGB triplet as defined in Appendix D. You can load a new document by using the location object. Reference anchors, forms, and links of a document by using the anchors, forms, and links arrays.

Properties:

- alinkColor is set to the ALINK attribute
- anchors is an array of all the anchors in a document
- bgColor reflects the BGCOLOR attribute
- fgColor is set to the TEXT attribute
- forms is an array of all the forms in a document
- lastModified is set to the date a document was last modified
- linkColor is set to the LINK attribute
- links is an array of all the links in a document
- location is set to the complete URL of a document
- referrer is set to the URL of the calling document
- title is set to the contents of the <TITLE> tag
- vlinkColor is set to the VLINK attribute

The following objects are also properties of the document object:

- anchor
- form
- history
- link

Methods:

- clear
- close
- open
- write
- writeln

Event handlers: None. (The onLoad and onUnload event handlers are for the window object.)

This property is found in the window object.

See also: frame and window objects

Property: E

This is the read-only Euler's constant and the base of natural logarithms.

Syntax:

```
Math.E
```

This property is found in the Math object.

See also: LN2, LN10, LOG2E, LOG10E, PI, SQRT1_2, SQRT2 properties.

Object: elements array

An array of objects corresponding to elements in a FORM.

Syntax:

```
formName.elements[index]
```

```
formName.elements.length
```

where formName is either the *name* of a form or an element in the forms array. The *index* is an integer representing an object on a form. All objects in a FORM are inserted in this array in the order they are created by Javascript. This array contains an entry for each object such as button, checkbox, hidden, password, radio, reset, select, submit, text, or textarea object in a form. For example, if a form has a two buttons and a text field, these elements are reflected as formName.elements[0], formName.elements[1], and formName.elements[2].

Properties:

- length is set to the number of elements on a form

This property is found in the form object.

Property: encoding

A string with the MIME encoding of the form.

Syntax:

```
formName.encoding
```

where formName is either the *name* of a form or an element in the forms array.

The encoding property initially reflects the ENCTYPE attribute of the <FORM> tag. You can overrides the ENCTYPE attribute *value* by setting the encoding property *value*. You can set the encoding property at any time.

This property is found in the form object.

See also: action, method, target.

Function: escape

Returns the ASCII encoding of an argument in the ISO Latin-1 character set.

Syntax:

```
escape("string")
```

where string is a non-alphanumeric string in the ISO Latin-1 character set. NOTE: The escape function is not a method associated with any object, but is part of the language itself. The *value* is the ASCII encoding of a character in the argument in the form of "%cc" where cc is the code. For example, escape("%21%23%26") is the same as "!#&".

See also: unescape function

Function: eval

The eval function evaluates a string as Javascript statements and returns a *value* from these statements.

Syntax:

```
eval(string)
```

where string represents a JavaScript expression, statement, function, or sequence of statements. The expression can include variables and properties of existing objects.

Method: exp

Returns e**number, where number is the argument, and e is Euler's constant,the base of the natural logarithms.

Syntax:

```
Math.exp(number)
```

where number is any numeric expression or the property of an existing object.

This method can be found in the Math object

See also: log, pow

Property: fgColor

A string for the foreground color of a document text.

Syntax:

```
document.fgColor
```

This property is found in the document object.

The fgColor property is expressed as a hexadecimal RGB triplet or as one of the string literals as shown in Appendix D. The *value* of this is set to reflection of the TEXT attribute of the <BODY> tag. The default *value* of You can override the *value* set in the fgColor property in either of the following ways by setting the COLOR attribute of a <FONT> tag or by calling the fontcolor method.

See also: alinkColor, bgColor, linkColor, vlinkColor and fontcolor

Method: fixed

Puts <TT> and </TT> tags around a string for a fixed-Pitch font

Syntax:

```
stringName.fixed()
```

where stringName is any string or a property of an existing object. This method can be found in the string object.

Method: floor

Returns the greatest integer less than or equal to a number.

Syntax:

```
Math.floor(number)
```

where number is any numeric expression or the property of an existing object.

This method can be found in the Math object.

See also: ceil

Method: focus

Gives focus to an object.

Syntax:

```
passwordName.focus()

selectName.focus()

textName.focus()

textareaName.focus()
```

where passwordName is either the *value* of the NAME attribute of a password, select, text, or textArea object. This method can be found in the password, select, text, textarea objects.

See also: blur, select

Method: fontcolor

Adds the <FONT COLOR=color> around a string.

Syntax:

```
stringName.fontcolor(color)
```

where stringName is any string or a property of an existing object. The color is a hexadecimal RGB triplet or as one of the string literals listed in Appendix D. This method can be found in the String object.

Method: fontsize

Adds the <FONTSIZE=size> tag to a string.

Syntax:

```
stringName.fontsize(size)
```

where stringName is any string or a property of an existing object. The size is an integer between one and seven. Use -Number or +Number to adjust the font size relative to the *value* set in <BASE-FONT>. This method can be found in the String object.

See also: big, small methods

Object: form object

The HTML object to collect user input in other objects.

Syntax:

Use standard HTML syntax to define a FORM:

```
<FORM

    NAME="formName"

    TARGET="windowName | frameName"

    ACTION="serverURL"

    METHOD=GET | POST

    ENCTYPE="encodingType"

    [onSubmit="function"]>

</FORM>
```

The NAME attribute the *name* of the form object. The TARGET attribute is set to the window that form replies will go to instead of the window that contains the form. The ACTION attribute the URL of the server to which form input information will be sent. The METHOD attribute can be set to GET or POST depending on how information will be sent to the sever by ACTION. The ENCTYPE attribute is set to the MIME encoding of the data sent. See RFC 1867 for details. You can get to a form object's properties and methods in one of these ways:

```
formName.propertyName

formName.methodName(parameters)

forms[index].propertyName

forms[index].methodName(parameters)
```

where formName is the *value* of the NAME attribute of a form object. The propertyName and methodName is one of the following *value*s listed in this section.

This object is found in the document object.

You can reference the forms in your code by using the forms array or by the the form *name*. The forms array contains an entry for each form object (<FORM> tag) in a document in source order. For example, if a document contains three forms, these forms are reflected as document.forms[0], document.forms[1], and document.forms[2]. The number of entries in the forms array is set in document.forms.length.

Elements in the forms array are read-only and can be *index*ed via the elements array in a form. Each item in the forms array is a form and has the following properties and methods.

Properties:

- action reflects the ACTION attribute
- elements is an array reflecting all the elements in a form
- encoding reflects the ENCTYPE attribute
- length reflects the number of elements on a form

Methods:

Each item in the forms array is a form and has the following methods:

- target
- submit

Event Handlers:

- onSubmit

The following objects are also properties of the form object:

- button
- checkbox
- hidden
- password
- radio
- reset
- select
- submit
- text
- textarea

Method: forward

Goes to the next URL in a history list.

Syntax:

```
history.forward()
```

This method can be found in the history object.

This method takes the same action as if a user chose the Forward button in the Navigator. The forward method is the same as history.go(1).

See also: back, go

Object: frame

Frames in a window are *index*ed with the frames array.

Syntax:

Use the following HTML syntax.

```
<FRAMESET

    ROWS="rowHeightList"

    COLS="columnWidthList"

    [onLoad="handlerText"]

    [onUnload="handlerText"]>

    [<FRAME SRC="locationOrURL" NAME="frameName">]

</FRAMESET>
```

The ROWS is a comma-separated list of *value*s for the row-height of the frame. The COLS is a comma-separated list of *value*s for the column-width of the frame. The SRC attribute is the URL of the document to be displayed in the frame. The NMAE attribute is *name* to be used as a target of any hyperlink jumps. The onLoad and onUnload event handlers are are handlers for the window object which contains the frames.

Here are some ways to use a frame object's properties:

```
[windowReference.]frameName.propertyName

[windowReference.]frames[index].propertyName

window.propertyName

self.propertyName

parent.propertyName
```

where windowReference is a variable, the windowVar from a window or one of the synonyms top or parent. The frameName is the *value* of the NAME attribute in the <FRAME> tag of a frame object. The *index* is an integer representing a frame object.

You can reference all the frame objects in an application via the frames array. The frames array has an entry for each child frame (<FRAME> tag) in a window that has <FRAMESET> tag. The order of frames in this array is the order in which they are created.

Here is the syntax to use when working with the frames array:

```
[frameReference.]frames[index]

[frameReference.]frames.length

[windowReference.]frames[index]

[windowReference.]frames.length
```

The frameReference or windowReferenceis a valid way of referring to a frame or frame. The *index* in integer to the item in the array. Elements in the frames array are read-only. The number of frames is in the frames.length property. The length property of a frame object is set to the number of child frames within a frame.

Properties:

- frames is an array of all the frames in a window
- name is the the NAME attribute of the <FRAME> tag
- length is the the number of child frames within a frame
- parent is a synonym for the current window or frame
- self is a synonym for the current frame
- window is a synonym for the current frame or window

Methods:

Each frame object has two methods:

- clearTimeout
- setTimeout

Event handlers: None.

See also: document and window objects

Method: getDate

Returns the day of the month for the specified date.

Syntax:

```
dateObjectName.getDate()
```

where dateObjectName is the *name* of a date object. The *value* returned by getDate is an integer between 1 and 31.

This method can be found in the Date object.

See also: setDate

Method: getDay

Returns the day of the week for the specified date.

Syntax:

```
dateObjectName.getDay()
```

where dateObjectName is the *name* of a date object. The *value* returned by getDay is an integer for the day of the week: zero for Sunday, one for Monday, two for Tuesday, and so forth.

This method can be found in the Date object.

Method: getHours

Returns the hour for the specified date.

Syntax:

```
dateObjectName.getHours()
```

where dateObjectName is the *name* of a date object. The *value* returned by getHours is an integer between 0 and 23.

This method can be found in the Date objects.

See also: setHours

Method: getMinutes

Returns the minutes in the specified date.

Syntax:

```
dateObjectName.getMinutes()
```

where dateObjectName is the *name* of a date object. The *value* returned by getMinutes is an integer between 0 and 59. This method can be found in the Date object.

See also: setMinutes method

Method: getMonth

Returns the month in the specified date.

Syntax:

```
dateObjectName.getMonth()
```

where dateObjectName is the *name* of a date object. The *value* returned by getMonth is an integer between zero and eleven. Zero for January, one to February, and so on.

See also: setMonth method

Method: getSeconds

Returns the seconds in the current time.

Syntax:

```
dateObjectName.getSeconds()
```

where dateObjectName is the *name* of a date object. The *value* returned by getSeconds is an integer between 0 and 59.

This method can be found in the Date object.

See also: setSeconds method

Method: getTime

Returns the numeric *value* corresponding to the time for the specified date.

Syntax:

```
dateObjectName.getTime()
```

where dateObjectName is the *name* of a date object. The *value* returned is the number of milliseconds since January 1, 1970 at 00:00:00. You can use this method to help assign a date and time to another date object.

This method can be found in the Date object.

See also: setTime method

Method: getTimezoneOffset

Returns the time zone offset in minutes for the current browser.

Syntax:

```
dateObjectName.getTimezoneOffset()
```

where dateObjectName is the *name* of a date object. Returns is the difference between local time and GMT. Compensates for daylight savings time.

This method can be found in the Date object.

Method: getYear

Returns the year in the specified date.

Syntax:

```
dateObjectName.getYear()
```

where dateObjectName is the *name* of a date object.

The *value* returned by getYear is the year minus 1900. For example, 1962 is returned as 62.

This method can be found in the Date object.

See also: setYear method

Method: go

Jumps to a URL in history list.

Syntax:

```
history.go(delta or "location")
```

The delta is an integer for a relative position in the history list. The location is a URL in the history list.

This method can be found in the history object.

See also: back, forward

Property: hash

A string beginning with a hash mark (#) that specifies a URL anchor *name*.

Syntax:

```
links[index].hash

location.hash
```

where *index* is an integer representing a link object. The hash property specifies a portion of the URL.

See RFC 1738 for complete information about the hash. This property is found in the link and location objects.

See also: host, host*name*, href, path*name*, port, protocol, and search.

Object: hidden

A text object that is invisible on an HTML form. A hidden object is used for storing intermediate *name/value* pairs in a form.

Syntax:

Use this syntax to define a hidden object:

```
<INPUT

    TYPE="hidden"

    NAME="hiddenName"

    [VALUE="textValue"]>
```

where the NAME attribute is set to the *name* property of the hidden object. The VALUE attribute is set to the initial *value* of the hidden object. You can get to the properties in a hidden field in one of two ways:

```
hiddenName.propertyName
```

```
formName.elements[index].propertyName
```

where hiddenName is the *value* of the NAME attribute of a hidden object and formName is either the *value* of the NAME attribute of a form object or an element in the forms array. The *index* is an integer for the element number on a form. The propertyName is one of the properties listed below.

Properties:

- name is set to the NAME attribute
- value is set to the current value of the hidden object

Methods: None.

Event handlers: None.

See also: cookie property

Object: history

This object has information on the URLs that the a user has visited from within a window.

Syntax:

To use a history object you can use this syntax:

```
history.methodName(parameters)
```

```
history.propertyName
```

The methodName or propertyName is one of these listed below.

Properties:

- length is set to the number of entries in the history object

Methods:

- back

- forward

- go

Event handlers: None.

See also: location object

Property: host

A string for the hostname:port portion of the URL.

Syntax:

To use these properties, you can use this syntax:

```
links[index].host

location.host
```

where *index* is an integer representing a link object.

The host property is a portion of a URL. The host property is the concatenation of the hostname, a colon and port properties. The colon is a delimiters. When a port property is null, the host property is the same as the hostname property.

This property is found in the link and location objects.

See also: hash, hostname, href, pathname, port, protocol, search

Property: hostname

Specifies the host and domain *name*, or IP address, of a network host.

Syntax:

To use these properties, you can use this syntax:

```
links[index].hostname

location.hostname
```

where *index* is an integer representing a link object.

The host*name* property is a substring of the host property. The host

This property is found in the link and location objects.

See also: hash, host, href, path*name*, port, protocol, search

Property: href

A string for a complete URL.

Syntax:

To use these properties, you can use this syntax:

```
links[index].href

location.href
```

where *index* is an integer representing a link object.

The href property specifies the entire URL. Not specifying a property
name for the location object is the same as using location.href.

This property is found in the link and location objects.

See also: hash, host, host*name*, path*name*, port, protocol, search

Property: *index*

An integer representing the *index* of an option in a select object.

Syntax:

```
selectName.options[indexValue].index
```

where selectName is either the *value* of the NAME attribute of a
select object. The *index*Value is the *index* into the select objeet's
array.

This property is found in the options array.

See also: defaultSelected, selected, selected*Index* properties

Method: indexOf

Gets the *index* within the calling string object of the first occurrence of the specified *value* when starting the search at from*Index*.

Syntax:

```
stringName.indexOf(searchString, [fromIndex])
```

where stringName is any string or a property of an existing object. The searchString is a string to search for. The from*Index* is the location within the calling string from where to start the search and must be any integer from 0 to stringName.length - 1. The from*Index* is 0 by default.

This method can be found in the String object.

See also: charAt, lastInde*x*Of methods

Function: isNaN

Evaluates an argument to determine if it is not a number.

Syntax:

```
isNaN(testValue)
```

where testValue is the *value* you want to evaluate. The isNaN function is a built-in JavaScript function intended for use on UNIX systems. The isNaN function returns true or false.

See also: parseFloat, parseInt functions

Method: italics

Puts <I> and </I> tags around a string.

Syntax:

```
stringName.italics()
```

stringName is any string or a property of an existing object.

This method can be found in the string object. Use the italics method with the write or writeln methods to format and display a string in a document.

See also: blink, bold, strike methods

Method: lastIndexOf

Returns the *index* within the calling string object of the last occurrence of the specified *value*. The calling string is searched backwards, starting at from*Index*.

Syntax:

```
stringName.lastIndexOf(searchValue, [fromIndex])
```

where stringName is any string or a property of an existing object and searchValue is a string or a property of an existing object, representing the *value* to search for. The from*Index* is the location within the calling string to start the search from. It can be any integer from 0 to stringName.length - 1 or a property of an existing object.

This method can be found in the String object.

See also: charAt, *index*Of methods

Property: lastModified

A string representing the date that a document was last modified.

Syntax:

```
document.lastModified
```

This property contains the date string of the time when the document was modified.

This is found in the document object.

Property: length

An integer that specifies a length-related feature of the calling object or array.

Syntax:

```
formName.length

frameReference.length

history.length

radioName.length

selectName.length

stringName.length

windowReference.length

anchors.length

elements.length

forms.length

frameReference.frames.length

windowReference.frames.length

links.length

selectName.options.length
```

The formName is either the *name* of a form or an element in the forms array. frameReference is either the *value* of the NAME attribute of a frame or an element in the frames array. radioName is either the *value* of the NAME attribute of a radio object or an element in the elements array. selectName is either the *value* of the NAME attribute of a select object or an element in the elements array. stringName is any string or a property of an existing object. window-Reference is a valid way of referring to a window, as described in the window object.

This property is found in the frame, history, radio, select, string, window objects as the anchors, elements, forms, frames, links, options arrays.

The length property is an integer that specifies the number of elements on a form, the number of frames within a frame (form 2 of the syntax). A frame that does not load a document containing a <FRAMESET> tag always has a length of 0. It can also specify the number of entries in a history object, radio buttons in a radio object, options in a select object, frames in a parent window or entries in one of the array properties or the length of a string. The length is always a read-only property. For a null string or an empty array, length is zero.

Method: link

Creates an HTML link to jump to another URL.

Syntax:

```
linkText.link(hrefAttribute)
```

where linkText is any string or a property of an existing object and hrefAttribute is any string or a property of an existing object.

This method can be found in the String object.

Use the link method with the write or writeln methods to create and display a hypertext link in a document. Create the link with the link method, then call write or writeln to display the link in a document. In the syntax, the linkText string is the literal text that you want the user to see. The hrefAttribute string represents the HREF attribute of the <A> tag with a valid URL. Links created with the link method become elements in the links array.

See also: link objects and anchor method

link object (links array)

A piece of text or an image identified as a hypertext link. When the user clicks the link text, the link hypertext reference is loaded into its target window.

Syntax:

To define a link, use standard HTML syntax with the addition of the *onClick* and onMouseOver event handlers:

```
<A HREF=locationOrURL

    [NAME="anchorName"]

    [TARGET="windowName"]

    [onClick="handlerText"]

    [onMouseOver="handlerText"]>

    linkText

</A>
```

where HREF specifies a destination anchor or URL. See the location object for a description of the URL components.

NAME names a tag that becomes an available hypertext target within the current document. If this attribute is present, the link object is also an anchor object. TARGET names the window that the link is loaded into. The windowName can be an existing window; it can be a frame *name* specified in a <FRAMESET> tag; or it can be one of the literal frame *name*s: _top, _parent, _self, or _blank. The windowName cannot be a JavaScript expression (parent.frameName or windowName.frameName). The linkText is displayed as a hypertext link to the URL. You can also define a link using the link method.

Use the following statement to use this property:

```
document.links[index].propertyName
```

where *index* is an integer representing a link object. The propertyName is one of the properties listed below.

This property is found in the document object.

Each link object is a location object and has the same properties as a location object. If a link object is also an anchor object, the object has entries in both the anchors and links arrays.

When a user clicks a link object and navigates to the destination document (specified by HREF=locationOrURL), the destination document's referrer property contains the URL of the source document.

Evaluate the referrer property from the destination document.

You can reference the link objects in your code by using the links array. This array contains an entry for each link object (<A HREF=""> tag) in a document in source order. For example, if a document contains three link objects, these links are reflected as document.links[0], document.links[1], and document.links[2].

To use the links array:

```
1. document.links[index]

2. document.links.length
```

where *index* is an integer representing a link in a document.

To obtain the number of links in a document, use the length property:

```
document.links.length.
```

Elements in the links array are read-only. For example, the statement document.links[0]="link1" has no effect.

Properties:

The href is the entire URL. The hash is an anchor *name* in the URL, and the host is the host*name*:port portion of the URL where host*name* specifies the host and domain *name*, or IP address, of a network machine. The port is set to the communications port number that the server uses for communications. The path*name* is the url-path portion of the URL. The protocol specifies the beginning of the URL, including the colon. The search string is a complete query string. The target is set to the same value as the TARGET attribute. The link.length is set to the number of links in a document

Taken together, these properties construct a URL in this manner:

```
protocol//hostname:port pathname search hash
```

Methods: None.

Event handlers:

- onClick
- onMouseOver

See also: anchor, link

Property: linkColor

A string specifying the color of the document hyperlinks.

Syntax:

```
document.linkColor
```

This property is found in the document object. The linkColor property is expressed as a hexadecimal RGB triplet or as one of the string literals listed in Color Values. This property is the JavaScript reflection of the LINK attribute of the <BODY> tag. The default *value* of this property is set by the user on the Colors tab of the Preferences dialog box, which is displayed by choosing General Preferences from the Options menu. You cannot set this property after the HTML source has been through layout.

See also: alinkColor, bgColor, fgColor, and vlinkColor properties

Property: LN2

The natural logarithm of two, approximately 0.693.

Syntax:

```
Math.LN2
```

LN2 is a constant, it is a read-only property of Math.

This property is found in the Math object.

See also: E, LN10, LOG2E, LOG10E, PI, SQRT1_2, SQRT2

Property: LN10

The natural logarithm of ten, approximately 2.302.

Syntax:

```
Math.LN10
```

LN10 is a constant, it is a read-only property of Math.

This property is found in the Math object.

See also: E, LN2, LOG2E, LOG10E, PI, SQRT1_2, SQRT2 properties

Object: location

Contains information about the current URL.

Syntax:

```
[windowReference.]location[.propertyName]
```

where windowReference is a window object, (or a synonym: top or parent). The propertyName is one of the properties listed here. A null property *name* is the same as specifying the href property (the complete URL). So, location.host specifies the path whereas, location by itself specifies the entire URL. The document *name* could be used instead of a window. Leaving out the windowReference defaults to the current window.

This property is found in the window and document objects.

The location object represents a complete URL. Properties of the location object are simply portions of a URL. Taken together, the properties of a location object form a complete URL. The properties are as shown earlier in the *link* object.

The location property of a document is entirely different from a location object. The *value* of document.location is read-only.

Methods: None.

Event handlers: None.

See also: history, location

Method: log

Gives the natural logarithm (in base e) of a number.

Syntax:

```
Math.log(number)
```

where number is a positive numeric number.

This method can be found in the Math object.

See also: exp, pow methods

Property: LOG2E

Returns the constant base 2 logarithm of e.

Syntax:

```
Math.LOG2E
```

This method can be found in the Math object.

See also: E, LN2, LN10, LOG10E, PI, SQRT1_2, SQRT2 properties

Property: LOG10E

Returns the constant base 10 logarithm of e.

Syntax:

```
Math.LOG10E
```

This method can be found in the Math object.

LOG10E is a read-only property of a Math object.

See also: E, LN2, LN10, LOG2E, PI, SQRT1_2, SQRT2 properties

Object: Math

A JavaScript built-in object for math functions.

Syntax:

```
Math.propertyName
```

```
Math.methodName(parameters)
```

where propertyName and methodName is one of the following properties.

Properties:

- E
- LN2
- LN10
- LOG2E
- LOG10E
- PI
- SQRT1_2
- SQRT2

Methods:

- abs
- acos
- asin
- atan
- ceil
- cos
- exp
- floor
- log
- max
- min
- pow
- random
- round
- sin
- sqrt
- tan

Event handlers: None

Method: max

Returns the greater of two numbers.

Syntax:

```
Math.max(number1, number2)
```

where number1 and number2 are two numbers or expressions that evaluate to numbers.

This method can be found in the Math object.

See also: min method

Property: method

A string in a form indicating how form field input information is sent to a server.

Syntax:

```
formName.method
```

where formName is either the *name* of a form or an element in the forms array. The method property should evaluate to either "get" or "post".

This property is found in the form object.

See also: action, encoding, target properties

Property: mimeTypes

An array of mimetype objects.

Syntax:

```
navigator.mimeTypes[index]
```

The length of the array is given in navigator.mimeTypes.length. The *index* is used to identify each mimeType that is supported in the current browser. The name, type, and description fields are given in a mimetype object each entry.

This property is found in the Navigator object.

Method: min

Returns the lesser of two numbers.

Syntax:

```
Math.min(number1, number2)
```

where number1 and number2 are two numbers. This method can be found in the Math object.

See also: max

Property: name

A string with the *name* of an object.

Syntax:

```
objectName.name

frameReference.name

frameReference.frames.name

radioName[index].name

selectName.options.name

windowReference.name

windowReference.frames.name
```

The *name* property is available in several objects and can be used as shown above. The *name* property is mostly used to reference objects. The objectName is either the *value* of the NAME attribute of an object such as a radio, frame, something that has frames, selectName, a window or an element in the elements array. The *name* property is a read-only property for window objects. For other objects, you can change the *value* of the *name* property. The *name* property is not the the label displayed on a button, reset, or submit object. The *value* property specifies the label for these objects. Every radio button in a single radio object has the same *name*. Each radio button in the object is eferenced by its position in the radio array.

This property is found in the button, checkbox, frame, hidden, password, radio, reset, select, submit, text, textarea, window and options array.

See also: *value*

Object: Navigator

A navigator object contains specific information about the Netscape Navigator. This object will not exist in other browsers.

Syntax:

```
navigator.propertyName
```

where propertyName is one of the properties listed below.

Properties:

- appCodeName lists the code name of the browser
- appName lists the name of the browser
- appVersion lists version information for the Navigator
- userAgent lists the user-agent header
- mimeTypes is a list of MIME types supported
- plugins is a list of Plug-Ins loaded in.

Methods : None.

Event handlers : None.

See also: link, anchors

Event Handler: onBlur

The onBlur event handler is called when a blur event occurs.

This is an Event Handler of select, text, textarea.

See also: onChange, onFocus event handlers

Event Handler: onChange

The onChange event handler is called when when a change event occurs. Use it to validate data after it is modified by a user.

This is an Event Handler of select, text, textarea.

See also: onBlur, onFocus event handlers

Event Handler: *onClick*

Called when a *click* event occurs.

This is an Event Handler of button, checkbox, radio, link, reset, submit.

Event Handler: onFocus

The onFocus event handler is called a focus event occurs.

This is an Event Handler of select, text, textarea

See also: onBlur, onChange

Event Handler: onLoad

The onLoad event handler is called after Navigator loads a window or all frames within a <FRAMESET>. Use the onLoad event handler in either the <BODY> or the <FRAMESET> tag.

With <FRAMESET> and <FRAME> tags,, an onLoad event within a frame occurs before an onLoad event within the <FRAMESET>

This is an Event Handler of window.

See also: onUnload

Event Handler: onMouseOver

The onMouseOver event handler is called when a mouseOver event occurs. You must return true from within the event handler if you want to set the status or defaultStatus properties with the onMouseOver event handler.

This is an Event Handler of link objects.

Event Handler: onSelect

A select event occurs when a user selects some of the text within a text or textarea field. The onSelect event handler executes JavaScript code when a select event occurs.

See the relevant objects for the onSelect syntax.

This is an Event Handler of text and textarea objects.

Event Handler: onSubmit

The onSubmit event handler is called s when a user submits a form and a submit event occurs. You use the onSubmit event handler to prevent a form from being submitted by returning false in the event handler. Any other returned *value* lets the form submit. If you forget to specify a return statement, the form is submitted.

This is the Event Handler of form objects.

Event Handler: onUnload

The onUnload event handler is called when an unload event occurs as you exit a document. With <FRAMESET> and <FRAME> tgs, an onUnload event within a frame occurs before an onUnload event within the <FRAMESET>. This is an Event Handler of window objects.

See also: onLoad

Method: open

Opens a input stream to write to using write or writeln methods.

Syntax:

```
document.open(["mimeType"])
```

where mimeType specifies of the following document types: text/html, text/plain, image/gif, image/jpeg, image/x-bitmap or plugIn. The "plugIn" is any two-part plug-in MIME type that Netscape supports. If the mimeType is text or image, the stream is opened to layout; otherwise, the stream is opened to a plug-in. If a document exists in the target window, the open method clears it.

Close the input stream with the document.close() method. The close method forces text or images that were sent to layout to display. After using document.close(), use document.open() again when you want to begin another output stream.

This method can be found in document objects.

If you do not specify a mimeType, the open method assumes text/html by default. The following is a description of mimeType: text/html is a document containing ASCII text with HTML formatting. The type of text/plain is a document containing plain ASCII text with end-of-line characters to delimit displayed lines. An image/gif is a GIF image as binary data, a image/jpeg is a JPEG image as binary data and a image/x-bitmap is a XBM bitmap image as binary data.

The mime type of plugIn loads the specified plug-in and uses it as the destination for write and writeln methods.

See also: clear, close, write, writeln

Method: open

Opens a new Web browser window.

Syntax:

```
[newWin = ][window].open("URL", "windowName", ["window-
Features"])
```

where newWin is the *name* of a new window. The URL specifies the URL or javascript:: code to open in the new window. The *name* is in windowName is the window *name* to use. The windowFeatures is a comma-separated list of any of the following options and *value*s:

- toolbar[=yes|no]|[=1|0]
- location[=yes|no]|[=1|0]
- directories[=yes|no]|[=1|0]
- status[=yes|no]|[=1|0]
- menubar[=yes|no]|[=1|0]
- scrollbars[=yes|no]|[=1|0]
- resizable[=yes|no]|[=1|0]

- width=pixels

- height=pixels

You may use any subset of these options as long as you separate options with a comma. Do not put spaces between the options.

In event handlers, you must specify the call to window.open() instead of just using an open() call.

This method can be found in window objects.

See also: close method

Property: parent

The parent property is a synonym for a window or frame whose FRAMESET is its parent.

Syntax:

```
parent.propertyName
```

```
parent.methodName
```

```
parent.frameName
```

```
parent.frames[index]
```

where propertyName is the [defaultStatus, status, length, *name*, or parent] property for a window, or [length, *name*, or parent] property when the parent refers to a frame object. The methodName is any method tied to the window object. The parent property is read-only. You can use parent.parent to refer to the "grandparent" frame.

This property is found in the frame, window objects.

Method: parse

Gets the number of milliseconds in a date string since January 1, 1970 00:00:00.

Syntax:

```
Date.parse(dateString)
```

where dateString is a string is set to a date such as "Jul 21, 1962","Feb 12, 1993 12:23:12".

This method can be found in the Date objects.

See also: UTC method

Function: parseFloat

Returns a floating point number from a parsed string.

Syntax:

```
parseFloat(string)
```

where string is a string that represents the *value* you want to parse. Characters are parsed up to the first character that is not a number or number symbol (-+,.).

See also: isNaN, parseInt

Function: parseInt

Returns a integer number from a parsed string.

Syntax:

```
parseInt(string [,radix])
```

where string is the *value* you want to parse and radix is an integer that represents the radix of the return *value*.

If the radix is not specified or is set to 0, then the first two character are interpreted as:

- "0x" implies a radix of 16 (hexadecimal).

- "0" implies a radix of 8 (octal).

- anything else as radix of 10 (decimal).

See also: isNaN, parseFloat functions

Object: password

A text field on an HTML form that displays (*) when text is typed in.

Syntax:

```
<INPUT

    TYPE="password"

    NAME="passwordName"

    [VALUE="textValue"]

    SIZE=integer>
```

where NAME is the *name* property of the password object. The VALUE is the initial *value* of the password object and SIZE is the number of characters allowed in the password object without the need for scrolling.

A password object is a form element and must be defined within a <FORM> tag. You can use a password object's properties and methods in one of these ways:

```
passwordName.propertyName

passwordName.methodName(parameters)

formName.elements[index].propertyName

formName.elements[index].methodName(parameters)
```

Properties:

- defaultValue is the VALUE attribute
- name is the NAME attribute
- value is the current value of the password object's field

Methods:

- focus
- blur
- select

Event handlers: None.

This property is found in the form object.

See also: form and text objects

Property: pathname

A string specifying the url-path portion of the URL.

Syntax:

```
links[index].pathname

location.pathname
```

The path*name* property specifies a portion of the URL. You can set this value at any time in a JavaScript program.

This property is found in the link and location objects.

See also: hash, host, host*name*, href, port, protocol, search properties

Property: PI

The constant PI (3.141595265358).

Syntax:

```
Math.PI
```

This read-only property is found in the Math objects:

See also: E, LN2, LN10, LOG2E, LOG10E, SQRT1_2, SQRT2

Property: plugIns

The array of items describing loaded plug-ins in Navigator.

Syntax:

```
navigator.plugIns[index]
```

The plugIns array contains items describing the name, file name, and length of each plug-in loaded in the Navigator browser. Each item can be listed with the *index*, the number of items in the array is found in navigator.plugIns.length.

This read-only property is found in the navigator object.

See Also: navigator.

Property: port

A string for the communications port that the server uses for communications.

Syntax:

```
links[index].port

location.port
```

The port property specifies a portion of the URL. The port property is a substring of the host property. The host property is the concatenation of the host*name* and port properties, separated by a colon. When the port property is not defined, the host property is the same as the host*name* property. You can set the port property at any time in your JavaScript application.

This property is found in the link and location objects.

See also: hash, host, host*name*, href, path*name*, protocol, search

Method: pow

Returns a base raised to the exponent power.

Syntax:

```
Math.pow(base, exponent)
```

The base and exponent are each a numeric expression.

This method can be found in the Math objects.

See also: exp, log

Method: prompt

Displays a Prompt dialog box with a message and an input field.

Syntax:

```
prompt(message, [inputDefault])
```

where message is any string or a property of an existing object. The inputDefault is a string, integer, or property for the default *value* of the input field. If you do not specify an initial *value* for inputDefault, the dialog box displays the *value* <undefined>.

This method can be found in the window object.

See also: alert, confirm

Property: protocol

A string specifying the beginning of the URL, up to and including the first colon.

Syntax:

```
links[index].protocol

location.protocol
```

where *index* is an integer representing a link object. The protocol property specifies a portion of the URL. The protocol indicates the access method of the URL (e.g. "http:", "ftp:").

This property is found in the link and location objects.

Object: radio

A list of radio buttons lets a user choose one button.

Syntax:

```
<INPUT

    TYPE="radio"

    NAME="radioName"

    VALUE="buttonValue"

    [CHECKED]

    [onClick="function"]>

    textToDisplay
```

The NAME specifies the *name* property of the radio object. All radio buttons in a group have the same NAME attribute. The VALUE is set to the *value* that is returned to the server when the radio button is selected and the form is submitted. The CHECKED attribute selects the radio button. You can access this *value* using the defaultChecked property. The textToDisplay is set to the label to display beside the radio button.

The syntax for this display is one of the following:

```
radioName[index].propertyName

radioName[index].methodName(parameters)

formName.elements[btnIndex].propertyName

formName.elements[btnIndex].methodName(parameters)
```

The radioName is the NAME attribute of a radio object. The *index* is an integer representing a radio button in a radio object. The formName is either the NAME attribute of a form object or an element in the forms array. The btn*Index* is the *index* into the radio button on a form. The elements array contains an entry for each radio button in a radio object. The propertyName and methodName lists each as listed below.

A radio object is a form element and must be defined within a <FORM> tag. All radio buttons in a radio button group use the same *name* property. To access the individual radio buttons in your code, follow the object *name* with an *index* starting from zero, one for each button the same way you would for an array such as forms:

```
document.forms[0].radioName[0] is the first,
```

```
document.forms[0].radioName[1] is the second, etc.
```

Properties:

- checked for selecting a radio button
- defaultChecked set to the value of the CHECKED attribute
- length set to the number of radio buttons in a radio object
- name set to the NAME attribute
- value set to the VALUE attribute

Methods:

- click

Event handlers:

- onClick

See also: checkbox, form, and select objects

Method: random

Returns a pseudo-random number between 0 and 1.

Syntax:

```
Math.random()
```

This method can be found in Math object.

Property: referrer

Setst the URL of the calling document when a link is *click*ed.

Syntax:

```
document.referrer
```

When a user *click*s on a link object to get a source document, the referrer property contains the URL of the document from which the user started on the link. You can look at the referrer property from the destination document to see where the user came in from.

This property can be found in the document object.

See Also: href

Object: reset

A reset button resets all elements in a form to their defaults.

Syntax:

```
<INPUT

    TYPE="reset"

    NAME="resetName"

    VALUE="buttonText"

    [onClick="handlerText"]>
```

The NAME attribute is the *name* property of the reset object. The VALUE is the text to display on the button face and is set to the *value* using the *value* property.

The following ways are available to use the reset objects:

```
resetName.propertyName

resetName.methodName(parameters)

formName.elements[index].propertyName

formName.elements[index].methodName(parameters)
```

The resetName is the NAME attribute of a reset object. The form-Name is either NAME attribute of a form or an element in the forms array. The *index* is an integer of a reset object on a form. The property-Name and methodName is one of these *value*s listed below.

This property can be found in FORM object.

A reset object is a form element and must be defined within a <FORM> tag. The reset button's *onClick* event handler cannot prevent a form from being reset; once the button is *click*ed, the reset cannot be canceled.

Properties:

- name is set to the NAME attribute
- value is set to the VALUE attribute

Methods:

- click

Event handlers:

- onClick

See also: button, form, and submit objects

Method: round

Returns the *value* of a number rounded to the nearest integer. If the fractional portion of number is greater than or equal to .5,the returned *value* is the next highest integer, otherwise it returns the next lower integer.

Syntax:

```
Math.round(number)
```

where number is any numeric expression. This method can be found in Math object.

Property: search

Creates a string starting with a question mark that contains query information in a URL.

Syntax:

```
links[index].search

location.search
```

where *index* is an integer representing a link object and the search property specifies a portion of a URL.

This is property of link and location objects.

See also: hash, host, host*name*, href, path*name*, port, protocol properties

Method: select

Selects the input area of the specified password, text, or textarea object.

Syntax:

```
objectName.select()
```

where objectName is the NAME attribute of a password, the text or textarea object or an element in the elements array. You can use the select method to highlight the input area of a form element to highlight a field and position the cursor in an text entry object.

This method can be found in password, text, textarea objects.

See also: blur, focus methods

Object: select

A selection list lets the user choose one item from a list. A

scrolling list lets the user choose one or more items from a list.

Syntax:

```
<SELECT

    NAME="selectName"

    [SIZE="integer"]

    [MULTIPLE]

    [onBlur="handlerText"]

    [onChange="handlerText"]

    [onFocus="handlerText"]>

    <OPTION VALUE="optionValue" [SELECTED]> textToDisplay

        [ ... <OPTION> textToDisplay]

</SELECT>
```

where NAME is set to the *name* property of the select object. The SIZE specifies the number of options visible when the form is displayed. Set SIZE to 1 for popup list. The MULTIPLE specifies that the select object is a scrolling list and not a selection list. The OPTION is set to a selection element in the options array. The VALUE is set to a *value* that is returned to the server when the option is selected when the form is submitted. The SELECTED is set to the default selection in the defaultSelection property. The textToDisplay specifies the text property (which is what is displayed in the list).

The following ways are available to use this object:

```
selectName.propertyName

selectName.methodName(parameters)

formName.elements[index].propertyName

formName.elements[index].methodName(parameters)

selectName.options[opIndex].propertyName

formName.elements[index].options[opIndex].propertyName
```

The selectName is set to the NAME attribute of a select object. The formName is either set to the NAME attribute of a form object or is an element in the forms array. The *index* is an integer set to the location of a select object in the elements array. The *opIndex* is an integer representing an option in a select object. The formName is either the NAME attribute of a form object or an element in the forms array. The *opIndex* is an integer is set to a select object on a form.

You can reference the options of a select object in your code by using the options array is used to reference the options in a select object. The options array contains an entry for each option in a select object (<OPTION> tag). To use the options array you can use of these properties:

```
selectName.options

selectName.options[index]

selectName.options.length

selectName.length
```

where selectName is the NAME attribute of a select object or an element in the elements array. The *index* is an integer representing an option in a select object. The length property is number of options in a select object or the size of the options array or the select object. The select object has properties that you can access only through the options array. These properties are also listed below. Elements in the options array are read-only.

Properties:

- length is set to the number of options in a select object
- name is set to the NAME attribute
- options is set to the <OPTION> tags
- selectedIndex is set to the index of the first selected option

The options array has these properties:

- defaultSelected is set to the SELECTED attribute

- index is set to the index of an option

- length is set to the number of options in a select object

- name is set to the NAME attribute

- selected lets you programatically select an option

- selectedIndex is set to the index of the selected option

- text is set to the textToDisplay that follows an <OPTION> tag

- value is set to the VALUE attribute

Note: The *select object* is a property of form and the *options array* is a property of *select objects*

Methods:

- blur

- focus

Event handlers:

- onBlur

- onChange

- onFocus

See also: form and radio objects

Property: selected

A Boolean *value* for the state of the current selection state of an option in a select object.

Syntax:

```
selectName.options[index].selected
```

where selectName is the NAME attribute of a select object and *index* is an integer representing an option in a select object. If an option in a select object is selected, the returned *value* is true otherwise it is false. The select object is immediately updated on the browser when you set the selected property.

This property can be found in the options array.

See also: defaultSelected, *index*, selected*Index* properties

Property: selected*Index*

An integer with the *index* of a selected option in a select object.

Syntax:

```
selectName.selectedIndex
```

```
selectName.options.selectedIndex
```

where selectName is the NAME attribute of a select object.

This property can be found in select object or options array.

Options in a select object are *index*ed from 0in the order in which they are defined. The display of the select object is immediately updated when you set the selected*Index* property.

See also: defaultSelected, *index*, selected properties

Property: self

The read-only self property is the same as the current window or frame.

Syntax:

```
self.propertyName
```

```
self.methodName
```

The propertyName could be one of the following: the defaultStatus, status, length, or the *name* property when self refers to a window object. The propertyName is the length or *name* property when self refers to a frame object. The methodName is any method associated with the window object.

The is a property of the frame and window objects.

See also: window property

Method: setDate

Sets the day of the month for a specified date object.

Syntax:

```
dateObjectName.setDate(dayValue)
```

where dateObjectName is the *name* of a date object. The dayValue is an integer from 1 to 31 representing the day of the month.

This method can be found in Date object.

See also: getDate method

Method: setHours

Sets the hours for a specified date.

Syntax:

```
dateObjectName.setHours(hoursValue)
```

The dateObjectName is the *name* of a date object and hoursValue is an integer between 0 and 23 for the hour.

This method can be found in Date object.

See also: getHours method

Method: setMinutes

Sets the minutes for a specified date.

Syntax:

```
dateObjectName.setMinutes(minutesValue)
```

where dateObjectName is the *name* of a date object and minutes-Value is an integer between 0 and 59 representing the minutes.

This method can be found in Date object.

See also: getMinutes

Method: setMonth

Sets the month for a specified date.

Syntax:

```
dateObjectName.setMonth(monthValue)
```

where dateObjectName is the *name* of a date object and monthValue is an integer between 0 and 11 for the months January (0) through December (11).

This method can be found in Date object.

See also: getMonth

Method: setSeconds

Sets the seconds for a specified date.

Syntax:

```
dateObjectName.setSeconds(secondsValue)
```

where dateObjectName is the *name* of a date object and the number secondsValue is an integer between 0 and 59 for the number of seconds to set.

This method can be found in Date object.

See also: getSeconds method

Method: setTime

Sets the *value* of a date object.

Syntax:

```
dateObjectName.setTime(timevalue)
```

where dateObjectName is the *name* of a date object and time*value* is an integer with the the number of milliseconds since the first of January 1970 00:00:00. Use the setTime method to help assign a date and time to another date object.

This method can be found in Math object.

See also: getTime

Method: setTimeout

Run some code after a specified number of milliseconds have elapsed.

Syntax:

```
timeoutID=setTimeout(expression, msec)
```

The timeoutID is an identifier that is used only to cancel the evaluation with the clearTimeout method. The expression is a string expression to be evaluated, normally a function call. The msec is a numeric *value* in millisecond units.

This method can be found in frame and window objects.

See also: clearTimeout

Method: setYear

Sets the year for a specified date.

Syntax:

```
dateObjectName.setYear(yearValue)
```

where dateObjectName is the *name* of a date object and yearValue is an integer greater than 1900.

This method can be found in Date object.

See also: getYear

Method: sin

Returns the sine of a number.

Syntax:

```
Math.sin(number)
```

The number is a numeric expression with the size of an angle in radians. The sin method returns a numeric *value* between –1 and 1, which represents the sine of the angle. Any number outside this range will cause sin to return 0.

This method can be found in Math object.

See also: acos, asin, atan, cos, tan methods

Method: small

Puts <SMALL> and </SMALL> tags around a string to be displayed.

Syntax:

```
stringName.small()
```

where stringName is any string or a property of an existing object.

This method can be found in String object.

See also: big, fontsize

Method: sqrt

Returns the square root of a number.

Syntax:

```
Math.sqrt(number)
```

where number is any non-negative numeric expression. If the *value* of number less than 0, the return *value* is always 0.

This method can be found in Math object.

See also: E, LN2, LN10, LOG2E, LOG10E, PI, SQRT2

Property: SQRT1_2 property

Set to the read-only *value* of the square root of 0.5

Syntax:

```
Math.SQRT1_2
```

This method can be found in Math object.

See also: E, LN2, LN10, LOG2E, LOG10E, PI, SQRT2 properties

Property: SQRT2

Set to the read-only of the square root of two.

Syntax:

```
Math.SQRT2
```

This method can be found in Math object.

See also: E, LN2, LN10, LOG2E, LOG10E, PI, SQRT1_2 properties

Property: status

Sets a priority or transient message in the status bar at the bottom of a browser window.

Syntax:

```
windowReference.status
```

The windowReference is a valid way of referring to a window. The status property is not the defaultStatus property. The defaultStatus property is set to the default message displayed in the status bar.

This property can be found in window object.

See also: defaultStatus property

Method: strike

Puts <STRIKE> tags around a string to be displayed as struck out text.

Syntax:

```
stringName.strike()
```

where stringName is any string or a property of an existing object.

This method can be found in String object.

See also: blink, bold, italics methods

Object : string

Contains a series of characters. The basic building block for creating strings.

Syntax:

```
stringName.propertyName
```

```
stringName.methodName(parameters)
```

where stringName is the *name* of a string variable and propertyName or methodName methodName is as listed below.

Properties:

- length is set to the number of characters in the string

Methods:

- anchor
- big
- blink
- bold
- charAt
- fixed
- fontcolor
- fontsize
- indexOf
- italics
- lastIndexOf
- link
- small
- strike
- sub
- substring
- sup
- toLowerCase
- toUpperCase

See also: text and textarea objects

Method: sub

Puts <SUB> tags around a string to be displayed as a subscript.

Syntax:

```
stringName.sub()
```

where stringName is any string or a property of an existing object.

This method can be found in String object.

See also: sup method

Method: submit

Submits a form.

Syntax:

```
formName.submit()
```

where formName is the *name* of any form.

Use the submit method to send data back to an http server. The submit method returns the data using either "get" or "post", as specified in the method property. The submit method submits the specified form as if a submit button was pressed.

This method can be found in form object.

See also: submit object and onSubmit event handler

Object: submit

A submit button on an HTML form. A submit button causes a form to be submitted.

Syntax:

```
<INPUT

   TYPE="submit"

   NAME="submitName"

   VALUE="buttonText"

   [onClick="handlerText"]>
```

where NAME is set to the *name* property of the submit object and VALUE is set to the *value* property and the label to display on the button face.

Use these ways to address the properties and methods of a submit object in a form:

```
submitName.propertyName

submitName.methodName(parameters)

formName.elements[index].propertyName

formName.elements[index].methodName(parameters)
```

where submitName is the NAME attribute of a submit object, the formName is either the NAME attribute of a form object or an element in the forms array, the *index* is an *index* into the element array on a form. The propertyName and methodNames are listed below.

Properties:

- name is set to the NAME attribute
- value is set to the VALUE attribute

Methods:

- click

Event handlers:

- onClick

See also: button, form, and reset objects, submit method, and onSubmit event handler

Method: substring

Returns a subset of a string object.

Syntax:

```
stringName.substring(index1, indexB)
```

where stringName is any string, *index*1 is any integer from 0 to stringName.length - 1, and *index*2 is any integer from 0 to string-

Name.length - 1.

This method can be found in String object.

Method: sup

Puts <SUP> tags around a string to be displayed as a superscript.

Syntax:

```
stringName.sup()
```

where stringName is any string or a property of an existing object.

This method can be found in String object.

See also: sub method

Method: tan

Returns the tangent of a number.

Syntax:

```
Math.tan(number)
```

where number is a numeric expression of the size of an angle in radians. This method can be found in Math object.

See also: acos, asin, atan, cos, sin methods

Property: target

Specifies the *name* of the window that responses go to after a form has been submitted to a server. For link objects it is a string specifying the *name* of the window that displays the content of a traversed link.

Syntax:

```
formName.target
```

```
links[index].target
```

where formName is either the *name* of a form or an element and *index* is an integer representing a link object. The *target* property initially is set to the TARGET attribute of the <FORM> and <A> tags;

however, setting target overrides these attributes. The target property cannot be assigned the *value* of a JavaScript expression.

This property can be found in form and link objects.

See also: action, encoding, method properties

Object: text

A text input field on an HTML form.

Syntax:

```
<INPUT

    TYPE="text"

    NAME="textName"

    VALUE="textValue"

    SIZE=integer

    [onBlur="handlerText"]

    [onChange="handlerText"]

    [onFocus="handlerText"]

    [onSelect="handlerText"]>
```

where NAME is set to the *name* property of the text object, the VALUE is set to the initial *value* property of the text object. The SIZE specifies the number of characters the text object can accommodate without scrolling.

You can access the properties of a text object in many ways:

```
textName.propertyName

textName.methodName(parameters)

formName.elements[index].propertyName

formName.elements[index].methodName(parameters)
```

where textName is the NAME attribute of a text object, and form-Name is either the NAME attribute of a form object or an element in the forms array. The *index* is an integer of the text object on a form. The propertyName and methodName are as listed below.

Properties:

- defaultValue is set to the VALUE attribute
- name is set to the NAME attribute
- value is set to the current value of the text object's field

Methods:

- focus
- blur
- select

Event handlers:

- onBlur
- onChange
- onFocus
- onSelect

See also: form, password, string, and textarea objects

Property: text

A string for the text that follows an <OPTION> tag in a select object.

Syntax:

```
selectName.options[index].text
```

The selectName is either the NAME attribute of a select object or an element in the elements array. The *index* is an integer is the number for the option in a select object.

This property can be found in the options array.

Object: textarea

A multiline input field on an HTML form.

Syntax:

Use standard HTML syntax to define the textarea object:

```
<TEXTAREA

    NAME="textareaName"

    ROWS="integer"

    COLS="integer"

    WRAP="off|virtual|physical"

    [onBlur="handlerText"]

    [onChange="handlerText"]

    [onFocus="handlerText"]

    [onSelect="handlerText"]>

    textToDisplay

</TEXTAREA>
```

The NAME specifies the *name* property of the textarea object. The ROWS and COLS set the physical size of the displayed input field in numbers of characters. The textToDisplay sets the initial *value* of the textarea object. A textarea can contain only ASCII text with, new lines. You can access this *value* using the defaultValue property. The WRAP attribute controls word wrapping inside the TEXTAREA. The *value* is "off" by default and lines are sent exactly as typed. The *value* "virtual" wraps in the display but are sent exactly as typed. The *value* "physical" wraps in the display and sends new-lines at the wrap points as if new-lines had been entered.

Here are some ways to get to the properties and methods:

```
textareaName.propertyName

textareaName.methodName(parameters)

formName.elements[index].propertyName

formName.elements[index].methodName(parameters)
```

where textareaName is the NAME attribute of a textarea object, and formName is either the NAME attribute of a form object or an element in the forms array. The *index* is an integer set to a textarea object on a form. The propertyName and methodName are as listed below.

Properties:

- defaultValue is set to the VALUE attribute
- name is set to the NAME attribute
- value is set to the current value of the textarea object

Methods:

- focus
- blur
- select

Event Handlers:

- onBlur
- onChange
- onFocus
- onSelect

See also: form, password, string, and text objects

Property: title

A string for the title of a document.

Syntax:

```
document.title
```

The title property is set to the *value* specified within the <TITLE> and </TITLE> tags. If a document does not have a title, the title property is null. The title is a read-only property.

This property can be found in document object.

Method: toGMTString

Converts a date to a string, using Internet GMT conventions.

Syntax:

```
dateObjectName.toGMTString()
```

The dateObjectName is either the *name* of a date object.

This method can be found in Date object.

See also: toLocaleString

Method: toLocaleString

Converts a date to a string, using the current locale's conventions. (Using getHours, getMinutes, and getSeconds will give more portable results, so avoid using the Locale function if you can.)

Syntax:

```
dateObjectName.toLocaleString()
```

The dateObjectName is the *name* of a date object.

This method can be found in Date object.

See also: toGMTString method

Method: toLowerCase

Returns a copy of the passed string *value* converted to lower case.

Syntax:

```
stringName.toLowerCase()
```

where stringName is any string or a property of an existing object. This method can be found in String object.

See also: toUpperCase method

Property: top

The read-only top property is the same as the top-most Navigator window.

Syntax:

```
top.propertyName
```

```
top.methodName
```

```
top.frameName
```

```
top.frames[index]
```

where propertyName is defaultStatus, status, or length property. The methodName is any method associated with the window object and frameName and frames[*index*] are ways to refer to frames.

The top property refers to the top-most window that contains frames or nested framesets. Use the top property to refer to this ancestor window.

This property can be found in the windows object.

See also: parent.

Method: toUpperCase

Returns a copy of the passed string *value* converted to upper case.

Syntax:

```
stringName.toUpperCase()
```

where stringName is any string or a property of an existing object. This method can be found in the String object.

See also: toLowerCase method

Function: unescape

Returns the ASCII string for the specified *value*.

Syntax:

```
unescape("string")
```

were string is a string contains characters in one of these patterns:

"%integer", where integer is a number between 0 and 255 (decimal)

"hex", where hex is a number between 0x0 and 0xFF (hexadecimal)

See also: escape function

Property: userAgent

A string with the the *value* of the user-agent header sent in the HTTP protocol from client to server.

Syntax:

```
navigator.userAgent
```

This property can be found in the navigator object.

See also: appName, appVersion, appCodeName, mimeTypes, plugins properties

Method: UTC

Returns the number of milliseconds in a date object since January 1, 1970 00:00:00, Universal Coordinated Time (GMT).

Syntax:

```
Date.UTC(year, month, day [, hrs] [, min] [, sec]);
```

where year is a year after 1900, month is a month between 0-11m date is a day of the month between 1-31, hrs is hours between 0-23, min is minutes between 0-59, and sec is seconds between 0-59.UTC takes comma-delimited date parameters and returns the number of milliseconds since January 1, 1970 00:00:00, Universal Coordinated Time (GMT).

This method can be found in Date object.

Property: value

A string that for the VALUE attribute of its object.

Syntax:

```
objectName.value
```

```
radioName[index].value
```

```
selectName.options.[index].value
```

The objectName is either the NAME attribute of a hidden, password, text, textarea, button, reset, submit or checkbox object or an element in the elements array. The radioName is the NAME attribute of a radio object. The selectName is either the NAME attribute of a select object or an element in the elements array. The *index* is an integer for the radio button in a radio object or an option in a select object.

See also: defaultValue, *name*, defaultSelected, selected, selected*Index*, text properties

Property: vlinkColor

A string specifying the color of visited links.

Syntax:

```
document.vlinkColor
```

This property can be found in the document object.

See also: alinkColor, bgColor, fgColor, and linkColor properties

Object: window

The top-level object for each document, location, and history object group.

Syntax:

```
winVar = window.open("URL", "windowName" [,"windowFea-
tures"])
```

To define a window, use the open method as shown above where win-dowVar is the *name* of a new window. The windowName is the window *name* to use in the TARGET attribute. See the open method for the windowFeatures. Windows' properties and methods can be addressed in at least these many ways:

```
window.propertyName

window.methodName(parameters)

self.propertyName

self.methodName(parameters)

top.propertyName

top.methodName(parameters)

parent.propertyName

parent.methodName(parameters)

windowVar.propertyName

windowVar.methodName(parameters)

propertyName

methodName(parameters)
```

where windowVar is a variable referring to a window object. The propertyName is one of the properties listed below.

Properties:

- defaultStatus is set to the default message displayed in the window's status bar
- frames is an array reflecting all the frames in a window

- length is set to the number of frames in a parent window

- name is set to the windowName argument

- parent is the same as the windowName argument can be used for a window containing a frameset

- self is the same as the windowName argument can be used for the current window

- status specifies a priority or transient message in the window's status bar

- top is the same as the windowName argument can be used for the top-most Navigator window

- window is the same as the windowName argument can be used for the current window

Methods:

- alert

- close

- confirm

- open

- prompt

- setTimeout

- clearTimeout

Event handlers:

- onLoad
- onUnload

See also: document and frame objects

Property: window

The window property is the same as the current window or frame.

Syntax:

```
window.propertyName
```

```
window.methodName
```

where propertyName is the defaultStatus, status, length, or *name* property when the calling window refers to a window object. The propertyName is the length or *name* property when the calling window refers to a frame object. The methodName is any method associated with the window object. The window property refers to the current window or frame. The window property is read-only.

This property can be found in the frame and windows objects.

Methods:

- write
- writeln

Writes one or more HTML expressions to a document in the specified window. The writeln method appends an extra carriage-return/linefeed to the output string whereas the write function does not.

See also: self property

Method: write or writeln

Used to write text to a document. The write method is the same as the writeln method, except the write method does not append a newline character to the end of the output.

Syntax:

```
document.write(expression1 [,expression2], ...[,expressionN])

document.writeln(expression1 [,expression2], ...[,expressionN])
```

where expression1 through expressionN are any JavaScript expressions or properties of existing objects. The write and writeln methods display expressions in a document window. You can specify any JavaScript expression with the write method, including numerics, strings, or logicals.

This method can be found in document object.

See also: close, clear, open methods

APPENDIX B
SOME HELPFUL WEB SITES AND NEWSGROUPS

Web Sites

Gamelan

`http://www.gamelan.com/`

The ultimate Java applet site also has a branch devoted to Java-Script scripts. Once you arrive, click on the JavaScript link.

JavaScript 411

`http://www.freqgrafx.com/411/`

Home of the JavaScript FAQ (Frequently Asked Questions) plus some pretty good tutorials.

JavaScript Tip Of The Week

`http://www.gis.net/~carter/therest/tip_week.html`

You guessed it. A new JavaScript tip each week. The archive of previous tips is worth looking at.

Netscape's JavaScript Resource Page

```
http://home.netscape.com/comprod/products/navigator/
version_2.0/script/script_info/index.html
```

A meta-index (index of indexes) with some good pointers to Java-Script resources on the Internet.

The JavaScript Index

```
http://www.c2.org/~andreww/javascript/
```

An excellent all-around site containing many ponters to JavaScript resources as well as its own archive of examples.

Live Software's Java and JavaScript Resource Center

```
http://jrc.livesoftware.com/
```

Some advanced JavaScript examples from the folks at Live Software.

Newsgroups

```
comp.lang.javascript
```

The main JavaScript newsgroup and a good place to get questions answered.

```
comp.lang.java
```

The main Java newsgroup but occassionally contains JavaScript-related postings.

```
comp.infosystems.www.authoring.html
```

A good place to resolve issues concerning HTML usage.

APPENDIX

C

DEBUGGING JAVASCRIPT

JavaScript is notoriously lax about reporting syntax errors and, when it does report errors, it is often not obvious where the problem lies. There are also quite a few subtle, and not so subtle, bugs in the Navigator 2.0, 2.01, and 2.02 browsers.

This appendix offers some help in debugging a few common JavaScript errors.

A Few Common JavaScript Error Messages

JavaScript error messages fall into two basic categories: syntax error messages and variable or function reference error messages. We can investigate the most common error messages by making some "mistakes" in our JavaScript scripts and observing the results when we try to execute them.

The format of JavaScript error messages is:

```
JavaScript Error: [full URL], [line #:]

[error message]

[erroneous statement]
```

The full URL is the complete URL of the file containing the error. This is normally the file we loaded into our browser; however, the error could be in an external JavaScript source file if we used the <SCRIPT SRC="..."> tag. In order to determine the line number of the error, JavaScript counts every line terminator starting from the <SCRIPT> tag. Blank lines with line terminators are counted as well. If you have multiple <SCRIPT> tags in your file, you'll have to look closely at the [erroneous statement] to determine which <SCRIPT>...</SCRIPT> contains the error, because Java-Script will report line numbers starting with the <SCRIPT> that encloses the error.

If the error occurs in an HTML statement, such as in an event handler that is part of a <BODY> tag, such as <BODY onLoad="clickme()">, JavaScript uses a somewhat more superficial error syntax that does not include the line number of the offending statement:

```
JavaScript Error: [full URL]

[error message]

[erroneous statement]
```

Unterminated String Literal

An often hard-to-find error is introduced if you have a long Java-Script string literal that spans multiple lines. Often, you'll be editing your JavaScript in a text editor, which may inadvertently add line termination characters into strings that span multiple lines. When you bring your JavaScript program back into Navigator, you get a syntax error even though your script "looks" the same as it always did. To illustrate, let's use the new script in Program C.1 called `version.html`, which writes the version of your Navigator browser in the browser window.

Program C.1: The `version.html` program writes the version of your browser in the browser window

```
<SCRIPT Language="JavaScript">

function GetVersion() {

        var place=0

        place=navigator.appVersion.indexOf(" ")

return (navigator.appVersion.substring(0,place))

}

document.write("<h2>You are running Netscape Navigator version
" +GetVersion()+"</h2>")

</SCRIPT>
```

If we place a carriage return after the word Navigator in the string literal, we get an error message even though the script looks ok.

```
document.write("<h2>You are running Netscape Navigator [hidden
CR here] version " +GetVersion()+"</h2>")
```

This produces two error message. Unterminated String Literal is the main one, but another error message, Missing) After Argument List, also appears as a side effect. Figure C.1 shows how the error messages appear in Navigator 2.0 for Macintosh.

One way to avoid this problem is simply to make sure your string literals never extend more than one line by assigning the string to a variable. In many cases, this makes your code easier to read as well. To illustrate, let's replace this statement:

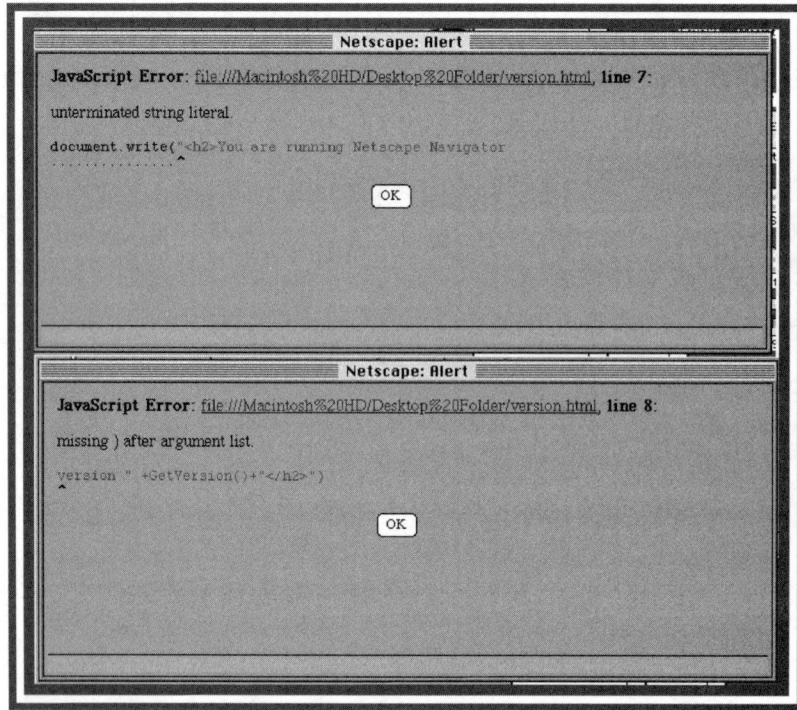

Figure C–1: An example of Unterminated String (Literal and Missing) After Argument List error messages

```
document.write("<h2>You are running Netscape Navigator [hidden
CR here] version " +GetVersion()+"</h2>")
```

with an equivalent series of assignment statements

```
var outstring = "<h2>" + "You are running Netscape"

outstring += "Navigator version" + GetVersion()+"</h2>"

document.write(outstring)
```

[OBJECT NAME] Has No Properties

Another common JavaScript error occurs when we improperly identify, or improperly reference, an object. Owing to the hierarchal nature of object references in JavaScript, object references can sometimes be quite long and, of course, mistakes happen. In addition, JavaScript is case sensitive, so it's easy to accidently make an error when typing an object name. The result is the ubiquitious [OBJECT NAME] Has No Properties error message, where [OBJECT NAME] is usually the mistyped object reference. To demonstrate, let's change the case of `appVersion` in our `version.html` to `appversion`, like so:

```
place=navigator.appversion.indexOf(" ")
```

Now, when we run the script, we get the error message:

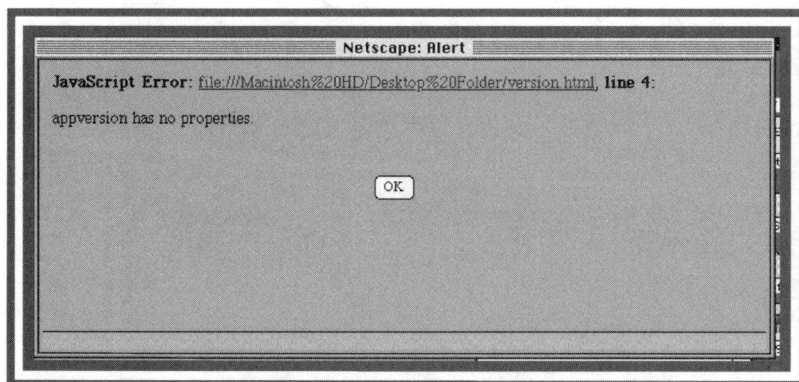

Figure C-2: An example of `[object]` `Has` `No` `Properties` error message

[VARIABLE NAME] Is Undefined

The error message `[VARIABLE NAME]` `Is` `Undefined` can occur in a variety of circumstances. One common scenario occurs when you leave off the function identifier when defining a function. If we go back to our `date.html` example and leave off the function identifier, like so:

```
FillDate() {

this.document.dform.dateandtime.value = new Date()

}
```

we generate the error messages in Figure C.3 upon execution.

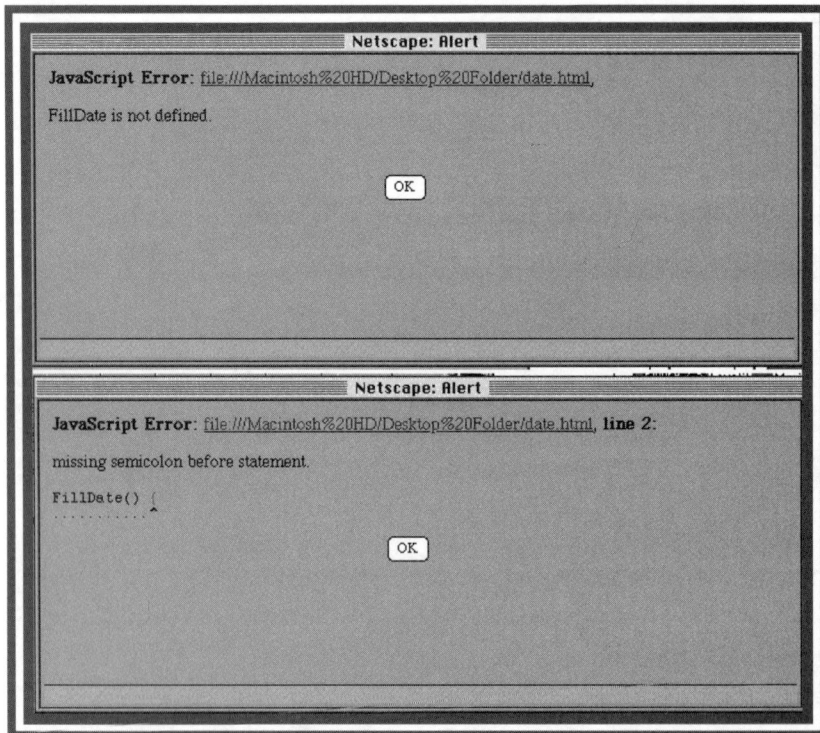

Figure C–3: An example of [variable name] Is Not Defined and Missing Semicolon Before Statement error messages

As a side effect, we also get the `Missing Semicolon Before Statement` error because Navigator now believes that `FillDate()` is part of an assignment statement.

APPENDIX D

USEFUL TABLES
AND OTHER INFO

ISO 8859-1 (Latin-1) Characters

Table D.1 shows all the Decimal and Hex codes for all the ISO Latin-1 characters. Note, in HTML, that any ISO Latin-1 character can be written as &#xxx;, where xxx is the decimal code of the character. Note that not all browsers recognize all the entity references listed.

Table D.1   Decimal And Hex Codes for All ISO Latin-1 Characters

Character	Decimal	Hex	Entity Reference	Character	Decimal	Hex	Entity Reference
NUL	0	0		SOH	1	1	
STX	2	2		ETX	3	3	
EOT	4	4		ENQ	5	5	
ACK	6	6		BEL	7	7	
BS	8	8		HT	9	9	
NL	10	a		VT	11	b	
NP	12	c		CR	13	d	
SO	14	e		SI	15	f	
DLE	16	10		DC1	17	11	
DC2	18	12		DC3	19	13	
DC4	20	14		NAK	21	15	
SYN	22	16		ETB	23	17	
CAN	24	18		EM	25	19	
SUB	26	1a		ESC	27	1b	
FS	28	1c		GS	29	1d	
RS	30	1e		US	31	1f	
SP	32	20		!	33	21	
"	34	22	"	#	35	23	
$	36	24		%	37	25	
&	38	26	&	'	39	27	
(	40	28		)	41	29	
*	42	2a		+	43	2b	
,	44	2c		-	45	2d	
.	46	2e		/	47	2f	
0	48	30		1	49	31	
2	50	32		3	51	33	
4	52	34		5	53	35	
6	54	36		7	55	37	
8	56	38		9	57	39	
:	58	3a		;	59	3b	
<	60	3c	<	=	61	3d	
>	62	3e	>	?	63	3f	
@	64	40		A	65	41	
B	66	42		C	67	43	

(continued)

Character	Decimal	Hex	Entity Reference	Character	Decimal	Hex	Entity Reference
D	68	44		E	69	45	
F	70	46		G	71	47	
H	·72	48		I	73	49	
J	74	4a		K	75	4b	
L	76	4c		M	77	4d	
N	78	4e		O	79	4f	
P	80	50		Q	81	51	
R	82	52		S	83	53	
T	84	54		U	85	55	
V	86	56		W	87	57	
X	88	58		Y	89	59	
Z	90	5a		[	91	5b	
\	92	5c		]	93	5d	
^	94	5e		_	95	5f	
`	96	60		a	97	61	
b	98	62		c	99	63	
d	100	64		e	101	65	
f	102	66		g	103	67	
h	104	68		i	105	69	
j	106	6a		k	107	6b	
l	108	6c		m	109	6d	
n	110	6e		o	111	6f	
p	112	70		q	113	71	
r	114	72		s	115	73	
t	116	74		u	117	75	
v	118	76		w	119	77	
x	120	78		y	121	79	
z	122	7a		{	123	7b	
|	124	7c		}	125	7d	
~	126	7e		DEL	127	7f	
--	128	80		--	129	81	
--	130	82		--	131	83	
--	132	84		--	133	85	
--	134	86		--	135	87	
--	136	88		--	137	89	
--	138	8a		--	139	8b	

(continued)

Character	Decimal	Hex	Entity Reference	Character	Decimal	Hex	Entity Reference
--	140	8c		--	141	8d	
--	142	8e		--	143	8f	
--	144	90		--	145	91	
--	146	92		--	147	93	
--	148	94		--	149	95	
--	150	96		--	151	97	
--	152	98		--	153	99	
--	154	9a		--	155	9b	
--	156	9c		--	157	9d	
--	158	9e		--	159	9f	
	160	a0		¡	161	a1	
¢	162	a2		£	163	a3	
¤	164	a4		¥	165	a5	
¦	166	a6		§	167	a7	
¨	168	a8		©	169	a9	
ª	170	aa		«	171	ab	
	172	ac		—	173	ad	
®	174	ae		¯	175	af	
°	176	b0		±	177	b1	
2	178	b2		3	179	b3	
´	180	b4		µ	181	b5	
¶	182	b6		·	183	b7	
,	184	b8		1	185	b9	
º	186	ba		»	187	bb	
_	188	bc		_	189	bd	
_	190	be		¿	191	bf	
À	192	c0	&Agrave;	Á	193	c1	&Aacute;
Â	194	c2	&Acirc;	Ã	195	c3	&Atilde;
Ä	196	c4	&Auml;	Å	197	c5	&Aring;
Æ	198	c6	&AElig;	Ç	199	c7	&Ccedil;
È	200	c8	&Egrave;	É	201	c9	&Eacute;
Ê	202	ca	&Ecirc;	Ë	203	cb	&Euml;
Ì	204	cc	&Igrave;	Í	205	cd	&Iacute;
Î	206	ce	&Icirc;	Ï	207	cf	&Iuml;
_	208	d0		Ñ	209	d1	&Ntilde;
Ò	210	d2	&Ograve;	Ó	211	d3	&Oacute;

(continued)

Character	Decimal	Hex	Entity Reference	Character	Decimal	Hex	Entity Reference
Ô	212	d4	&Ocirc;	Õ	213	d5	&Otilde;
Ö	214	d6	&Ouml;	x	215	d7	
Ø	216	d8	&Oslash;	Ù	217	d9	&Ugrave;
Ú	218	da	&Uacute;	Û	219	db	&Ucirc;
Ü	220	dc	&Uuml;	Y	221	dd	&Yacute;
_	222	de	&THORN;	ß	223	df	&szlig;
à	224	e0	&agrave;	á	225	e1	&aacute;
â	226	e2	&acirc;	ã	227	e3	&atilde;
ä	228	e4	&auml;	å	229	e5	&aring;
æ	230	e6	&aelig;	ç	231	e7	&ccedil;
è	232	e8	&egrave;	é	233	e9	&eacute;
ê	234	ea	&ecirc;	ë	235	eb	&euml;
ì	236	ec	&igrave;	í	237	ed	&iacute;
î	238	ee	&icirc;	ï	239	ef	&iuml;
∂	240	f0	&eth;	ñ	241	f1	&ntilde;
ò	242	f2	&ograve;	ó	243	f3	&oacute;
ô	244	f4	&ocirc;	õ	245	f5	&otilde;
ö	246	f6	&ouml;	÷	247	f7	
ø	248	f8	&oslash;	ù	249	f9	&ugrave;
ú	250	fa	&uacute;	û	251	fb	&ucirc;
ü	252	fc	&uuml;	y	253	fd	&yacute;
_	254	fe	&thorn;	ÿ	255	ff	&yuml;

Color Table For JavaScript

The string literals in Table E.2 can be used to specify colors in the JavaScript `alinkColor`, `bgColor`, `fgColor`, `linkColor`, and `vlinkColor` properties and the `fontcolor` method. You can also combine the Red, Green, and Blue hexadecimal values in the table below. For example:

```
document.linkColor="F0F8FF"
```

sets the document link color to the first color in the table, aliceblue.

You can also use the string literals to set the color in HTML tags, for example:

```
<BODY BGCOLOR="bisque">
```

and to set the COLOR attribute of the FONT tag, for example,

```
<FONT COLOR="blue">color</font>
```

Table D.2   The Red, Green, and Blue Values Are in Hexadecimal

Color	Red	Green	Blue
aliceblue	F0	F8	FF
antiquewhite	FA	EB	D7
aqua	00	FF	FF
aquamarine	7F	FF	D4
azure	F0	FF	FF
beige	F5	F5	DC
bisque	FF	E4	C4
black	00	00	00
blanchedalmond	FF	EB	CD
blue	00	00	FF
blueviolet	8A	2B	E2
brown	A5	2A	2A
burlywood	DE	B8	87
cadetblue	5F	9E	A0
chartreuse	7F	FF	00
chocolate	D2	69	1E
coral	FF	7F	50
cornflowerblue	64	95	ED
cornsilk	FF	F8	DC
crimson	DC	14	3C
cyan	00	FF	FF
darkblue	00	00	8B
darkcyan	00	8B	8B
darkgoldenrod	B8	86	0B
darkgray	A9	A9	A9

(continued)

Color	Red	Green	Blue
darkgreen	00	64	00
darkkhaki	BD	B7	6B
darkmagenta	8B	00	8B
darkolivegreen	55	6B	2F
darkorange	FF	8C	00
darkorchid	99	32	CC
darkred	8B	00	00
darksalmon	E9	96	7A
darkseagreen	8F	BC	8F
darkslateblue	48	3D	8B
darkslategray	2F	4F	4F
darkturquoise	00	CE	D1
darkviolet	94	00	D3
deeppink	FF	14	93
deepskyblue	00	BF	FF
dimgray	69	69	69
dodgerblue	1E	90	FF
firebrick	B2	22	22
floralwhite	FF	FA	F0
forestgreen	22	8B	22
fuchsia	FF	00	FF
gainsboro	DC	DC	DC
ghostwhite	F8	F8	FF
gold	FF	D7	00
goldenrod	DA	A5	20
gray	80	80	80
green	00	80	00
greenyellow	AD	FF	2F
honeydew	F0	FF	F0
hotpink	FF	69	B4
indianred	CD	5C	5C
indigo	4B	00	82
ivory	FF	FF	F0
khaki	F0	E6	8C
lavender	E6	E6	FA
lavenderblush	FF	F0	F5

(continued)

Color	Red	Green	Blue
lawngreen	7C	FC	00
lemonchiffon	FF	FA	CD
lightblue	AD	D8	E6
lightcoral	F0	80	80
lightcyan	E0	FF	FF
lightgoldenrodyellow	FA	FA	D2
lightgreen	90	EE	90
lightgrey	D3	D3	D3
lightpink	FF	B6	C1
lightsalmon	FF	A0	7A
lightseagreen	20	B2	AA
lightskyblue	87	CE	FA
lightslategray	77	88	99
lightsteelblue	B0	C4	DE
lightyellow	FF	FF	E0
lime	00	FF	00
limegreen	32	CD	32
linen	FA	F0	E6
magenta	FF	00	FF
maroon	80	00	00
mediumaquamarine	66	CD	AA
mediumblue	00	00	CD
mediumorchid	BA	55	D3
mediumpurple	93	70	DB
mediumseagreen	3C	B3	71
mediumslateblue	7B	68	EE
mediumspringgreen	00	FA	9A
mediumturquoise	48	D1	CC
mediumvioletred	C7	15	85
midnightblue	19	19	70
mintcream	F5	FF	FA
mistyrose	FF	E4	E1
moccasin	FF	E4	B5
navajowhite	FF	DE	AD

(continued)

Color	Red	Green	Blue
navy	00	00	80
oldlace	FD	F5	E6
olive	80	80	00
olivedrab	6B	8E	23
orange	FF	A5	00
orangered	FF	45	00
orchid	DA	70	D6
palegoldenrod	EE	E8	AA
palegreen	98	FB	98
paleturquoise	AF	EE	EE
palevioletred	DB	70	93
papayawhip	FF	EF	D5
peachpuff	FF	DA	B9
peru	CD	85	3F
pink	FF	C0	CB
plum	DD	A0	DD
powderblue	B0	E0	E6
purple	80	00	80
red	FF	00	00
rosybrown	BC	8F	8F
royalblue	41	69	E1
saddlebrown	8B	45	13
salmon	FA	80	72
sandybrown	F4	A4	60
seagreen	2E	8B	57
seashell	FF	F5	EE
sienna	A0	52	2D
silver	C0	C0	C0
skyblue	87	CE	EB
slateblue	6A	5A	CD
slategray	70	80	90
snow	FF	FA	FA
springgreen	00	FF	7F
steelblue	46	82	B4

(continued)

Color	Red	Green	Blue
tan	D2	B4	8C
teal	00	80	80
thistle	D8	BF	D8
tomato	FF	63	47
turquoise	40	E0	D0
violet	EE	82	EE
wheat	F5	DE	B3
white	FF	FF	FF
whitesmoke	F5	F5	F5
yellow	FF	FF	00
yellowgreen	9A	CD	32

URL Character Encoding Issues

(Taken from RFC 1738)

Characters used in URLs must be encoded if they have no corresponding graphic character within the US-ASCII coded character set, if the use of the corresponding character is unsafe, or if the corresponding character is reserved for some other interpretation within the particular URL scheme.

No Corresponding Graphic US-ASCII:

URLs are written only with the graphic printable characters of the US-ASCII coded character set. The octets 80-FF hexadecimal are not used in US-ASCII, and the octets 00-1F and 7F hexadecimal represent control characters; these must be encoded.

Unsafe Characters

Characters can be unsafe for a number of reasons. The space character is unsafe because significant spaces may disappear and insignificant spaces may be introduced when URLs are transcribed or typeset or subjected to the treatment of word-processing programs. The characters "<" and ">" are unsafe because they are used as the delimiters around URLs in free text; the quote mark (""") is used to delimit URLs in some systems. The character "#" is unsafe and should always be encoded because it is used in World Wide Web and in other systems to delimit a URL from a fragment/anchor identifier that might follow it. The character "%" is unsafe because it is used for encodings of other characters. Other characters are unsafe because gateways and other transport agents are known to sometimes modify such characters. These characters are "{", "}", "|", "\", "^", "~", "[", "]", and "`".

All unsafe characters must always be encoded within a URL. For example, the character "#" must be encoded within URLs even in systems that do not normally deal with fragment or anchor identifiers, so that if the URL is copied into another system that does use them, it will not be necessary to change the URL encoding.

Reserved Characters

Many URL schemes reserve certain characters for a special meaning: their appearance in the scheme-specific part of the URL has a designated semantics. If the character corresponding to an octet is reserved in a scheme, the octet must be encoded. The characters ";", "/", "?", ":", "@", "=" and "&" are the characters which may be reserved for special meaning within a scheme. No other characters may be reserved within a scheme.

Usually a URL has the same interpretation when an octet is represented by a character and when it encoded. However, this is not true for reserved characters: encoding a character reserved for a particular scheme may change the semantics of a URL.

Thus, only alphanumerics, the special characters "$-_.+!*'(),", and reserved characters used for their reserved purposes may be used unencoded within a URL.

On the other hand, characters that are not required to be encoded (including alphanumerics) may be encoded within the scheme-specific part of a URL, as long as they are not being used for a reserved purpose.

INDEX

A

B

F

G

H

I

J

L

M

N

S

T

U

V

variable 62

W

window.confirm() 260
with statement 95
write 247
writeln 247

New Backstage Studio™

The **power** to build a **meaningful relationship** with every **potential customer** on the **Web.**

Free Trial!

Macromedia Shockwave

Presenting the power of the Macromedia Backstage™ Studio, the only Web site creation tool that combines easy WYSIWYG multimedia web page layout with sophisticated application development.

Now you can create a powerful application in a fraction of the time it would take to write a CGI script. An application that generates HTML on the fly, delivering unique Web pages with personalized information your customers need.

All of which makes Backstage Studio the key to building strong one-to-one relationships with your customers on the Web.

New Backstage Studio is a true visual environment based on object technology. You can create complex Web sites containing Shockwave™ and Java multimedia, discussion groups, forms to e-mail and database connectivity—all with no programming required.

It includes Backstage Designer for Web page authoring, Backstage Manager for remote Web site maintenance, Backstage Object Library for rapid application development, and Backstage Server for application deployment. All integrated into one seamless package. And of course, it also works with

your favorite Web server.

With Backstage Studio, you create unique Web pages based on the visitor preferences stored in your database. You'll talk to your customers on a one-to-one basis, giving you a real, competitive edge.

To see Backstage Studio in action, download our free demo version at http://www.macromedia.com/.

Who knows, this could be the beginning of a million lifelong customers.

http://www.macromedia.com/
1-800-945-4054*

MACROMEDIA®
Tools To Power Your Ideas™

LICENSE AGREEMENT AND LIMITED WARRANTY

READ THE FOLLOWING TERMS AND CONDITIONS CAREFULLY BEFORE OPENING THIS CD PACKAGE, *HANDS-ON NETSCAPE CD—WINDOWS 3.1*. THIS LEGAL DOCUMENT IS AN AGREEMENT BETWEEN YOU AND PRENTICE-HALL, INC. (THE "COMPANY"). BY OPENING THIS SEALED CD PACKAGE, YOU ARE AGREEING TO BE BOUND BY THESE TERMS AND CONDITIONS. IF YOU DO NOT AGREE WITH THESE TERMS AND CONDITIONS, DO NOT OPEN THE CD PACKAGE. PROMPTLY RETURN THE UNOPENED CD PACKAGE AND ALL ACCOMPANYING ITEMS TO THE PLACE YOU OBTAINED THEM FOR A FULL REFUND OF ANY SUMS YOU HAVE PAID.

1. **GRANT OF LICENSE:** In consideration of your purchase of this book, and your agreement to abide by the terms and conditions of this Agreement, the Company grants to you a nonexclusive right to use and display the copy of the enclosed software program (hereinafter the "SOFTWARE") on a single computer (i.e., with a single CPU) at a single location so long as you comply with the terms of this Agreement. The Company reserves all rights not expressly granted to you under this Agreement.

2. **OWNERSHIP OF SOFTWARE:** You own only the magnetic or physical media (the enclosed CD) on which the SOFTWARE is recorded or fixed, but the Company and the software developers retain all the rights, title, and ownership to the SOFTWARE recorded on the original CD copy(ies) and all subsequent copies of the SOFTWARE, regardless of the form or media on which the original or other copies may exist. This license is not a sale of the original SOFTWARE or any copy to you.

3. **COPY RESTRICTIONS:** This SOFTWARE and the accompanying printed materials and user manual (the "Documentation") are the subject of copyright. The individual programs on the CD are copyrighted by the authors of each program. Some of the programs on the CD include separate licensing agreements. If you intend to use one of these programs, you must read and follow its accompanying license agreement. You may not copy the Documentation or the SOFTWARE, except that you may make a single copy of the SOFTWARE for backup or archival purposes only. You may be held legally responsible for any copying or copyright infringement which is caused or encouraged by your failure to abide by the terms of this restriction.

4. **USE RESTRICTIONS:** You may not network the SOFTWARE or otherwise use it on more than one computer or computer terminal at the same time. You may physically transfer the SOFTWARE from one computer to another provided that the SOFTWARE is used on only one computer at a time. You may not distribute copies of the SOFTWARE or Documentation to others. You may not reverse engineer, disassemble, decompile, modify, adapt, translate, or create derivative works based on the SOFTWARE or the Documentation without the prior written consent of the Company.

5. **TRANSFER RESTRICTIONS:** The enclosed SOFTWARE is licensed only to you and may not be transferred to any one else without the prior written consent of the Company. Any unauthorized transfer of the SOFTWARE shall result in the immediate termination of this Agreement.

6. **TERMINATION:** This license is effective until terminated. This license will terminate automatically without notice from the Company and become null and void if you fail to comply with any provisions or limitations of this license. Upon termination, you shall destroy the Documentation and all copies of the SOFTWARE. All provisions of this Agreement as to warranties, limitation of liability, remedies or damages, and our ownership rights shall survive termination.

7. **MISCELLANEOUS:** This Agreement shall be construed in accordance with the laws of the United States of America and the State of New York and shall benefit the Company, its affiliates, and assignees.

8. **LIMITED WARRANTY AND DISCLAIMER OF WARRANTY:** The Company warrants that the SOFTWARE, when properly used in accordance with the Documentation, will operate in substantial conformity with the description of the SOFTWARE set forth in the Documentation. The Company does not warrant that the SOFTWARE will meet your requirements or that the operation of the SOFTWARE will be uninterrupted or error-free. The Company warrants that the media on which the SOFTWARE is delivered shall be free from defects in materials and workmanship under normal use for a period of thirty (30) days from the date of your purchase. Your only remedy and the Company's only obligation under these limited warranties is, at the Company's option, return of the warranted item for a refund of any amounts paid by you or replacement of the item. Any replacement of SOFTWARE or media under the warranties shall not extend the original warranty period. The limited warranty set forth above shall not apply to any SOFTWARE which the Company determines in good faith has been subject to misuse, neglect, improper installation, repair, alteration, or damage by you. EXCEPT FOR THE EXPRESSED WARRANTIES SET FORTH ABOVE, THE COMPANY DISCLAIMS ALL WARRANTIES, EXPRESS OR IMPLIED, INCLUDING WITHOUT LIMITATION, THE IMPLIED WARRANTIES OF MERCHANTABILITY AND FITNESS FOR A PARTICULAR PURPOSE. EXCEPT FOR THE EXPRESS WARRANTY SET FORTH ABOVE, THE COMPANY DOES NOT WARRANT, GUARANTEE, OR MAKE ANY REPRESENTATION REGARDING THE USE OR THE RESULTS OF THE USE OF THE SOFTWARE IN TERMS OF ITS CORRECTNESS, ACCURACY, RELIABILITY, CURRENTNESS, OR OTHERWISE.

IN NO EVENT, SHALL THE COMPANY OR ITS EMPLOYEES, AGENTS, SUPPLIERS, OR CONTRACTORS BE LIABLE FOR ANY INCIDENTAL, INDIRECT, SPECIAL, OR CONSEQUENTIAL DAMAGES ARISING OUT OF OR IN CONNECTION WITH THE LICENSE GRANTED UNDER THIS AGREEMENT, OR FOR LOSS OF USE, LOSS OF DATA, LOSS OF INCOME OR PROFIT, OR OTHER LOSSES, SUSTAINED AS A RESULT OF INJURY TO ANY PERSON, OR LOSS OF OR DAMAGE TO PROPERTY, OR CLAIMS OF THIRD PARTIES, EVEN IF THE COMPANY OR AN AUTHORIZED REPRESENTATIVE OF THE COMPANY HAS BEEN ADVISED OF THE POSSIBILITY OF SUCH DAMAGES. IN NO EVENT SHALL LIABILITY OF THE COMPANY FOR DAMAGES WITH RESPECT TO THE SOFTWARE EXCEED THE AMOUNTS ACTUALLY PAID BY YOU, IF ANY, FOR THE SOFTWARE.

SOME JURISDICTIONS DO NOT ALLOW THE LIMITATION OF IMPLIED WARRANTIES OR LIABILITY FOR INCIDENTAL, INDIRECT, SPECIAL, OR CONSEQUENTIAL DAMAGES, SO THE ABOVE LIMITATIONS MAY NOT ALWAYS APPLY. THE WARRANTIES IN THIS AGREEMENT GIVE YOU SPECIFIC LEGAL RIGHTS AND YOU MAY ALSO HAVE OTHER RIGHTS WHICH VARY IN ACCORDANCE WITH LOCAL LAW.

ACKNOWLEDGMENT

YOU ACKNOWLEDGE THAT YOU HAVE READ THIS AGREEMENT, UNDERSTAND IT, AND AGREE TO BE BOUND BY ITS TERMS AND CONDITIONS. YOU ALSO AGREE THAT THIS AGREEMENT IS THE COMPLETE AND EXCLUSIVE STATEMENT OF THE AGREEMENT BETWEEN YOU AND THE COMPANY AND SUPERSEDES ALL PROPOSALS OR PRIOR AGREEMENTS, ORAL, OR WRITTEN, AND ANY OTHER COMMUNICATIONS BETWEEN YOU AND THE COMPANY OR ANY REPRESENTATIVE OF THE COMPANY RELATING TO THE SUBJECT MATTER OF THIS AGREEMENT.

Should you have any questions concerning this Agreement or if you wish to contact the Company for any reason, please contact in writing at the address below.

Robin Short
Prentice Hall PTR
One Lake Street
Upper Saddle River, New Jersey 07458

This product includes a set of Macromedia Shockwave™ Plug-Ins for Director®, Freehand™ and Authorware®, the standard for dynamic multimedia on the world-wide web. For further information regarding Shockwave, including upgrades and add-ons that may be available, please check out the Shockwave Technology section on the Macromedia world-wide web site (http://www.macromedia.com/Tools/Shockwave).

Government restricted rights legend: "This software is 'Restricted Computer Software.' Use, duplication, or disclosure by the U.S. Government is subject to restrictions as set forth in this Agreement and as provided in DFARS 227.7202-1(a) and 227.7202-3(a) (1995), DFARS 252.227-7013 (OCT 1988), FAR 12.212(a)(1995), FAR 52.227-19, or FAR 52.227-14, as applicable."